D1303506

Management and Control in the Mutual Savings and Loan Association

Management and Control in the Mutual Savings and Loan Association

Alfred Nicols
University of California,
Los Angeles

Lexington Books
D.C. Heath and Company
Lexington, Massachusetts
Toronto   London

Copyright © 1972 by D.C. Heath and Company.

All rights reserved. No part of this publication may be reproduced or transmitted in any form or by any means, electronic or mechanical, including photocopy, recording, or any information storage or retrieval system, without permission in writing from the publisher.

Published simultaneously in Canada.

Printed in the United States of America.

International Standard Book Number: 0-669-83238-3

Library of Congress Catalog Card Number: 73-39752

Table of Contents

List of Tables

List of Figures

Preface

Though I had been active a number of years in conducting studies of the savings and loan industry in California and elsewhere, the thought of attempting a book did not enter my mind until 1963. A former colleague and friend, Dr. Philip Neff of Westwood Research, suggested that I look into the seminal study just published by Professor Edward Shaw of Stanford. Indignant industry spokesmen were reported in the papers to be frothing at the mouth so perturbed were they with Shaw's apparent *lesé majesté*. It seemed that not every sentence on every page had proclaimed the industry's splendid achievements. Indeed, he had fearlessly castigated the California section of the industry.

Shaw's conclusions were seriously presented. They were thought-provoking and debatable. As I progressed in my analysis of the industry, I turned to a different aspect—but not one that had been ignored by Shaw. This was the role of the large and mature mutuals. They were a different breed from the conventional stock savings and loan association as well as the ordinary industrial and financial corporation in the United States. I began to question how they had come into existence; how they had survived; and the special role they had come to play as a financial intermediary.

The work of understanding the mutual took considerably longer than I anticipated when I began my studies. I was aided by a number of individuals—not only Dr. Philip Neff—but also Armen Alchian of UCLA and Reuben Kessel of the University of Chicago. Professor George Stigler also permitted me to present a paper reporting on the problems the investigation had faced. A later draft of the findings were presented at the San Francisco meetings of the American Economic Association in December 1966. Professors George Stigler and Reuben Kessel read substantial parts of the original study and made a number of helpful comments.

Funds for the study were generously provided by the Bureau of Business and Economic Research, The Institute of Urban Land Economics, and the Division of Research, all now parts of the Graduate School of Management at the University of California, Los Angeles. The Eli Lilly Fund and the Earhart Fund provided funds both for travel to secure data and for research assistance; Professor Alchian's workshop on property rights also provided an opportunity for presentation of some of the more difficult problems. Computer work was done by the Western Data Processing Center (UCLA).

In the course of the work I was aided by a number of very able research assistants and former students. Hans Burchard v. Harling, now of Daimler-Benz, was the first of a long line of persevering statisticians; Thomas May did original work on nepotism and management changes; David Shinn made lengthy calculations and carried out a number of highly original tests for estimating the extent of advertising as utilized by mutuals and stock. William Bliss, Jeff Willardson and Richard Cooper also served as valuable research assistants.

The study has benefited from a series of discussions over a considerable period of time with Professors Jora Minasian and Jack Lishan of the University of Southern California. In addition, Professor Minasian read the entire manuscript and made many helpful suggestions for tightening the argument and eliminating a number of diversions which while intriguing for the theory of managerial infrastructure were of less significance in a monograph on the savings and loan industry. Professors Frank Puffer, Irving Pfeffer, Don Ratajczak, Robert Williams, and Michael Granfield offered me many valuable suggestions. Ray Jessen gave me sensible insights on the statistical procedures.

I particularly wish to acknowledge my gratitude to Mary Ryan, the Director of the Government Publications Room at the University of California, Los Angeles Library. Over what seemed to be an eternity, she found government sources for me; permitted me to keep them for extended periods; and aided and abetted this study far more than she can ever realize.

The Central Stenographing Service of UCLA provided an enormous amount of typing. Miss Susan Garrick in the Graduate School of Management performed the necessary typing corrections as the manuscript was altered from day to day and year to year. I am grateful to all of these generous souls who have contributed to the completion of this work.

During the course of the work I talked with a number of officials of savings and loan associations, the Federal Home Loan Bank Board, the San Francisco Federal Home Loan Bank, the National Association of Mutual Savings Banks, the Division of Savings and Loan for the State of California, and a number of other individuals active in the industry and mortgage and savings markets. Though none of these individuals can be held responsible for the opinions expressed, I am grateful for the time they gave me.

Both the late Bart Lytton and Charles Wellman gave me many helpful leads. J. Walter Lautenberger of the California Commissioner's office provided me with the data that was not otherwise available. Ben Goland of the Los Angeles office of the Federal Home Loan Bank of San Francisco was always generous with his time and help in explaining to me the pitfalls of the data problems. It is doubtful if without his aid I could have ever come to understand the inconsistencies of the data differences as reported by the state of California and the Federal Home Loan Bank Board. Allen W. Winger of the San Francisco Bank also went to endless trouble in providing me with data otherwise inacccessible. Goland, Lautenberger and Winger represent the highest type of civil servant. Indeed, each truly considered himself a "servant" of the public and spared no efforts in making this study possible. If they be bureaucrats, democracy need have no fear for its future.

A long list of busy and important individuals took time from their concerns to provide me with information. Preston N. Silbaugh, a former California Commissioner and now the chief officer of Beverly Hills Federal, was most constructive in our discussions of the industry. I also benefited from talks with industry attorneys: H.O. Van Petten, Leon Scales, Jerry Fine, Robert Gooch, William K. Glikbarg, and William F. McKenna. The following savings and loan officials gave help at various times: Kenneth D. Childs of Southern California Savings and Loan Association, Robert Butz of Home Savings, Philip Barnett of California Federal, George Thatcher of Surety, Elwood Teague of United Savings, Robert L. Kringen of Union Federal, Edward Lindley of Palomar and J.E. Hoeft of Glendale Federal. Joseph Clawson, an eminent industry economist, also offered a number of intriguing hypotheses.

Arthur Shaw provided a number of critical suggestions and many pleasant hours over lunch. Timothy Dwyer introduced me to some of the problems "money brokers" face in dealing with the savings and loan industry. Finally, I had stimulating conversations with John Stafford of the United States Savings and Loan League in Chicago and Saul B. Klaman of the National Association of Mutual Savings Banks in New York. All of these individuals helped me to achieve some understanding of the industry and the savings and mortgage markets.

1 Introduction

The mutual association is the dominant form of organization in the savings and loan industry, which is the principal intermediary of funds for purchase of existing homes and construction of new homes. It is astonishing that so venerable and significant a financial intermediary has been so little studied and received such scant attention. A distinguishing characteristic of the mutual is the apparent omnipotence of management, which rarely accounts for its actions and policies as it must in the conventional stock corporation. Though the saver provides the funds which the association lends, he *owns* only his savings. Referred to as a member, he typically surrenders his proxy to management upon the opening of the account. Because there are no association owners to whom the management must report, there are likewise no owners to whom profits or net earnings are distributed.

The notion that a mutual savings and loan association is owned by the member-savers is not supported by recent legal findings. Nor is it true that it is directed by them. Decisions with respect to both goals and operations are made by management in a context which converts power into direct pecuniary wealth. But since the industry also permits—at least in certain states—the conventional stock-owned savings and loan association, an excellent opportunity exists for a comparison of managerial units with shareholder-owned enterprise.

The management-dominated mutual is almost a classic instance of the relatively modern theory that *control* in large-scale American enterprise has, because of the wide diffusion of shares, passed to a nonowning management elite. If the theory of management domination is correct, there would be no observable differences in the operating results of stock-owned establishments as compared to mutuals. If, on the other hand, it should turn out that the differences are both significant and lasting, the "diffusion-loss of control" hypothesis would have to be rejected. The differential results would be derived from a viable ownership factor that has maintained a critical "control" in the corporation—unlike the membership myth in the mutual savings and loan association.

The managers of mutual establishments can be likened to "self-perpetuating autocracies." The origin of their power lies in two apparently diverse features. First, the mutual is derived from the benevolent and democratic cooperatives of nineteenth century America. Empirically and pragmatically shaped by the requirements of individuals of modest means, lacking the requisite capital to either construct or purchase homes, the mutual association, even to this day, maintains the concept of a society or association of members. To preclude control falling

1

into the hands of those with more capital, each saver is allowed one share for every one hundred dollars of savings up to a maximum of fifty shares. The growth of associations into units with assets, at least for the largest, of over one half a billion dollars has so diffused the ownership of shares that effective day-to-day control has passed into the hands of management, as in large coporations. However, unlike the corporation, there is no effective way for anyone to challenge his decisions or power.

Similar to the mutual savings and loan association—and unquestionably the direction in which it is moving—is the mutual savings bank. The latter has never had to contend with the fiction of members. The savers are not said to own the mutual savings bank or the reserves. Policy is determined by a board of trustees who presumably act in the interests of all the depositors, "not only now but yesterday and tomorrow."[1] No proxies are collected from savers. The trustees are presumably on their good behavior, benevolent in their intentions as well as responsible in their fiduciary capacity. Because the control of proxy rights has effectively concentrated management in the hands of the chief executive officer, the mutual savings and loan association does not differ practically from the mutual savings bank—at least so far as the rights and powers of the savers are concerned.

The savers do not in law or fact own the association; they do not in fact control it or the management. Though the management controls the association, it does not own it in the sense that it has a proprietary right which can be sold. All income over and above the necessary expenses for operation and additions to reserves[2] is supposed to revert to the savers in the form of dividends. The operative phrase here is, however, "necessary expenses for operation and additions to reserves."

But though management has power, it is not an owner. This means that a "reasonable" wage and necessary expenses are all that it can properly allocate to itself. It cannot capitalize nor take the profit nor share in it. Yet, it neither is induced nor compelled to give profit in any form to the savers. Since it cannot appropriate the profit directly, it has less reason to seek profits than if it could appropriate profits. Its purposes are less tied to the welfare of the investors. The lack of clear-cut ownership rights externalizes objectives: the firm becomes an instrumentality rather than an institution with an end in itself. In this, it is not too unlike those related institutions, the regulated public utility and the nationalized or socialized public firm owned by the state. But there is a difference—an important one—the managers of the mutual are not civil servants.

The mutual management is to a remarkable extent free from political as well as economic restraints. To cite one rather obvious contrast: both salary and the amenities that go with the job are considerably greater than that received for similarly placed officials in the civil service. Indeed, it is no accident that civil servants often become savings and loan officials rather than that the latter should become civil servants. The only restraint on both salaries and amenities which go with a management position in a mutual is that they "be reasonable." What they share in common with the publicly owned national enterprises is in absence of an ownership interest. Neither the general public which supposedly owns the nationalized institution nor the savers in a mutual savings and loan association take part in the selection of management or the choice of policies. Though senior officials in nationalized enterprise often hold their positions because of political connections, they are frequently changed with the ebb and flow of political currents. The organizations, however, are generally run by senior civil servants of permanent tenure. This means that policy is determined by officials who are hardly likely to be replaced; and who are certainly not responsible to the electorate. In fact, the mutual managers are even less controlled. The difference is only one of degree: the mutual manager possesses considerably greater autocratic power. But even he must remain on the good side of the politicians in the form of the various regulatory agencies which establish the general policies for the behavior of the industry.

That such a management-dominated organization should have developed is more a tribute to the naivete of its founders than to the ingenuity of the management. It was, and continues to be, thought that a mutual institution is superior to an enterprise solely devoted to profits. Removal of ownership interests and the pursuit of private profit was believed to make the institution more successful. But the criterion for success was neither specified nor related to the actual enterprise established. Presumably a mutual is more concerned with social goals than is the traditional private profit-seeking establishment. Incidentally, it was believed able to attain these goals because management would not be diverted by a profit orientation and would be of "local" origins. This last qualification is significant. The 1961 Report of the Federal Home Loan Bank Board, which regulates all member institutions, refers to the System as designed "to meet a long existing need in many communities throughout the Nation for *local* institutions that would supply adequate thrift and home financing facilities."[3]

The goal of the mutual is "to finance the purchase of existing homes and the building of new homes." That a mutual institution should be the optimal instrument for this purpose is not obvious. But there is some historical support in the fact that other financial intermediaries did not provide funds for home construction and home financing for low-income families unable to make the customary large down payments.[4] The profit-oriented units had other more profitable uses for their funds.[a]

Coincident with the establishment of the mutual on a nonproprietary basis was the implicit belief that because of the benevolent purposes of both the founders and their management, competition would not be necessary. Mutuality was sufficient. Removal of the private profit motive would simultaneously remove the necessity for its control by competition. Surely if there were no

---

[a]Commercial banks are traditionally oriented towards *short term* credit and until 1913 national banks were not permitted to make mortgage loans.[5]

profits, there would hardly be an incentive for collusion to rig prices or establish monopoly. Mutuality with the inherent altruism of its management would bring about the stated goals of securing funds at a low cost to support home financing and home ownership.

The present study examines the promise and the reality of mutuality. Though a venerable and esteemed institution, it is but one of several alternatives. To what extent should it have been regarded as superior? To what extent has it turned out to be superior? Such questions remind us that judgments are not possible until goals, alternatives and tests for judgment have been specified.

At the outset a modest, but critical hypothesis will be offered: not that the mutual enterprise is more successful or superior to the traditional profit-seeking firm, but rather that ownership makes no difference for performance. The continued survival of both mutual and stock savings and loan establishments, at least superficially, appears to suggest just that. But that would be so only in a freely competitive environment where there were no differential barriers imposed through governments. In any case, the alleged superiority of mutuality must be testable in some form. The initial critical hypothesis is ownership makes no difference for performance. If this is rejected, we have something to investigate.

But there is more to the mutual than the relatively simple issue of its alleged superiority over more traditional ownership forms. The denial of private profits and, by implication, competition requires further examination. How is the controlling element, management, motivated? On the surface, it does not appear to share in the internal success of the establishment. It may benefit, however, in the form of higher wages and amenities which go with a top position. But this is so for all suppliers of inputs. It is precisely in this element that the distinguishing facet of the mutual is revealed. The management is, in a sense, as external to the firm as any other supplier. It is the prospects of the firm's making profits which internalize the management objectives and thereby create the traditional firm. The mutual is a quasi-firm because it both lacks the objectives of the firm, i.e., profits, and has objectives not internal to the firm. The model for the quasi-firm specifies the restraints on the management and implies the hypotheses about the behavior of mutuals.

Though the mutual seemed to require neither profits nor competition, it has in practice leaned heavily on the restrictive power of public regulatory agencies for suppression of competition. Apparently, the philanthropic benevolence of management has not always made competition gratuitous. Indeed, the frenzy with which competition has been suppressed suggests the possibility that mutuality is not viable in a competitive environment.

The problem facing management in the mutual is the conversion of its power into personal gain of some form. That management can do this is clear and obvious since there is no internal check or power capable of frustrating it. Under the restraint that the management cannot take out profits or *sell* control, the ordinary and most apparent avenues open to management are (1) to share in the success of the firm through salary increases; (2) to take a larger share of the establishment's income in the form of amenities; and (3) to divert income to other proprietary firms owned by the managers. In the first two instances, expenses are increased with obvious effects on both the output of the firm and the accumulation of new capital. The ability to increase expenses must depend upon an absence of competitive cost-cutting and price competition. But these avenues are of limited value while differences in tax treatment between annual income and long-term capital gain create pressures for management to divert income from the firm to outside establishments.

Thus, in the first instance, because management does not share in profits, there is no owner interest nor is there a profit capitalization incentive as in the conventional firm. On the other hand, the nonproprietary firm manager has reason to seek to divert income from the firm. The procedure for this third avenue is found in the development of subsidiaries wholly or partially by management. Such proprietary establishments siphon off income that might have gone to the original mutual savings and loan association. But they can only do so if the income is larger than that customarily associated with a competitive and minimum return. If the latter was only just earned, there would be nothing to siphon off.

Diversion requires the prior existence of an extraordinary noncompetitive margin or differential ability among managers. Three reasons drive a mutual away from competition: (1) since management does not receive profits, it will have no reason to follow the conventional marginalist procedures associated with profit maximization; (2) in order to divert income, there must first be income in excess of the normal costs of providing the service or products; (3) to ensure the emergence and permanence of extraordinary income, mutuals rely upon the assistance of government in the form of regulatory agencies. Competition is restricted by artificial barriers to entry and by regulations which penalize and inhibit competitors. The intimate and close relationship between the mutual sector of the industry and the government is no accident. Regulation in the public interest is simply a euphemism for monopolistic restriction.

Ordinarily, governmental barriers to entry and price supports are successful only in creating a permanent state of disequilibrium. Each incumbent is encouraged to expand with the result that supply exceeds demand, e.g., overcapacity among the airlines. But with the quasi-firm, the situation is different. The excess-supply disequilibrium is not permitted to appear. On the contrary, given the protection against competition, quasi-firm managers restrict their offerings and thrive on a disequilibrium of the opposite type, excess demand.

It is not to mutual management's interest to permit price to ration. Frustrated borrowers are compelled to make competitive offers not for the services of the savings and loan association but for the service of the management-owned affiliate. By this means, monopoly profit is diverted to management. Because management does not own part of the association, i.e., it lacks internal ownership interests, it rationally creates external ownership interests—external to the firm. A conflict of interest appears when there is absence of arm's length bargaining between the firm and its suppliers.

Noncompetitive income is diverted by means of affiliates *owned* by management. But even were the ownership of such affiliates not permitted, the disequilibrium-diversion mechanism would be brought into operation. Thus in another classical instance of the quasi-firm, the university, tickets to sell-out performances, e.g., a Rose Bowl game, are not sold at equilibrium prices but at substantially smaller prices so that demand habitually exceeds supply. Since rationing is necessary, the ticket agent makes tickets available on a basis which enhances either his personal wealth or provides power for which prices are paid at a future date in return for today's favor. The point is simply that the conversion of management's power into personal gain of some form is not only inevitable but is associated with deliberate creation of disequilibrium or shortage situations. The quasi-firm is a source of inflation in that it restricts sales and thereby requires nonprice rationing. Where the traditional firm produces and expands, the quasi-firm limits sales at nonmarket clearing prices.

California stock savings and loan associations play an extremely important part in the foregoing study. Indeed, it may be said that they serve the function of acting as the "control" group for the evaluation of the performance of mutual associations. In order to understand the reasons for this special status, it is necessary to consider the market structure in the industry.

The savings and loan industry is similar to Caesar's Gaul in that it is divided into three parts. First, there are the savings and loan associations operating under federal charter all of which are "mutuals." As Table 1-1 indicates, with $69.6 billion in assets at the end of 1966, their share of total assets of all members of the Federal Home Loan Bank System was 52.6 percent. Second, the mutuals, operating under the various state charters, at the end of 1966 had $35.7 billion in assets which was 26.7 percent of the total industry. The third and least in total size, but fastest growing sector of the industry, was the state-chartered savings and loan associations of the stock type. Table 1-1 reveals that they have shown a phenomenal increase in assets since 1955: from $4.0 billion to $28.6 billion or 615 percent. During the same period, their market share increased from 10.5 percent to 21.3 percent. To a considerable extent, this part of the industry is California-based. With $17.1 billion in assets at the end of 1966, that state had 62 percent of all the assets of stock associations. Many stock associations are owned by public holding companies[6] of which there are 30, all in the West. However, as a result of the Spence Act (September 1959), deposit insurance is denied associations acquired by a corporation already owning other associations..[7] Nine public holding companies own more than one association. At the end of 1962, 23 public holding companies in California owned 51 associations whose assets included 56 percent of the assets of all state-chartered associations.

Table 1-1

Savings and Loan Asset Growth, U.S., 1955-66: By Types of Ownership and Regulation

	1955	1966	% Increase
U.S.*	36.0	$133.9 billion	272
Federals	20.0	69.6 billion	248
State Mutual	12.0	35.7 billion	198
State Stock	4.0	28.6 billion	615
Relative Shares			
Federal/U.S.	53.2	52.6	
State Mutual/U.S.	36.3	26.7	
State Stock/U.S.	10.5	21.3	

*All members of the Federal Home Loan Bank System.
Source: United States Savings and Loan League. Savings and Loan *Fact Book* 1963, Chicago 1963, Tables 65, 66, pp. 52, 76-77; *Fact Book* 1967, Chicago, 1967, Tables 39, 40, p. 52.

This study is divided into four sections. The first presents evidence that differences in ownership affect the operating characteristics of savings and loan associations. Next, the development and relation of the industry to the government is reviewed. The third section offers a theory of managerial diversion in the mutual. The fourth part discusses the problems involved in measuring relative performance with respect to expenses and profits. The regression techniques utilized, though more sophisticated than those relied on in earlier chapters, provide complementary findings. Inasmuch as they are consistent with each other, the total effect is to establish the conclusion that there are substantial differences in the behavior of associations based upon the presence or absence of a meaningful ownership or property interest. Where stock is held, it is voted; expenses are lower; profits are higher and growth faster than in organizations dominated by management.

In mutuals, management has created a proprietary infrastructure with elaborate relationships between the latter and the association. All are characterized by an absence of arm's length bargaining. The relative infrequency of such infrastructures either in stock savings and loan associations or conventional industrial companies indicates that the widely held view that diffusion of stock ownership is a sufficient condition for management domination is false. If diffusion was sufficient to transfer control to management, we would expect to find industrial enterprise entangled with the infrastructure common to mutual savings and loan associations. The fact that industrial enterprise bears such a close resemblance in this respect to the stock savings and loan association rather than the mutual indicates that management has not had the power to divert corporate income. The outstanding characteristic of the modern economy is not the time-hallowed separation of ownership from control due to diffusion, but the development of a *class* of managers without property—not in stock corporations but in mutuals, nationalized firms, governments, labor unions and nonprofit institutions such as universities and foundations.

Part I: Some Distinguishing Characteristics of the Mutual Savings and Loan Association

2

The Relative Performance of Mutual as Compared to Stock Savings and Loan Associations

The next few chapters compare the performance of the mutual savings and loan associations to stock associations. Obviously, expenses represent one of the more important tests of relative performance. The reason for their separate consideration is that, due to the absence of property arrangements with respect to management, the mutual savings and loan association is not a conventional "firm." As a quasi-firm, it must be treated in terms of the different arrangements both with respect to the legal constraints and economic objectives of the various components, *viz.*, management, savers, borrowers and suppliers.

At issue here is the manner in which the mutual association differs from the typical corporation. In recent years, it has been said that the latter is managed by individuals without ownership—the much discussed separation of ownership from control in the modern American stock corporations. Due to the wide diffusion of ownership, the large American corporation was alleged to be effectively controlled by a management which had substituted its goals for that of the shareholders.[1] Now, if this is correct, one would hypothesize that there would be no differences between the performance of mutual savings and loan associations and management-dominated stock savings and loan associations.

But the effort to test the hypothesis that management controls large corporations by comparing stock with mutual savings and loan associations requires additional qualification. It is necessary, first, to demonstrate that the stock associations examined correspond to the large-scale corporations. To the extent that they are both young and closely controlled by owner-managers, the Berle and Means hypothesis would be inappropriate. If, on the other hand, management in stock associations deal with a large number of widely diffused stockholders, no one of which holds sufficient stock for control, inferences from the savings and loan industry are appropriate.

But, even in the event that the stock associations represent owner-managers, it is worthwhile to consider the impact of different ownership arrangements and relationships between savers and managers as well as between savers, managers and shareholders. Does it make a difference that management in a mutual possesses absolute power and is not responsible to member-savers? Thus, when confronted with differences in behavior and operating results, it is legitimate to attribute the differences to the differences in the ownership arrangements. If evidence is shown that the mutual has encouraged practices that a stock association would not follow, this bears on the hypothesis that there are significant differences. To illustrate, the maximizing of nonpecuniary income in the mutual

11

is attributable to (1) the absence of property arrangements; (2) the diversion of income to the infrastructure; and (3) the inability or unwillingness to build up net worth as indicated by the differences between California federal and stock associations. Accordingly, the interest in this chapter is *actual* as opposed to *mythical* differences between the mutual and stock form of organization. In doing so, it is hoped that light will be shed on the more general problem involving the dictum which relates to a separation of control from ownership in the modern American corporation.

On the Alleged Superiority of Mutuality

In their early days, the superiority of the mutual form of organization was restricted in its claim and fairly obvious. As with any test of efficiency, the critical element lies in the purpose. Thus, mutuals were organized to provide funds for home building. To the extent that stock forms of organization did not have this objective, the mutual may have been more efficient. But this is a restricted specification of relative efficiency. The nineteenth century joint stock companies were formed with the objective of making profits. It was completely irrelevant that those profits might be earned in building railroads, steel mills or clipper ships. The important requirement was that the capital invested was designed to yield a maximum return. The organization of mutuals had a much more restricted objective, *viz.*, the financing of homes and new construction. Because stock organizations had more lucrative alternatives, they were not in the housing market and should not be compared to mutuals.

The original mutual association was a democratic cooperative in which all the member-savers shared in the decision making. However, with the development of a separation between the savings and the lending function as well as the expansion of the economy, a professional class of managers developed. They not only ran the association but, in the course of time, converted the member-saver from an active participant in the association's affairs into what, in effect, is nothing more than a creditor. The saver in the modern savings and loan association, mutual or stock, is no different than the holder of a time or savings deposit in a commercial bank. Thus, there developed a vacuum so far as "control" in the mutual savings and loan association was concerned. Management took control; it can perpetuate its control; yet it lacks legal claim to both the ownership of the savings and loan association and the profits. Given this seizure of absolute control by management, information is sought on the extent to which the member-saver benefits or loses. To what extent does this form of organization represent a viable and efficient form of organization as compared to alternatives, particularly the more conventional stock organization?

The question is the extent to which a management free of voters, i.e., shareholders, can be more or less efficient. It is to be noted that such a question actually has no relationship to the idea of mutuality. That this should be so is rather remarkable. Yet, it is the result of the development of a professional management class in an institution where diffusion of membership is the consequence of a legal arrangement which limits the number of votes held by any one member to 50. The difference between the shareholder in a stock corporation and that in the mutual is simply that inasmuch as the latter is limited to 50 votes or an investment of $2,500, any effort by one member to take an active part in the management; or to throw out the present management, is likely to cost considerably more in terms of his own individual effort and expense than any gain he can derive. The costs of conducting a proxy fight are easily in the hundreds of thousands of dollars.[a] With accounts insured up to $20,000 and, with the limit on the number of votes, the expected costs far outweigh the gain.

In addition, if dissatisfied with management, the member-saver has an option denied the shareholder in the conventional stock corporation. At any time, because of his creditor status, he may *demand* immediate payment of his savings. He may, if he wishes, transfer those savings to another association which provides a management he prefers. Shareholders do not have this privilege. Should a shareholder be dissatisfied with the management, it is probably because dividends have been reduced or the value of the stock has declined or both. But he cannot claim *his original investment*. The impact of a reduction in a dividend may take the form of a reduction in the value of the stock so that a part of his capital is wiped out. Inasmuch as he may have an investment of from several thousand to several hundred thousand, it becomes a matter of great concern that the shareholder should organize other shareholders in an effort to make the management more responsive to shareholder goals; or failing that, seek to depose that management. Ultimately, a shareholder may be forced to take a loss by selling his stock. But, the only investor in a depreciated stock is he who anticipates that he will be able to concentrate votes sufficient to depose the management; and by increasing the earnings of the corporation enhances the value of the stock.

Managerial Compensation and Mutuality. A curious and inconsistent view held by managers of mutual associations and government officials is that compensation to the officers of the mutual association should be higher than that for officers in the stock association. Inasmuch as the mutual management does not have property rights, he must be compensated by a higher salary as well as through receipt of various amenities. In order to secure the most efficient management, inducements in compensation are said to be a substitute for stock options.

Now this reasoning is clearly inconsistent with the mutual idea. To the extent that mutual management receives income in lieu of stock, it is difficult to see

---

[a]After his successful battle for the control of the New York Central, Robert R. Young submitted a bill for $1.3 million to cover his costs for proxy solicitation. He later settled for $300,000.[2]

how the mutual differs or is more efficient. An alleged advantage of the mutual is that, lacking the necessity to pay dividends to shareholders out of profits, saver-members will receive greater income on their savings accounts. But if their management receives direct pecuniary and indirect nonpecuniary offsets to make up for the lack of stock options, the differences from the stock association would be dissipated.

This leads to another question. Suppose the evidence supports the hypothesis that there are no differences between mutual and stock associations. One apparent reason for an absence of differences is that the mutual management receives in salary and nonpecuniary benefits amounts roughly equal to the entire profit of a stock association. If this were the case, the differences between the two types of associations would be mythical rather than actual. To the extent the mutual management receives income equivalent to profit in a stock association, there is clearly no meaning in the idea of mutuality. The philosophy of mutuality is not only contradicted; it would lack economic reality.

Separation of Control from Ownership. In the typical large-scale American corporation, the owners are separated from the management. A picture is presented of an autocratic management feathering its nest pursuing goals other than profit maximization. In one model, management is said to substitute a goal of sales maximization on the grounds that as sales increase, management compensation can thereby be inflated.[3] But it is not clear that the stockholders are as impotent as has been portrayed in some of the more recent contributions on this subject. One has only to compare the public discussion of managerial decision making both in the financial press and in the annual meetings with the iron curtain of secrecy which surrounds decision making in the mutual association. The differences with respect to information that relates to the mutual association as compared to the publicly-owned American corporation are so striking as to cast some doubt on the hypothesis that diffusion of ownership in the modern industrial corporation has been associated with managerial seizure of power.

Indeed, one of the laments of chief officials in stock saving and loan associations is that institutional shareholders particularly brokers, have exerted continual pressure upon management. Rarely have these shareholder groups been content to accept management's word for forecasts as to future trends in the industry. Nor do they acquiesce in a management refusal to answer relevant questions with respect to the balance sheet and income statement. Management has not been permitted to become indifferent to institutional reaction to performance of the enterprise. In contrast, a management which also owns stock has to be interested in the questions raised by shareholders. The latter's evaluation determines the price of the stock and, therefore, not only the value of the managerial investment but also the flow of new capital to the enterprise. When the stock price is high, less stock need be sold. The dilution of ownership is correspondingly less.

Absence of Ownership in Mutuals

In contrast, it seems that under the present legal interpretation the mutual association is not owned by the savers. The attitude of executives of mutual savings and loan associations and mutual savings banks is that the reserves are owned by the corporation rather than by the savers. This is similar for mutual insurance companies. It has been noted that there is a significant distinction between the early savings and loan associations which were terminating, voluntary, and purely private in character. "They were not charged with the public interest . . . the terminating type and the modern permanent mutual type cannot be equated."[4]

The liquidation of the member-savers rights in the mutual has its origin in a rationale developed with respect to claims to reserves. It is insisted by management spokesmen that it is necessary to build reserves for future losses:

If a mutual company were obliged to distribute as dividend during a policy term all the premium income in excess of losses and expenses, it would never be in a position to accumulate surplus and contingency reserves to meet anticipated emergencies. Neither is the company in any sense a partnership, nor can policyholders either during the term that policies are in force or afterwards compel distribution of surplus, contingency reserves, or any other form of safety fund the company may have accumulated.[5]

Reference to the legal decisions involving mutuals generally relates to insurance companies which have the same problems with management as mutual savings and loan associations. In the *White Fuel Corporation vs. Liberty Mutual Insurance Company*, the court said that the decisive question is whether a mutual insurance company can accumulate surplus funds for general strengthening of the company, "for which funds it is not obliged to account to those who were policyholders during the period of accumulation."[6] The court (a Massachusetts court) answered in the affirmative saying that accumulation is necessary "to give financial stability and continuity to mutual companies equivalent to that given stock companies by the capital stock and thus to assist the mutual principle as a whole to survive in the insurance business."[7]

In another case, *Greef vs. Equitable*, the court ruled that the principle which controls the disposition of surplus earnings of stock corporations is applicable to this mutual insurance company

In those cases it has often been held that until dividends have been declared a stockholder has no right of action at law to recover any part of the fund applicable to that purpose, and that when directors have exercised their discretion in regard thereto the courts will not interfere unless it is bad faith or willful neglect, or abuse of such discretion . . . we find nothing in the policy which requires the defendant to distribute its entire surplus among its policyholders.[8]

The courts have ruled that the surplus belongs to the corporation *as distinct from the policyholders*. The assets including the reserves and surplus are owned by the company and not by the policyholders and on conversion policyholders have prior right to subscribe to new stock. But policyholders have no right to the distribution of surplus funds. For the typical saving and loan mutual, "we find here also the principle firmly established that in a perpetually chartered savings and loan association the reserve belongs to the corporate entity as distinct from its members."[9] "Such a reserve fund is created to take care of contingent liabilities and losses occurring in the future." But the interest of the "owner" of a perpetually chartered mutual corporation in the corporation's reserves is purely *nominal* as affirmed by the Supreme Court of the United States in an Ohio case involving a mutual savings bank. The surplus is primarily a reserve against losses and secondarily a repository of undivided earnings. In England, it is to be noted, reserves have no independent existence.

"Our own federal supervisory authorities, likewise, take the position that the reserves are permanent, are institutionalized and are the property of the corporation rather than of the individual members and are to be used for general corporate purposes."[10]

Furthermore, it has been observed that membership in a mutual involves a creditor-debtor relationship. In addition, the insurance of accounts makes the reserves a contract between the corporation and the Federal Savings and Loan Insurance Corporation only. "Reserves are not deferred earnings but are what the regulators in substance say they are—a depreciation account for the sole purpose of absorbing losses which our experience tells us in due course will inevitably occur."[11]

Management Changes. It has often been suggested that the large mutual federal savings and loan associations are actually no different from the public holding companies. Evidence bearing on this subject will be discussed in the present context. Additional kinds of evidence will be developed later in the chapter.

Because the management of the mutual controls the association, he need not report to the member-saver. He has no difficulty in maintaining his authority. It is expected that management changes in mutuals would be relatively rare as compared to stock associations. In the latter, management presumably is judged by performance and when that performance fails to measure up to expectations, e.g., with respect to results relative to other associations, management is likely to be replaced.

Table 2-1 presents data with respect to the changes in management comparing California federally and state-chartered mutuals to state-chartered stock associations. A change in management is defined as a change in the president or listed manager. The table shows both the number of changes during the year, i.e., occurrences, as related to the number of associations in that ownership category. In addition, the ratio of the first column to the second indicates the number of

Table 2-1

Changes in Management: California Federal Associations Compared to Stock Associations[1]

Year	Federal[2]			Stock[2]		
	No. of Management Changes	No.[3] Mutual Ass'ns	No. of Management Changes / No. of Ass'ns	No. Management Changes	No. of[3] Stock Ass'ns	No. of Management Changes / No. of Ass'ns
1950-1951	2	92	2.2	13	74	17.6
1951-1952	8	91	8.8	7	78	9.0
1952-1953	8	89	9.0	18	76	10.5
1953-1954	8	84	9.5	11	82	13.4
1954-1955	8	82	9.8	13	93	14.0
1955-1956	4	79	5.1	16	104	15.4
1956-1957	3	78	3.8	23	109	21.1
1957-1958	5	82	6.1	28	123	22.8
1958-1959	2	82	2.4	31	140	22.1
1959-1960	4	80	5.0	37	136	27.2
1960-1961	3	78	3.8	36	143	25.2
1961-1962	6	77	7.8	45	169	28.1
1962-1963	3	76	3.9	45	162	27.8
1963-1964	4	79	5.1	53	177	29.9
	68	1149		366	1657	
Median Value			5.1			21.8

Total No. of Changes ÷ Total No. Ass'ns   5.9%   22.1%

1. Data refer to California state-chartered of which stock associations held 97% of the assets.
2. Data derived from Federal Home Loan Bank of San Francisco, Roster of Members, 1950-1965.
3. Includes only associations with one calendar year after receiving their charters.

management changes as a percentage of total possible changes. The median value reported for the stock associations was 28.8%; for the mutual associations it was 5.1%. Totaling the data reveals that for 68 occurrences or management changes in mutual associations, there were 1,149 nonoccurrences. For stock associations, there were 366 occurrences as compared to 1,657 nonoccurrences. Taking the number of changes as a ratio to the number of associations in the particular year, the values for the mutual associations were 5.9% as compared to 22.9% for the stock associations.

The null hypothesis that there is no difference with respect to the proportion of management changes in the federal associations as compared to the stock associations was tested as against the one-sided alternative that the proportion among the stock associations is higher. The test was set at the 1% level. Since the upper tail 1% rejection level for K, the standard normal variable, is 2.326, the null hypothesis is to be rejected for any larger value of K: that such a value would be due to chance is less than one in a hundred. A computation revealed K to be equal to 11.7. Therefore, the alternative hypothesis that management changes will be more frequent among stock associations is accepted. After all, it is not surprising that the management would find it easy to maintain control in an organization in which the member-savers are creditors with little incentive and power to participate in decision making. There are no effective challenges to management because there is no incentive to organize on the part of the creditor member. On the other hand, stock associations are similar to conventional corporations and face the same pressures for increased earnings and dividends. Their performance is judged as compared to the performance of other managers in other industries managing the invested dollars of shareholders.[b]

Nepotism. It is expected that since nepotism is both a nonpecuniary reward and a tax-free form of inheritance, it would be larger in mutuals. In lieu of both high salary and stock in the association, the management uses power to place relatives and friends in key positions, thereby permitting them to draw both pecuniary and nonpecuniary benefits. Similarly, management can pass on control of the association to relatives in the event of anticipated death or retirement. An inheritance tax need not be paid simply because legally there is no "ownership" by management.

The ubiquity of nepotism in the mutual association is attested to by a statement by John de Laittre, a former member of the Federal Home Loan Bank Board. He indicated in a talk before the United States Savings and Loan League that he had succeeded his father and grandfather in the Farmers and Mechanics Savings Bank in Minneapolis (a mutual savings bank).

Nepotism is defined as a relationship of the chief executive officer or in a few

---

[b]The occurrences and nonoccurrences reported by federal and stock associations for *each year* were tested also in terms of the null hypothesis. The latter was rejected at the 1% level.

instances, chairman of the board to other officers. The relationship is simply the same last name and obviously understates the degree of nepotism because it fails to include in-laws or relatives with different surnames. Data were collected for four years both to ascertain changes in trends and to avoid reliance upon merely one observation.

Table 2-2 summarizes the results dichotomized into occurrences and nonoccurrences of nepotism. In 1955, the California stock associations reported 23 incidents and 109 nonoccurrences or a ratio of 21.1%; the mutual associations showed 22 incidents and 56 nonoccurrences at 39.3%. The standard normal variables and probability that they would be exceeded are also shown for the years 1955, 1960, 1963 and 1967. Similar data are provided for Los Angeles associations. With the exception of the state data for 1967, the differences between the mutuals and the stock are statistically significant. Mutuals also showed a higher incidence of nepotism when the data were aggregated for the four years. In Los Angeles, the ratio of occurrences to nonoccurrences was 48.9 as compared to 16.0 for the stock.

These results may actually understate the incidence of nepotism in mutuals for another reason. Stock savings and loan associations were generally organized by one individual who secured a dominant part of the stock. This means that he could take advantage of the tax laws by training members of his family in a business they were later to inherit. Where the stock is widely distributed, there would be less tolerance of this practice for the obvious reason that shareholders prefer to hire only the most efficient officers.

It is to be expected that a mutual run in the interests of its members would show the same intolerance. It follows that it is not sufficient that mutuals show no greater nepotism than stock There should be less because *some* stock are closely controlled, thereby permitting owner-managers to employ members of their family. Our expectation is accordingly that mutuals would show *less* not similar nepotism to stock. An identical incidence would be expected only in the event that all stock associations were widely held.

Inasmuch as the test is for the null hypothesis that there are in fact no statistically significant differences between the mutual and stock, no recognition is made of the above factor in stock associations. It is not only that stock associations differ among themselves with respect to the proportion of shares held by the managers, but there is indeed reason for anticipating the practice of nepotism. On the other hand, there is no reason for expecting to find nepotism among mutuals that are run in the interests of their members. Mutuals should show less nepotism not more. It is therefore significant that the incidence of nepotism among them ranged from 71% to 291% more in the eight comparisons. Had they been run according to the principles of mutuality, the opposite would have been anticipated.

Table 2-2
Nepotism[1] in California: Mutual Associations Compared to Stock Associations

	Number of Occurrences of Nepotism	Number of Nonoccurrences of Nepotism	Occurrences / Nonoccurrences	Standard Normal Variable "k"	Probability that Standard Normal Variable is Exceeded
1955					
Los Angeles					
Mutual	12	25	48.0%		
Stock	9	47	19.1%	1.593	.0554
California					
Mutual	22	56	39.3		
Stock	23	109	21.1	1.666	.0480
1960					
Los Angeles					
Mutual	11	24	45.8		
Stock	7	60	11.7	2.344	.0095
California					
Mutual	21	55	38.2		
Stock	24	144	16.7	2.311	.0104

1963					
Los Angeles					
Mutual	12	23	52.2	2.440	.0073
Stock	11	62	17.7		
California					
Mutual	24	53	45.3	4.260	.0010
Stock	26	150	17.0		
1967					
Los Angeles					
Mutual	11	22	50.0	1.997	.0228
Stock	9	56	16.1		
California					
Mutual	18	65	27.7	1.390	.0823
Stock	25	154	16.2		
Totals					
Los Angeles					
Mutual	46	94	48.9	9.640	.0010
Stock	36	225	16.0		
California					
Mutual	85	229	37.1	4.028	.0010
Stock	98	557	17.6		

Source: Federal Home Loan Bank of San Francisco, Roster of Members: 1955 and 1963.
Notes: 1. Defined as same last of any officer with either managing officer, chairman of the board or president.

SAINT PETER'S COLLEGE LIBRARY
JERSEY CITY. NEW JERSEY 07306

Management and the Diversion Mechanism

A mutual is only to be understood in terms of the options and constraints on management as it attempts to convert power into both personal wealth and nonpecuniary benefits. Constraints on management's ability to seize potential profit directs the organization towards "second best" alternatives. This raises a question of whether such alternatives, or fringe benefits as they are known, are as effective incentives as direct monetary incentives. Clearly, "second best" alternatives are by definition less desirable. To that extent, more is required in order to derive a given input from management. It is significant that the president of the largest federal savings and loan association in the nation has urged that the authorities consider the conversion of the federal or mutual associations into stock associations. Obviously, such a transformation would have to be based on a showing of some net benefit to the economy. That an official of a large mutual would make the recommendation testifies to the rather obvious differences that exist between the two kinds of organizations.

It has generally been recognized that in the savings and loan industry, mutual salaries are tied to size. It makes considerable sense to pay the manager of an association with assets of more than \$100,000,000 a higher salary than an association with assets of \$10,000,000. Kendall has commented that "savings and loan managers also recognize that the larger their institution becomes, the greater is its ability to compensate those on the executive staff responsible for the services rendered by that institution ... since most institutions are mutual in character, these factors—the growth and responsibilities and earning assets—become highly important motivations to management."[12]

Indeed, the relationship between size and compensation has also been explored with respect to the conventional stock corporation. Baumol has developed a hypothesis with respect to the large industrial corporation which substitutes *sales* maximization for profit maximization.[13] Referring to an oligopolistic, noncompetitive model, he postulates that large-scale management seeks to maximize sales or revenue under the constraint that it must maintain competitive dividends and earnings in order to secure new funds from the capital market. It is pertinent to cite his comment that "the mutual life insurance companies, for whom profits are not even readily defined, may be particularly obvious sales maximizers."[14]

To the extent that mutual management links compensation to size in the form of total sales or revenue, it might be expected that the Baumol model would be applicable to the savings and loan industry. In comparing a profit-maximizing firm to a sales-maximizing firm "the (long-run) sales maximizer must end up the larger while the profit maximizer produces more income for its stockholders."[15] The evidence with respect to relative growth of stock associations as compared to mutual associations does not confirm the Baumol hypothesis. Nor is it supported when mutual associations in California are compared to stock associations. In both cases, stock associations have grown at considerably faster rates than mutual associations. Now this difference may not necessarily invalidate the Baumol hypothesis. This is because stock associations in California, as well as in other states, have generally been managed by their owners. Where the stock is not widely diffused, the classical profit-maximizing model is applicable. Differences are attributable to type of organization.

The Baumol model would be more appropriate for the large industrial corporation where the stockholders are widely diffused so that no one can exert influence on the management. For reasons indicated elsewhere, as well as for the evidence to be presented in this chapter, the Baumol hypothesis has to be rejected. The evidence indicates that there are differences in the operating results of mutual or management-dominated associations as compared to stock associations—even where the stock is widely distributed among the shareholders. Diffusion is not a sufficient condition for management control in that it permits the substitution of management goals for owner goals.[16]

So far as this study is concerned, it is sufficient to compare stock associations to mutual associations with respect to at least one of the tests, growth. As a later chapter goes into this matter in more detail, it is sufficient to merely summarize here. The test of the Baumol hypothesis is found in the relative rates of growth as between mutual and stock associations. The differences are significant and substantial. Whether or not the management of the stock associations is responsive to the shareholders is irrelevant. The fact is that there are differences and that these differences were suggested by the hypothesis with respect to variations in the types of ownership. Thus, though the evidence may not necessarily directly bear on the Baumol hypothesis, it most certainly is relevant that due to the differences in ownership, there will be differences in operating results as measured by expenses, growth rate, maximization of sales, profits, etc.

Buildings and Furnishings. Table 2-3 shows office buildings and furniture as a percentage of average assets for both federally-chartered and state-chartered associations in those states permitting the stock form for the year 1962. In nine of the eleven states, the ratio for the stock associations was below that for the federal associations. In Texas where the ratio is higher, it is to be noted that the stock share of the state-chartered is 77%. The contribution of the state mutuals to this ratio exerts some influence on the outcome. So far as Wyoming is concerned, the probable reason is that as the stock associations are new, they have had to build capacity in advance of the market.

It may be important that investment in furnishings is limited in certain states, e.g., California: state-chartered associations are not permitted to invest in furniture, fixtures, furnishings, equipment or leasehold improvements to an amount greater than 20% of the nonwithdrawable capital if the premises are owned; nor larger than 30% if the premises are leased.[17]

Table 2-4 shows buildings and office furnishings as a percentage of networth

Table 2-3
Office Buildings and Furniture as a Percentage of Average Assets

| | 1962 | |
| | Office Building (net) plus Furniture and Fixture (net) as a Percentage of Average Assets | |
State	Federal	State[1]
Arizona	2.94	2.83
California	1.83	1.49
Colorado	2.65	2.25
Idaho	1.49	0.20
Kansas	1.95	1.10
Nevada	3.62	1.20
Ohio	1.75	1.49
Oregon	1.91	1.79
Texas	2.16	2.24
Utah	1.91	1.70
Wyoming	2.30	3.54
Mean	2.23	1.80
USA	1.76	1.49

Source: Federal Home Loan Bank Board, combined financial statements: Members of the Federal Home Loan Bank Systems, 1962, Washington, D.C.
Notes: 1. Insured Associations

Table 2-4
Building and Office Furnishings as a Percentage of Net Worth, 1964: California Federal Associations Compared to Stock Associations

	Buildings and Furnishings[1]	Net Worth	Buildings and Furnishings Net Worth
Federal	157,762	528,463	29.9%
Stock	186,112	1,125,425	16.5%

Source: Federal Home Loan Bank Board. *Combined Financial Statements*, 1964, Washington, D.C.
Notes: [1] In thousands of dollars.

for 1964 for California federal associations compared to stock associations: the federal associations had 29.9%, the stock associations 16.5%. The federal associations expenditures on such items relative to net worth was 80.0% higher than that of the stock associations. Had the federal associations achieved a ratio equal to that of the stock associations, their investment in building and office furnishings would have been $87.2 million. This would have made for a savings of $70.6 million and would have increased net worth by 13.4%. Now given the rate of return to net worth which was achieved by the California stock associations at

25%, this would have meant an extra return for that year of $17,650,000. Inasmuch as the federal associations paid out $218,000,000 in dividends that year, the extra $17,650,000 would have increased dividends by 8%, which is to say each saver would have received an additional eight cents per dollar of savings. In five years, the $88,250,000 savings would have grown at similar rates of return to $268,000,000 or roughly 22% more than the dividends paid by federal associations in 1962. The significance of these data with respect to funds tied up in building and furnishings is that both the liquidity and the net worth of the association is reduced. When such funds are available, there is just that much less necessity for expensive resort to the Federal Home Loan Banks for liquidity. Furthermore, funds in net worth as part of reserves and surplus represent interest-free reserves and become earning assets.

It is possible to estimate the expenditure on buildings and furnishings as a form of amenities for the management by the use of the regression analysis. Though there were the usual problems of multicollinearity, statistically significant regression coefficients were obtained for two variables, number of savings accounts and loans made. The data for the thirty-eight mutual areas related to the five years, 1961 through 1965. The resulting regression coefficients were later used to derive the estimated expenses for mutuals with the same product mix as Los Angeles and San Francisco. A mutual estimate for buildings and furnishings was substituted for the actual buildings and furnishings on the grounds that mutual expenditures for these purposes would differ from stock.

Table 2-5 reports the results of these multiple regression procedures. While the coefficients of determination were high, and in four of the five years over 0.94, there was a decline each of the last three years. The standard error of estimate increased each year beginning from just over 4.1 the first year and rising to 9.7 the fifth year.

Table 2-5
Regression Equations for "Buildings and Furnishings," Mutual Savings and Loan Associations, 38 Areas, 1961-65

	Regression Coefficients and Standard Errors				
	Constant Term	Number of Savings Accounts	Loans Made	R^2	Standard Error of Estimate
1961	−0.97004	0.01285 (0.00343)	0.05012 (0.00656)	0.9515	4.14006
1962	−0.83503	0.01606 (0.00357)	0.04457 (0.00605)	0.9478	4.92372
1963	−1.41696	0.02100 (0.00383)	0.04114 (0.00594)	0.9381	6.26169
1964	−2.05649	0.01636 (0.00501)	0.06036 (0.00880)	0.9277	7.61910
1965	−4.00717	0.00286 (0.00987)	0.10631 (0.01962)	0.8998	9.71402

Source: Federal Home Loan Bank Board, Federal Home Loan Bank of San Francisco and California Division of Savings and Loan.

Table 2-6

Comparison of Actual Investment on Building and Furnishings by Los Angeles and San Francisco Stock Associations to Estimates Derived from Multiple Regression Equations Board on Identical Product Mix, 1961-65

		Actual Investment	Estimated Investment	Excess of Estimated Over Actual	Estimated / Actual	Excess / Standard Error of Estimates
1961	LA	53,595	88,263	34,668	164.7%	8.37
	SF	12,812	20,290	7,478	158.4%	1.81
1962	LA	72,639	121,412	48,773	167.1%	9.91
	SF	15,208	25,835	10,627	169.9%	2.16
1963	LA	86,769	160,100	73,331	184.5%	11.7
	SF	20,147	34,472	14,325	171.1%	2.29
1964	LA	99,215	208,700	100,985	209.8%	14.3
	SF	20,869	73,307	53,438	351.3%	6.88
1965	LA	113,068	260,748	147,680	230.6%	15.2
	SF	31,401	94,407	63,006	300.6%	6.49

Sources: Federal Home Loan Bank Board, *Combined Financial Statements*, 1961-65; Federal Home Loan Bank of San Francisco, *Roster of Members*, 1962-66.

Table 2-6 presents a comparison of actual investment on buildings and furnishings by Los Angeles and San Francisco stock associations to estimates derived from mutual regression equations based on identical product mix. In each instance, the mutual with the same product mix would have spent more on such items. The excess of the estimate over the actual stock investment is shown along with the ratio of the former to the latter. The final column shows the ratio of the excess to the standard error of estimate. For each year, the differences are statistically significant at the ninety-nine percent level for Los Angeles. The San Francisco differences are significant at the ninety-five percent level. It is clear that management is taking some part of its nonpecuniary income in the form of attractive furnishings as compared to the stock associations.

Mortgage Brokerage Services

Control of an established and large mutual savings and loan association offers opportunities to the management not available to the general public. For example, in Los Angeles, eastern insurance companies seek sources to originate mortgages. Naturally, they want individuals with experience. The management of a federal association obviously has achieved the expertise and experience that goes with both originating and servicing those mortgages. He is a natural candidate for the role of mortgage correspondent to the eastern companies. But, in addition, there is another reason why the privately-owned affiliates of the management of the mutual savings and loan may be favored in the choice of mortgage correspondent by the insurance company. It is in the nature of a payoff simply because the savings and loan association has at its disposal the insurance to protect homes against fire. It is no accident that at one time the president of the largest federal savings and loan association also owned with his brother-in-law the largest mortgage banking organization in Southern California. Nor was it any less peculiar that another large federal association was run by the owner of one of the largest mortgage companies in the area.

But there are problems in this network of affiliations.[18] The most obvious is the self-dealing and "conflicts of interest" which can arise when it becomes profitable to the management of the mutual savings and loan association to send the best mortgages (at a good price, of course) to the insurance companies. Since savings and loan holding companies are censured when this occurs, it would seem to be, *a fortiori*, equally the case for the mutual infrastructure.[19]

There is, in addition, another arrangement open to the diversified mutual which involves a conflict of interest.[20] Because the management can decide which insurance company will receive the business generated by the savings and loan activities with respect to home insurance, insurance companies can and do offer inducements for the business which is paid for in higher insurance costs. The most obvious, apart from a mortgage correspondent position, is a loan to the management or to his relatives and friends. Inasmuch as the savings and loan association, and in particular the mutual association, is precluded from making loans to officers other than that restricted to their private residence, control over placing of the home insurance business provides the management with excellent opportunities for securing not only the correspondent business but also loans under the most favorable terms. Such business arrangements are a consequence of positions held by management in the mutual and are not available to ordinary borrowers. Stock owner-managers have no motive for raising insurance costs. Indeed, the pressure is to lower them!

Insurance. Whenever an association acquires a mortgage or makes a loan on a dwelling, it is necessary that that dwelling be insured against destruction due to fire. In a sense, since the money loaned is the association's, there is no reason why the association should not specify the insurer. But, the insurance agents, competitive with savings and loan associations, have objected to an alleged coercion of borrowers. Pressure by California insurance agents has secured an addition to the California insurance code prohibiting coercion of borrowers by lender with respect to the choice of insurance agents or company.[22]

The insurance business is lucrative in that the association or the management not only has no solicitation expenses, because the borrower is already on the premises, but the management or agency may also receive the renewal and other forms of insurance, e.g., auto, life, etc. It is generally believed in the industry that this insurance business is pure profit since there are no expenses in connection with placing the business on *his* agency's books. Not only are the borrowers "captive," but as the officers of the association transact the loan, there is nothing to stop them from wearing another hat on and simultaneously selling insurance. The expenses for placement of the insurance business is borne by the association while the receipts go to the privately-owned affiliate.

The insurance business offers many attractive features. On $20 million in mortgages, if the average size of the mortgage is $10,000, there are 2,000 units to be insured. The premium is roughly about $30 on $100 for three years or $20,000 a year and is all "gravy." Obviously, the association employees must also be part of the insurance infrastructure. It is their responsibility to make sure that the mortgage is protected against fire by insisting on the purchase of insurance.[c]

Bank Deposits. In 1964, 4.13% of the assets of federally-chartered associations in Los Angeles were held in the form of cash on hand or in commercial banks. The five largest federals with an average $642 million in assets, each averaged $27 million. With certificates of deposits selling at 4%, the return would have been $1 million. If the management of the large federal decides to forego interest[d] in favor of a demand deposit, it is obvious that a bank would have little difficulty in showing gratitude.[e]

The placement of savings and loan association cash flows is not inconsiderable. When "loans repaid" are added to net savings for 1964, the five largest federals would have had about $148 million in-flow and the next five $56 million. Commercial banks can create many opportunities for acknowledging their gratitude for such deposits. Lines of credit readily become available to the savings and loan association officials, and may be used to purchase options for speculative land appreciation—an arrangement not permitted officers of the savings and loan associations with their own institutions. Business associates in other areas of investment, on the reference of the savings and loan official, may secure loans for which they would otherwise not qualify. Whether it be commercial bank deposits or the sale of insurance, escrow, or trustee relationships is immaterial; management is in a position to use the margin between prices and costs as a bargaining arrangement similar to "tie-in" sale. Shaw comments that

ties with the infrastructure are not compatible with economy in operating savings and loan associations. Prices charged to associations for services and affili-

[c]The late Howard Ahmanson, President and owner of Home Savings and Loan Association, the largest savings and loan association in the nation, originally entered the savings and loan industry from the insurance business.

[d]The New York Legislative Inquiry of 1905 (the Armstrong Committee) revealed that the large New York insurance companies had maintained unduly large cash balances in banks in which both their offices and the companies themselves were heavily involved.[23]

[e]"The varieties of situations in which directors use their position to obtain credit either directly from their institutions or indirectly by depositing their firm's funds in another institution which in turn extends them credit are numerous. These transactions are being uncovered with increasing frequency as defaults rise."[24]

ates do not always appear to be competitive market prices. Rather they seem to be shallow prices for distributing revenues between associations and their affiliates according to the preferences of top management.[25]

It is the contention of this study that there are differences in the infrastructure arrangements as between mutual and stock associations. The mutual alone is constrained towards diverting income from the association to the privately-owned subsidiaries. The objective of the stock association is relatively simple, maximization of profit. It makes no difference where the profit is earned. In the mutual association, it is necessary to secure the business for the affiliates. It is not desirable, in terms of management goals, that the business should go to the association in the absence of the "tie-in" feature. Therefore, to secure the business on terms profitable for the infrastructure, management requires the establishment of nonmarket clearing prices.

At prices where demand exceeds supply, management can "trade off" by rationing a service in return for securing the related business for its affiliates. In contrast, no such constraint operates for the stock association.

This does not mean that stock associations will not also own affiliates: they are incidental only to the main business, home financing. The advantage from owning an affiliate, e.g. insurance, is that since the homes must be insured to protect the association's loans and, inasmuch as the borrower is on the association premises or in the loan office, the additional costs for the insurance business are nonexistent or best nominal. But, the stock association has no reason to insist on the insurance business. A diversion mechanism is neither an integral or a necessary part of the operation. Nor is it consistent with objectives relating to the exercise of property rights in a profit oriented milieu.

Diversion of Fee Income. In the period 1960 to 1964, the California federally chartered savings and loan associations did about the same proportion of construction lending relative to "loans made" as the California stock associations. Inasmuch as the main source of fees is in construction lending where the rates are higher, it is to be expected that a ratio of fees to "loans made" should roughly be identical for both federal stock associations. In 1962, the California stock associations, ratio of fee to "loans-made" was 3.14; the California federal association 2.32. In 1963, the ratio for the stock associations was 2.77 and the federals, 2.14.

Had the federal association reported the same proportion of fees to "loans made" as the stock associations, they would have earned $15.1 million more in premiums in 1962; and $15.0 million more in 1963. This would have come to $218,810 per federal association in 1962; and $211,420 in 1963. Or this difference expressed as a percent of average savings capital would have allowed for an 0.32 increase in the dividend paid in 1962 and 0.27 more in 1963. Or, to express it another way, the difference came to 47% of compensation paid in 1962 and 40% in 1963.

But the real significance of this difference in the ratio of fees to "loans made" is to be seen by comparing the difference to the five largest, ten largest, and fifteen largest federal associations. The federal associations had roughly the same proportion of construction loans as compared to "loans made" as stock associations. Therefore, they should have secured the same ratio. It is suggested that the reason they did not is that the fees were absorbed by affiliates or subsidiaries owned by the management of the federal associations: the fees received by federal associations were less by the amount of that diversion. If we allocate the fees as proportional to asset size, each of the five largest federal associations would have diverted $1.2 million; or each of the ten largest $825,605; and each of the fifteen largest $654,480.

Estimated Value of Related Activities. An effort is made here to estimate the income derived from the infrastructure. The net income for 17 California public holding companies may be compared to the net income of their 43 associations to provide income attributed to the infrastructure. The assumption is that accounting procedures are roughly similar for the holding companies and associations which report income to the California Savings and Loan Commissioner. The difference in net income between the holding companies' and associations' income originates in related activities such as insurance, escrow, land development, mortgage brokerage and title companies. The value of the related activities, based upon net worth of associations owned by the holding companies, came to 2.61% (see table 2-7). It is suggested that if the income of the mutual associations in California were truly owned by the savers, they would have received a comparable amount. That they did not, indicates the failure of mutual goals to be achieved as a consequence of a diversion to management. Obviously, had the mutuals acted as the stock, price to borrowers would have been lower and the estimates also lower.

The discrepancy between the net income reported by the holding companies and that reported by their individual associations came to $10.6 million. When this is related to their net worth less their capital stock (to make them comparable to federals which have no stock), the non-association income came to 2.61%. Thirty-five Los Angeles federal associations had a net worth of $331.3 million. Assuming that they would have been as efficient as the holding companies, their affiliates in related lines would have earned an estimated $8.6 million. The average net income per federal would have been $247,045. That is, each chief officer would have earned that amount.

The importance of this source of income for the managing officer in a mutual is more strikingly revealed by concentrating on the larger associations. Using the same ratio, the chief officers of the largest five associations would have received on the average $976,297. The executives of the next largest five would have earned an estimated $254,183. These estimates represent funds that might have gone into the mutual. It is apparent that control of a mutual is exceptionally valuable.

Table 2-7

Estimate of Net Income from Public Holding Companies Affiliated Savings and Loan Associations, 1963

Net Income[1]	
17 Holding Companies	$90,622,000
Net Income[2]	
43 Associations	80,055,000
Income from Related Activities	10,567,000
Holding Companies: 43 Associations'	
Net Worth at Beginning of Year	405,291,000
Income/Net Worth	2.61%
35 Los Angeles Federals[3]	
Net Worth	331,287,000
Estimated Value of Affiliates on	
basis 17 Holding Compnies %	8,646,591
Average to Each Federal Chief Officer	247,045
Average to 5 largest Federal Chief Officer	976,297
Average to next 5 largest Federal Chief Officer	254,183

Notes

1. Holding Company Reports.

2. California Division of Savings and Loan.

3. FHLB, Roster of Members, 1964.

3

Differences in Expenses and Operating Characteristics

Performance cannot be judged simply by one test or even one set of similar tests. An evaluation of the relative performance of mutual and stock savings and loan associations must recognize the diversity in the goals of the two types of organization. Tests appropriate for the mutual might have no meaning for the stock association. To illustrate, it is conventional to look at expenses. This is appropriate in considering a mutual savings and loan association because expenses represent the principal *direct* method of compensating management. In the stock association, expenses are minimized only in a *ceteris paribus* sense. They are justifiably incurred when the additional revenue associated with them is larger. In a profit-maximizing institution, marginal calculation will justify additional expenses when the additional revenue is larger.

It is necessary to consider a number of tests and to keep in mind not only the objective of the study but also the purposes of the organization in terms of both managerial and owner or membership goals. Expenses and net income are often expressed as a ratio to assets. This would appear to be a desirable or meaningful procedure when a comparison between different geographical areas such as cities or states is sought. The difficulty is that the ratio which compares expenses to assets is not meaningful unless the *ceteris paribus* assumption is maintained, i.e., the product mixes are equal. Otherwise, the difference in the expense ratio reflects the differences in the product mix rather than differences in efficiency or relative performance.

So far as the objectives of saving members in an association are concerned, tests frequently used are the ratios of net income and dividends to average savings capital. Both would be necessary since the former indicates what amount was available for savers while the latter that actually received. Another test important for savers, concerned with the relative safety of their deposit as well as regulatory authorities interested in performance, is "capital adequacy" as measured by the ratio of net worth to savings. Again, there is a problem in comparing mutuals to stock associations which arises because of the lack of an ownership interest in the mutual. Because the management does not own any part of the net worth of the organization, it has less incentive to enhance it. Ratios of profits or net after dividends to net worth will not have the same meaning in the mutual association.

An indication of the importance of nonpecuniary goals is found in the ratio of office buildings plus furnishings to net worth. A related test is provided by current expenses on buildings and furnishings as a percentage to gross operating income or net income. The difficulty with using income as a denominator is identical to that from using assets or savings capital: a disproportionate weight is attached to past transactions. In 1962, member associations in the United States reported a ratio of interest income to gross operating income of 84%. If the average turnover of mortgages is 14% and interest rates are fairly stable, 72% of the gross income would have originated from transactions made in previous time periods. A way of avoiding this difficulty might be for certain services to take another ratio, *viz*., compensation as a percentage of fees, on the theory that since fees represent, to a considerable extent, the actual activity for the current year, they would be more appropriate. Here again, there are difficulties in that these are also a way of adjusting mortgage interest and do not exclusively relate to expenses. Variations between associations and characteristics differing between regions with respect to the perfection of competition would effect the level of fees. The fee is also considered an indication of the monopoly power of associations in a particular area rather than an indication of capital shortage; and, therefore, a part of true interest.[a]

Operating Characteristics: Ratios

The hypothesis is that the mutual in contrast to the stock will report a rate of growth associated both with lower gross operating income and lower dividend rates paid to savers. The relevant comparisons are (1) between the California federal and stock associations; and (2) the California stock associations as compared to the remainder of the United States (which is dominated by the mutual form). The reason for the two comparisons is that the California federally-chartered associations have had to develop some of the attributes of the stock associations in order to survive. Unlike mutuals elsewhere in the nation, they must compete with stock associations. Consequently, the differences between California federals and California stocks would not be as large as that between the latter and mutuals outside of California.

Table 3-1 presents the operating results for 1962 and 1963 with respect to certain ratios: new loans to average assets, expenses to average assets, gross operating income to average assets, fees to loans made, dividends to average savings capital, and allocations to reserves and surplus to average net worth. The significant aspect of the differences is the higher ratio of activity as measured by "new loans" or "loans made" as compared to average assets for the California

---

[a]Speaking of fees and charges "a second element is monopoly profit that an association can extract from a borrower whose alternative loan opportunity are few or nil . . . Fees and charges give (mortgage rate of interest) flexibility inconspicuously and reversibly. They perform the function for mortgage rate that premiums, now essentially disallowed, once performed for share rates and that individual promotion performs for both. Where mortgage markets are especially subject to fluctuating demand for loans, one can expect a high proportion of fees and charges to interest revenue or associations."[1]

Table 3-1

Operating Characteristics: U.S. Compared to California, Mutual and Stock Associations*

	New Loans ÷ Average Assets	Expenses ÷ Average Assets	Gross Op. Income ÷ Ave. Assets	Fees ÷ Loans Made	Dividends ÷ Average Saving Cap.	Allocation to Reserve and Surplus ÷ Ave. Net Worth
1962						
U.S. less California Insured Members FHLB	21.3	1.14	5.55	1.49	4.01	12.6
California Federals	31.8	1.28	6.38	2.32	4.59	18.1
California Stock	41.3	1.31	7.10	3.14	4.84	22.0
1963						
U.S. less California	21.2	1.17	5.48	1.29	4.04	9.3
California Federals	34.9	1.36	6.31	2.14	4.72	11.8
California Stock	45.1	1.42	6.60	2.77	4.78	15.4

stock associations. Not only are they twice that for the United States without California, but they represent another 33% higher amount as compared to California federals in the same market area.

Expenses. It has been noted that expense data must be interpreted with caution. The major qualifying factor is that the purposes of the manager may differ because of the type of ownership. Accordingly, the judgment of performance has to consider not only one test such as expenses but also other tests which relate to both other activities of the association and other objectives of the association.[b]

Emphasis in a mutual is on expenses rather than profit; and is directed to both managerial compensation as well as the indirect nonpecuniary benefits arising out of the manager's position. When California federal associations are compared to stock associations in 1962, the latter with a new loan volume of $3.8 billion was twice the federals with $1.8 billion. Yet the stock associations' expenses at $119.3 million were only 62% larger than the federals expenses at $73.8 million (Table 3-2). On the basis of a variance of Parkinson's law, expenses are what income permits.

Table 3-2
Expenses and Activities: California Federals Compared to Stock, 1962[1]

	Federal	Stock	Stock as a % of Federal
New Loans[2]	$ 1.838	3.752	201.4
Expenses[3]	73.8	119.3	161.7

Notes: 1. In millions.
2. Federal Home Loan Bank of San Francisco.
3. Federal Home Loan Bank Board, Combined Financial Statements, Washington, D.C., 1962.

The Trend in Expenses, 1950 to 1964. When the ratio of total operating expenses is averaged[c] for the years 1962-1964 and compared to the average for 1950-1952, the United States without California showed an increase of 434% (see Table 3-3). The increase in annual activity as measured by "loans made" was 285%. The number of mortgage accounts increased by 122% and the number of savings accounts 186%. Since the major item in expenses is loan origination, it is significant that the increase in expenses was 52% higher than the increase in "loans made." California stock expenses increased 1296%, while "loans made"

---

[b]In suggesting that there are no significant internal economies of scale, Grebler and Brigham contend that such holds "regardless whether operating efficiency is measured by costs, returns on assets, or profits, and regardless whether or not public holding company affiliates are treated as one institution."[2]

[c]To eliminate the influence of an "unusual" year.

Table 3-3
Trends in Expenses as Related to Other Variables, 1950-1964: PERCENTAGES

	Expenses	"Loans Made"	Assets	Number of Mortgages	Number of Savings Accounts
U.S. less California	434	285	457	122	186
California Federals	499	390	609	277	336
California Stocks	1,296	1,363	1,702	554	1,039

Source: Federal Home Loan Bank Board, *Combined Financial Statements*, 1950-1964.

rose 1363%. The ratio of incremental expenses to incremental loans was 0.95 for the stock as compared to 1.52 for the United States without California. Where expenses increased by 434% for the United States, assets increased 457%. In contrast, the California stock association expenses increased 1296% and assets 1702%.[d]

The expense-to-asset ratio for insured savings and loan associations in the United States in 1950 was 1.29; in 1963 it was 1.21. But the ratios of "loans made" to assets fell from 38.9% to 27.6%, i.e., a 27.6% drop. Construction loans as a ratio to assets fell from 13.8% to 7.9% (a 43% drop). The mutuals' expenses were increasing not only at a considerably higher rate than "loans made" but also at a higher rate than the number of mortgages and savings accounts which required servicing. In contrast, expenses for the California stock associations increased somewhat less than "loans made" and substantially less than the percentage increase in assets. The percentage increase in expenses for the California federals was similar to the United States: it was also larger than the increase in "loans made" and close to the increase in assets, suggesting that expenses were increased in line with the maintenance of a stable expense to asset ratio. Expenses were what income and assets permitted.

The table reveals that the mutuals increased their expenses much more than the stock when compared to the growth in "new loans." The number of mortgages they serviced increased but 28% of expenses; 43% of "loans made"; and 27% of assets. Between 1950 and 1964, expenses in the United States less California increased more than three and a half times that of the increase in the number of mortgages and almost two and a half times the increase in the number of savings accounts. In contrast, expenses among the California stock associ-

---

[d]There is a possible shortcoming in these comparisons that could be attributable to variations in the average size of "loans made" by the California institutions as compared to the remainder of the country. On the basis of estimated changes in average mortgage size 1950-1964, U.S. (less California) was 82.1% of California. California stock "loans made" were deflated with the result that the increase in expenses came to 115.8% of the increase in new loans. Notwithstanding the adjustment, the U.S. increase was 31.5% more than this deflated estimate.

ations increased only 30% more than the percentage increase in the number of savings accounts and were two and a half times the increase in the number of mortgage accounts as compared to three and a half times for the mutuals in the remainder of the United States.

The increase in expenses cannot be explained by the increase in the number of mortgages or savings accounts. It is simply rational behavior by management in a mutual association: the increase in assets is a basis and apparent justification for increasing compensation. This is only one of the mechanisms by which the mutual management exercises power. It also represents a diversion of association income from savers and thus defeating the purposes of mutuality.

Mutuals follow a pattern, where as assets increase, management claims the possible savings through an increase in expenses. Expenses are kept in line with assets so that the expense-to-asset ratio is reasonably stable. The increase in assets might have allowed for an increase in net income for savers but, inasmuch as savers have to be paid only the money market rate, management simply increases compensation, fringe benefits and diversion possibilities.

The Decline in "Loans Repaid"

A significant factor in accounting for the lag in "loans made" as compared to expenses is that over the period, 1950-1964, there was an increase in the average life of mortgages from 4.3 years to 6.9 years. This is a 62.2% jump. During the same period, the average loan balance measured in dollars, increased 165% from $3,644 in 1950 to $9,463 in 1963.

Table 3-4 shows the ratio of mortgages paid off as a percentage of the loan balance at the beginning of the year for the period 1954 to 1962 for California as compared to the United States without California. Inasmuch as both the California federals and stock are in the same market, the turnover rates are not surprisingly different: data are reported for California as a whole. The meaning

Table 3-4
Mortgages Paid Off as a Percentage of Loan Balance,[1] 1954-1962

	1954	1955	1956	1957	1958	1959	1960	1961	1962	Average
California	28.4	34.7	27.4	23.5	22.5	25.2	21.0	34.4	19.5[2]	26.3
U.S. less California	21.4	25.1	21.0	17.6	17.6	17.4	14.5	13.8	14.0	18.1

Source: Federal Home Loan Bank Board, Combined Financial Statement: Members of the Federal Home Loan Bank System, 1953-62, Washington, D.C. Federal Home Loan Bank Board, Savings and Home Financing Source Book, 1963, Washington, D.C.
Notes:
1. At beginning of the year.
2. Corrected for net participations.

of this substantial and continuous decline in the turnover rate in recent years is illustrated in the following example. Suppose the turnover rate in the initial period represents 30% of "mortgages held" at the beginning of the year. In order to maintain the mortgage portfolio at the same size, it would be necessary to make new loans at a 30% rate. If the mortgage portfolio was $100 million, $30 million in "new loans" would be required. If, however, the growth rate is rather moderate at 5%, only $5 million more is necessary. The consequence of a decline in "loans repaid" or turnover rate from 30% to 20 is that it only is necessary to add $20 million in loans or one-third less to maintain a constant size.

It is possible to continue the same rate of "new loan" activity without increasing expense since the reduction in the turnover rate frees expense for $10 million in additional loans and makes the growth rate 15%. This can be achieved with no actual increase in expenses. Or put another way, the association could have maintained the portfolio at $100 million while reducing expenses by the amount no longer required to be spent on securing $30 million worth of mortgages. The lower expenses are a result of the 33 1/3% decline in "loans repaid."

Ceteris paribus, a decline in the ratio of "loans repaid" to the mortgage balance or a decline in the ratio of "loans made" to that denominator should reduce expenses since the associated activities would be correspondingly reduced. The decline in this turnover ratio made it possible for savings and loan associations to achieve the fantastic growth rates of the last 15-year period. But though an increasing portion of the "loans made" went for growth as compared to replacements, the increase in expenses was 52% higher than the increase in "loans made." The shift to growth was not sufficient to take up the full amount that would have been saved in expenses. It is clear that management diverted part of the savings from the association. The lower turnover rate permits both growth and the opportunity for higher expenses with respect to either compensation, amenities, etc. Had management simply chosen to maintain the association at the same size, the decline in the turnover rate would have permitted a reduction in expenses with a higher net income for savers; or it could have transferred the savings from lower expenses to its own pocket.

Expenses and Growth. When a savings and loan association is capable of reducing and minimizing expenses, the return or earnings are that much greater. As reserves or net worth is enhanced, a basis is provided for further growth. It has been said that if savings and loan associations were taxed similar to commercial banks, the dividend rate would have to be cut one-fourth of a percent. "Our business would grow faster if we could put more into reserves. . . . If our ability to put money into reserves is impaired, this will hold back the growth of the business, for we can grow only to the extent that we put money into reserves."[3]

The accumulation of earnings in the form of reserves means that part of the total assets are represented by interest-free funds, i.e., the savings and loan association has created a capital fund as a consequence of both favorable lending conditions and efficiency. Not only does the accumulation of this capital fund make it possible for the association to grow but also increases the ability to pay higher dividends. Thus, it is important to compare the operating results with respect to net income for the federal associations as compared to the stock association. Table 3-5 reports the results for three years. The stock associations showed higher ratios of net income to average savings in all but two of the cases in each of the three years. In the two states where the federal appeared to do better, part of the result may be attributed to the fact that the data for the state-chartered in Kansas also include state mutuals which make up 31% of the assets; and in Texas 23% of the assets.

Table 3-5
Net Income as a Percentage of Average Savings: Stock States, Federal Associations Compared to Stock Associations

| | 1960 | | 1961 | | 1962 | | 1963 | |
	Federal	Stock	Federal	Stock	Federal	Stock	Federal	Stock
Arizona	5.02	5.06	4.95	4.84	5.41	5.79	5.29	6.17
California	5.57	6.33	5.75	6.51	6.10	7.18	5.69	6.16
Colorado	5.08	5.13	5.24	5.49	5.51	6.04	5.06	5.25
Idaho	4.78	5.72	4.89	5.41	5.19	5.43	4.92	5.14
Kansas	4.93	4.72	5.07	4.90	5.40	5.07	4.94	4.87
Nevada	5.60	5.92	5.48	7.30	5.67	12.64	5.87	8.70
Ohio	4.48	4.79	4.55	4.80	4.74	5.05	4.58	4.67
Oregon	4.76	4.82	5.04	5.31	5.09	6.38	4.88	5.18
Texas	4.88	4.84	4.91	4.95	5.08	5.43	4.96	5.07
Utah	4.80	5.12	5.19	5.23	5.84	5.80	5.12	5.07
Washington	4.79	5.83	5.03	5.57	5.25	5.79	4.99	4.91
Wyoming	–	–	4.84	6.42	4.94	5.70	4.75	5.53
U.S.	4.64	4.92	4.88	5.09	5.11	5.45	4.85	5.12

Source: Federal Home Loan Bank Board, *Combined Financial Statements*, 1959-63, Washington, D.C.

Volume of Operation. It has been suggested previously that measurement by total assets is misleading since the volume of assets in no way reflects the activity at any one period. To illustrate, an association of $100 million in assets may "originate" $20 million in loans annually, while another association of similar asset size or even less might originate $40 million "new loans." Obviously, the latter association will have higher expenses. Table 3-6 presents "new loans" or "loans made" as a percentage of average mortgages "held" for the stock state 1960-62. The ratios for the federally chartered associations are compared to those for the stock associations. It is clear that in each of the years the stock associations have been more active with respect to "new loan" activity. This

Table 3-6
New Loans as a Percentage of Average Mortgages: Stock States 1960-62

	1960		1961		1962	
	Federal	Stock	Federal	Stock	Federal	Stock
Arizona	24.3	36.8	24.5	43.5	32.8	61.9
California	30.1	38.9	33.9	45.2	38.0	48.2
Colorado	29.1	28.9	37.8	29.4	34.4	34.3
Idaho	17.8	33.8	20.7	25.8	26.4	23.1
Kansas	22.3	25.8	22.6	29.2	22.6	31.3
Nevada	24.7	42.4	31.3	55.8	35.6	115.8
Ohio	19.1	29.5	28.8	28.5	19.0	32.4
Oregon	31.8	26.0	32.5	41.4	29.0	30.6
Texas	23.8	27.9	23.6	30.6	24.8	31.3
Utah	36.9	27.6	36.5	32.2	42.5	35.1
Wyoming	–	–	32.4	176.8	28.8	92.9
U.S. Members	25.6		27.5		28.7	

Source: Federal Home Loan Bank Board, Source Books, 1959-1962.

activity also brought them higher gross operating and net incomes as related to average savings.

Net Income. Net income is governed by the same factors determining gross operating income. In 1962, 18.3% of the operating income of the California stock associations had its source in fees, as compared to 11.5% for the federal associations and 6.5% for all federal associations in the United States. To the extent that California federal associations maintain the same proportion of construction loans as stock associations, some part of the difference in the fee-to-income ratios may be accounted for by the diversion mechanism characteristic of management in the mutual association.

Another factor contributing to difference in income is a mutual preference for greater liquidity. This may mean that they will keep larger idle cash accounts in commercial banks. Management seeks tie-in arrangements for which kickbacks are received in the form of favorable loans at low or no interest from suppliers and others providing services for the association.[e] One reason for preferring liquidity is simply that a conservative management is less vulnerable to risk and thus potential threats to the maintenance of control.

An important factor in income differences is the ratio of mortgage loans to savings capital. When associations make use of the Federal Home Loan Banks for advances, they increase the ratio of mortgage loans to savings. This also raises the proportion of "loans made" in the total mortgage portfolio. The increased

[e]The saying is, "If you scratch my back, I will scratch yours."

volume generates additional fees which in turn increase income. Table 3-7 indicates the ratio of mortgage loans to savings capital 1960-1962 and compares the federal to the state-chartered associations in states permitting the stock association. The state associations in all but two of the states,[f] by greater use of their borrowing power, were able to also increase net income (Table 3-5).

Income is also positively associated with "participation" sales. Thus, when a savings and loan association in California sells all or part of a mortgage to an eastern association, it not only keeps the origination fee but also receives a payment for servicing the loan. Associations arranging participations receive an

Table 3-7
Mortgage "Held" as a Percentage of Savings: Federal Compared to Stock Associations, Stock States, 1960-62

	1960 Ratio		1961 Ratio		1962 Ratio	
State	Federal	State	Federal	State	Federal	State
Arizona	106.5	113.6	106.5	122.2	111.2	126.5
California	109.1	115.6	109.1	118.1	110.3	119.1
Colorado	102.0	108.0	103.2	111.8	107.3	112.8
Idaho	102.3	107.4	101.2	105.3	104.8	101.8
Kansas	106.5	103.9	107.3	105.4	111.1	107.6
Nevada	99.3	103.4	95.8	120.9	99.2	171.2
Ohio	97.8	98.4	98.5	97.9	98.0	97.5
Oregon	103.9	107.8	102.4	119.0	103.0	115.2
Texas	100.2	101.5	98.8	103.0	101.3	105.8
Utah	103.2	111.6	106.0	113.8	112.3	116.0
Wyoming	100.0	300.0	99.5	176.5	100.0	134.1

Source: Federal Home Loan Bank Board, *Combined Financial Reports* and information made available in Washington, D.C.

Table 3-8
"Net" Participation Sales, 1959-64: California Federal Compared to Stock Associations

	Net Participation Sales	Mortgages 12-31-58	Participation as a % of Mortgages
Federals	453,201	2,633,041	26.9%
Stock	965,996	3,406,528	39.6%

Source: Federal Home Loan Bank of San Francisco.

---

[f]The stock influence is reduced because the only data available related to "state-chartered" associations which in some states included a substantial proportion of state-chartered *mutuals*, e.g. Kansas 69%, Ohio 54%, and Texas 77%.

"override" which often yields a rate of return as high as 10%. Table 3-8 reports on the total "net" participation sales for the period 1959-64 for California federal and stock associations. At 39.6%, the stock is 10.2 points higher or 47.2% more. With only 29% more in mortgages, it "sold" 90% more in the six years.

Ideological factors may account for some part of the difference with respect to utilization of the participation program. But eastern associations, concerned with the outflow of local savings attracted by the higher dividend rates paid in the west are compelled to search out higher-yielding mortgages. Their solution to this problem is the participation program in which they purchase California and other high-yielding western mortgages. Some concern has been voiced that this program should not be pushed too far. Kendall in his monograph notes that "association executives generally feel that home loans, once made, ought to be retained by the individual association until repayment . . . the relationship between the borrower and the financial institution ought to be continuous and that the buying and selling of loans should be a relatively minor part of savings and loan operations.[4]

To summarize, gross and net income can be increased by activity, i.e., by generating more business during the year, e.g., "new loans," higher rates of growth, greater use of borrowings from the Federal Home Loan Bank, participations and more lucrative higher-yielding construction loans.

"Spreads." "Spread" is defined as gross operating income less the sum of dividends paid to savers plus interest paid on advances. It is usually expressed as a percentage of average assets or average savings capital. The advantage of the spread ratio is that it provides an idea of the margin which the association, or the aggregate of associations in a region, possesses between gross operating income, which reflects the mortgage market, and the cost of savings and other capital. It is the amount available to cover expenses. The remainder is available for reserves and surplus. It may have a greater significance for mutuals inasmuch as it indicates the total amount management can claim for compensation and amenities. It should be noted, however, that the spread itself is partially determined by managerial decision: gross operating income may be less when management prefers to take less fees in negotiations with managerial-owned mortgage bankers or brokerage firms. In an integrated operation, management might allow the subsidiary a higher price on mortgages transferred to the association.

The spread has some superiority to "net income" in that it does indicate the maximum return available to the management of the mutual. "Net income" is defective for the reason that management actually has no purpose in expanding it *per se* since it would cost management by reducing compensation and amenities. Just as with expenses, there are defects. Where a mutual reports the same expenses as a stock association, greater efficiency is not necessarily indicated: fewer "new loans" may be generated; or it might service less mortgages on its own account. To this extent, spread is preferred as a test of efficiency particularly if interest is in the return to investments.

Data showing the differences between the federal and stock association in three stock states are indicated in Table 3-9. For the period 1962 and 1963, spread is expressed as a percentage of average assets. In both years, the stock associations reported consistently and substantially higher spreads than the federal associations within the same states. This higher spread may be attributable to a number of different factors. The most obvious is the differences in product mixes. The stock were more active in the "new loan" market. They generated not only higher fees but benefited to a larger extent from rising mortgage rates. With relatively more "new loans," their average mortgage yields rose as compared to the federals. The significant difference is not that the product mix of the stock associations favored higher spreads but that they *chose* a product mix which produced a higher spread. It is clear that the stock associations were more interested in increasing monetary return.[g]

Table 3-9
"Spread"[1] as Percentage of Average Assets, 1962, 1963: Selected Stock States

	1962	1963
Arizona		
Federal	2.28	2.20
Stock	2.99	3.19
California		
Federal	2.36	2.28
Stock	3.04	2.58
Oregon		
Federal	2.15	2.03
Stock	2.98	2.76

Note: 1. Spread = Gross Operating Income less (Dividend + Interest on Advances).
Source: Federal Home Loan Bank Board, *Combined Financial Statements*, 1962, 1963.

Performance with Respect to Dividends
Paid to Savers

If there is one test of the impact of mutuality with respect to relative performance, it is the rate paid to the saver-member. This may be expressed either in terms of the advertised rate or the yield of dividends paid to average savings capital. The 1963 report of the National Association of National Savings Banks indicated that "because all net earnings of mutual savings banks are distributed

[g]Curiously enough, Professor Shaw appears to suggest that there is an inverse correlation between spread and efficiency: referring to the federal associations, he finds that "they do appear to be more efficient allocatively, if only because they maintain lower spreads between average interest yield on assets and average interest cost of savings capital." It would appear that his judgment fails to allow for the variations in product-mix which would account for the variation in spread. If so, the *ceteris paribus* condition is not satisfied and the judgment is without relevance.

to depositors except for additions to protective reserves, the mutual form of organization has proved to have distinct advantages for the saver."[6] It has also been noted that commercial banks would not be expected to pay as high a rate as the savings and loan associations simply because of the difference in ownership.

One reason is that the commercial banks are owned by stockholders and they are trying to make a profit on the operation of the bank, including the savings department. Most of the savings and loan associations, on the other hand, are mutual institutions; they are anxious to pay as much as they can to the saver, and hold back only what prudent judgment relative to loss in reserves dictate. For that reason, if for no other, I think there will always be a difference between what banks and savings and loan associations pay.[7]

The ideological preference for the mutual form is somewhat naive. Clearly, there are alternatives, particularly competitive enterprise. But the most favorable circumstances for mutuals or cooperatives embraces a restricted monopolistic market. In such conditions, it is possible that establishment of a mutual as an alternative to the monopoly may reduce the "monopoly profit" which would have gone to nonsavers. But Shaw does not see it this way: "mutualism is not preferable to decentralized private enterprise in a competitive context."[8] In a competitive market, the member-savers must attract efficient management. This requires them to offer management more than it can earn in alternative opportunities. But, since by definition, the competitive rate of return is just sufficient to maintain the resources in that industry, and not larger than alternative opportunities, it would be necessary that the mutual pay competitive salaries comparable to the alternative opportunities. This means that at its best, mutuality cannot improve upon the competitive market. The viability of mutuality depends upon a restrictive monopolized market. It is not fortuitous that the mutuals have worked closely with governmental authorities in restricting entry into the industry as well as foreclosing numerous opportunities for the various competitive strategies.[h]

The second problem concerns the evidence. Do mutuals in fact pay higher rates than profit-oriented enterprise, i.e., enterprise where property rights are explicitly spelled out. It is one thing to compare mutual savings and loan associations to privately-owned commercial banks and conclude that the latter have not been effectively competitive. But there are a number of alternative reasons, both historical and economical, which explain their situation vis-a-vis the mutual savings and loan association and have nothing to do with the fact that banks are owned by shareholders. Historically, the banks had more attractive alternative opportunities for investments. More recently, they have operated under a set of restrictive regulations which both inhibits their competition for savings as well as

---

[h]This is not to say that the incentive to restrict competition would not have existed in the absence of the mutual.

for mortgage lending. Here, the principal issue concerns the competitive performance of *stock* associations in the same competitive market as the mutual associations.

Table 3-10 shows dividends as a percent of average savings capital 1960 to 1963. The federal are compared to the stock associations in the stock states. The only two states where the federal yield was higher were Kansas and Utah where the stock associations were relatively small and new. The results are also obscured by the fact that as much as 30% of the assets in those states was controlled by state-chartered mutual associations.

Further evidence is that provided by the rate increase that went into effect during the April quarter of 1965 in California. The stock associations were the first to raise their rates as reported by the Wall Street Journal.[9] It is significant that one was a rather small one with $6 million in assets. "Although federally

Table 3-10

Dividends as % Average Savings Capital, 1960-1963 Federal Compared to Stock Associations: Stock States

States Permitting Stock Form	1960 Federal	1960 Stock	1961 Federal	1961 Stock	1962 Federal	1962 Stock	1963 Federal	1963 Stock
Arizona	3.78	3.81	3.83	3.76	4.46	4.54	4.36	4.60
California	4.42	4.45	4.39	4.45[2]	4.59	4.73[3]	4.72	4.78
Colorado	4.05	4.09	4.07	4.18	4.33	4.42	4.33	4.51
Idaho	3.83	4.04	3.82	3.93	3.94	3.99	4.22	4.08
Kansas	3.87	3.89	3.85	3.90	4.10	4.08	4.12	4.14
Nevada	3.95	3.90	4.11	4.61	4.11	4.54	5.01	5.26
Ohio	3.64	3.84[5]	3.76	3.89[5]	3.89	4.04[5]	3.97	4.06
Oregon	3.90	3.99	3.89	3.98	3.96	4.04	4.08	3.88
Texas	3.90	4.01	3.91	3.94	4.06	4.16	4.23	4.23
Utah	3.84	3.81	3.87	3.86	4.24	4.22	4.48	4.32
Wyoming	3.73	—[1]	3.80	4.40	3.99	4.24	4.01	4.30
Mean[4]	4.05	4.27	4.09	4.24	4.27	4.35	4.39	4.49
U.S.								
All Members	3.86		3.85		4.13		4.17	
Less Stock	3.79		3.78		4.09		4.02	

Source: FHLBB, *Combined Financial Statements*, 1960-1963.

Notes:

1. No stock associations at this time.

2. Adjusted from FHLBB data which reported only for 3 quarters. See Grebler, *Mortgage Markets*, p. 114.

3. Adjusted from FHLBB data which reported for 5 quarters. Ibid., p. 114.

4. Weighted.

5. Stock associations only.

licensed savings and loan associations usually lag behind the state-chartered institutions in savings rate increases, at least one, Coast Federal, increased its rate to 4.95 from 4.9 compounded and paid semi-annually."[10] The stock associations, in contrast, had gone to 5.09. Three associations, part of Financial Federation, a public holding company, Community, Atlantic and Sierra led the increase. In addition, two other stock associations, the First Savings and Loan Association and University Savings and Loan Association jumped to 5% or more.

Advertising and Dividend Competition

A survey of eastern advertising promotion by California associations was made through using the New York *Times* first Sunday edition of every quarter for the period 1955 to 1963. The purpose was to determine the extent of advertising and the magnitude of the rates offered by California stock and mutual savings and loan associations. It was anticipated that favorable interest differentials coupled with effective advertising techniques were partially responsible for the relatively larger growth rate of stock associations during that period.

The number of individual associations (Table 3-11) advertising increased tremendously in 1960. In 1955, Fidelity Federal was the only association advertising in the *Times*. The declining use of brokers (due to governmental restric-

Table 3-11

Number of Advertisements by California Associations in the Sunday Edition of the *New York Times*, 1955-63, First Sunday of Each Quarter

	First Quarter		Second Quarter		Third Quarter		Fourth Quarter		Total for Year	
	Mutual	Stock	Mutual	Stock	Mutual	Stock	Mutual	Stock	Mutual	Stock
1955	1	0	1	0	1	0	1	0	4	0
1956	1	1	1	1	1	4	1	2	4	8
1957	1	2	1	1	1	3	1	2	4	8
1958	1	6	1	5	2	5	2	1	6	17
1958	4	6	3	5	2	5	3	0	12	16
1960	3	7	3	10	4	12	3	8	13	37
1961	4	13	5	12	6	17	4	13	19	55
1962	5	23	5	18	6	27	5	13	21	81
1963	1	2	6	15	5	24	3	13	15	54
Totals									98	276

Total Number of Associations Advertising during the Period

Mutual   11

Stock   59

tion) probably accounted for the growth in a number of associations using the newspaper media for obtaining funds. For the period, 11 mutual associations advertised as compared to 59 stock associations. It is not necessary to adjust for the larger number of stock associations inasmuch as the number of federal associations capable of advertising in the *New York Times* was not substantially different from the number of stock associations. Though the number of stock associations at the beginning of the period was 93 as compared to 84 mutual associations, at least 100 of the stock associations and 30 of the federal associations were not large enough to place ads economically in the *New York Times*. This meant that in terms of potential advertisement, the federal associations had roughly about the same number of opportunities as the stock associations. Thus, at the end of 1959, there were 21 mutual associations with assets over $50 million and 28 stock state-chartered associations. There were 45 stock associations with assets over $25 million and 34 mutual associations.[11] For all practical purposes, not more than 28 stock associations was likely to have advertised in the *New York Times* as opposed to 21 mutual associations. Twelve observations for the mutuals and 59 for the stock indicate that the latter's use of advertising media reflects policy rather than the number of associations.

The number of associations, both mutual and stock, placing advertisements in the *New York Times* each year is shown in Table 3-12. Also shown is the total number of associations in each category as well as the relative frequency of advertisements. With the exception of the first year, the stock showed higher percentages. When the results are aggregated, the incidence of advertising by the stock at 11.5% is twice that of the mutual, even though the mutuals are typically both older and larger.

Table 3-12

Number of California Associations Placing Advertisements Each Year in the *New York Times*, 1955-1963

	Mutuals			Stock		
Year	Number of Associations Advertising	Total Number of Associations	% Advertising	Number of Associations Advertising	Total Number of Associations	% Advertising
1955	1	82	1.2	0	93	0
1956	1	79	1.3	4	104	3.8
1957	1	78	1.3	4	109	3.7
1958	2	82	2.4	9	123	7.3
1959	4	82	4.9	8	140	5.7
1960	4	80	5.0	22	136	16.2
1961	7	78	9.0	21	143	14.7
1962	10	77	13.0	41	169	24.3
1963	9	76	11.8	26	162	16.0
Total	39	714	5.5	135	1.179	11.5

If we take 714 as the maximum possible number of associations that could have advertised over the period for the mutuals and 1,179 as the maximum possible for the stock, it follows that there were 675 nonoccurrences for the mutuals and 1,044 for the stock. (Table 3-13) A standard normal variable of 4.29 was obtained which meant that the probability that a difference of 100% between the two performances could be attributed to chance was less than one in ten thousand. In other words, there is a significant difference between the mutuals and the stock with respect to the use of advertising. It is no wonder that the stock grew so much faster.

In terms of absolute numbers, the fewer the number of associations advertising, the greater the probability an individual association has of being selected over another, *ceteris paribus*. The greater the number of associations from a particular classification (i.e., stock versus mutuals) advertising in an issue, the greater the probability of their selection. Stock associations had both these probabilistic advantages over mutual during this period.

It was anticipated that interest-conscious savers would supply funds to the association which offered an advantageous rate differential relative to other associations. Most of the time, the rates offered were similar. Table 3-14 indicates, however, that in recent years stock associations on the whole offered higher rates than those of the mutuals. While it is not certain that the rate advantages held by stock associations at a particular moment was maintained throughout the period, the data do indicate that new savers would more likely place their funds in stock associations. Typically, the stock associations emphasized higher dividends.

Advertising, though often wrongly condemned by economists, plays an extremely important role under the usual circumstances of imperfect markets. The generally negative attitude stems from an assiduously indoctrinated preference for pure and perfect markets. Given the conditions postulated, advertising is not permitted to perform a useful function. But judgments with respect to adver-

Table 3-13

Frequency of Advertising by California Mutual and Stock Associations, 1955-1963 in the *New York Times*

	Number Advertising	Number Not Advertising	Total Number[1] of Possible Events, 9 years	% Advertising
Mutual	39	675	714	55
Stock	135	1.044	1.179	11.5
Totals	174	1.719	1.893	9.2

Notes:

1. Total number includes only those associations in existence one full calendar year. This number is summed for each year to give the total number of "possible" events.

Table 3-14
Rates Offered by California Associations in *New York Times*, 1955-1963

Year	Quarter	Rate	Mutual	Stock
1955	First	3.5	1	–
	Second	3.5	1	–
	Third	3.5	1	–
	Fourth	3.5	1	–
1956	First	3.5	1	–
	Second	3.5	1	1
	Third	3.75	–	1
		4.0	1	3
	Fourth	4.0	1	2
1957	First	4.0	–	1
	Second	4.0	–	1
	Third	4.0	–	3
	Fourth	4.0	1	2
1958	First	4.0	1	6
	Second	4.0	1	5
	Third	4.0	2	5
	Fourth	4.0	2	1
1959	First	4.0	4	6
	Second	4.0	3	5
	Third	4.0	2	2
		4.5	–	3
	Fourth	4.0	–	–
		4.5	1	–
1960	First	4.5	3	7
	Second	4.5	3	10
	Third	4.5	4	11
		4.6	–	1
	Fourth	4.5	3	7
		4.6	–	1
1961	First	4.5	4	9
		4.6	–	1
	Second	4.5	5	11
		4.6	–	1
	Third	4.5	6	16
		4.6	–	1
	Fourth	4.5	4	13
		4.6	–	1
1962	First	4.5	1	10
		4.6	4	12
		4.75	–	1
	Second	4.6	1	–
		4.75	4	16
		4.8	–	2
	Third	4.75	6	20
		4.8	–	7
	Fourth	4.75	4	7
		4.8	1	6

Table 3-14 (cont.)

Year	Quarter	Rate	Mutual	Stock
1963	First	4.8	1	2
		4.85	–	–
	Second	4.8	6	13
		4.85	–	2
	Third	4.8	3	2
		4.85	2	20
		4.9	–	1
		5.0	–	1
	Fourth	4.8	2	–
		4.85	1	12
		4.9	–	1

tising, which implicitly assume the purely competitive alternative, are hardly relevant for actual market situations. It is to be noted in this connection that the California Savings and Loan Commissioner in laying down standards of superior performance stated, among other things, that an association must "have held advertising costs in check."[12]

It is implicitly assumed that between two associations everything is identical with the exception that because one of the associations has a lower ratio of advertising to savings, it is superior or more efficient. This is obviously not the case. Where one association might raise the rate in order to attract more savings, another association might work within a given rate structure and penetrate the market through advertising and promotion. In view of the widespread ignorance with respect to individual savings and loan association performance as well as the lack of information possessed by savers, advertising performs a useful function. It is no different from other efforts aimed at increasing the amount of information in the marketplace.

Given the lack of complete information, the effort to disseminate information with respect to alternative sources of supply and alternative prices serves an extremely important marketing function. It is a well-known proposition in marketing that though a particular marketing channel may be eliminated, the marketing function and costs involved continue. Very often, the substitution of one marketing channel for another will involve higher expenses, not lower expenses. But such an investment may often be worthwhile if more revenue results.

Efforts to repress advertising are often part of a scheme aimed at monopolistic restriction. It is no accident that the American Medical Association[13] frowns on advertising as unethical. The objection is not to the advertising so much as to the fact that advertising is competitive. So far as the Medical Association is concerned, all forms of competition with respect either to fees or advertising is unethical. A similar cartel attitude has been adopted in the savings and loan industry to restrict the competition from the higher dividend associations of the Far West. The rationale behind restricting the advertising of out-of-state associations is that it is an interference with the local savings market. Instances have been reported in which the federal regulatory authority has cracked down on California associations for advertising in local midwestern and eastern newspapers. In view of the critical position occupied by the regulatory authorities, no management, at least in a mutual, wishes to antagonize those whose goodwill is necessary for the maintenance of his position.

Table 3-15, showing advertising as a percentage of average assets in 1962, compares the federal to the stock associations in the stock states. Generally, the stock associations have allocated a relatively larger amount as measured on average assets to advertising. This is in line with their emphasis upon higher growth rates and higher dividends.

Table 3-16 shows advertising as a percentage of both average savings capital and new savings in 1962 for the larger cities. It is to be noted that whereas the Los Angeles Standard Metropolitan Statistical area has the highest ratio of advertising to total savings, the ratio of advertising to new savings is not out of line. At least three other cities show a ratio of advertising to new savings higher than Los Angeles. This additional ratio is included because it is more relevant since the purpose of the advertising is to attract new savings. Another measure would be advertising to net savings.

When the 40 largest standard metropolitan statistical areas are ranked in terms of their ratios of advertising to average savings capital, Los Angeles is

Table 3-15

Advertising as a % of Average Assets, 1962–Federal Compared to Stock Associations, Stock States

	Federal	State[1] Chartered
Arizona	0.15	0.27
California	0.16	0.21
Colorado	0.14	0.24
Idaho	0.14	0.11
Kansas	0.12	0.12
Nevada	0.04	0.40
Ohio	0.12	0.10
Oregon	0.12	0.22
Texas	0.09	0.13
Utah	0.22	0.20
Wyoming	0.11	0.35

Source: Federal Home Loan Bank Board, *Combined Financial Statements*, Washington, D.C., 1962.

Note:

1. The only data available were for state-chartered associations in Kansas, Ohio, Texas and Utah. Mutuals represented a substantial proportion.

Table 3-16

Advertising as a Percent of Average Savings Capital and New Savings, 1962:
Selected Cities

	Advertising ÷ Savings	Total Savings Rank	Advertising ÷ New Savings	New Savings Rank
Chicago	.085	13	.474	3
Cincinnati	.094	12	.393	8
Detroit	.146	6	.297	12
Indianapolis	.134	9	.419	5
Los Angeles	.252	1	.424	4
Miami	.147	5	.239	13
Milwaukee	.119	10	.409	6
Minneapolis	.212	2	.565	1
New York	.084	14	.181	14
Philadelphia	.108	11	.313	11
Pittsburgh	.137	8	.476	2
St. Louis	.149	4	.398	7
San Francisco	.191	3	.321	10
Washington	.140	7	.325	9
Median	.137-.140		.393-.398	

Source: Federal Home Loan Bank Board, *Combined Financial Statements*, 1962.
Note:
1. Los Angeles stock associations' ratio of advertising to new savings was 4.79.

second; Phoenix (another stock city) is first; San Bernardino is third and San Francisco is eighth. But when advertising is related to new savings capital, Los Angeles is close to the average with its rank of 15; Phoenix is 22nd; San Bernardino is 13th and San Francisco is 26th.

The stock associations were much more active in making expenditures on advertising than are their mutuals in California in the period 1960-1965. Table 3-17 reveals that the ratio of federal advertising outlays to stock outlays declined from 56.1 to 38.6 in the five-year period. The federals also only made 45.3 of the total expenditures.

Table 3-18 compares compensation and savings growth for the two types of organization for the same period. Though the federals took almost two-thirds in compensation, they generated only one-third of the savings increase of the stock. In 1960, their compensation was 80.8% of the stock and total savings 72.7%. It is clear that compensation did not produce the growth in savings for them that it did for the stock. Had the federal compensation been in line with the savings increase, it would have been $69.1 million less. Dividing by the average number of federals during the period, the excess compensation would have come to $959,486. This represents the diversion value to each association.

Table 3-17

Comparison between California Federals and Stock Associations with Respect to Expenditures on Advertising,[1] 1960-1965

	1960[2] Advertising	1960-1965[2] Total Expenses of Advertising	1965[2] Advertising
Federal	$ 7,746	57,947	10,722
Stock	13,799	127,853	27,766
Federal Stock ÷	56.1	45.3	38.6

Notes:

1. Source: Federal Home Loan Bank Board, *Combined Financial Statements*, 1960-1965.
2. In thousands.

Table 3-18

Compensation and Savings Growth: California Federal Compared to Stock Associations, 1960-1965[1]

	Savings[2] 1960	Compensation[2] 1960	Savings Growth[2] 1960-1965	Total Compensations[2] 1960-1965
Federal	3,739,368	24,269	3,162,280	210,186
Stock	5,145,900	30,018	8,863,476	326,405
Federal Stock ÷	72.7	80.8	35.7	64.4

Notes:

1. Federal Home Loan Bank Board, *Combined Financial Statements*, 1960-1965.
2. In thousands.

Mortality Rates

A simple test of managerial competence or irresponsibility of an association is its survival as a managerial unit. A survey was made with respect to savings and loan associations in Los Angeles and Orange Counties in the period 1950-1968. The two counties properly represented one market area. Many of the large associations in Los Angeles also have branches in Orange County. There were 47 federal associations: nine converted to the stock form during the period. Of this number, there were three mortalities or eliminations so that the rate is 6.4% (Table 3-19). Of the stock associations, there were six closings out of a hundred and three or 5.8% rate. The mortality rate among federals does not appear to differ from the stock rate.

There is in addition an alternative explanatory variable so far as the closings

Table 3-19
Mortalities, Los Angeles Federal Compared to Stock, 1950-1968

	Number of Mortalities	Number of Associations	Mortalities as a % of All Associations
Federal	3	47	6.4%
Stock	6	103	5.8%

Source: Federal Home Loan Bank of San Francisco, Roster of Members, 1951-1969.

were concerned—alternative to the hypothesis of ownership. Five of the six stock associations were new: the oldest, Washington Savings and Loan Association had opened in 1958; the other four in 1961 to 1962. Obviously, it is to be expected that both newer and smaller associations would experience greater difficulties in the tight money markets which have prevailed in recent years. At the least, they would find the going rougher than the older established institutions.

But a ratio expressed strictly in terms of the number of associations may be misleading in that a closing or failure is not identical in every case. We are not dealing here with a homogeneous unit. When a large institution closes, the impact on savers is all out of proportion to the loss for a relatively new and smaller institution. In order to weight for this factor, the ratio of the assets of the failing association to total assets was taken at the time of the closing (Table 3-20). They have been added for each year to gain a composite percentage figure for the relative importance at the time of the closing. The federal associations showed 14.7% as compared to 2.7% for the stock associations. The difference is large enough to support the hypothesis that the greater *number* of closings among the stock is attributable to their relative youth.

Both unweighted and weighted proportions were subjected to the standard statistical test in terms of the null hypothesis that there is no difference in mortality rates as between mutuals and stock as against the alternative that the proportion is higher among the stock. The test was taken at the five percent level. The standard normal variable, K at $-.238$ and 1.26 were less than the upper-tail five percent rejection level for K at 1.645. Therefore, the null

Table 3-20
Weighted Mortality Rates,[1] Los Angeles Federal Compared to Stock, 1950-1968

Federal	14.7%
Stock	2.7%

Source: Federal Home Loan Bank of San Francisco, Roster of Members, 1951-1969.
Note:
1. Assets of failing association as a percent of all associations at the time of failing.

hypothesis is accepted: differences with respect to mortality between stock and mutual associations are not indicated.

4 Relative Growth Rates

Growth is referred to as a tradition of the savings and loan industry.[1]

Savings and loan executives believe that the growth of their institutions is necessary to serve the public interest . . . when individual communities have their own pools of savings available for home mortgage loans, they are not entirely dependent on far away lenders and the local market is usually better served.[2]

Apart from the rather questionable argument favoring a protected market, a contradiction should be noted, viz. the growth of an association or area is often accompanied by an increase in rates designed to attract additional savings. California has received as much as 19% of its savings[3] from out-of-state savers.

At times, savings and loan executives tend to rate each other on the basis of the asset size or the relative growth of their respective institutions. . . . The growth of physical facilities, savings sources, lending opportunities, employee staffs, and so on, are manifestations of the superior ability of the specific institution to serve the people in the community and to meet the public welfare objectives of the institution.[4]

It is generally recognized that growth does represent at least one of the tests of performance. It is noted that

savings and loan managers also recognize that the larger their institution becomes, the greater is its ability to compensate those on the executive staff responsible for the services rendered by that institution. Since most institutions are mutual in character, these factors—the growth and responsibility and earning assets—become highly important motivations to management.[5]

Recently, growth has been subject to sharp criticism. Shaw sees no reason why California associations should grow faster than associations elsewhere: were the market for savings and mortgages perfect, equal rates of growth would have occurred. The relevance of this judgment for actual markets is not altogether clear. One might as well state that had Germany not been defeated in World War II, Germany would not have been defeated! The markets for savings and mortgages are not perfect: rate differences occur; and lenders and borrowers do not regard distant associations, mortgages, and savings accounts as perfect substitutes for nearby ones. Grebler and Brigham believe that a high growth rate is probably associated with the expectation of further growth so that the growing association "will probably have a tendency to build excess capacity at current levels of operation. This excess capacity adds to overhead and results in higher cost ratios."[6] A second and "probably more important reason for expecting growth to be associated with higher costs is the fact that a rapidly growing association will have a relatively large portion of new loans and deposits during any accounting period."[7] But this can be seen in a different perspective when reference is made to the entire product mix of the association or region. Expenses originate in the total new loan activity rather than simply the growth. New loans reflect changes in "loans repaid" (i.e., the turnover rate), as well as the net growth. After allowance for the other variables was considered, it was found that the associations with the higher new loan ratios did not have higher expenses. Nor was performance inferior.

A distinction need be made here between two aspects of the mutual. First, there is the question of the income diverted to management. Second, there is the impact of the differences in ownership on the economy. The stress so far has been on the diversion. But the differences in growth are startling: the mutuals in California grew 28% of the stock association; and 45% of the stock states, not including California, over the period 1955-64. With a lid on growth, the mutuals were able to create an opportunity for increasing expenses of the type they preferred.

The effect is exactly the same as in monopolistic restriction. Nor is it particularly surprising that mutuals grow. After all, monopolies also grow when both demand and its elasticity increases. Indeed, in the Baumol model, the management-dominated enterprise generates a higher volume of activity than simple monopoly. But even though the savings and loan market is restricted by entry regulations and other governmental impediments to competition, the alternative to management domination in the mutual is not a simple monopoly operated by owner managers. The industry has been substantially more competitive than a monopoly model would suggest; and the stock associations have taken advantage of the opportunities for increasing their penetration of that market. Because the mutual management must resort to second-best choices, all requiring noncompetitive margins, the necessary emphasis on tie-ins, rationing and discrimination reduced their rate of growth as compared to stock associations.

The Dampening Influence of Higher Expenses

The higher expenses of mutual savings and loan associations are to be attributed to the constraints on property rights. Not only is net income thereby reduced so that less is available for savers in the form of dividends, but with less to lend, mortgage interest rates are forced up. This in turn means that the additions to reserves are smaller so that, other things remaining the same, interest-free reserves are that much less.

These are all the necessary concomitants of a management-dominated enterprise. Given the higher compensation, the greater expenses on amenities and the diversion mechanism, fewer opportunities exist to facilitate growth. This is particularly so with respect to reserves because they provide the basis for profitable growth. Too much of management's activities is involved in adding redundant personnel, building privately-owned ancillary institutions and restricting the lending to borrowers willing to negotiate "tie-in" contracts. The increased expenses are at the cost of net income and thus additions to those reserves which provide a basis for further growth.

Tax Incentives and Property Ownership. Inasmuch as management has no property rights in the savings and loan association, he does not have the same set of options available with respect to the distribution of his tax burden. It is no accident that the pressure for growth should have been greater in California. The transfer of net earnings to tax deferred reserves depended on two items: (1) the ratio of the present reserves to savings; and (2) the ratio of net earnings to savings. Until 1963 an association was permitted to transfer tax-deferred earnings up to 12%. The trend in earnings rose until 1963, even though they represented a potential tax transfer. As the California associations' earnings were higher than elsewhere, they were very close to the 12% level. Any increase in earnings would have made them subject to the tax unless they had been able to increase the savings denominator. They met the problem of taxation by increasing the savings base which, in turn, increased the permissible transfer of earnings. The way to circumvent a tax during those years was to increase their rate of growth. The greater the net earnings and the closer the reserves to the 12% limit, the higher the incentive to increase savings so as to absorb tax deferred reserves.

Given the 12% tax deferral reserve, an association would have had to increase its savings by 8.33 times net earnings. (The latter were 2.35% for 1962 on 1961 year-end savings.) Savings would have to have grown by 19.6%. In eastern savings and loan associations, with smaller net earnings at 0.98%, the necessary increase in savings came to but 8.3%. Thus the greater growth of the California stock associations is attributable to an attempt to avoid a tax at the new 20% rate. This, *prima facie*, is not a factor in a mutual since management does not pay the tax. The generally slower growth of federals in California and elsewhere is accounted for by the lack of pressure to avoid taxes. It is a paradox that while the tax treatment of savings and loan associations made it profitable to grow, regulatory authorities objected to what is essentially rational behavior. Growth exists entirely apart from any problems from increasing risk, and is simply the consequence of tax constraints operating under a system of private property.

Market Share Changes in California. For California, the market share of the federally-chartered associations fell from 58.1% of total assets in 1950 to 33.7% in 1964 (Table 4-1); the California stock associations increased their market share from 41.9% to 66.3%. This result is consistent with the hypothesis that the mutual associations will show a retarded rate of growth. Had the mutual associations been equally competitive, there would have been no reason why there should have been such a substantial decline in their market share.

Or put another way, the greater aggressiveness of the stock associations is indicated in an increase in their market share of about 60%. It is possible that the mutuals with the larger market share in 1950 might have acted in line with the dominant firm theory. Preferring the "quiet life," they may have passively permitted the stock to expand at their expense. These restrictive policies are appropriate only to monopolies.

Had the mutuals been competitive with the stock associations, they would have maintained their market share. It follows that the decreasing market share is evidence of either a lack of competitive ability or a decision to permit the stocks to grow so that the mutuals could more fully exploit the remaining market along monopolistic lines.

Table 4-1

Changes in Market Share, 1950-1964: California Federal Compared to Stock Associations

		(000s)		
	Total Assets 1950	% of Market	Total Assets 1964	% of Market
Federal	862,079	58.1	8,049,360	33.7
Stock	621,418	41.9	15,812,722	66.3
Total	1,483,497	100.0	23,863,082	100.0

Growth in the *Number* of Associations

Growth may be measured in a number of different ways. The change in assets or savings capital, net worth, or, for the industry, the number of associations. Profitless growth, on the other hand, would appear to support the Baumol hypothesis that managerial objectives have superceded the objectives of the owners. Where firms are only growing in assets and net worth (i.e., reinvested profit), it is often the case that entry into the industry is restricted by one means or another.

An increase in the number of associations would reflect more favorable earnings opportunities for that form of organization or more liberal chartering policies. The Federal Home Loan Bank Board has been far more liberal in issuing new charters and branches than have states with stock associations. Indeed, the most severely limiting factor with respect to the federals has been the capital requirements. It has been difficult to raise capital for new federals as there are preferable alternative uses. Given an equal opportunity to organize a stock association, in which ownership or private property is developed, individuals have naturally opted for the stock association. There is little reason an individual would invest capital in a mutual he cannot control when he has the alternative of "owning" one. Neither the mutual nor the stock is immediately profitable: capital must be tied up for some time. Those with capital, therefore, demand ownership and the right to share in the profits.

Table 4-2 shows the growth in the number of associations in the period 1955-64 by type of ownership and regulation. The number of federally-chartered associations grew by 17.7% while the state-chartered mutual declined by 12.7%. In contrast, the state-chartered stock associations increased in number from 400 to 785—a 96.3% increase. For the United States as a whole, the increase in the number of associations was relatively small at 2.9%.

Table 4-3 shows savings and loan association asset growth for 1955-67 by types of ownership and regulation. While the federal associations' assets increased 277%, the state mutual increase was less at 178%. The state stock associations had a much greater increase at 645%. In terms of relative shares, the federal share of the total United States market fell from 55.5% to 53.3%. The state mutual share fell from 33.5% to 25.6%. The state stock associations share increased from 11.0% to 21.1%. In terms of the number of associations and assets, the stock form has been much preferred with respect to new organizations and to ability to win a larger share of the total savings and loan industry.

Within the states permitting stock associations, the stock states consistently outperformed the federal associations on a year-to-year basis. Table 4-4 shows the percentage increases in assets for the federally-chartered as compared to the stock associations for the four years 1959-60, 1960-61, 1961-62, and 1962-63. The general pattern is one of considerably greater growth of assets for the stock associations.

Table 4-2

Growth in Number of Associations, 1955-64 by Type of Ownership and Regulation

	1955[1] Number	1964 Number	% Increase
Federal	1,683	1,481	+17.7
State Mutual	3,988	3,482	−12.7
State Stock	400	785	+96.3
U.S.	6,071	6,248	+ 2.9

Source: U.S. Savings and Loan League Fact Books, 1956, 1965.
Note:
1. 1955 is the first year for which data relating to the stock associations can be secured.

Table 4-3

Savings and Loan Asset Growth, 1955-67: by Types of Ownership and Regulation

	1955	1967	% Increase
U.S.*	36.0	$141.4 billion	371%
Federals	20.0	75.3 billion	277%
State Mutual	12.0	33.4 billion	178%
State Stock	4.0	29.8 billion	645%
Relative Shares			
Federal/U.S.	55.5%	53.3%	
State Mutual/U.S.	33.5%	25.6	
State Stock/U.S.	11.0%	21.1	

*All members of the Federal Home Loan Bank System.

Table 4-4

Percent of Growth of Assets 1959-63: Stock States, Federal Compared to Stock

	1959-60		1960-61		1961-62		1962-63	
	Federal	Stock	Federal	Stock	Federal	Stock	Federal	Stock
Arizona	15.0	22.0	18.5	50.8	27.1	42.0	13.1	54.9
California	13.3	22.3	16.5	29.1	18.1	27.6	16.3	31.4
Colorado	13.5	16.2	14.5	22.5	15.3	21.8	10.1	22.1
Idaho	7.2	26.3	13.3	23.5	12.8	6.5	14.1	15.8
Kansas	13.9	13.2	13.6	17.7	15.5	16.5	12.5	14.4
Nevada	13.2	20.8	19.5	327.1	16.3	183.9	20.9	67.0
Oregon	12.9	27.7	16.5	39.5	13.6	17.2	11.5	10.3
Texas	19.3	15.3	15.4	22.1	14.2	21.0	15.0	17.7
Utah	11.5	8.6	14.9	14.7	16.4	15.2	14.0	21.8
Washington	10.9	21.5	15.6	42.8	12.7	30.1	12.7	16.6
Wyoming	15.1	–	17.0	414.2	12.1	100.0	8.9	34.7

Source: Federal Home Loan Bank Board, *Combined Financial Statements*, 1959-63.

Shaw has commented with respect to California that new federal charters are

rarely sought or granted to a small minority of firms, of high average age, and the result has been a high concentration of savings capital and assets in this minority. Of 69 federal associations, seven operate 50 branches or half of the state total for federal associations and six other firms maintain 20 branches.[8]

It is not likely that today's investor would make an investment with strings attached to his right to withdraw savings while at the same time he shared voting privileges with those who had that right.

This leads to the question of how the federals were started initially. The irony is that they originated in the depression when capital was scarce. But this was because many of the federal associations were conversions. It is hypothesized that conversions represented a convenient method for the management to rid itself of the original investors, thereby gaining a free hand in the control of the organization.

There was another enticement to becoming a federal in the thirties. For every dollar of savings, the new federal association received three dollars from the federal government. It is significant that new federal savings and loan associations have not been organized in states where investors are permitted the alternative of organizing a stock association. The federal association may not be viable in a competitive market since it cannot compete with other capital instrumentalities such as industrial corproations, commercial banks or stock savings and loan associations. The present large well-organized federal associations are the beneficiaries of discrimination dating from the thirties coupled with an opportunity for young men without capital. Capital was provided by the government at a time when alternative industrial opportunities were limited.

Another reason for the paucity of new federal associations is that established federal associations have made it certain that the new capital would not be available from the government. The United States Treasury no longer provides three dollars of funds for every one dollar of savings in the new federal association. The absence of this inducement reveals the power of established federal associations in restricting the development of new competition.

Some indication of the opportunities presented in the savings and loan industry in states permitting stock associations is revealed by Table 4-5 which shows the growth in the number of associations in stock states in the period 1950-64. The change in the number of associations for the federally-chartered is compared to the changes in the stock associations. In most cases, the data with respect to number of associations refer to state-chartered associations. This is appropriate when the stock associations make up as much as 80 to 90% of the assets as well as the number of associations within the state. When the asset share as well as number share was substantially less, data for the stock associations alone were used where it was available. With the exception of Virginia, the increase in the number of federal associations was either insignificant or negative. Even in Virginia, where a rather substantial increase of 47.6% was revealed, the stock associations increase was larger at 191%.

The Sources of Growth

Growth has its sources in many diverse elements. The hypothesis here relates growth as one performance test to the type of organization: it is believed that property rights will influence it. This is because the stock form of organization

Table 4-5

Growth in Number of Associations, Stock States 1950-64: Federal Compared to Stock[1]

	1950		1964		Increase		% Increase	
	Federal	Stock[3]	Federal	Stock	Federal	Stock	Federal	Stock
Arizona	2	2	2	12	0	10	0	500
California	74	81	69	203	−5	122	− 6.8	151
Colorado	23	16	20	35	−3	19	−13.0	119
Idaho	8	0	8	3	0	3	0	*
Kansas	28	37	29	62	1	25	3.6	168
Nevada	1	0	1	5	0	5	0	*
Ohio	132	104	136	112	4	8	3.0	71
Oregon	21	0	19	9	−2	9	−9.5	*
Texas	83	47	86	175	3	128	3.6	272
Utah	6	4	6	9	0	5	0	125
Virginia	21	11[2]	31	32[2]	10	21	47.6	191
Washington	35	1[2]	35	12[2]	0	11	0	1200
Wyoming	9	0	9	3	0	3	0	*

Source: Federal Home Loan Bank Board, *Combined Financial Statements*, 1950, 1964; U.S. Savings and Loan League, Fact Books, 1956-1964.

*None in 1950

1. Data for stock refer to *all* state-chartered associations unless otherwise specified. In most cases, stock proportion of total state-chartered assets over 90%.

2. Stock only.

3. Members of Federal Home Loan Bank System.

offers incentives to owners encouraging them not only to minimize expenses but also to take advantage of profitable opportunities by growth. For it is the growth of their organization which makes their investment profitable. Indeed, one of the major criticisms of the California industry, particularly the public holding companies, is that they have made growth an end in itself to the detriment of their savings accounts for which they have a fiduciary responsibility. The foregoing evidence provides ample support for the conclusion that, whatever the faults of the stock association, they cannot be attributable to a too conservative or stagnant attitude towards growth.

Greater Efficiency. A major factor in the growth of an association in an area is the efficiency attained in financial intermediation. Associations, capable of both innovating with respect to cost items while also maintaining a close watch on expenses, can with a given income level earn a higher net enabling them both to pay higher dividends and to make larger additions to reserves. Enlargement of the latter provides the association with interest-free reserves which in turn permit additional lending and thereby more income. Given the tax advantage which existed until 1963, there were many reasons an association would be encouraged to grow.

Inasmuch as stock associations are oriented towards profits while the mutual associations place constraints on management diversion and absorption of profits, it is to be expected that the stock associations would attempt to dampen down expenses. In the mutual, it is rational policy for the management to take the benefits from his dominance in the form of higher compensation, amenities and ultimately the use of the complicated diversion mechanism discussed earlier. Whether the management increases his salary and amenities or diverts income to privately-owned affiliates, it is to his interest to have the association assume the expenses arising from dealing with the affiliate. To this extent, expenses are increased and net earnings reduced for the association. The accumulation of interest-free reserves will be less than found in a similarly located stock association. The evidence shows that this has been the case.

Out-of-State Funds. Grebler and Brigham have noted that the stock associations and public holding companies in California have on the whole made a superior contribution to the interregional flow of funds by making "far greater use of out-of-state funds relative to their total savings capital than do the federally-chartered institutions."[13] This performance is attributed almost entirely to the large proportion of such funds employed by the public holding company associations. The latter reported a ratio of 24% as compared to 10% for the federally-chartered associations.

One of the more obvious ways for reducing expenses and creating the conditions conducive to further growth is to reduce the costs of borrowed funds. To the extent that the public holding companies made use of debentures, they have done so only when the costs involved were less than they are on new savings which involve both the dividend rate and promotional and brokerage costs. Another indication of the greater aggressiveness of stock associations in minimizing their total expenses was given in Table 3-7 which showed mortgage loans as a percentage of total savings, comparing the federal to the stock associations for a three-year period. In each case, the higher ratio of mortgages to savings indicates a greater use of borrowed capital by the stock associations. The significance of this higher ratio is that the stock associations only went to the Federal Home Loan Banks and commercial banks because borrowing costs were less than from savers. It is curious that more frequent use of the Federal Home Loan Banks by the stock associations should be condemned since one of the alleged assets of the Federal Home Loan Bank System is that the Banks were created for just this purpose.

Willingness to Take Risks

One reason for the higher growth rates of stock associations has been a greater willingness to take risk. On the other hand, it is said that to avoid trouble the management of a mutual will not expose himself to risk. He may not wish to increase vulnerability by acquisition of potentially delinquent mortgages which will threaten ability to meet the published dividend rate. If this occurs, the regulatory authorities enter to replace the management.

Nor is it surprising that mutuals both in California and elsewhere should condemn the California stock associations for a growth which is at the mutuals' expense whenever the stock increase the dividend rate. The mutual either loses savers so that expenses increase relative to total accounts; or it must increase dividends and thus reduce the spread which must cover additions to reserves and operating expenses. The mutual is in a dilemma when faced with such a choice. But the preference is clearly for the quiet life—sudden and unexpected changes are not desired; nor is there a wish to see the apple cart upset.

There is an intimate linkage between the responsibilities of management in the mutual and the objectives of management. By following conservative policies, risk of danger is minimized. There is little likelihood of regulatory investigation since there is less probability of trouble developing with respect to loan foreclosures. Thus, it is clear why mutuals object to the more competitive dividend-increasing and rate-advertising stock associations.

Some idea of the willingness to incur risk may be gained from Table 12-12 where the percentage of conventional mortgages to mortgages for 1964 is shown. A wide variation is reported: Massachusetts had the low of 58.4% as compared to California at a high of 96.0. The balance of mortgages are government-guaranteed or insured, i.e., VA or FHA. With government-insured loans, the association can hand the loans over to the government agency and thus its own losses and expenses from delinquency and foreclosure are correspondingly reduced.

Shaw has a similar view with respect to mutuals, noting that they "report lower average ratios of net worth to savings capital, but their relatively low growth yields on assets suggest that their risks are more conservative."[14] But one must consider the other side of the coin. While the risks the stock association may appear to take seem larger, there is a more than compensating offset in the receipts. As Grebler and Brigham pointed out, the increased costs of growing firms "are more than offset by their higher revenues."[15] Thus, even though costs may be increased as when there is a higher ratio of scheduled items to assets,[a] the critical test with respect to whether the risk is justified is not the ratio of scheduled items to assets or the expenses, but rather the overall performance with respect to additions to net worth over time. Even if the stock associations had increased risks and thus, over time, taken greater losses, it would not follow that they were less efficient or that their growth was economically unwarranted. Against the losses and greater frequency of foreclosed real estate, there is the higher incomes earned through higher interest rates, fees, commissions and premiums. If the stock associations have maintained a higher rate of growth over time, and have made relatively greater contributions to net

---

[a]Scheduled items are loans delinquent, real estate owned and acquired through foreclosure, loans to facilitate sale of real estate owned and contracts of sale.

worth, it would appear not that they took greater risks but that the decisions were profitable decisions and optimal with respect to the allocation of a scarce resource, savings capital.

It has been said that because stock associations have a higher ratio of scheduled items as well as a higher rate of failures, they are less efficient. It has already been noted that the rate itself is not to be taken on its face value. Due to differences in the laws and institutions in different states, it is possible to *profitably* foreclose on properties in certain states, while it is unheard of in other states. Account must be taken of these important differences in the legal framework between the states. But even more significantly, a high failure rate in itself is not an altogether meaningful test. Industries which have relatively low failure rates are not necessarily the most efficient industries. The failure rate among banks since 1934 has been very low, but it does not follow that commercial banking is efficient. On the contrary, the banking authorities have been severely criticized for their policy of not permitting banks to fail. Without the possibility of failure, there can be no corrective to inefficiency. A competitive mechanism works only when not only the efficient firms are rewarded, but the inefficient firms are penalized through a failure to survive. It is not altogether to the credit of the mutual savings bank industry that there have been no failures in the last fifty years.[16]

The uses of Federal Home Loan Bank advances and borrowed money by mutuals as compared to stock associations has varied over the years. A Stanford Research institute report found that in 1959

the relatively large holdings of advances and borrowed money by the largest federally-chartered associations reflect the greater emphasis placed by them on low cost borrowing to match their large holdings of low yield government obligations and cash. The smaller first mortgage loan holdings, as compared with those of the big stock associations, are not due to lack of lending opportunities, since all federal and most stock associations with over $100,000,000 in assets are located in capital short Southern California. Both groups have also been in business for many years and have had adequate time to accumulate larger portfolios of mortgage loans. Thus the lower holdings of first mortgage loans of the large federal associations is apparently due to a management policy of preferring to some extent, high liquidity of assets to high yield.[17]

By 1964, the ratio of Federal Home Loan Bank advances to assets for the California federals was 6.90 as compared to 9.33 for the stock associations. On the average, they were less aggressive in their borrowings for expansion. While a decision in favor of less borrowing can be justified on conservative grounds, it is also consistent with monopolistic restriction and it fits into the general model where a mutual will be more selective or discriminating in the choice of borrowers. By being exclusive, the mutual rations loans and creates great opportunities for the tie-in type of transactions to be indicated in later chapters.

Part II: Development and Regulatory Climate

5

The Mutual Saving and Loan Association: Nature and Development

The development of the mutual savings and loan association is also the development of the savings and loan industry. Early associations were almost completely of the mutual form.[a] They had their origin in the inability of low-income families to raise the necessary capital to either build or purchase a home. Groups banded together into an association of members pledging to make contributions for a share or combination of shares. As funds accumulated, members in turn would draw on them. Repayments and the inflow of pledged savings constituted the two sources of funds. The society or association was democratically controlled usually at monthly meetings. It was relatively small and often met in the back of a store or church. There was, of course, no professional management.

The early associations were established to meet a need for financing that had not been recognized by existing financial institutions[b]—mainly commercial banks.[c] To this day, and probably for additional reasons, banks do not concentrate their attention on this market. It has been stated that the consequence has been that the savings and loan industry operates in a "sheltered market."[4] Whether it is so, the reasons require further examination. One point is undeniable: the original savings and loan associations were the sole source for financing homes for families without sufficient capital. Commercial banks had other investments both shorter in term and more profitable. That they should have ignored this market is neither surprising nor irrational.

It is rather significant that the funds saved and invested by the savings and loan associations in home financing would have yielded greater returns in alternative investments. That the societies chose home financing is indicative of an overwhelming preference on the part of the "members" for home purchase.

---

[a]"Saving and Loan Associations in United States are direct descendants of the British Building Society. The Building Societies were the outgrowth of "friendly societies"—small, local cooperative groups whose members made weekly contributions which entitled them and their families to benefit in the event of death, illness, accident, fire, sometimes employment, or certain other major calamities."[1]

[b]"The original savings and loan associations were small local cooperatives, organized solely to handle savings and make real estate loans. All members were both savers and borrowers, and the associations were dissolved when each had received and repaid his loan. The associations operated with very little competition from other financial institutions."[2]

[c]During this period, commercial banks were not a substitute for savings and loan associations since neither the "volume nor terms of the loan which these lenders were willing and able to supply" were satisfactory to wage earners in cities. "A related requirement of the wage earners was a satisfactory means of accumulating their savings. Few financial institutions existed to take savings in small amounts."[3]

Their zeal may be compared to that which built churches, private schools, community centers and YMCAs.[d] The local needs of their members and communities were always of paramount concern.

But not only were the commercial banks uninterested in financing homes for individuals lacking sufficient capital for large downpayments, they were not interested in attracting savings in the small amounts[e] that savings and loan associations habitually sought. They have complained about the costs of keeping small accounts and even today find it irksome that more than fifty percent of their savings accounts come to but three percent of total savings.

After a rather checkered career, reflecting the typical ebb and flow of American economic development, the savings and loan industry in 1900 settled down in the United States as an almost exclusively mutual organization. Licenses were issued by each state government. With few exceptions, they were mutual in character. Precedent favored this arrangement. Unfortunate experience with stock associations, national in character, led to an aversion for that form; and the desire to meet "local needs" favored the mutual arrangement. The number and relative importance of the stock associations was so small that it could be safely stated that the industry had chosen the mutual form. After the crisis of the thirties, the federal government stepped in with its Federal Home Loan Bank System.[f] Though members of the latter need not be mutuals, the federal savings and loan associations which were established and chartered were set up that way. Existing state mutuals were permitted to convert into federals. There were many advantages. The most important was that for every dollar of saving capital originating with the association, the federal government provided three.[7] This was at the peak of the popularity of mutuality. It lasted until about 1950 when the first large postwar building boom got underway.

I. Part-time Management

Until 1950, the typical savings and loan association was small, mutual and essentially a local institution. Its growth over the past century had led to the recognition that efficient operation required professional management. But for many

[d]One prominent savings and loan official has stated that the reasons that one might start a mutual saving and loan association are very similar to those which would motivate those initiating a Y.M.C.A.[5]

[e]It was noted by one commercial banker that "At one large commercial bank, accounts under $500 constitute well over half of the total number of accounts but comprise only three and one-half percent of total savings balances. Unquestionably, the great bulk of these small accounts are unprofitable, this is true for the average bank."[6]

[f]The Federal Home Loan Bank Act was approved July 22, 1932, and required that the Federal Home Loan Bank Board establish regional federal home loan banks and the districts they would serve. The banks were to provide additional liquidity and funds for mortgage lending by making advances to member institutions as needed to meet unusual or heavy withdrawals and credit demands.

ventional corporations rest upon the control of that vote, restriction of sale inevitably leads to some other form of nonmarket-clearing. The right to select, nominate and vote for control in the institution carries with it a certain value in excess of a zero price. These rights have effectively been sterilized in the mutual association by substitution of an alternative privilege to savers, viz., the right to withdraw savings on demand. Such a right which insures the value of their capital investment has meant that both the efficiency and activities of the management group are hardly relevant.

Management control in the modern Mutual Savings and Loan Association has been associated with the appearance of ancillary corporations developed to permit management to divert income or to convert power into financial return. An elaborate infrastructure has been based on the initial savings and loan activities. Inasmuch as management is oriented toward this infrastructure, the association has come to play a secondary role. The tail now wags the dog. It is as if the United States government existed for the sole benefit of either the Republican or Democratic party. The notion is obsolete; but the problem to be discussed here is somewhat different. It is not so much that management runs the mutual for its own benefit but rather that it is restricted in its choices: the latter are second best and inefficient.

The Insurance Corporation Acts for the Saver. The restraint on the saver as an owner originates in his relation to the regulatory authority. The latter is either a state agency or the Federal Home Loan Bank Board. In most instances, it is, at least, the latter. It is the Board if it is a federal savings and loan association. It is also the Board or its creature, the Federal Savings and Loan Insurance Corporation, where the association is federally insured. All federal associations are mutuals, and all state associations, insured by the Corporation, come under federal regulations. State mutuals and stock associations also are supervised by their respective state regulatory agencies as well.

Because of the insurance, it is thought that the Board or the Insurance Corporation acts for the members.[p] Insurance obligates it to take an active interest in the activities and portfolios of the various associations.[q] It interprets its function as that of a traffic policeman who has to direct the flow of traffic and prevent

---

[p]It has been observed by Arthur H. Courshon, National League of Insured Savings and Loan Associations: "The current Board (Federal Home Loan Bank Board) has taken the position that the shareholders in a mutual institution are represented by the Board. They are not represented by themselves."[20]

[q]The president of the Federal Home Loan Bank of Little Rock which serves the five states of Arkansas, Louisiana, Mississippi, New Mexico and Texas stated: "It is difficult for me to understand why in the role of the insuring agency, the insurance corporation should assume a $70 billion liability without any right to say what shall or shall not be done in an institution which it insured."[21]

snarl-ups. The general philosophy seems to be that trouble originates in conflicts-of-interest situations. To a remarkable extent, it is preoccupied with them almost to the exclusion of other problems.

Inasmuch as management has sought to justify control of the association in terms of its responsibility as a trustee in managing the reserves in the interests of both past and future savers, the role now claimed for the Federal Savings and Loan Insurance Corporation (FSLIC) would appear to represent some duplication if not conflict. Through insurance of accounts, the insurance corporation necessarily assumes a risk which the saver member would ordinarily have undertaken. To that extent, there is some basis for the claim that the corporation acts for the member. But there can be no question of the management safeguarding the saver's capital, presumably as against claims by present savers as against reserves. If the FSLIC acts for the member, the question is whether or not management is in fact responsible. And, further, does the insurance corporation actually act as a surrogate for owners or saver members? If so, is there evidence indicating that the activities of the insured savings and loan associations are scrutinized in all respects.

There is some rather astonishing evidence that the FSLIC acts for the saver member only to a limited extent. Examiners are concerned with liquidity and solvency; with the classical conflict of interest situation; and with rather obvious increases in delinquencies and foreclosures that may ultimately affect the association's solvency and thus involve a risk to the insurance corporation. But aside from these rather obvious areas, the government officials say that they are not interested in executive salaries or expenses. If an association is both solvent and not involved in obvious conflict-of-interest lending, the insurance corporation official is not concerned with the level of salary. This is rather remarkable for it indicates that the government does not truly act as a saver-member or shareholder-owner. For it is perfectly obvious that the latter would exert pressure on management with reference to executive salaries, expenses, earnings and profits. Mutual spokesmen, quick to note the pressure of stockholder or owners on management, claim that such pressures have no place in a savings and loan association.

One legal authority concluded that "a shareholder has a vote until he cares to exercise it, and then he ceases to have a vote, if the board so decides."[22]

The metamorphosis of the mutual into something that is not a mutual is perhaps better understood in the following rationalization by the executive director of the United States Cooperative League who claimed that it was necessary to protect "the beneficial ownership . . . of the depositors—not only now but yesterday and tomorrow."[23] It is as if democracy must not be permitted in the "people's democracies" of Eastern Europe in order to preserve the democracy of the past and the future. That is, the slightest breath of democracy would be too shattering for such a rare flower. This has all been said before: one must fight a war to end all wars and to preserve the peace, etc.

Freedom from Shareholder Pressure. Though these constraints on the members effectively preclude *mutual* control and ownership, there are undoubtedly good arguments for doing so. Their merit rests, however, on grounds that effectively stifle the mutual as a viable organization—for whatever the form of organization it is, it is not a mutual. Arguments that justify elimination of control by members not only suppress the mutual element but protect management from the necessity of accounting for its actions. It is frequently claimed by proponents of the mutual organization that through the mutual form, the association is not up for grabs by the wrong people.[r] It could be similarly argued that elections are not necessary in the United States either on the grounds that the wrong people might get into office. In other words, the proposition submitted is nothing more than an attempt to justify totalitarian dictatorship. Presumably the right people are presently in control. In any case, if they are not the right people, there is hardly likely to be any means short of insolvency for replacing them. The only way to get rid of them is through elimination of the association.[s] There is nothing members can do because the mutual form of ownership provides no mechanism for replacement of either incompetent managers or for representation on the Board of minority views by the members or shareholders.

Mutual management also proudly boasts that their associations need not show earnings designed to inflate stock prices.[t] Presumably lacking the pressures of stockholders seeking more earnings and therefore higher values for their stock, they can follow more conservative and prudent policies. The other side of the coin is that they can do exactly what they please: pay themselves noncompeti-

---

[r]Mr. Riordan of the National Association of the Mutual Savings Bank has stated: "We feel that the savings of the community are too important to become the prize in any recurrent struggles for management control between warring groups. We feel that the depositor's interest can best be taken care of by this, as I say, harsh trustee system of standards, plus strict supervision."[24]

[s]In a proxy contest involving the motion picture producer MGM, a federal court ruled the manager may use a limited number of employees and spend company funds in defending itself against an insurgent stockholder group. The management had hired expensive attorneys, a public relations firm and proxy soliciting groups. The president, Robert O'Brien argued that if he couldn't use company money to stay in power "the test for corporate control would become individual wealth." The richer contestant "would win almost by default because of the inability of long term executives to raise the large amounts" needed to wage a proxy contest. Judge Sylvester Ryan refused the insurgents request for a preliminary injunction on the grounds that the dissident failed to show how they would suffer serious injury. In effect, this court at least rejected market standards as represented by wealth in favor of the right of the management to use the company funds to perpetuate itself in control even apart from its ability to get the backing of more than half of the shareholders.[25]

[t]Mr. J.E. Hoeft, Chairman of the Board, and President of Glendale Federal Savings and Loan Association of California, an association with assets over $600 million, said: "I don't think you can possibly run a conservative, or run a savings and loan association in the character in which it is operated for 130 years with an eye on the stock market . . . and you cannot make pronouncements, you cannot make loans, you cannot do operating problems on the basis of trying to hold the value of the price of your stock up on a New York stock exchange. I don't think it can be done."[26]

tive salaries, take extraordinary expense accounts and divert association income to their privately-owned subsidiaries. It is true that they are not up for grabs by the wrong people. The trouble is that there is no assurance that the wrong people have not already obtained control. And there is absolutely no way to replace them once they have gotten control.

The possibility of lengthy and expensive proxy battles frightens the mutual managements with good reason. Such tests exert a form of discipline they would prefer not to experience. Certainly, they could hardly continue with some of the activities they now practice, e.g., owning firms doing business with the association.[u] Their success in avoiding proxy fights as occur in stock corporations only testifies to their ability to avoid a rough but necessary form of discipline. The effects of such evasion will be revealed in subsequent chapters. It suffices to say at this juncture that their success here is not an unmixed blessing so far as economic efficiency is concerned.

The Savings and Loan Association as A Local Institution. Regulatory boards and savings and loan officials stress the local character of the industry.[v] It is often repeated that the associations are locally oriented, geared to local needs and jealous of their local character.[w] Thus the Committee on Banking and Currency described savings and loan associations "as locally owned financial institutions organized primarily for the purpose of promoting thrift and home ownership."[30] Annual Reports of the Federal Home Loan Bank Board,[31] which governs member associations, use similar terms. Indeed, when a California association goes beyond its local market to seek savings in other parts of the country, it is likely to bring down upon itself the wrath of the Board for creating instability in a local eastern or midwestern savings and loan market. California

[u]A Deputy Attorney General in California, Marshall S. Mayer, states: "At present certain activities of directors fall into a shadowy area of conflict. Frequently savings institutions employ corporations to conduct specialized activities for them. It is not unusual for an association to employ a corporate agent to originate loans and to pay this agent a percentage on each approved loan. The directors of the corporate loan agent and the directors of the savings association in some cases would reveal identical membership. It is difficult to distinguish the substance of this transaction from that conduct which if done directly would be felonious . . . Associations also often employ corporations to perform escrow, insurance, trustee and real estate sales functions. It is not unusual for directors and officers of the association to be financially interested in these firms."[27]

[v]"Throughout the history of savings and loan associations, legal and regulatory measures more often than not have been designed to preserve the local character of the institutions. In order to insure that mortgage money from the local source will be available for just about every section of the country, Congress has restricted savings associations to home financing field function and to the support of home ownership in relatively limited geographical area."[28] The 1961 Report of the Federal Home Loan Bank Board stated that the system was designed "to meet a long existing need in many communities throughout the nation for local institutions." Report 1961, Washington, D.C., p. 55.

[w]The Home Owners Act of 1933, Section 5 (A) refers to the establishment of "local mutual thrift institutions" in establishment of federal savings and loan associations "thereby giving primary consideration to the best practices of local mutual thrift and home financial institutions in the United States."[29]

advertising of a higher share rate in that community is said by the Board to disrupt stable market conditions. Preservation of the local character of the industry appears to be a euphemism for prevention of a competitive allocation of savings.[x]

There is, however, some basis in the emphasis on the local aspects of the industry. Most of the loans and savings deposits are local. One study in California showed that the bulk of loans were in an area of from five to twenty-five miles from the association: 45 percent by number and 47.2 percent by dollar volume.[33] Another 16.2 percent by number and 19.1 percent by dollar volume were in the next 25 miles so that 68.3 percent of the loans, at least in Los Angeles, were from five to fifty miles away. Inasmuch as the sample embraced 88 associations, it is likely that the mortgage demand for funds for any *one* association would be very elastic—the more so for a relatively small association.

With respect to savings, the same study revealed that 37 percent of Los Angeles associations' accounts were within two miles of the offices; 62 percent within five miles. It appears also that for a small association there is a relatively large potential supply of savings that does not have to be within the five-mile area. Whether it can be tapped depends on whether the small association can hold a higher dividend rate than its rivals. If it cannot, savings will consequently be limited by oligopolistic considerations, i.e., recognition of rival retaliation.

The stress on the local market and its stability has become almost an article of faith to the regulators.[y] Lacking a rational system for regulatory decisions, they have eagerly seized on the apparent necessity for preservation of local stability. As the most serious threat to that stability is competition, they have been quick to condemn all its manifestations as causing chaos in a local market. Nor has the Board acted consistently: while it has censured advertising by California associations in Eastern markets, it has encouraged Eastern associations to

---

[x]Cf. the observation of Professor Shaw, "Some aspects of regulation reflect the archaic principal that savings and loan associations are (or should be) neighborhood cooperatives for savers and home buyers, detached from the profit motivation of normal capital markets; that saving should be used locally; that management cannot accurately appraise property beyond easy travel limits of horse and buggies." Also referring to the California mortgage market it is noted that "market areas are detached to a degree from each other and still more remote economically from market areas elsewhere. Because mortgages are less homogeneous and less mobile than shares, impediments are higher on mortgage than on share markets. 'Local Savings for Local Homes' is a rallying cry in defense of these laws."[32]

[y]The Federal Home Loan Bank Board is not altogether consistent: local ownership may be desirable for those who are to be regulated but for regulators, i.e., Federal Home Loan Bank Board, it is a different matter. The regional system of 11 federal home loan banks was apparently established with the intention to develop full private ownership and local control. "Actually government control is complete."[34] The Federal Home Loan Bank Board selects both the chairman and the vice chairman from among the directors and officers which are elected by the Board of Directors and are subject to federal approval by regulations with respect to the system. In contrast, the original theory was designed to set up a decentralized system with emphasis on *local* rule. Any perusal of investigations of the Federal Home Loan Bank Board makes it abundantly clear that the significant decisions are made at Washington by the Board and not by the individual banks.

purchase California mortgages through the participation program as well as out-right purchase. Yet, the effect^z is identical in that funds are diverted from the purchase of Eastern mortgages in favor of California mortgages. Of course, the Eastern savings and loan association can rationalize its action: out-of-state purchases are desirable in order to secure necessary diversification. It may be desirable to avoid having too many eggs in one basket. But the fact remains that when an Eastern association purchases a California mortgage, it also diverts funds from the local market and it is denying local needs.

Though the Board may stress the local nature of the industry, it has hardly done much to enforce its policies. The managements of mutuals are in an autocratic position and when they have chosen to turn their backs on local needs, there is little the Board has done about it. Indeed, in the rare instances the Board has moved ostensibly to protect local interests, it has protected the local association from outside competition—all, of course, at the expense of the local community. By forcing California associations to withdraw from competitive advertising, the Board has denied the local savers opportunities with respect to market information and higher returns for their savers. Apparently, an industry devoted to *local* home financing is to mean nothing more than protection of the local monopolists or oligopolists from distant competition.[35]

Another reason has been advanced: ". . . when individual communities have their own pools of savings available for home mortgage loans, they are not entirely dependent on far-away lenders and the local market is usually better served."[36] That this should be so is by no means obvious. If the local supply fails to meet the local demand, either because of rapid growth or monopolistic restriction, the price of money will rise. The dependence on far-away lenders is eagerly sought by borrowers in order to keep the price down. A monopolist obviously does not want foreign money in the market. He therefore condemns it as foreign and demands protection of the local thrift institutions. In the same way, he does not want to see his source of savings tapped by others since he has to pay that much more; and has to be that much more competitive.[37] The truth of the matter is that the ideal of a mutual association, with each saver and borrower a member in intimate contact with each other and serving local needs, is hardly appropriate to the modern mutual savings and loan association. Commercial bank spokesmen have pointed out that "savings banks and savings and loan associations have developed far beyond their original local character and their original objective of serving the specialized needs of groups of individuals banded together for mutual benefit. Today they are aggressive business enterprises, operating over large areas and across state lines and actively competing with commercial banks by offering many of the same services."[38]

It is a far cry from the original ideal to the modern large mutual actively involved in large scale construction lending. Such enterprises are not mutual;

^{z}Since March 1957 associations have been permitted to participate in conventional mortgage loans held by other institutions. At the end of 1966 mortgages involved in participation came to 5.7 percent of total mortgages held.

they are not democratic; nor are they geared to *local* thrift and home financing. On the contrary, they represent power blocs closely intertwined with insurance, mortgage brokerage and trustee companies owned by their managements. Strangely enough, they are less mutual than their competitors,[39] the stock savings and loan associations. The latter have stockholders with some interest in election of officers and the determination of policy. The allegation that stock associations keep an eye on the stock market testifies to some influence; and they have been known to rise up and discharge their top management.

The Relative Success of Mutual Savings and Loan Associations as Compared to Other Cooperatives. Cooperatives have not been successful in the United States. The tremendous growth shown by mutual savings and loan associations is an anomaly requiring explanation. The greatest triumph—if not the only—of the mutual cooperative form has been restricted to two sectors, the financial and the agricultural. Mutuals have prospered as savings banks and savings and loan associations, and as agricultural cooperatives. In the latter two, the federal government has provided a significant assistance. In agriculture, the encouragement of cooperative forms of organization has been a continuing policy for many years.[a] Differential and favorable tax treatment has virtually eliminated the private middleman in favor of the cooperative form. Exemption from prosecution under the antitrust laws has permitted group activities not otherwise tolerated. Similarly, in banking and savings and loan markets, the government controls entry through the new chartering. Newcomers must prove that they will not cause injury to existing institutions. Given this requirement, it is a wonder that new establishments ever appear.

But where the government does not license and where competition is not restricted, cooperatives have failed to make much of a market penetration. In retailing, where a great contribution was expected, cooperatives are conspicuous by their rarity.[b] They have not proved either an efficient instrument nor a viable competitor simply because the industry was and is competitive and progressive. The mutual form has had nothing to offer. Indeed, it lacks survival value. It is not too much to suggest that it could not have survived because it could not tolerate competition. That it prospered in financial and agriculture markets is not surprising. Either it was the beneficiary of special tax benefits or the industry (for other reasons) restricted competition. The necessary conditions for its survival and success are that competition should be restricted; and special discriminatory benefits from the government must be forthcoming.

[a]The Clayton Act of 1914, in amending the Sherman Anti-Trust Act, exempted agricultural cooperatives of the mutual and nonstock variety from the antitrust laws. The Capper-Volstead Act of 1922 both permitted the organization of producers of agricultural products to engage in interstate commerce, and specified the method of organization of such associations.

[b]If sales of farmers' supplies are excluded, the total value of business performed by retail consumer cooperatives is probably less than one fifth of one percent, "with the bulk of this accounted for by gasoline service stations and food stores."[40]

Profit-Sharing Plans. While it may seem strange, in view of the origins of the mutual, it is not altogether surprising that profit-sharing plans have emerged in some of the federally-chartered associations. To the extent that all profits are shared among employees, differences from the stock would be reduced. Employees would simply act as owners. In cases where this has been tried, each employee is given a share proportional to his share of the total amount paid in compensation. Unlike the stock association, the share does not entitle him to vote at meetings or share in the control of the mutual. He would seem to be given an ownership interest in the form of the share in the profits but not in the control. The latter is still reserved by management to itself.

That management should favor such plans is not altogether irrational. First, recognition and acceptance of the plan constitutes a first step in giving management, along with other employees, an ownership right in the more traditional sense of sharing in the profits. And in sharing the profits with employees lower in the echelon, management is no worse off—and possibly because of restriction on entry and the existence of the diversion mechanism, it is better off than a similarly situated management in a stock corporation. Second, management continues in absolute control of the organization.

But there are differences. Unlike a stock association, management will not opt for reinvestment of earnings. To do so would be to surrender a dollar of present income for not even a promise. It has no claim to the reserves which are built up from future profits. At best, it may only share the future earnings with other employees or increase the managerial wage as a result of growth. Furthermore, there are alternative methods which yield management more.

In contrast, a stock association would reinvest its earnings. First, so long as reserves were less than 12% of savings, they can be invested as tax-deferred. The full amount is available for investment and, hopefully, additional earnings. Second, the rate of return to net worth or reserves has been higher in the savings and loan industry than in alternative areas. In the three years, 1960-62, insured associations in the United States, minus California, earned 12.2% on average net worth. Both reasons would appear to militate against the establishment of an employee profit-sharing plan. It is better to reinvest earnings in the association than to share profits. That these plans have been created by mutual managements in prosperous times indicates a lack of identity between the association as a rational profit-seeking institution and the mutual with its constraints on the payment of profit to management and the employees.

Finally, a question may be asked concerning the right of employees to share in the profit. They are on a salary basis which means that the incomes received are contractual. They take no more risks than employees in other establishments. The sharing in profits provides them with an ownership interest. If they have become owners, what has happened to the saver-members? And in what way do employees have precedence over savers in the claim to residual earnings?

Development of profit-sharing suggests a take-over of the mutual. To the extent that the employees have a right to the residual earnings (rather than the shareholders), they may be said to have achieved an ownership stake in the association without the necessity of saving or investing. In that case, they are no longer mutuals but rather worker-owned enterprises—but with a qualification. The workers are not equal. Nor are the shares of profit limited along mutual lines to a maximum of 50; nor do worker-owners share in the management decision making. It is also pertinent to recall that it was thought necessary to protect "the beneficial ownership . . . of the depositors—not only now but yesterday and tomorrow." How are the past and future employees protected? What are the rules for distribution of profit? And, if past and future depositors have ownership rights, why are they not consulted with respect to the institution of profit-sharing among the employees?

It is difficult to escape the conclusion that profit-sharing explicitly, even blatantly, spells finish to mutuality. That the savers ever had ownership interests seems to be recalled only when (1) mutuals want to distinguish themselves from the stock associations; and (2) mutual management seeks special and protective regulation as against their competition. The typical mutual savings and loan association of the 1970s is not a mutual. It is not controlled and not owned by its saver-members. It is an instrumentality of management; and is wholly oriented towards objectives external and foreign to the original objective of mutual and democratically owned and controlled associations. It is, of course, different from the stock form; but has even less in common with the original conception of the mutual.

6 Regulation and Competition

Regulation has generally been a substitute or alternative for competition. The theory apparently has been that, inasmuch as the industry is regulated, competition is not only unnecessary but to be avoided. It is a potential threat to the solvency of the regulated. Perhaps the principal reason for reducing or suppressing competition is, that in the absence of rational criteria for decision making, the task for the regulated is eased. In the words of one of the regulators, inhibition of competition precludes the development of sour apples. This simply means that the apple cart is not to be upset. Regulators do not care to deal with the uncertainties created by competition—particularly in industries with high rates of innovation. The regulator's basic creed begins with the preservation of the status quo. When novelty and change is suppressed, there are fewer problems. Thus the regulators cannot be faulted.

The consequence is that liquidations are reduced or eliminated; or, at the worst, those in trouble are quietly taken over by complementary associations. The rationale is that failure can neither be tolerated nor recognized: the interests of savers must be protected. A guarantee that liquidations will not be permitted is, of course, a guarantee to management that, so long as it is not *too* inefficient and does not get into trouble, protection will be provided against the competition of troublemakers.

One Eastern savings and loan official, in commenting how the East resents advertising in their papers of the higher West Coast dividend rate, noted that other approaches are available "to curb ill-considered actions regarding dividend rates. One is promotion. Our business originated many savings promotion schemes, which, as might be expected, got a little out of hand. One institution in the East gave away a Cadillac automobile, and a few gave away Plymouths and Fords. Ultimately we got ourselves a regulation that imposes a limit of $2.50 on the cost of any giveaway for an addition to an existing account or the opening of a new account."[1]

The industry had "seen the need for some types of restraints and has worked for them in its own interest."[2] What is the effect of regulation?[3] Are we to believe that regulators resemble the heroine of the famous musical comedy, "Annie Get Your Gun?" Paraphrasing the song, anything "the market can do, regulators can do better." One is reminded of the definition of a diplomat: regulators solve problems which never would have arisen had there been no regulators.

But one mutual official, John Stafford, said that regulation was not a solution:

No sooner had we gotten into effect the $2.50 regulation on premiums, which we were highly in favor of, than our competitor savings banks, operating under the jurisdiction of the state, began giving away $3.50 premiums . . . some of the regulations that we enforce upon ourselves turn out drastically different in effect from what we anticipate.[4]

Apparently, there is a diversity of attitude with respect to the control of competition with respect to the dividend rate. Former chairman of the Federal Home Loan Bank Board, McMurray, indicated that a ceiling on dividends "would discriminate against savings association shareholders as compared with other dividend receivers and would destroy the very essence of mutuality. Moreover, a rate ceiling would not solve the fundamental problem of providing funds in capital-scarce areas or the transferring of funds from capital-surplus areas."[5] Another official, Fred T. Greene, President of the Indianapolis Federal Home Loan Bank observed that:

When I went to Indianapolis 25 years ago, Detroit was the business center of the bank district; it was much larger than Los Angeles, which you know is now much larger than Detroit. Obviously housing the people who moved from the Midwest and other regions into Los Angeles required a lot of home mortgage money. To get this home mortgage money in competition with other investments and in competition with the rest of the country, it was necessary to pay a high rate. I should not like to see a regulation limiting dividends that savings and loan associations can pay, because this allocative function would be lost.[6]

The question of concern in this chapter is the extent to which regulation improves on a competitive allocation. How is success recognized? How are the failures of regulation identified? And what alternative methods are present for meeting the problems regulation is supposed to solve?

The prevailing attitude on competition is somewhat ambivalent. It may be compared on the one hand to the medieval pursuit of the Holy Grail—"always sought but never found." On the other hand, it is often viewed as potentially so destructive that it is not to be tolerated. Thus Shaw has stated that, "The banking system has a propensity to suicide only thwarted by firm public regulation."[7]

Perhaps a psychoanalyst would suggest that there is no real difference in these two approaches. The preference for competition is likened to a "death wish": it is defined in so exacting and rigorous form that it could never be found—except, possibly, in textbooks. Often, the necessary *ceteris paribus* requirements of the pure model are forgotten. Transportation costs and other types of distribution costs are said to reflect either market imperfection or the absence of competition. But it is a question whether this is an altogether fruitful approach. One is reminded of the scholars who condemned Kepler's elliptical orbits on grounds that as they were not circles, they could not be perfect; and because God is a perfect being, He would never have made such orbits! Actually, the question of their "perfection" is not particularly relevant. The Keplerian hypotheses were adopted simply because they were better predictions.

But apart from problems of psychoanalysis and astronomy, too much attention has been focused on the alleged "imperfections" of competition; not enough has been directed to the usefulness of a theory which so often is defined so as to have so little relevance for actual markets. Pure competition in its more rigorous form is about as useful as a handbook for clergymen on how to stay out of brothels.

This point is stressed because the case for regulation is frequently based on the alleged imperfections and shortcomings of the market. Differences in prices received by California savings and loan associations compared to national averages, as well as other parts of the country, are considered to be "the most telling index of suboptimal resource allocation."[8] It is to be noted (1) that it has not ever been shown that unequal prices and returns necessarily rule out competition; and (2) that regulation will improve upon resource allocation.

But it is not correct to conclude that price inequality implies imperfections in the competitive process unless the *ceteris paribus* condition is met. Consider government insured and guaranteed mortgages through the FHA and VA. The risk is not eliminated through these features; the rates in different cities have varied and to that extent reflect different *assessment* or risk.[a] In spite of government protection, there is always the possibility of delinquency and foreclosure costs with the consequent loss in income. Thus, the variations in risk make not only for different prices but indicate that the differently located mortgages are not identical products.[b] One does not have to fall back on the crutch of Shaw's "differentiated oligopoly"[10] to understand this variation.

Oligopoly and the Necessity to Regulate

In view of the theory of oligopoly, it is strange that regulations should be thought necessary. If oligopoly provides testable hypotheses, it is most notable

aSaul B. Klaman, *Post War Market*, pp. 95-98. In connection however with the "shares" of savings and loan associations, Professor Shaw finds that "it is rather remarkable that demand obligations insured by the federal government sell at different prices within national, state and even town market areas. Shares are shares: they are homogeneous, in the manner of savings bonds. The market impediments that differentiate Los Angeles shares from San Francisco shares from Phoenix and Miami shares, or association A from association B shares serve no social benefit and have the sole result of fracturing a common market into oligopolistic sub-markets. The consequence must be, as we shall indicate, misallocation of national savings."[9] Structure, pp. 29-30.

bThere are related and similar long-term differences on short-term commercial bank rates between cities.

that because of the recognition of mutual dependence, competition is avoided. That is, oligopoly is thought a sufficient condition to preclude competition. This being so, one may ask why regulations are necessary in order to prevent the outbreak of destructive or ruinous competition.

The Control of Entry. Control over entry[c] of newcomers and therefore competition is frequently thought necessary in order to prevent "dangers to the solvency of the weaker institutions."[12] Through regulation of entry competitors are protected from competition.[d] Obstacles are placed in the way of receiving charters to operate a savings and loan association. It has been reported that in California bonuses of $50,000 or more[e] are paid through certain law offices to receive charters.

The 1963 Report of the Federal Home Loan Bank Board states that "in determining the applicant's eligibility for insurance, consideration is given to a number of factors. Of prime importance, as the number of insured facilities and the degree of resultant competitive increase, is the question of need for an additional insured institution in the area and the related question of the probability of its growth and success without *undue injury to the existing insured institutions.*" As is characteristic in regulation, "need" all too often becomes identified with the protection of competitors from any form of competition. "Undue injury" comes to mean prevention of competition. Little concern is

---

[c]Grebler and Brigham observed "that the competitive structure of the California savings market is unquestionably characterized by oligopoly. This is an inevitable consequence of restricted entry into the savings deposit business and is reinforced for banks by ceilings on the rates that they are permitted to pay on time deposits and for savings and loan associations by the FSLIC regulation which prevents new institutions from paying higher dividend rates than those prevailing in a local market area.[11]

[d]It has been said that "free competition requires acceptance of the proposition that weaker uneconomic units unable to meet the tests of the markets should be permitted to fail. But since a bank failure means destruction (or at best, temporary unavailability) of circulating medium, those aspects of competition which weaken (or are thought to weaken) banks and make them susceptible to failure are restricted or severely regulated . . . commercial banks are prevented from engaging in price competition for demand deposits (payment of interest) and severely restricted at engaging in such competition for saving deposits." Grebler and Brigham platitudinously note "free entry into the business of intermediation is barred for sound reasons" related to the protection of the public. On the other hand, Professor Phillips observes "if the competitive force of new entrants are to be relied upon to achieve efficiency, free entry in banking must take the two-way meaning attached to it in competitive theory—freedom of entrance and exits. More exits, of course, is precisely what regulation and supervision, including restrictions on entry, are designed to prevent. As a result the banking structure has responded very slowly to inefficient operators and to geographical shifts of the industry."[13]

[e]Professor Shaw observes with respect to California that "the state gives a fortune now with each new charter. It supplies charters monopolistically, and it limits the supplies so tightly that market value is much higher than required initial capital. The state donates its monopoly profit to the successful charter applicant instead of tax payers." It has been reported that in the early 1960s industry estimated that "the price in which new charters demanded would be in balance with new charters currently being granted" would be in excess of one million dollars.[14]

shown for the injury to the users or buyers of the service denied the opportunity to purchase at the lowest prices under the most favorable terms.

Regulators Favor a Locally-Oriented Industry. The Home Owners' Loan Act of 1933, Section 5(a) refers to the establishment of "local mutual thrift institutions" and created federal associations "thereby giving primary consideration to the best practices of local mutual thrift and home financing institutions in the United States."[15] In 1959, both savings and loan leagues supported the Holding Company Act because "control of savings and loan associations should be kept in the hands of local citizens—rather than out-of-town investors."[f] Presumably, such safeguards are designed to remove the local interests from "outside interference," a pejorative description of competition.

Regulation to Reduce the Risk of Insolvency. There are some curious contradictions in this particular reason for regulation. It has been noted by both Professors Shaw,[17] Grebler and[18] Brigham that competition has failed to achieve optimal resource allocation in this industry. Now, to the extent that noncompetition implies monopoly, it would follow that the risk of failure due to the competition would be reduced or eliminated. Again, what reason is there for regulation in a situation where competitive failures are highly improbable? Either the industry is competitive and therefore prone to competitive successes and failures thereby involving risk; or if the industry is dominated by monopolistic elements, the risk problem would be absent.

The Contradictory Nature of Regulation. One is tempted to paraphrase Marx's reference to the "inherent contradictions of capitalism." An instance of how regulation leads to contradictions is provided in the announcement that any association might engage in direct lending in any place in the country up to five percent of its assets.[19] At the same time, the rule governing participation was altered so that an association selling a participation would have to increase its share to 50 percent of the mortgage.

Another contradiction is in the favorable tax environment for savings and loan associations which permitted a tax deferral on earnings until 1963. Clearly, the privilege of transferring earnings to this tax-deferred reserve encouraged growth[g] in that it permitted increasing earnings to go into the tax deferred

---

[f]"The examining and regulatory authorities appear to be fairly well imbued with the philosophy of saving associations as local, home, financial institutions . . . Restrictions on the powers of savings associations, especially on the lending side, might be considered serious drawbacks by casual observers. The geographic lending area, the types of dwellings on which mortgage loans may be made, the services which may be offered to the public and the types of accounts which may be held are restricted."[16]

[g]"Some instruments of regulation prod the industry to growth. For example, federal law has made tax relief contingent on growth in savings capital and mortgage loans—an incentive to promotion at the expense of economy."[20]

reserve funds. Nonetheless, the Federal Home Loan Bank Board found reasons to object[h] to growth.

The most serious contradiction involved in regulation is that control over entry and the regulation of competition through limits on the use of brokers' savings[i] and limits on premiums[j] associations can offer to new savers reduce competition. In other words, a disequilibrium is created as with any other type of monopolistic arrangement. The situation may be compared to the price support program in agriculture which encourages chronic surpluses. In such circumstances, each savings and loan association seeks growth in order to take advantage of the noncompetitive return. This occurs even when mortgage rates are falling simply because it is profitable to a competitive firm. There is nothing perverse in this as suggested by Grebler and Brigham.[24] Independent competitive decisions are a response to restrictive price and thereby multiply the problems of control and regulation. Instead of reducing risk and discouraging expansion, the regulations have an effect opposite to that intended.

The most serious problem arising from regulation is the extent to which the regulatory agencies feel compelled to arbitrarily determine the extent of competition to be tolerated. This is illustrated in the various efforts at shackling the dimensions of competition, e.g., in the suppression of premiums offered by savings and loan associations, the use of broker savings[k] and threats against increases in the share rate on savings. In seeking to inhibit these competitive forms, there is grave danger that the most vigorous (and in some areas the only) kind of competition possible is suppressed. It is, indeed, ironical that the regulatory authorities are urged to promulgate additional new regulations in the interests of preserving competition. Ironical because the most probable result of such regulations is its suppression!

[h]A Board member, Michael Greenebaum, stated that "almost without exception problems originate in rapid growth . . . the impairment of the assets of most of these associations shows a consistent pattern—a drive for rapid growth stimulated by a high dividend rate."[21]

[i]Referring to 1961, it is reported that "there was also serious discussion at the Federal Home Loan Bank Board of regulating fees and discounts on mortgage loans as part of an effort to stabilize rates on savings in localities where high income from such charges gave certain associations *advantages over their competitors* in bidding for savings . . . the clamor for a regulation of broker savings accounts had come from the business, where the majority of the associations did not use the device and believed that the broker's advertising of higher rates placed them at a disadvantage."[22] (italics supplied)

[j]"In order to foster fair competition within the savings and loan industry by eliminating certain practices developed under existing gift sales the Board on June 14, 1963 amended the *rules and regulations for insurance of accounts* to prevent persons other than the associations from engaging in certain activities directly affecting the association's operations by prohibiting insured institutions from accepting savings solicited through such practices."[23]

[k]Mr. Greenebaum, a member of the FHLBB, denied that out-of-state savings was savings in the ordinary sense. Noting that a large percentage of some associations' savings inflow comes from other parts of the country, he observed that "this money is not local. It is not savings in the sense that you or I or the ordinary man on the street construe savings. It has been attracted here in large quantity because of the slightly higher yield being offered."[25]

During the tight money situation which developed in mid-1966, stock associations in California broke through the 5 percent ceiling. Federal savings and loan associations failed to follow them. Two stock associations, Home Savings and Loan Association, the largest and later Lytton, were the leaders. It was reported in the newspapers that "the Federal Home Loan Bank Board has effective rate control through denying associations advances when the rate exceeded what the Board considers to be the prevailing level in its area . . . within a few days, it is believed, the Board hopes to crack down on associations that exceed its new 5 percent regular passbook ceiling in California, but the legal technique to be used" is not decided. "An association going above the new 5.25 percent," one Washington source said, "will get itself into hot water."[26]

Home Savings and Loan, the first of the area savings and loan associations to go to 5 percent from 4.85 percent, did so earlier in April 1966. The president, the late Howard W. Ahmanson, stated that the decision to raise the rate "was based on the fact that savings and loan associations must pay competitive rates if they are to fulfill their basic function of encouraging thrift and home ownership."[27] The chairman of the Federal Home Loan Bank Board, John E. Horne, condemned these increases saying "many banks have increased rates on consumer certificates of deposit to 5.5 percent and some savings and loan associations have sought to gain *unfair advantage* at the expense of competitive institutions by escalating rates. These circumstances have combined to create serious inequities in the Board's policy of stabilizing dividend rates of member institutions."[28] It was reported that "the federals generally have been trying to hold the line to 5 percent. The 48-member conference of federal savings and loan associations announced that it supported requests by the administration to give the regulatory agency control over rates."[29]

One professor and former Savings and Loan Commissioner has observed that the "industry thrives in a setting of Federal and State controls and regulations."[30] That it "thrives" is hardly astonishing since the regulation of both entry and competitive behavior guarantees a noncompetitive or monopoly return. A more important question would have been whether the housing industry and the economy "thrives"? "Federal and state savings and loan regulation has prevented capital from moving *freely* between geographical markets because of lending-distance limitations; and it has prevented savings and loan associations, which collect into usually large amounts the savings of millions of households from exercising a sufficiently wide range of choice in the types of lending in which they may engage."[31]

The power to regulate entry and competitive behavior means that the income of associations and particularly the management is more dependent on the good will of the regulators than on internal efficiency or market forces (since the latter may be forestalled and controlled). Thus, the good manager is not necessarily the one who keeps his expenses down. He needs to be highly skilled in winning the support of the regulatory authorities in keeping out unwanted new competitors, and punishing aggressive associations prone to unleash undesirable competitive activities.

Insurance and the Suppression of Competition

Federal insurance of savings and loan associations may have been a potent factor in the tremendous growth relative to other financial intermediaries. It meant that savings would be protected as at commercial banks. In return for the insurance of their deposits, the associations have been subjected to a variety of regulations involving audits and dividend policy that must tend to question the value of insurance.

The newly insured association is not permitted to raise his dividend rate above the competitive rate during his first five years.[l] Presumably this requirement is designed to make him more prudent. But inasmuch as newcomers must grow, they have no option but to compete. Thus, the impact of regulation is the suppression of competition. More lately, the Federal Home Loan Bank Board has secured legislation enabling it to set maximum rates. The sole purpose of this power has been the elimination of competition for savings by means of dividend rate.[m] Not only has the Board the power to set maximum rates but in addition it has used its power over the individual associations to deny advances to associations which failed to heed its views on maximum dividend rates.[n]

A ceiling on dividends does not of course completely eliminate competition. It is obvious that when restrictions are placed on price competition, the competitive forces are diverted into nonprice channels. The question for optimality in resource use is whether the alternative competitive form performs as well as that replaced. Presumably, given a choice between alternatives, an independent unit will choose the more profitable or more efficient or least costly in terms of the function to be performed. Accordingly, when this optimal choice is foreclosed, the firm is forced to the "second best"—the function is either not performed as effectively or involves higher expenses. It should be noted that in this industry competition takes many forms embracing simultaneously both price and nonprice forms.[33] There is, therefore, a presumption that a ceiling or restriction on certain kinds of competition means that alternative forms of competition will be pursued at a higher cost to the firm, industry and the economy.

---

[l]This is a condition for the insurance of accounts by the federal savings and loan insurance corporation.

[m]". . . a maximum time deposit rate imposed by regulation Q below the rate schedule which would be reached in a nonregulated market is the economic equivalent of a collusive agreement among competitors to exert monopsonistic powers."[32]

[n]The refusal of advances to associations raising rates beyond certain levels has been the policy of the Federal Home Loan Bank Board and uniformly adopted by the individual Federal Home Loan Banks.

The consequence of the elimination of competition with respect to dividends has been a not unsurprising disequilibrium in the industry. The savings and loan industry cannot control mortgage rates since they are set by supply and demand forces in a market where there exists other powerful financial intermediaries. But the cost of their input is at least protected against intraindustry competition. And, since the same law giving the Federal Home Loan Bank Board power to set maximum dividend rates also continued Federal Reserve power over time and saving deposit rates of the commercial banks, the cost of input is effectively insulated from competition for at least two of the major intermediaries. It follows that when mortgage rates are sufficiently high, a savings and loan association has an incentive for expansion. Whether it merely pockets the noncompetitive spread or seeks to expand will depend upon internal incentives. But the ceiling on the cost of a major input is responsible for a permanent disequilibrium between supply and demand. Mortgage rates are not and cannot be controlled, even though the price the two major institutions pay for savings is controlled. Consequently, there is no adjustment or inducement to place more savings in those institutions, and thus bring about a new equilibrium. Whatever adjustments may come, they will be adventitious and fortuitous.

There are other effects, but they are peculiarly related to the major ownership characteristics of this industry, i.e., the mutual arrangement. Inasmuch as those in control, the management, do not own, they do not have the same incentives that a normal profit-seeking firm would have. As will be discussed later, disequilibrium is the "mutual" way of life. Though disequilibrium is rationally welcomed, it is hardly indicative of a *rational* allocation of resources in a profit economy.

The Federal Home Loan Bank Board's behavior with respect to the 1958 examination of Alice Savings and Loan Association of Alice, Texas, is illustrative. The investigator, Schmoker, received the following instructions from the District Supervisory Agent N.S. Oakes: "Uncover all information possible in connection with any secondary financing by other of the Mullen companies. We are anxious to determine how this association can invest its funds at the rates that are being obtained."[34] A special investigation was prompted by the decision of Alice Savings and Loan Association to raise its dividend rate when other associations in the area were lowering their rates. It would appear that the theory underlying the Board's action was that the ability of the more competitive association in raising its rate represented *prima facie* evidence that there was a violation of the rules and regulations with respect to proper lending. Presumably, no association could possibly pay a higher dividend rate without an infringement of one of the rules. Oakes reasoned that if Alice Savings and Loan Association could pay higher dividends it had to be because they were receiving better mortgage rates. Yet, the evidence indicated that they were falling throughout the District. "In my judgment we have felt that oftentimes it is possible for any institution, by making a full loan, whether it has a second behind it or whether it is based on appraisal, to get a little better rate on it than it could if it were a long percentage loan."[35]

While the judgment may be correct, it is to be noted that it represents a substitution of an administrative opinion for the individual savings and loan association management. It is difficult to say when an association may be assuming too much risk; but it is questionable whether the administrator's forecast of supply and demand conditions is necessarily superior to management. Oakes' reasoning suggested that 90 percent loans meant borrowers would have little equity—particularly, if there was a second mortgage, this would permit the association to receive a higher rate than earned by a competitive institution. Though Oakes denied that it was his habit to punish institutions for increasing the rate, he did say "that it is not good for the overall picture."[36] It is, however, difficult to reconcile this denial of punishment with the rather obvious harassment which went on with respect to Alice Savings and Loan Association.[o]

From the view of the regulatory authority, an independent increase in rate would undoubtedly lead to an investigation along the lines outlined in the case of Alice Savings and Loan Association. In this particular case, the Federal Home Loan Bank Board looking for "a conflict of interest" claimed to have found it: John M. Wyman, the director of supervision of the Federal Home Loan Bank Board, offered the definition "the use by director or officer of an association of his fiduciary position in such a manner as to realize or invite personal gain."[38] Undoubtedly, the definition is both acceptable and meaningful. But it is not clear why the Board went after Alice Savings and Loan Association while ignoring the rather obvious conflicts of interest occurring among federal associations whose managements own subsidiaries that conduct business with their associations.

Close Relations between Mutuals and the Regulatory Authority. Mutuality has a "sacred cow" status. This has been achieved and preserved because of the fiction of "mutuality." But it is no longer mutual in *ownership* nor do the members share in the management. The special status with the government has only been maintained because of the archaic notion that a mutual represents a purer organizational form, unsullied by profit seeking and competitive materialism.

This close and intimate relationship with the government has other important and not altogether fortunate results. For reasons that will be made clearer in subsequent chapters, management requires freedom from competition to convert

---

[o]Oakes also said "if you have one institution over here that can only obtain 6 percent for prime loans, another institution here that can obtain 7 on all of its prime loans . . . we would want to know how this institution—it may be because of outstanding service, it may be because of managerial personality, it may be because of a fuller loan than this institution is making . . . if a substantial volume of any institution's loans are for 100 percent of appraisal of purchase price or more, then it is entirely possible that the lending institution, if it can arrange for the first and second, can obtain a much higher than the prevailing or competitive rate might be, entirely possible."[37]

a power position into personal gain: competition must be severely inhibited—if not eliminated altogether.[p] In their aversion to competition, they are not unlike the owners of more traditional firms. But unlike the latter, mutual managers cannot gain from competition. On the contrary, *some* property-oriented firms can "profit" from competitive behavior. The result is that mutual management's first interest is the maintenance of an anticompetitive policy on the part of the regulators. It is not enough to restrict entry: outbreaks of competition must be severely dealt with—even punished so that they cannot be permitted to further upset the applecart.[q]

The surest way to guarantee that competition will not break out is through maintaining at all times a close relationship with the regulatory authorities. When his own fortunes depend far more on what that authority permits or fails to suppress, it is hardly surprising that the mutual should consider this his primary activity.[r] Indeed, he is far more significantly affected by regulatory policies than by the internal efficiency of his firm. First, free from the worst excesses of competition, he is not required to be efficient. Second, his return, in one form or another, is closely intertwined with regulatory policy and action. Third, as an employee of a nonprofit establishment, he is much closer to the civil servant than is the owner-manager of a stock savings and loan association. Resentment for stock associations in this industry, on the part of the government officials as well as mutual management, is part of a general aversion for profit seeking and competition. The mutual manager works at maintaining intimate relations with public officials. It is more to his interest than either high profits

---

[p]Innis M. Oakes, president of the Federal Home Loan Bank of Little Rock, testified at the hearings concerning the Alice Savings and Loan Association of Alice, Texas, that he attended a regional meeting in which there was a heated discussion of dividends. "Mr. Pryor, it is true, as to the other managers in the district, urged us to take action in the case of Alice Savings and Loan Association. I don't deny the fact that there is much prodding that goes on in the district. It is not a difficult matter to find many institutions that are forever calling us asking us to take some action against some of their competitors. That is quite a common practice in the district. I devote much time on the telephone listening to the complaints from competitors suggesting that regulations should be adopted to regulate the competitor in this town or that town or across the street."[39]

[q]Mr. Hoeft, a mutual executive, expressed his apprehension with respect to competition: "I think you only have to pick up the *Wall Street Journal, New York Times,* any papers from the East and see the effect of *unbridled advertising* from others outside of the East for money, especially from California and the Nevada associations. Frankly, I doubt very much whether this savings bank is going to continue to pay a 4-7/8 rate for any length of time. They are probably doing it under pressure to protect their institution from raiding of the advertising associations in the western part of the United States. When you see advertising like 4-7/8 and so on, it depends on which kind of computer you use. I think it *unfair to those eastern institutions.*"[40]

[r]"Among all the devices used by the government to promote monopoly, public security, or public interest, regulation is in some respects perhaps the worst."[41] The combination of private management for profit with public boards to determine prices and profit "invites corruption of government by creating a situation in which the private profits of the private owners depends as much upon their ability to influence the regulatory authority as upon other considerations. Executive talent is diverted from the task of organizing efficient production to the task of influencing public relations."[42]

for the association or low expenses because he is not the beneficiary whereas, with restricted competition, a world of possibilities are open to him.

Antipathy of Regulatory Officials
for Stock Associations

The principal regulatory authority in the savings and loan industry is the Federal Home Loan Bank Board in Washington. Not only does the Board set policies for the Federal Home Loan Bank System with respect to its twelve regional banks but it also controls the insuring agency of the system, the Federal Savings and Loan Insurance Corporation. It is not too surprising that with 80% of the assets of the industry controlled by mutuals, the Board members should be particularly responsive to their needs as well as complaints. The most intimate relationship exists between the mutual sector of the industry and the Board in Washington. At times, it has almost seemed as if the Board had a pathological hatred of stock associations and public holding companies.

One official, William E. Husband, General Manager of the Federal Savings and Loan Insurance Corporation, commented in 1959: "Holding companies have no place in a savings and loan business . . . in the long run they will do you irreparable harm." He cited a case of a holding company organized by selling 100,000 shares at $1.00 apiece to insiders. They borrowed $10.7 million from a bank to which they also gave an option to buy 42,500 shares at $1.00. This money gained was used to buy control of a savings and loan association. To repay the loan, less than three months later, stock was sold to the public at $23.50. It has since paid a 5% dividend three times, split the stock 2 1/2 for one. The stock was now selling between $50 and $60 a share. "So you might say 'Who lost?' and I will say: In the long run, the reputation of the savings and loan business lost."[43]

The general attitude of the federal authorities with respect to the stock association seems to be based on at least an implicit, if not at times explicit, condemnation of business run for profits and with ownership interests. It is difficult to account for this hostility. Perhaps some part of it arises out of envy. The regulatory authorities observe individuals in the industry they regulate growing exceptionally wealthy. The regulatory authorities receive salaries considerably less than those earned by top management in even the large mutual associations. The almost paranoid hatred government officials feel is not unique to the savings and loan industry. It may be ubiquitous among all bureaucrats and reflects an attitude towards a business and private property system.

Another reason is that the stock associations are aggressively competitive. They not only compete for savings in their own local territories but also advertise in distant markets, e.g., California associations have actively sought savings in New York and other large Eastern cities. One savings and loan official, the late Bart Lytton, observed that "some 40% of our money comes from the East."[44]

The president of First Charter Savings and Loan Association in Los Angeles, Anthony Frank, stated that his California dividend is related to what happens in the East which supplies 18% of his savings and loan money. "We have to maintain a differential. If they do cut the rate in the East then it may have the effect of bringing them down here."[45]

Stock associations and public holding companies have shown a remarkable ingenuity in circumventing some of the bureaucratic regulations. By doing so, they have generated new sources of funds. Great Western, one of the largest, has done this for its subsidiary savings and loan associations at a rate much smaller than the long-term money which it receives from depositors. Notes have been sold to commercial and industrial corporations expiring in 270 days but payable on demand before that. The price is 3.5% for less than 90 days; 4% for 91 to 180 days; and 4.5% to a full 270 days. Corporations must buy a minimum of $100,000. At one time, as much as $12,000,000 had been sold and up to that point no corporate buyer had demanded early payment.

The Spence Act (September 1959) denied insurance to federally-insured associations subsequently acquired by a corporation controlling more than one federally-insured association. In effect, this prohibited further mergers or acquisitions by a holding company. But it did not restrain the opening of new branches. One holding company official commented, "I have never been able to establish in my own mind a logical reason for the enactment of this legislation, inasmuch as at the time of its passage there were no allegations of misdeeds or abuses on the part of the then existing holding companies."[46]

Typical of the regulatory attitude towards holding companies is a comment by the Annual Report of the Federal Deposit Insurance Corporation in 1944 that "holding companies not only tend to become monopolies but increase the problem of supervision."[47] Holding companies, and the womb from which they sprang, stock associations, are not only anathema to the regulatory authorities, they are allegedly monopolistic in intent and effect.[s] At least this is the rationale for the deep-seated hostility felt for them.[t]

The federal officials' deep distrust of the stock association as a manifestation of private property is accompanied by a very different attitude toward the mutual. Very often, regulatory officials will resign their government posts to

---

[s]Mr. Horne, Chairman of the Federal Home Loan Bank Board, has stated that all the problem cases in the national savings and loan industry are due to California holding companies because, unlike mutuals, they seek to maximize profits. It is allegedly because of their interest in the price of their stock that they would seek to build up current earnings by taking unnecessary risks. The idea is that for a given doubling of earnings from $3 to $6 a stock which sells at ten times earnings would move from $30 to $60.

[t]Former chairman of the Federal Home Loan Bank Board, Joseph P. McMurray, discussing the Holding Company Bill, indicated that "it is not intended to be a primitive bill. We do not regard holding companies per se adversely. We do believe if they wish to function in a financial area which is regulated, they should be subject to review and to that degree of regulation which assures the protection of their financial subsidiaries. Industry cannot function with some subject to control and others largely in an open-ended framework."[48]

take high salaried positions plus amenities in federal associations. In addition, there is a community of interest between the regulators and the mutuals in that the latter are far less regulated than the state-chartered stock associations, e.g., those in California. Until recently, federal regulations did not extend to checks on appraisals. The principal concern of the Federal Home Loan Bank Board and Bank officials has been potential conflicts of interest for officials of federal associations.

Regulation in the Interests of Mutuals. Regulators feel more in common with the salaried management of mutuals.[u] Whatever the reasons, they rarely pass up the opportunity to lash out at the "profit-seeking" growth-minded "joint stock companies."[50] Many of the regulations of the last decade have been designed to hold in check the competitive intensity of stock associations, particularly those in California. Limits on participation sales have been tied to what has been labelled excessive growth. Restrictions on the use of broker savings to 5 percent of assets has been rationalized on the grounds that it was necessary to prevent some future flight of "hot money."

Board member Greenebaum has commented that "the strength of the savings and loan association movement . . . and its phenomenal growth over the past 20 years has been correctly attributed to the essentially local nature of the saving and home building industry. Common sense dictates caution in modifying this pattern. You must weigh the volatile nature of nonlocal funds carefully against their short-term and perhaps illusory advantage."[51] One former president of the United States Savings and Loan League has stated: "Suppose you were the manager of a savings and loan association on the West Coast with, say, $5,000,000 or $10,000,000 of broker money in your portfolio, and one day you received a call from a broker saying that the XY Savings and Loan Association in Seattle, Washington, has just gone up to 4 3/4 percent and that if you do not go up to 4.75 percent he is going to pull out his money and send it up there. That is what some associations could face. The regulation seeks to protect the business against such squeeze plays."[52] The research director of United States Savings and Loan League commented: "What we did, or hope we did, was to remove the broker's ability to mobilize funds . . . it was dangerous to have one person exercise potentially extensive control over an association."[53] The cure may however have been worse than the disease. Instead of permitting the broker to make the decision with respect to the placement of the money, that decision was concentrated in Washington at the Federal Home Loan Bank Board level. Regulatory authority was substituted for the conflicting and responsible decisions of a more impersonal marketplace. A survey of broker savings accounts in California asso-

---

[u]George Stigler has trenchantly suggested and sought to prove that "regulation is acquired by the industry and is designed and operated primarily for its benefit. The state's power to coerce provides "the possibilities for the utilization of the state by an industry to increase its profitability."[49]

ciations show that of those which remained open at the time of the survey, there was "a tendency to remain relatively stable in size."[54] Other findings were that the turnover rates of broker savings and local savings were approximately equal; and average broker savings accounts at the time of being opened were more than three times as large as the average local savings accounts. With respect to accounts of both types which have been closed, each remained open for approximately the same length of time. Direct savings placements by out-of-state savers was about twice that of broker savings and may be just as active and potentially mobile as broker savings since they are held, obviously, by rate-conscious savers. Thus, the regulations with respect to the brokers may be relatively ineffective in precluding an outflow of funds.

Effectiveness of Regulation of Mutuals

In the absence of a proprietary interest exercised by shareholders in controlling management, the only possible deterrent to managerial diversion, short of insolvency, is effective government regulation. It has been noted earlier how those familiar with the operation of mutuals have dismissed the savings and loan method with its membership voting as "pious in its assertions but illusory in practice."[55] It is urged that "the savings of the community are too important to become the prize in any recurrent struggles for management control between warring groups."[56] In order to meet the question of how the depositors' or savers' interests are to be safeguarded, it has been suggested that they can "best be taken care of by this, as I say, harsh trustee system of standards, plus strict supervision—plus recognition of the fact—and this is involved in strict supervision that a mutual savings bank has historically been considered a quasi-public institution."[57]

There are a number of weapons a hostile regulator can use against competitive or maverick associations, e.g., denial of applications for branches; allowance of new branches and new associations across the street from the condemned associations; lengthy and expensive examinations as apparently occurred in the case of the Alice Savings and Loan Association of Alice, Texas; and denial of Federal Home Loan Bank advances to the association as may have been threatened in the latter. The president of Alice testified before a Congressional Committee that he had been subjected to some rather high handed and bizarre methods: harassment consisted of lengthy examinations which saw an increase in their costs from $782 in 1957 to $12,383 the next year. One year after the examination, the president of this association which had $17.6 million in assets was indicted for an alleged theft of $260 from the association. Three months later, a warrant of arrest was made out; and after another three months, the case was dismissed without a hearing.

Industry regulation favors the mutual. It would be too much to say that it tolerates the stock form; it can hardly abide it. There is one law for the stock and another for the mutual, as is illustrated by the investigation of the public holding companies in 1959.[59] An infrastructure was revealed to the public and censured. Yet, not one word was said about the infrastructure of mutuals[v] where management "owns" a variety of firms doing business with and competing with the associations. This rather remarkable double standard is hardly surprising. Both the savings and loan industry and the regulatory apparatus are mutually oriented. The mutual can do little wrong; the stock little good. Elimination of certificates of deposit from "liquid" reserves is a case in point. Presumably, a rational procedure for a profit-oriented firm, they are anathema in an industry dominated by mutuals.

But short of insolvency, there is little in the record to suggest that incompetent, self-perpetuating, autocratic and self-dealing management have been replaced—let alone chastized by the regulatory authorities. The Long Beach Federal Savings and Loan Association seizure in 1946 and again in 1960 related to a long-standing feud between the management and the Federal Home Loan Bank Board with respect to the appointment of a president for the Federal Home Loan Bank of Los Angeles.[w]

In a certain sense, there is bound to be an identity of interest between the regulating authorities such as the Federal Home Loan Bank Board or the state savings and loan commisioner's office and the managerial officers in the mutual savings and loan associations. Both are salaried managers. While the savings and loan official has considerably greater discretion than the government official, the organizational structure of the mutual does not permit him to participate directly in the earnings. Yet, not infrequently opportunities arise in which the managing officer in a mutual association must be replaced. There may be no direct heirs or relatives to take charge of the mutual. Under these circumstances, nothing could be more natural and at the same time more odious than for a member of the regulating hierarchy to resign to become chief official in a mutual. In direct salary, the change is of the order of magnitude from $18,000-$20,000 to $50,000-$75,000 a year. In addition, there are, of course, opportunities for side income through control over the infrastructure. Table 6-1 gives some conception of the employees in the Federal Home Loan Bank Board who have taken either

---

[v]"No information however was gathered with regard to possible outside interests of managers and officers of state mutuals or federally chartered associations."[60]

[w]Congressman Holifield alleged "the record of the previous hearings will show that the Long Beach Association was seized in 1946 at Mr. Fahy's order, and under Mr. Ammann's conservatorship, because they would not accede to the appointment of a Mr. Twohy from the Home Loan Bank Board's staff as president of the Twelfth Regional Bank, which was in Los Angeles at that time. The bitterness of that personal fight precipitated the first seizure."[61]

Table 6-1

Employees with Salaries of \$7,500 per Annum or More, Who Have Resigned in the Past 10 Years to Accept Position in Savings and Loan Associations or Federal Home Loan Banks

Name and Position	Salary	Separated	Reason for Resigning
	Federal Home Loan Bank Board		
O.K. LaRoque, Board member	\$15,000	March 1951	Return to Federal Home Loan Bank of Greensboro.
A.C. Newell, special representative.	10,600	April 1953	To accept position of vice president, Federal Home Loan Bank of San Francisco.
J.W. McBride, assistant to chief supervisor.	8,360	June 1953	To accept position of vice president, Federal Home Loan Bank of San Francisco.
J. Alston Adams, Board member.	15,000	June 1953	To accept position of president, Federal Home Loan Bank of San Francisco.
Brendon O'Dwyer, reviewing examiner.	8,040	October 1953	To accept position with Enterprise Federal Savings & Loan Association, Annapolis, Md.
J. Aldrich Hall, General Counsel.	12,900	October 1955	To accept position with Security Federal Savings & Loan Association, St. Petersburg, Fla.
Gerald Whistler, financial analyst.	7,785	June 1956	To accept position with Federal Home Loan Bank of San Francisco
W.W. McAllister, Board Chairman.	20,500	September 1956	To return to San Antonio Savings & Loan Association, San Antonio, Texas.
Albert Crew, Director of Bank Operations.	11,880	April 1957	To accept position of treasurer, Federal Home Loan Bank of Cincinnati.
Ashby T. Gibbons, auditor	8,990	June 1957	To accept position of treasurer, Federal Home Loan Bank of Indianapolis.
R.C. Dickerhoff, financial analyst.	8,810	April 1959	To accept position with First Federal Savings & Loan Association, Cumberland, Md.
Jack Ferguson, financial analyst.	10,370	August 1959	To accept position with Federal Home Loan Bank of Little Rock.
	Division of Examinations		
F.E. Haigis, district examiner.	\$ 8,760	November 1952	To accept position with Manchester Federal Savings & Loan Association, Manchester, N.H.

Table 6-1 (cont.)

| Name and Position | Division of Examinations | | |
	Salary	Separated	Reason for Resigning
L. Earl Woodford, chief examiner.	10,535	September 1955	To accept position with Home Savings & Loan Association, Youngstown, Ohio.
Grover C. Kirby, assistant chief examiner.	7,570	September 1955	To accept position with Decatur Federal Savings & Loan Association, Decatur, Ga.
Charles Dillon, Savings and Loan examiner.	8,430	October 1955	To accept position with Community Federal Savings & Loan Association, Overland, Mo.
W.I. Kamm, savings and loan examiner.	7,570	April 1956	To accept position with Coast Federal Savings & Loan Association, Los Angeles, Calif.
John W. Kleeb, chief examiner.	10,320	May 1956	To accept position of vice president, Federal Home Loan Bank of San Francisco.
William A. Patton, savings and loan examiner.	7,570	June 1956	To accept position with Petersburg Mutual Building & Loan Association, Petersburg, Va.
Karl Schoenecker, savings and loan examiner.	7,680	February 1957	To accept position with Home Building Loan Association, Milwaukee, Wis.
Thomas J. Garvey, savings and loan examiner.	7,570	October 1957	To accept position with Federal Home Loan Bank of Chicago.
Carl Mathena, savings and loan examiner.	7,570	October 1957	To accept position with Akron Savings & Loan Association, Akron, Ohio.
James Miller, assistant chief examiner.	8,990	November 1957	To accept position with Citizens Federal Savings & Loan Association, Bellefontaine, Ohio.
George W. Maple, savings and loan examiner.	8,570	June 1958	To accept position with Franklin Federal Savings & Loan Association, Columbus, Ohio.
Donald H. Taylor, chief examiner.	12,770	August 1958	To accept position with Federal Home Loan Bank of Cincinnati.
Carolus D. Little, savings and loan examiner.	8,330	April 1959	To accept position with First Federal Savings & Loan Association, New Smyrna Beach, Fla.

Table 6-1 (cont.)

| Name and Position | Division of Examinations | | Reason for Resigning |
	Salary	Separated	
Ervin Berlinger, savings and loan examiner.	8,330	May 1959	To accept position with Dollar Federal Savings & Loan Association, Columbus, Ohio.
M.G. Glissman, savings and loan examiner.	9,890	June 1959	To accept position with Home Mutual Savings & Loan Association, San Francisco, Calif.
R.J. Strecker, chief examiner.	12,770	July 1959	To accept position of vice president, Federal Home Loan Bank of Pittsburgh, Pa.
R.E. Reimer, savings and loan examiner.	8,570	July 1959	To accept position with Home Savings & Loan Association, Rockford, Ill.
E.T. Westgaard, savings and loan examiner.	9,890	September 1959	To accept position with Clearfield Federal Savings & Loan Association, Philadelphia, Pa.
R.G. Kellenbach, savings and loan examiner.	9,890	October 1959	To accept position with Federal Home Loan Bank of Portland.
Federal Savings & Loan Insurance Corporation			
Robert C. Rush, special representative.	$10,280	October 1956	To accept position with Federal Home Loan Bank of New York.
Tull Ryall, financial analyst.	7,510	September 1958	To accept position with Northern Virginia Savings & Loan Association, Arlington, Va.

Source: Investigation of the Federal Home Loan Bank Board, Alic - Pt. 1-A, op. cit., pp. 741-42.

positions in associations which they had formerly regulated or have gone to the District Federal Home Loan Banks which technically are owned by member associations. The game of musical chairs played between *regulating* officials and the *regulated* is not unique to this industry. The differences in salary and opportunities for additional income are well known.

On the one hand, employees of the Board can harass the member associations. They can indeed make the managing officer's tenure irksome and expensive: as in the Alice seizure, a man can be tried in the harsh light of publicity, so that both he and his association are persona non grata in a community. On the other hand, management in the mutual associations have much to offer government officials responsible for regulating the industry. Whenever openings arise in a mutual association or in the District Federal Home Loan Bank, the most obvious candidates will be former Board employees. They are familiar with the industry as well as with other bureaucrats. Additional intimate relationships benefit the regulated and the regulators where attorneys take transient positions with the Board. It is not uncommon to find them working from two to four years in Washington in both advisory and executive positions with respect to approval of charters for new associations and for branches. When their term of office is over and they return to home, it is frequently seen that they have secured the most lucrative accounts in representing associations on whom they have generously bestowed branch charters a few years before in their role as Board officials.

Regulation has consisted in the establishment of a cartel policy designed to please the majority of the members.[x] The price to the economy is the suppression of independent and competitive behavior. So long as the association remains solvent, there is little incentive for the regulator to become obnoxious so far as the management of the mutual is concerned. On the other hand, to the extent that he maintains good relationships with the associations, there is the ultimate hope that he will make the transition from government to the more lucrative role of a chief operating officer in an association. There is one further point: State commissions, the Federal Home Loan Bank Board and Federal Home Loan Bank officials are paid by the industry. An arrangement in which the industry pays the regulatory officials makes about as much sense as having dope pushers pay policemen to keep competitors out of their local preserve. The net effect is a mutual toleration of inefficiencies at the two levels of savings and loan management and regulation.

Regulation is not a surrogate for competition or a check on the efficiency of the management of mutuals. Actually, regulation is to a great extent nothing more than a form of window dressing to persuade savers that the management is efficient and morally responsible in a fiduciary sense. In this sense, the link between mutuality and regulation may be compared to the English freebooters of the sixteenth and seventeenth centuries who shared their loot with Queen Elizabeth and later royal monarchs. Or put more strongly, regulation legalizes the managerial exploitation of the saver. This is indicated in the extent to which the Federal Home Loan Bank Board is responsive to mutuals in their opposition to competitive increases in the share rate. The Board protects the mutuals because of an identity of outlook between mutuals and regulation. Mutuals oppose

---

[x]In this connection, note the comment by Harry Schwartz, economist of the Federal Home Loan Bank Board: the Board should not favor uniform share or dividend rates for savings and loan associations throughout the nation. He reasoned that a uniform rate would force down the California rates and thus increase the profits going to associations of the "stock" type.[62]

higher dividends to savers because they eat up funds that would not only go into reserves but into the infrastructure. To the extent that reserves are reduced, the position of management becomes more precarious; it is that more vulnerable to vigorous rate competition.

Regulation and the Rate of Return

Inasmuch as the savings and loan industry is a regulated industry, it is worthwhile to consider the impact of regulation on the rate of return. A naive expectation is that a regulated industry, protected from free competition of new firms, would experience less risk and threats to solvency. The rate of return would obviously be reduced: with less risk, less return is justified. If regulation is not merely a euphemism for monopolistic restriction, the justification that the industry cannot stand competition must take the form of reducing the rate of return in line with the deliberately fostered policy of restricting competition. The lower interest charges of public utilities on their bonds reflect the reduced risks they undergo in regulated industry.

But the earnings of a mutual savings and loan, as reflected on the net worth, are misleading. Mutual associations do not have the same incentive structure for increasing the net worth. Their management increase compensation, expenses and diversion possibilities. Some idea of the rates of return *allowed* in the savings and loan industry can be derived from the California stock associations' performance. Two reasons make the performance indicative of the value of regulation in what is otherwise a mutual industry. In the first place, federal requirements with respect to the allocation of net income to reserves have made the California federal associations maintain reserves relative to savings capital in the same ratio as the stock associations. The denominator, "average net worth," is not different. In addition, since they are competitive with the stock associations, stock performance indicates the potential rate of return for mutuals. It is inferred that a similar return must or could have been earned by the California federals. The performance of the California stock associations is a satisfactory index for the potential diversion of federal associations.

Table 6-2 shows rate of return after taxes 1960 and 1963 for savings and loan associations as compared to commercial banks, leading manufacturing corporations and all corporations. The federals do not show a rate of return equivalent to the California stock associations though they are in the same market. The difference may be attributed to their higher outlays on compensation, amenities and the operation of the diversion mechanism. In all four categories, the stock savings and loan association rate of return was higher. Of course, part of the difference for 1960 is attributable to the fact that until 1963, savings and loan associations were practically exempt from corporate taxes. This means that a more appropriate measure would have been rate of return prior to taxes. In

Table 6-2
Rate of Return,[1] after Taxes 1960, 1963

	1960	1963
California Stock Associations[2]	19.5	14.4
California Federal Associations[2]	12.8	11.2
U.S. Federal Associations[2]	11.5	9.1
U.S. Less California[2]	10.9	9.3
Insured Commercial Banks[3]	10.4	9.2
Leading Manufacturing Corporations[3]	10.6	11.5
All Corporations[3]	9.1	9.5

Notes:

1. Net after taxes and dividends to average net worth.

2. Federal Home Loan Bank Board, *Combined Financial Statements*, 1960, 1961, 1963 and 1964, op. cit.

3. National City Bank, Monthly Review, April, 1961, 1964.

1963, after the new tax regulations had gone into effect, the critical comparison is with the California stock savings and loan associations. Because of constraints on mutuals this is the potential return. It is significant that a regulated industry should have earned not only 40% more than *all* corporations in the nation but almost 60% more than commercial banks and 25% more than leading manufacturing corporations. While returns for the California federal associations and the U.S. federal associations are not significantly greater than either manufacturing corporations or all corporations, it must be remembered that as mutuals some adjustment should be made for the amount diverted and in expenses. If we allow for 30% higher expenses in 1963, the adjusted rate of return is 13.8% which is fairly close to the California stock return and 19% higher than the average reported for manufacturing corporations and 42.3% more than that for "all corporations."

Contrary to expectation, this regulated industry, instead of receiving a smaller rate of return because the risks of competition were reduced, if not entirely eliminated, earned more! The moral is that if an industry wishes to increase profits, it would do well to have itself regulated by the government. The hue and cry sometimes raised concerning the adverse impact of regulation on profits may represent nothing more than misplaced emphasis as well as misunderstanding. At least for those able to survive the regulation, the benefits are indeed attractive. Not only is the estimated rate of return higher, but the rigors of unrestrained competition are eliminated. Thus, the hazards from uncertainty, innovation and instability in market shares are reduced. Regulation is an exceptionally low price to pay for such privilege. The next step beyond regulation is, from the view of management, simply to mutualize. Once that is achieved, there is no longer necessity for sharing the return with what used to be called the legal property owners.

Part III: The Theory of Managerial Diversion

7

Management Control and the Fiction of Mutuality

The first mutual savings and loan associations were neither profit oriented nor management dominated. The Oxford Provident in 1831 required that its "members" subscribe for not less than one and not more than five shares at five hundred dollars a piece. A member was entitled to borrow five hundred dollars for every share held. The original concept included "the voice of the shareholder in the management policy."[1] Directors were usually chosen from the members who met face to face and knew each other intimately. The enterprise was essentially cooperative and democratic. Professional management was not only antithetical to this philosophy but was a luxury not to be afforded.

Public Service vs Profit

The men who organized these first associations were dedicated to the importance of home financing for moderate-income families. They went about their business in the same way they organized their churches and colleges; and with a similar dedication and zeal. Identical in spirit to those individuals of a later generation who organized community service clubs and YMCAs, they possessed a strong conviction that such institutions were a necessary part of any society. It has been stated, even today, that one would start a mutual for the same reason one would start a "Y"—to provide a community service. "An association is not an economic unit. It is a social organism."[2]

The reference to the religious motivation of the founders of the original savings and loan associations is not to be taken lightly. It is no accident that in the frustrating and sorry history of socialistic and cooperative ventures in America, the few successful projects have been tied in one way or another to a religious organization.[3] At the core of the mutual organization is a religious zeal—even fanaticism—which has defied economics and the "main chance." Homes for the members of their association or community were only slightly lower on the scale of priorities than churches and schools.

The original ideal of shareholder democracy in making loans at monthly meetings to members involved an allocation of funds to areas in which the rate of return was considerably below that to be earned elsewhere. In a free society, this is possible. Hence, investments and gifts for school and churches. But it is by no means obvious that such investments are superior—or inferior: they are perfectly consistent with free choice. They may be considered philanthropic gifts.

But it is incorrect to suggest that savings are therefore better handled through mutual institutions. If one wants to subsidize an institution that is his privilege. It is sufficient that it survives (because of his subsidization); but nothing is demonstrated with respect to relative efficiency since the profit and the non-profit organizations are not on equal terms. Survival demonstrates that the non-profit association is wanted; not that it is more efficient.

But if profit is not sought, what can be said of the goal of home ownership? Do mutual institutions perform more effectively with respect to this goal than profit seekers? The evidence which is reported elsewhere[4] suggests that they do not. They are less successful in collection of savings and less efficient in inter-mediation between savers and borrowers for home purchase. Furthermore, if they are truly uninterested in profits, they have no basis for making rational decisions with respect to competing demands for loans. Undoubtedly, they could survive; but only through[a] the addition of extra investment dollars emanating from the zeal for mutuality.

Mutuality and Property Rights. The question of ownership in a mutual is not clear. It is sometimes said that the earnings "after expenses" (including taxes) and provisions for necessary reserves for safety of deposits, will be distributed entirely to depositors.[6] Referring to the trustees of mutual savings banks, Congressman Moulter said, they "are held to high standards of trust and barred from making personal profit in conflict of interest situations."[7] In contrast to stock-owned commercial banks, who are responsible to their stockholders rather than their depositors, the mutual savings banks "consider that their basic reason for operations is to reward savers for their thrift. In other words, the sole motivation of the savings business is to stimulate thrift and offer the saver the highest reward possible, after allowing for adequate reserves to protect the safety of the depositors' funds."[8] Inasmuch as mutuals are not run for profit, neither competition nor competitive excesses are to be anticipated. Nor in the context of mutuality would insurance of deposits appear to be necessary. It may be suggested that insurance does serve a function. But it is not to protect the savers. They are already protected first by mutuality which means they do not have to fear the outbreak of competitive excesses promoted by the desire of profits; and second, government control of entry further restricts the competition from new-comers seeking to break into a protected market. On the contrary, what the insurance features accomplish is that apart from making the savings and loan association comparable to the commercial bank, the management is relieved of

---

[a]In referring to the dependence of private colleges on gifts, President Lloyd E. Warner of Colorado College observes that "there has never been a year in any strong private college . . . that the final fiscal outcome did not depend upon gift income to make up the difference between expenses and general revenues . . . it is a well-established fact of the private-college way of life, just as it is part of the way of life of the local symphony or museum."[5]

liability to the shareholders. The insurance corporation assumes that liability for him.[b] Management is given a free hand to make something of its power.

Thus, in the first instance, the mutual is said to have a different goal than profits. Not only has management relieved itself of the necessity for paying profits to savers: it has also succeeded in ridding itself of liability for what happens to those savings. It is rather remarkable that, on the one hand, management can deny that it seeks profits while, on the other hand, it has been free to develop an infrastructure of wholly owned private subsidiaries geared to earning profits as a consequence of something less than arm's length dealing with the savings and loan association.

The rejection of competition has had its source in the alteration and dispossession of property rights in the savings and loan association. The mutual has been a means for eliminating specific clear-cut owner control relationships. Competition is rejected and ruled out as gratuitous because ownership is important. But it is a different kind of ownership. The ownership or property right which gives profit to the owner is rejected in favor of mutual or social ownership. This is supposed to serve as a substitute for competition. Since the savers are not owners, nor interested in profits or management, control passes to the management. Responsible to no one and a self-perpetuating autocracy, it is free to do what it pleases. It shows its disdain for the savers' property rights and profit seeking by the establishment of management-owned private subsidiaries which survive as management creatures.

What then is the effect of mutuality? The expenses they incur cannot be less than those incurred by competitive firms. The latter can earn only a minimal return equal to alternative opportunities. But since the public's savings are protected, it is probable that expenses will be higher. This is because there is no competitive corrective to inefficiency. Elsewhere, we have investigated the hypothesis that mutuality is socially beneficial in that savers would receive more and borrowers pay less. In closing, we refer to Berle's judgment that stock ownership is the "worst way" to meet the problem of organizing the nation's savings. "Competition is a great principle, but there is a limit to its usefulness when you are competing for deposits. Stockownership and stockowner-controlled management encourage overcompetition for deposits . . . The mutual form is more logical when you are dealing with savings, and I think it is not an accident that the mutual form has been in both the insurance and savings bank field on the whole more successful."[10]

The Passing of Shareholder Control in the Mutual. The democratic mutual with a "shareholder voice in the management" was a product of the initial savings and

---

[b]The president of the Federal Home Loan Bank of Little Rock which serves the five states of Arkansas, Louisiana, Mississippi, New Mexico and Texas stated: "It is difficult for me to understand why in the role of the insuring agency, the insurance corporation should assume a $70 million liability without any right to say what shall or shall not be done in an institution which is insured."[9]

loan associations of a century or more ago. The number of "members" was small as was the amount of funds handled and loans made. Decisions were not difficult and could be made at the monthly meetings. Management was at best part-time, and easily controlled by the body of the members. In any event, the danger for which the members felt the greatest apprehension was handled by the limitation of shares or votes of any one member to fifty. This regulation was designed to preclude the wealthier members from exercising control by virtue of owning more shares. It effectively made for a diffusion of the membership. But it had an unforseen result when (a) the association began to grow; and (b) the savings member was separated from the borrower-member.

As the association grew in size and prospered, part-time managers gave way to a professional management which was not only employed full-time, but had acquired an expertise in dealing with the intricacies of both savings and mortgage markets. The decisive change was after World War II as the assets of the industry increased some tenfold. Curiously enough, certain aspects of the change from part-time small-scale operations have continued into the present large-scale enterprise; some control assets worth over $500 million and more than six hundred full-time employees.

In the worst days of the depression, after the Federal Home Loan Bank System was started, the Board in order to encourage the establishment and survival of the new federal associations (which were all mutual) encouraged individuals in related fields such as lawyers, mortgage brokers, insurance and trustees to take on the management of associations as a part-time activity. The business of the association was not sufficient at this time for the typical association to support a full-time manager. "Hundreds of examples could be cited where outstanding success has been achieved in the development of savings and loan associations with a substantial portion of the compensation coming from sidelines, but related activities."[11] The tail now wags the dog.

Though ultimate power is still supposed to reside in the shareholders, the latter typically surrender their proxies to management when opening an account. Indeed, it is not neceesary that they surrender their proxies since so few attend meetings and have such little interest. Management is in control simply because there are so many savers; all of them are relatively slight compared to the total; and they are creditors who can "demand" repayment at any time.

The Paradoxical Role of Profits. Spokesmen from the mutual side of the business often attack their rivals, the stock companies, because of their interest in profit making.[c] Mutuals are said to be superior because they have different goals: they are primarily interested in home financing; they are not watching the stock market; they are not interested in profits but rather the safety of the funds

---

[c]Harry Schwartz economist to the Federal Home Loan Board, has stated that the stock savings and loan associations seek risky loans in order to increase yield and therefore earnings which have the effect of "pumping up the stock prices in the open market . . . such an institution is not just interested in the saver, it is interested in its equity price."[12]

they invest for their savers. It is their proud boast that unlike the stock associations, profits plays no role in the mutual.[13] But that is all it is—a boast.

But when both the savings and loan industry and the mutual is viewed broadly as to embrace all the related activities[d] involved in the generation of savings and home financing, it is rare to find a mutual savings and loan association that is not intimately linked to profit seeking in one form or another.[e] Kendall observed that the managers came from the real estate business and casualty insurance.[16] The mutual savings and loan association supplied the funds, but the ancillary activities are and were not mutual. "If you secure mortgage money for a home owner, you have a good chance of getting this premium of the home insurance." And as a second generation of savings and loan managers developed, "the basic motivation was that this financial entity permitted subsidiary lines to expand, and these could be owned. Thus a profit motive was there to attract talent into the savings and loan business."[17]

The infrastructure with its linkages to real estate operations, mortgage brokerage, insurance[f] trustee and title is owned by the management and entirely geared to profit seeking. One can only speculate on how much confidence should be placed in a management which periodically tells its savers that their business is not directed to such mundane objectives as profits. Such statements would carry more weight if the management saw fit to divest itself of its linkages to profit-oriented infrastructure.[g] Certainly, the latter is neither necessary for the savings and loan industry nor for the mutual form.

On the other hand, the infrastructure is of great significance to the management. It is the vehicle by which extraordinary profits arising in protected, non-competitive markets, can be transferred to management. Mutuality ensures management absolute control; infrastructure is the mechanism for diversion.[h]

---

[d]"In the savings and loan industry, the so-called corporate opportunity prevails, whereby, for example, the director of the savings and loan association can also be the principal officer and director of an insurance company, which insures—provides the fire and hazard insurance on some, at least, of the mortgages that are written. This is not possible in most savings banks states. I know it is completely prohibited in New York."[14]

[e]"The pattern of alliances affects federal as well as state associations though the former lack the facility of the holding company in collecting affiliates . . . It appears to be the prospect of private profit in ancillary enterprise that motivates the same display of aggressive entrepreneurship in some mutuals as in stock associations."[15]

[f]John M. Wyman, Director of Supervision for the Federal Home Loan Bank Board, testified before the House Committee on Government Operations that "where considerable influence has been brought to bear" on borrowers in purchasing their insurance with an affiliate of the association "the effort has been made to bring about the revisions of policy, because in some of those instances there was no doubt that outright coercion was being applied to borrowers. We have endeavored to have that discontinued."[18]

[g]It has been noted that where management does not have collateral income from owing the insurance agency the executive compensation per million dollars of assets is higher. This means that the insurance or related activities subsidizes the savings and loan industry.[19]

[h]"Ties with the infrastructure are not compatible with economy in operating savings and loan associations. Prices charged to associations for services of affiliates do not always appear to be competitive market prices. Rather they seem to be shadow prices for distributing revenues between associations and their affiliates according to the preferences of the top management."[20]

The mutual form deprives the saver of both a say in management and a property right. In addition, since there is no check on managerial decision making, management is in a position to create a self-perpetuating autocracy with an elaborate superstructure of relationships with wholly owned profit-seeking affiliates.[i]

Viability of the Mutual Form. As the mutual grows in size, it becomes more difficult and finally irrational for the savers to participate in management. The professional managers are thereby in a position to set up ancillary, privately-owned organizations which both provide and receive services from the association. The savers can neither secure the information nor veto the decisions of the management.

Both the fifty-share limitation as well as the limitation of insurance to $15,000 clearly restrict the amount of savings in one association. It is obviously preferable to spread larger sums between as many associations as will provide the individual with full insurance coverage. So far as his votes are concerned, and given the $20,000 limitation, suppose the cost of inefficient management is one-half of 1% on total assets in a $100,000,000 association. Assuming all savers have accounts up to $20,000, each of the 5,000 savers would receive an additional amount of $100 or yield an extra 0.5%.[j] However, due to the "open-end" feature of selling "shares" in a savings and loan association, any savings that would result from more active participation by savers in the management would have to be shared with new savers entering that association to take advantage of the extra yield. It is difficult to see how a saver would thereby rationally take any interest in the management of the mutual association.

Mutuals have appeared for these two reasons—either to meet the needs for home financing when it was not otherwise available, and as a device to extricate management from stockholder control. It is the product of either a shortage of mortgage funds or a management take-over. It has survived and flourished in a market situation involving both government protection and favoritism. But they have failed to grow as rapidly as have their stock competitors among savings and loan associations. It is not difficult to see why this should be so. Unlike the situation facing the organizers of a new mutual one hundred years ago, the needs for home financing are met not only by mutuals but also by stock savings and loan associations, commercial banks and insurance companies. The competition is tougher; and the need not as great.

It is significant that the only other major fields in which mutuals have appeared are food retailing and agriculture. In the former, they have not been entirely successful—at least in the United States.[k] The reasons for this lack of

---

[i]"The industry is impressing its own pattern of imperfect competition on other elements of the real estate infrastructure. Its alliances with the infrastructure divert it from preoccupation with competitive, efficient and safe intermediation."[21]

[j]In 1966, the average size account for the United States was $2,706.[23]

[k]"Left to stand upon their own feet and face to face with private retailers, the cooperatives seem to be seriously limited. It is only those private retailers who do not operate efficiently that may find the cooperative a significant competitive factor."[24]

success in retailing and also for its survival in agriculture are relevant to both the savings and loan industry and mutual saving banks. Retailing has been marked by intense competition, first from chain stores and later from supermarkets. High volume and low margins of profits in a competitive industry distinguished by continual innovation have hardly even permitted the mutual or cooperative to establish a beachhead. On the other hand, special discriminatory tax treatment with respect to agricultural cooperatives[l] has been associated with the decline of all forms of profit-seeking middlemen. The lesson to be learned by the contrasting results between food retailing and agriculture is that the mutual is not a viable form; bur rather a hot-house plant dependent for survival on government protection from competition as well as subsidization.

The necessary condition for successful mutuality or cooperation is prior monopolistic restriction. The cooperative may then distribute the gains in the form of patronage refunds. Thus, the mutual insurance is a classic form with its "participating policies." The ability to pay dividends[m] is initially derived from restrictions on entry either through a refusal to charter new mutuals[n] or through artifically high capital requirements.[26] Exemption from antitrust laws[o] is a further source of income. But the main gains from the organizational form are concealed by the diversion mechanism. If any one wanted the profits, he could make more in a shorter time by organizing a stock company (if state laws permitted it).

If the mutual is not a viable form in a free competitive market, how is it that it has survived alongside the stock form? The answer is first that the market has not been free, and second, the mutual has not survived too well. The pressure for Federal Home Loan Bank Board control of dividend rates, additional and novel regulations concerning reserves for fast-growing savings and loan associations and restrictions on the use of broker-generated savings to five percent of assets, has come almost exclusively from the eastern part of the United States (i.e., east of the Rockies) where savings and loan associations are almost exclusively mutual in form.

Parallel developments in the insurance industry are not without meaning. The casualty field is entirely dominated by the stock form, whereas in life insurance, the mutual has been either the product of restrictive legislation (which has limited the chartering of new) or conversion of stock. The bulk of mutuals owed

---

[l]The cooperative has an advantage through its ability to avoid taxes on patronage refunds which paid or allocated (even though retained) "may be excluded from the gross income . . . in determining its taxable income."[25]

[m]That is, amounts in addition to interest paid on capital (an opportunity cost to members) and managerial salaries.

[n]"One reason the majority of new life insurance companies are organized as stock companies is that a statutory requirement for that type of insurer are more easily met than for a mutual insurer."[27]

[o]Up until the Southeastern Underwriters decision by the Supreme Court in 1944, it was believed that since insurance was not commerce, the Sherman Act did not apply. (322 US

their initial success to the stock form.[p] In a sense, they were born large. But they have not maintained their position; during the last thirty years, the stock life insurance companies have grown faster.[q] (See Table 7-1)

Table 7-1
Relative Shares of Mutual and Stock Life Insurance Companies

| | 1939 | | 1966 | |
	Mutual	Stock	Mutual	Stock
Number of Companies	25%	75%	9%	91%
Assets	80%	20%	70%	30%
Insurance in Force	74%	26%	55%	45%

Source: Investigation of Concentration of Economic Power, *Study of Legal Reserve Life Insurance Companies*, op. cit., p. 13; Institute of Life Insurance, *Life Insurance Fact Book, 1967*, (New York), p. 98.

Significance of Shift of Power to Management. The management of the mutuals have not lacked skill in rationalizing their seizure of power. In replying to a question as to what voice a depositor would have in electing and removing a director in a mutual savings bank, one official denied that he would not have any voice. "And, I think it is a very serious question as to whether people in that position, without any risk, really should be given voting power."[31] But the question, in the present context, is not whether the saver takes a risk but rather the lack of mutuality in an organization where the saver has "no voice" in the control. It is not a mutual in the nineteenth-century cooperative sense. It is also true, as the same spokesman said, the saver would not "have a voice as a depositor in a commercial bank." But again, that is hardly relevant since commercial banks are not and have not claimed to be "mutuals."

Mutual management, as well as their proponents in political office, claim that their position somehow gives them not only a special status but a sanctity in their dealings that is alien to run-of-mill enterprise. Congressman Moulter felt

533) The subsequent McCarran Act established that the Federal Anti-trust Acts should apply to the insurance business only "to the extent that the business is not regulated by state law." Though life insurance rates are not regulated in the sense they are controlled in certain fire and casualty lines, reserve requirements in life insurance assures the adequacy of rates.[28] Clearly, the most effective device for inhibiting competition has been in the practice of Insurance Commissioner license revocation because of rebating. It has also been observed that "the principal life insurance companies have for several years undertaken to eliminate rate competition by means of intercompany agreements and "gentlemen's understandings."[29]

[p]Slightly over half of the Federal savings associations were the product of conversions.[30]

[q]With respect to new business written, the mutuals gathered 51% in 1913 and only 26% in 1962 (see Best's Life Reports).

that the trustees of the mutual savings banks were "held to high standards of trust and barred from making personal profit in conflicts of interest situations."[32] While the statement is undoubtedly correct in a strict sense, there are so many possible interpretations of "conflict of interest" that it is not difficult for a trustee to personally profit from his position—just as it is not difficult for a congressman to build a personal estate far in excess of his salary as a congressman.

All too often, "conflict of interest" becomes a bludgeon by which administrators can attack associations that refuse to cooperate with an implicit cartel policy. It was shown in the matter of Alice Savings and Loan Association that an association which sought to pursue an independent and aggressively competitive policy became vulnerable to this charge of "a conflict of interest." The investigator, Schmoker, had instructions: "uncover all information possible in connection with any secondary financing by other of the Mullen companies. We are anxious to determine how this association can invest its funds at the rates that are being obtained."[33] Mullen was the head of the Alice Association and a conflict of interest between the association and his related companies was investigated. Furthermore, this was a "stock" association.

It is freely admitted that management control is both complete and self-perpetuating. "Practically, in a savings and loan association, they are responsible if there is misconduct, because more or less, if they operate within the rules, and they do their job, once the proxies are taken by the existing management, they become more or less a permanent thing, whether they are permanent in fact, or they take new ones every couple of years. And the management that is there perpetuates itself actually the way the mutual savings banks do."[34]

Impact of Management Control

The impact of the management seizure of control may be divided into two classes of problems. First, its significance for the survival and special treatment of the mutual organization, which has been discussed earlier. Second, the checks, if any, upon the decision-making apparatus as exercised by an omnipotent management. It has been noted by at least one director of the Federal Home Loan Bank Board that " . . . in certain cases, a managing officer of an association, by his control of proxies, which in effect are given in perpetuity, militates against the display of independence so vital to the performance of a director's duties."[35] Thus, management control of proxies permits him to eliminate, when he so chooses, any director who will not rubber stamp his policies. For such reasons, the FHLB is "taking a fresh look at the abuse of such a practice, to determine whether it is feasible to impose rules designed to avoid one-man control."[36] It has been eight years since this statement and little has been done. It is sufficient, however, to note that the power continues and is probably inherent in the mutual as it now exists.

In a similar industry, insurance, the Temporary National Economic Committee (TNEC) observed: "On the basis of the evidence deduced, it cannot be said that the policyholders have any control over the management of the mutual companies. The putative rights of the policyholders to select and elect directors are of no practical value. The directors are completely self-perpetuating."[37] A questionnaire reported that 65% of the mutual insurance companies did not mail special notice of elections to directors, and of policyholders receiving them only 22% sent proxies. In the 1937 elections in the twelve leading mutuals, 0.55% eligible votes were cast. Those voting were usually employees and agents who signed the names of policyholders to the ballots. The study concluded that the alleged claim that a mutual is run by its policyholders is nonsense since it is not possible to "oust" the management. In this sense,[r] there is a difference from the conventional stock firm since in the latter, management is often ousted; and, what may be more important, there is the possibility of starting a "fight" to gain control of the proxies, thereby making management responsive to stockholders.[r]

It is true that the same TNEC Report did not find insurance companies of the stock type different. In any case, empirical tests are available for consideration of the hypothesis that stock insurance companies are not different from mutual ones. It is sufficient to note in passing that the marked increase in the relative share of the life insurance business written annually by stock companies during the last fifty years (see Table 7-2)[s] suggests a difference in both goals and operational procedures that is consistent with the ownership hypothesis.

Stigler's survivor technique relates to the problem of determining the optimum firm size. "If the share of a given class falls, it is relatively inefficient, and in general is more inefficient the more rapidly the share falls."[38] This "survivor technique" is also applicable to the problem concerning the optimum type of ownership arrangement in an industry, e.g., mutual ownership as compared to conventional stock ownership.

Many modern economists criticize the classical view of a management responsive to its stockholders. Carl Kaysen refers to the "ideology of corporate management" which considers the owners as "one among a number of client groups whose interests are the concern of management: labor, consumers and the "public" forming the others . . . The stockholders allegedly exercise little or no power of choice themselves."[39]

---

[r]It is ridiculous to criticize the stock associations for "having an eye on the stock market" while at the same time insisting that their management is invulnerable to shareholder criticism. The stock market is nothing more than the organized expression of shareholder opinion, both approving and disapproving.

[s]The table refers to relative growth rates for the fifteen largest companies in each of the two categories from 1910 to 1965. As has been noted earlier, the history of the insurance industry reveals a continued process of mutualization from stock companies. This development which is generally in one direction, i.e., from stock to mutual, and not from mutual to stock, is to be explained by hypotheses as suggested above.

Table 7-2

Market Shares of 15 Largest Mutual Insurance Companies Compared to 15 Largest Stock Insurance Companies[1] in New Business Written, 1910 and 1965

	1910[2]	Market Share	1965[2]	Market Share
Mutuals	$1,742	61.8%	59,852	28.5%
Stock	144	5.1%	30,429	14.5%
U.S.	2,821		210,229	

Source: Spectator Year Book 1915; Best's Life Insurance Report 1966, Fortune Directory, The 500 Largest, 1966.

Notes:

1. These are the fifteen largest mutual insurance companies and stock companies in 1965 as reported in terms of assets by the *Fortune Directory for 1966*.

2. In millions of dollars.

John Lintner, however, found ample evidence supporting the conventional view of management responsiveness to shareholder demands. Even those executives who were in minority in viewing the interests of the company as distinct from the interests of the shareholders "and who seemed least concerned with their responsibilities to frame dividend policies in the best interests of the shareholders as such, were generally concerned with the decline in favorable proxies and in the weakening of their personal positions which they believed would follow any failure to reflect a 'fair share' of such added earnings and dividends."[40]

Diffusion of Ownership not Sufficient for Management Control. Diffusion of ownership is a common characteristic shared by both the mutual savings and loan association and the conventional corporation of the stock type. Indeed, it has been eloquently argued that the diffusion of ownership in the modern corporation is responsible for a separation of management or control from ownership.[41] If this were so, it would follow that the mutual is in no way different from any other organization. Or to put it another way: the ownership of shares or property in a stock corporation has no significant effect upon the behavior of the corporation.[†] Fortunately, the savings and loan industry provides an appropriate testing ground for that hypothesis since at least in California, as well as in eighteen other states, both types of organization exist. Since they perform identical functions under reasonably similar economic conditions (and governmental constraints), differences in their behavior could be reasonably attributed to the

---

†While recognizing that it is an "unquestioned fact" that there is a "very substantial separation of effective control from the bulk of ownership," Lintner questions, "whether their corporations and their managers are—or more precisely whether they act as if they were—increasingly free from shareholders' influence and of classical market restraints." His evidence and analysis casts considerable doubt on the original hypotheses offered by Berle and Means.[42]

presence or absence of property rights, i.e., to the difference between the stock form as compared to the mutual form.

The managers of the stock associations, whether they are privately or publicly held, retain a large, if not preponderant, ownership interest. Thus, any differences as compared to the mutual would shed no light on the thesis of Berle and Means. The critical comparison is rather that exhibited by the mutual associations as compared to managements in typical large-scale industrial and financial corporations in other industries. Mutual savings and loan associations are dominated by their managements in the most literal way. They need account for their actions to neither stockholders nor savers. It is expected that if the managements of the typical industrial and financial corporations had succeeded in wresting control from the owners, they would have created infrastructures similar to that found among the mutual associations.

Though ownership *may* be diffused in the stock corporation, it is not *legally* diffused as a mutual. In the latter, the fifty-share constraint, as well as the insurance maximum, encourages an increase in the number of accounts rather than their size. In the stock, new issues, public sales, splits, etc., may diffuse the ownership. But, as has been often observed, large blocks of stock may be held so that effective control is preserved in the hands of owners other than management.[u]

The progressive dilution of each mutual member's voting weight can also be brought about by a management policy of growth. Not just growth for its own sake (as is frequently discussed in the industry); but a growth which makes management control inevitable and unassailable. Given favorable mortgage market conditions, management could dilute (or "diffuse") the membership simply by substitution of broker savings attracted from other areas by higher dividend rates. Management need not concern itself with the proxies simply because the great distance from the particular institution's location makes attendance at meetings even less probable than attendance of nearby members. That such savings are restricted to five percent of assets in no way diminishes their importance.[v] They still represent a substantial number of votes in a "mutual" association. Savings may also be attracted by aggressive advertising. Thus, whatever the means used, management has at its command a variety of techniques which may be used to concentrate the requisite number of proxies to meet any threat to its position.

The stock company, on the other hand, has a permanent capital. While after

[u]"A figure of ten to one of assets controlled to assets owned is often realistic."[43] Ten percent ownership is consequently a sufficient concentration to make management listen and also to secure representation on the Board of Directors.

[v]A rule limits broker savings to 5% of assets. In California where they are important, it was reported that, in 1960, 45% of the federal, which are mutual, associations had broker savings. In addition, 38% of the savings accounts held in federal associations in Southern California were for savers more than five miles away from the association. It seems obvious that such individuals would not be likely to attend an association meeting.[44]

proper consideration, meetings and vote-taking, capitalization may be increased, it is neither automatic or within the arbitrary decision-making power of management. This permanent capital has also a value dependent on the performance of the firm and thus the management. As a stock is bought and sold, it is compared daily to other firms with similar investment and in similar markets. If management is not up to the mark, the value of the stock fails to reflect current and expected earnings. If the shareholders are not on the ball and fail to vote out the management, others seeing unexploited opportunities for this firm can buy the stock. Depressed price levels reflect ineffective or irresponsible management. As the holdings of the new buyers accumulate, there is ultimate expectation that enough shares will be concentrated to vote out the management.[w]

Absence of the fifty-share maximum in the stock corporation clearly makes the position of management more uncertain than it is in the mutual. Any large block of stock can combine with other large blocks or seek to attract other stockholders to its banner. If the management performance or slate is not lily-white or, if there is evidence of "self-dealing" such as diversions to management-owned affiliates, stockholder groups can fight to secure proxies so as to replace the management;[x] or the firm's shares may be purchased by another firm.[47] Such a fight is not possible in the mutual. Indeed, the mutual spokesmen claim that this is one of their advantages over the stock form. In the mutual, the "wrong people" are not allowed to take over. More will be said of this argument later. It is sufficient here to note that the mutual offers no safeguard that the "wrong people" are not in control. Nor that it is not the "right people" who are seeking control.

The Management Rationale for Seizure of Power

Management has offered a number of reasons why power has been thrust upon it and why any alternative would be undesirable. The oldest argument with the best historical authentication is the familiar one that "no one person just by money alone can come in and put in several million dollars and get more votes that he is entitled to."[48] Other reasons are prevention of the wrong people from gaining control; dislike of profit-motivated enterprise as well as the accompanying risks; and indifference, ignorance and unworthiness on the part of the public because it takes no risk. Each will be discussed in turn.

---

[w]It has been observed that "the shareholder votes will tend to move into the hands of those who know best how to maximize their use value. Any inclination towards disagreement among shareholders about how the company should be managed tends to be halted automatically, as one side will simply buy out the other."[45]

[x]Manne observes that the cost of making the effort is a constant but if the size of the holdings diminish, it rises relative to that individual holding. That is, there are returns, to scale in this endeavor.[46]

Prevention of "Dollar" Voting. This is the basis for restriction of the number of shares to any one member to fifty. Its basis is historical and it is closely tied to an active member participation in management decision making. In short, it is an archaism derived from the time when mutuals were truly mutuals. The object was clearly to keep control with the members on a somewhat qualified majority-voting basis. It was not a simple "one man-one vote" mechanism because it allowed up to fifty votes. But all members were encouraged to invest up to this maximum with the effect in practice that an equalitarian democracy would prevail, and that it would not be superceded by dollar voting.

The Mutual Association is not "up for grabs" by the wrong people. Berle and others have expressed apprehension that a financial intermediary should be:

"up for grabs" by any group able to mobilize enough capital to make a drive for it . . . there is nothing I am more afraid of than the small financial institution, relatively small whose stock can be bought for a block of money capable of being mobilized by some stock exchange group or some aspiring financial wizard. Such situations always strike me as insecure.[49]

The fear is that the stock may be purchased for a nominal sum by a group of unscrupulous speculators interested in nothing more than turning a quick profit. The papers are full of incidents of this sort. But though these things do occur, it by no means follows that they are financial institutions uniquely associated with the stock. Nor does it imply that intermediation must be limited to the mutual type. There are alternative methods for handling the specific problem. The most obvious is to apply the same standards to ownership changes as are now applied to the granting of new charters. The controller of the currency has actually moved in this direction. But if safeguards are required to prevent the seizure of financial institutions by unworthy individuals, it is equally important that management now in control be subject to scrutiny as to its competence and integrity. If it is necessary to protect the public savings against unworthy newcomers, it is even more important to protect the public savings from unworthy incumbents—and from an inefficient management which has achieved a status of a self-perpetuating autocracy. Mutual spokesmen should first put their own house in order. They should face up the fact that as regulation is now practiced, there is no way to ensure savers that they will have honorable and competent managers.

The main reason for managerial opposition to "take-over" by the "wrong people" is that other people are by definition the "wrong people." Mutuality has represented first a means of guaranteeing the "succession" for the present management.[y] Second, it has been a device to permit management to retain

_____

[y]In the case of Prudential, a near majority of insurance company's stock rested in the Fidelity Trust Company. After the death of the founder, John F. Dryden, "The Fidelity's directors sought to use their voting power to oust the existing management and to put in their own representatives.[50] It was the recognition by management groups that it might be harder to keep track of stock controls, than policyholder proxi controls" that led to the mutualization of Prudential.[51]

control by precluding outside groups from purchasing the stock from heirs or present owners.[z] Third, in some cases (the large life insurance companies), it represented a means for capitalizing and securing the benefits of accumulated surplus and undistributed profits. Fourth, a means for precluding conflicts between stockholders and shareholders or member in the distribution of profit. All these areas of conflict quite simply have been resolved by mutualization; control has been vested in management so that it could autocratically distribute the profits to itself in whatever form the few constraints directed.

Independence from the Stock Market and Necessity for High Earnings. It has been suggested that another advantage of the mutual is that management does not have to have an eye on the stock market.[a] Consequently, its decisions will be more prudent since there is no reason to increase earnings in order to inflate the value of stock. The frequent references to the detrimental influence of the stock market on savings and loan associations is based both on a theory that the drive for earnings encourages unsound lending[b] and a hostility for Wall Street in general. Perhaps the antecedents derive from the populist agitation of the nineties and in the attack on the "economic royalists" during the thirties. But whatever the validity of the objections to Wall Street, the attack is undeniably sound tactics for a management which seeks to maintain a self-perpetuating autocracy.

If the stock associations are successful in earning more profits, it is because they are more successful in providing savers and borrowers with the kind of services and loans they want. While there is no necessary conflict between profit and the public interest, emphasis on "short-run" profits may entail an absence of prudence in lending. In such circumstances, it is not profit which is at fault so much as shortcomings in management. The mutuals would argue that profit-seeking management and ownership is inherently incapable of prudent investment; that the safety of the funds will necessarily be sacrificed to inflate earnings and stock prices. They fear that the ultimate result is a black eye for the entire industry—mutual and stock alike. Thus, Berle concludes that "the mutual form is more logical in dealing with savings" and "it is no accident that the

---

[z]Management interests first advanced the mutualization idea for Equitable Life Insurance Company in 1905 "as a device for unseating Mr. James Hazen Hyde," the son and heir to the stock owned by the founder of that company.[52]

[a]One of the great entrepreneurs of the California mutual movement has commented: "I don't think you can possibly run a conservative, or run a savings and loan association in the character in which it has operated for one hundred and thirty years with an eye on the stock market . . . you have to run it in the public interest."[53] "Ours is a *Federal* savings and loan association operated under a Federal Charter, supervised by an agency of the United States Government; *not* a stock company or affiliated with any holding company which could require that pronouncements, loan policies, and other matters of policy be formulated with an eye on the stock market."[54]

[b]Harry Schwartz of the Federal Home Loan Bank Board in referring to the argument that the stock associations seek the high-risk loan in order to increase yield and therefore earnings said it is a device for "pumping up the stock prices in the open market. Such an institution is not interested in the saver; it is interested in its equity price."[55]

mutual form has been in both the insurance and savings bank field on the whole more successful."[56]

The crucial or operative word in the above judgment is "successful." If it only means that mutuals have a better record with respect to failures, it is somewhat questionable.[57] But whatever the failure rate, the reasons are not exclusively related to the mutual form of organization. Entry is restricted while incumbents, as a matter of self-interest and political pressure, are compelled to take over the liabilities of failing companies.[c] But more important: success in maintaining a low attrition rate is hardly indicative of economic efficiency—of optimality in the allocation of economic resources.[d]

The other side of the argument with respect to the market and ownership rights is that they impose a discipline on management. An observation of a bank official with respect to mutuals is pertinent: "The threat of proxy fights does not exist . . . Proxy fights exert a certain amount of discipline in the case of stock institutions."[60] "Stockholders demand information. Large stockholders can threaten proxy fights. Institutional investors and large brokerage firms seek out the relevant information and probe into the activities of management both in its official and private manifestation."[61] The absence of such disciplinary pressures in the mutual can be conducive of nothing but inefficiency.

Savers do not distinguish between Mutual and Stock. In order to make out their case for management control, their proponents have argued too much. If savers are ignorant and uninterested in management of their mutual, the association ceases to be mutual. One might as well speak of democracy as that government without elections. But if voters do not vote, it is difficult to see how the government can express their will. A democracy without elections makes as much sense as Hamlet without the Prince of Denmark.

It is important to agree in fundamentals. Both proponents and critics of the mutual concur that saver-members do not attend meetings. That being so, they can hardly participate in decision making. In California, an executive of a *federal* association (which are all mutual) has observed: "I am not persuaded that the public can ever be educated to the difference between federal and state-char-

---

[c]As the basis of insurance settlement, the California Savings and Loan League cites the law with respect to the Federal Savings and Loan Insurances Corporation: "In the event of a default by any insured institution, payment of each insured account in such insured institution which is surrendered and transferred to the corporation shall be made by the corporation as soon as possible either (1) by cash or (2) by making available to each insured member a transferred account in a new insured institution in the same community or *in another insured institution* in an amount equal to the insured account of such insured member . . ."[58]

[d]"If the competitive force of new entrants is to be relied upon to achieve efficiency, free entry in banking must take the two-way meaning attached to it in competitive theory—freedom of entrance and exit. Forced exit, of course, is precisely what regulation and supervision, including restrictions on entry, are designed to prevent. As a result, the banking structure has responded very slowly to inefficient operators and to geographical shifts in demand."[59]

tered institutions (stocks), and in truth, the difference as seen through the eyes of our savers and borrowers, is practically nil."[62] In seeking to justify assumption of control on the above grounds, management has effectively removed the basis for mutuality. Mutuals do not exist. Therefore, organizations referring to themselves as mutuals should be deprived of their special privileges. They should be compelled to conform to standards appropriate to the activities they perform and the functions they serve. Examination of the latter must consider the question of whether they are serving any useful function once it is admitted that they lack the characteristics of mutuals.

Management and "Industrial Statesmanship." Industrial statesmanship presumably consists in adapting the action of the firm to a set of goals incompatible with simple profit maximization. It is obvious and generally conceded that it can arise only in noncompetitive markets. Market power achieved by virtue of large size, both absolutely and relatively, is one of the prerequisites. Or industrial statesmanship is expected, if not demanded, in those areas where competition has been restricted by institutional arrangements, such as government regulation or the mutual form of organization. "The traditional economic view of the drawback of market power has been the achievement of monopoly profit by the restriction of supply. But it need not do so."[63]

Only a firm possessing market power or freedom from competition is in a position to refrain from following the rules for profit maximization. "While the firm in the highly competitive market is constrained to seek out the maximum profits, because the alternative is insufficient profit to ensure survival, the firm in the less competitive market can choose whether to seek maximum profit or be satisfied with some 'acceptable' return and to seek other goals . . . The firm may seek a variety of goals: 'satisfactory' profits, and 'adequate' rate of growth, a 'safe' share of the market, 'good' labor relations, 'good' public relations, and so forth."[64]

The question is whether a management or corporation in pursuit of a configuration of goals or in an attempt to please divergent interests can do so in a meaningful way. What is the evidence with respect to the effectiveness of management in satisfying the objectives of these various groups? Not only is it material to consider this question as to managerial effectiveness with respect to the goals, but it is also necessary to weigh the impact of these goals on the more general social and economic objectives which bear on efficient use of scarce resources. It is quite possible that substitution of a more complicated set of goals results in a loss of both economic and social efficiency.[e]

---

[e]Kaysen observes that where "the pressure of competition does not force prices down to costs, costs themselves have a tendency to rise: internal management checks alone cannot overcome the tendency to be satisfied with costs when the overall level of profits is satisfactory."[65]

On the day that Fannie Mae was fully converted into private ownership, its President Raymond H. Lapin said, "We will continue to be as profitable as we have been in the past." But he noted, "we certainly don't have any intention of maximizing our earnings either."[66] Apart from the contradiction, it would appear that "social" goals were to take precedence over earnings. Unfortunately, no schema was indicated that would provide for their reconciliation in the event of conflict.

The question raised is really an old problem stated in new form. Given a freedom from the discipline which market forces exert, the management in the corporation has a power both for good or evil. It may be that management "need" not maximize profits; but it is equally the case that management need not use the corporation for what might be called socially desirable ends. Much depends on the character of the men that enter and achieve control.

The leaders of the mutual savings and loan association may be drawn from idealistic nonconforming young men and women seeking an alternative to the corporate way of life. Or they may be drawn from those lacking the opportunities to make headway in the more conventional type of corporation as in the mid-depression 1930s. But there is a third class which seeks to take advantage of both the privileged position occupied by the mutual savings and loan association and the lack of shareholder democracy. It seeks to exploit a managerial position of tremendous power and prerequisites.[f] In this case, the major defect of managerial control derives from the absence of the competitive discipline. There is simply no compelling reason why management should operate at optimal efficiency. Thus Kaysen, who has done much to call attention to the great powers possessed by modern management, has also raised some legitimate doubts with respect to the responsible use of that power. "It is not sufficient for the business leaders to announce that they are thinking hard and wrestling earnestly with their wide responsibilities, if, in fact, the power of unreviewed and unchecked decision remains with them, and they remain a small self-selecting group."[68] In short, the leaders do not have to make their actions conform to what others believe to be desirable social and economic goals. They have the power both for good and evil. They both exercise that power and select their own successors. It is not surprising that the successors should follow in the outlines laid down by their predecessors.

Finally, it is necessary to have regard for the effectiveness of an unchecked managerial institution in accomplishing economic and social goals. It is not sufficient to claim that the goals are good and in keeping with longstanding traditions of mutuality. The important issue concerns whether the twentieth

---

[f]Referring to the leadership problem in the union, Chamberlain observes that "a second class of people from whom unions, in the circumstances they now find themselves, are likely to draw their leaders is the class of adventurers . . . Probably most such adventuring will simply take the form of internal political manipulation for personal advantage."[67]

century mutual performs more or less effectively than do its alternatives. Fortunately, there are institutions and data at hand which supply answers to this question. With the savings and loan industry embracing both the mutual and the stock type of operation, a comparison with respect to performance is possible. As indicated elsewhere, the mutuals grow less rapidly, incur higher expenses and earn less than the stock enterprises.

8 The Quasi-firm: Management-Dominated Enterprise

Up to this point, we have treated the mutual savings and loan association as a viable economic institution economically and organizationally distinct from the more conventional stock companies. To a large extent, the principal differentiating characteristic has been the absence of stockholders capable of exerting pressure on management in the interests of profits. Proponents of the mutual form have said that what distinguished their enterprise was that in place of profits it sought to encourage habits of thrift and the promotion of home financing. The essential differences lay in (1) the objectives; and (2) membership participation in decision making.

Enough was said in the previous chapter to indicate that this view of mutuals is both mythical and inappropriate to what passes as today's mutual savings and loan association. The latter is not run by its members; nor is it unique in encouraging savings and home finance. Profit-oriented institutions in both banking and savings and loan have been equally successful in recent years. This chapter considers the goals of management-dominated enterprise and the constraints operating on management arising from the legal and historical antecedents in mutuality.

Absence of Property Rights

At the outset, we are confronted by the fact that management has no property rights in the firm. Thus, we have a remarkable—but not an historically unusual—situation in which due to the ineffectiveness of mutuality, management has assumed absolute power yet has no claim to property and thus to the residual earnings or profits. Nor, surprisingly, have the saver-members: they provide the capital but are in no position to claim the profits. They are without power and are consequently treated as every other creditor. They are paid a dividend which is enough to keep the association competitive with other associations and slightly in excess of what banks historically pay on time deposits. The "spread" between gross income and dividends paid to savers, apart from money and loan market considerations, depends on managerial discretion. It may be extensive where diversionary possibilities to management-owned affiliates are unlimited; and slim where the opposite is true. In any case, management is confronted with a variety of options which are the consequences of a major constraint, viz. the absence of a property right which precludes management's direct seizure of profits.

131

The firm is not directed along simple marginal profit-oriented lines, but rather it goes off on tangents suitable to other objectives. Since those goals take precedence over that of the conventional firm, costs are likely to be incurred which are antithetical to profit maximization. The assumption of such costs by the enterprise is similar to an externality in that they are external to the management. They are shifted on to the enterprise.

It is not surprising that a management-dominated association should differ from a conventional stock association oriented towards profit seeking. It is the mechanism of management's response to both its power position and the constraints it faces which is of interest here. The problem for management is simply one of converting power into either pecuniary wealth or other forms of power which yield satisfaction or utility. Management cannot take the profit as a profit and because it has absolute power within that constraint, the only question is which form or combination of forms is optimal? One input is management's own time. Thus, given the income a manager is paid, he will minimize his own expenditure. One choice is to select the least costly assets, as measured in terms of what must be done to acquire them. He may rationally (from his point of view) sacrifice association income to inflate the value of his salary relative to the necessary expenditure of effort. Or again, since he will not wish to cut his expenses since they include both salary and amenities, he will oppose competition since it invariably reduces the margins available for these purposes. Salaried managers generally prefer monopoly (or an absence of competition) since it reduces what they must do and increases the probable return. In contrast, a profit-oriented firm will compete because of the expectation that it is *more* profitable. As Baumol has observed, a management-dominated enterprise has nothing to gain and much to lose from following the competitive will-o'-the-wisp.[1]

Differences Between Mutuals and Stock

The first consideration is the establishment of whether there are actually differences between the mutual and the stock, the quasi-firm and the orthodox firm. A former California savings and loan commissioner and now an official of a mutual believes that

... apart from the accident of legal ownership, there are striking similarities between stock and mutual associations. . . . (There is) no valid reason to set mutual associations apart from stock associations. The motives of their management are also a private enterprise motive, and they bear absolutely no resemblance to the romantic stereotype of yesteryear. Their management is self-perpetuating and its interest is in growth as a means of greater compensation or as a source of profit to affiliates.[2]

Two types of observations suggest that the difference between mutuals and stock is illusory. The first notes as in the above citation that managers of the mutual are equally profit-oriented. We have earlier discussed this argument, noting that while that is undoubtedly so, there is a very important distinction in the nature of the constraints to which they must conform. The mutual management has no claim to ownership and thus profits in the association. Since it is a power without property rights, it is exercised by diverting association income. It is unnecessary for the management of stock associations to resort to such procedures. The suggestion that the difference is largely an illusion implies that ownership or an absence of property rights does not matter. In any event, the hypothesis is testable. As has been shown elsewhere, the diversity of results as between the two organizational forms is statistically significant and substantial.

The second type of observation refers to the diffusion of ownership[a] in the typical stock corporation.[b] It has been noted by a number of students that ownership and control in the modern corporation are separate. The widespread use of proxies and the failure of many stockholders to vote suggest that stock corporations are not very different from mutuals. Management is said to control while the stockholder hardly differs from a creditor.[c] But these judgments obfuscate the issue because they fail to clarify the nature of the ownership problem. By implicitly identifying control with management, they fail to recognize an ultimate or residual control provided by ownership. That they are vastly different is seen in both the different behavioral characteristics and operating results of stock and mutual savings and loan associations. If managers "controlled," stockholders would not only not differ from savers, but they would receive no return.

Other than salaries and amenities taken at the place of employment, management would benefit by sharing in profits. But how? It could acquire shares, but this would require stockholder approval. It is not expected that the latter would

---

[a] " . . . it is no historical accident that control over so much of our business activity is in the hands of persons whose financial commitment represents only a small proportion of their firms' asset value . . . the issue of the stock can be considered simply as an effective (though tax expensive device for borrowing money)." "With the development of the corporate form of organization the vast body of stockholders have lost effective control over the organizations of which they are the legal proprietors."[3]

Dempsetz makes a similar judgment: "Shareholders are essentially lenders of capital and not owners . . . What shareholders really own are their shares and not the corporation . . . the President of the corporation and possibly a few other top executives own the corporation."[4]

[b] It has been stated that the 350,000 shareholders in the United States Steel Corporation "cannot remove a management which is failing to maximize profits . . . even when some individual stockholders follow the management's actions closely and raise objections to them, they can seldom prevail against the passive majority on management's side."[5] But another point of view insists that passive owners do not mean an absence of owner influence. Shares count not heads in corporate voting. "Owners with less than a persuasive minority may gain authority through the very proxy channels associated with management control."[6]

[c] Olson observed that since "the income of the corporation is a collective good to the stockholders, and the stockholder holds only a minute percentage of the total stock, like any member of the latent group, he has no incentive to work in a group interest. Specifically, he has no incentive to challenge the management of the company however inept or corrupt it might be."[7]

give their assent if the effect was simply to deprive them of their own rights.[d] On the other hand, to the extent management does secure shares, an identity of interest is created with the shareholders which is not possible in a mutual because there are not ownership rights to "share."

If management "owns" the corporation, presumably it would be able to sell the property, i.e., it could capitalize its stake in the corporation. But there are few, if any, cases of management accomplishing this feat, while there is ample evidence of corporate shareholders offering management an inducement to identify with them, viz., through bonus plans, stock options and profit sharing. Management control of the corporation would be expected to show up in seizure of the profits in some form. Possibly, it would act as does the management of the mutual. The latter is constrained to (1) resort to diversions through the use of affiliates; (2) deal with suppliers at less than "arms' length"; and (3) to exhibit different behavioral characteristics with respect to nepotism and frequency of management changes. On these two points alone, the stock savings and loan associations revealed less nepotism and greater frequency of managerial changes.

But "control" by the management of a stock corporation must originate in gaining control over the proxies. Only then does management accumulate the necessary votes. In this sense, it may be said to "own." But this kind of "ownership" is to be contrasted to the more conventional ownership. The "control" of the proxies is held on good behavior[8] and is no more ownership than that which a trustee achieves in acting for a trust. Both control; but the power is delegated by a set of rules which limit the authority of the trustee.

If management actually "owned," it is to be expected that the old owners would be dispossessed by the issue of new stock which dilutes the original owners' ability to withdraw proxies. Yet, according to Baumol, it is the opposite which occurs. Competition forces firms to grow. They require more funds than they can generate from earnings. The cash-hungry owner of a growing firm will be tempted to issue stock. In order to make the sale, they will have to pay competitive dividends. Therefore, they must show high earnings. Unlike the management-owned or the mutual, management in a publicly-held corporation has to act in the stockholder interests. When it fails to do so, earnings diminish, stock values fall and the corporation becomes vulnerable to "raids"[e] designed to replace that management with one which seeks to realize the full potentiality of

---

[d]In order to make the individual member of a mutual savings and loan association powerless, the management has only to raise the dividend rate. Even though this increase is competitively met by his rivals the immediate effect is to attract new saver members into his association. The importance therefore of the one member's vote is correspondingly reduced by the influx of new voters. In addition, the claim to net earnings and reserves is also diluted.

[e]Shareholders buy shares because the vote is worth something and because they have reason to believe that management will maximize profits. "Market reaction to corporate earnings and dividends is certainly not ignored by management. A protracted decline in the price of the stock may occasion purchasers looking toward a bid for control through proxy solicitation."[9]

the firm's market position. This is not possible in a mutual. Nor are mutuals threatened with proxy fights.

The executive in a stock company can have his compensation geared to changes in profits as is done in General Motors and many other large corporations. Other indexes are market share, sales and expenses which to some extent create an identity of interest between the executive management and the stockholders. It is true that the stock option may represent infinitesimal increases in the stock so that management might prefer to take its profit in terms of amenities. But inducements such as better retirement, fringe benefits, etc., can also be geared directly to the increase in profit as opposed to the profit per se. Furthermore, the competent executive, who is demonstrably successful, even in a firm or industry where there are no stock or bonus plans, establishes a reputation which in turn may secure better offers from other firms and industries. In contrast, management changes are few and far between in the mutual savings and loan associations. Not only are there no "owners" seeking better management, present managers cannot be replaced.

Separation of Management from Ownership Significant only where Noncompetitive Returns. In a competitive market, the return is only just sufficient to maintain the present resources: were it larger, additional resources would be attracted; and if smaller, some resources would not be replaced. The shareholders of the corporation must receive a return comparable to what they would earn for similar risk in alternative investments. If they were nothing more than creditors, their return would be no larger than the holders of bonds; but the risk of capital loss would have to be no larger.

Similarly, the competitive return to management would be no more than a competitive wage, i.e., no more or less than he could earn in an alternative industry. Since both his wages and the dividend is controlled by market forces, it would make no difference that ownership of shares were separated from control of the firm. The manager could not pay a smaller dividend; nor could he pay himself a higher wage.

Separation of management from ownership is significant only when management does have choices: the manager may have sacrificed part of the profits for higher compensation to himself; less arduous performance of his duties; greater expenditures on the amenities with which he surrounds himself when employed; and, possibly, use of a diversion mechanism. All such choices imply the absence of competitive pressures. Even the statement of the necessary conditions for the "separation" model suggests its incompatibility with the Baumol model in which it was competition that forced the manager-owner into sharing his stock and hence ownership. " . . . each share which is sold drives deeper the wedge that will separate the 'ownership' of this firm from its management." Competition further forces the process: "When one firm uses every available source of credit to finance its expansion, its rivals must follow suit if their market share is not to decline."[10] The businessman who holds out against the issue of stock will have less funds to bid for resources in inflation and thus will suffer a decline in market share. On the other hand, noncompetitive firms would obviously be under less pressure to enter the market for capital funds. Possibly, they could secure the necessary funds from their own monopoly profits.

If management effectively controls the corporation simply because ownership has become widely diffused, it is to be expected that management would capture the monopoly return[f] through high salaries, amenities and diversion. The shareholders could obviously do nothing. It follows that absence of these three behavioral characteristics indicates either (1) the industry is competitive so that management has no options; or (2) the shareholders "control" the management.

Diffusion of Ownership and Management Control

The general argument follows Berle and Means.[12] The greater diffusion of ownership is said to have thrust control onto management. Hence, it follows that the ordinary joint stock company is no different than the mutual. But to the extent that diffusion has led to less active participation by owners in the control of their corporation, it is *a fortiori* easier for a relatively small minority interest to seize control. Thus, a recent report on events in Libby, McNeil & Libby tells of its president resigning because foreign stockholders with about one-third of the stock are "trying to run" the corporation. For "all practical purposes," they are said to have secured control.[13]

The very same power that allegedly accounts for management seizure also operates so as to permit minority control. Management is not likely to ignore a concentrated block of stock even though it is less than fifty percent. If it does, it runs the danger of a proxy fight which it can lose because of the amount already in the hands of this shareholder or group of shareholders.

But the apparent control of the corporation through possession of proxies should not be taken as literal evidence that management "owns" the corporation—or can run it against the interests of the shareholders. It has been suggested earlier that management may have this power only on sufferance and on a trustee basis of good behavior or good operating results. In one crucial way, the management of the stock corporation differs from that of the mutual savings

---

[f]In a very interesting treatment of the modern corporation, Henry Manne notes that "the separation of ownership and control may allow the managers gain . . . for example, the managers may be able to conceal the fact of monopoly profit from the shareholders of the corporation . . . such 'concealing' has precisely the same economic effect as simple managerial inefficiency. In fact, the latter can even be the form in which the managers choose to take additional 'compensation.' " Business expense is one way to conceal "expensive office furnishings, lavish expense accounts, company yachts, time off from day-to-day business concerns, and a variety of other nonpecuniary rewards."[11]

and loan association. Shareholders can join together; they can sell their stock;[g] they can throw out the management. They have done so—while there is no evidence of saver-members throwing out its management.

The thesis advanced some three decades ago by Berle and Means that diffusion of ownership among a large number of shareholders had effectively separated ownership from control in the modern corporation has been widely accepted. With the exception of Professor Lintner's[15] notable study contesting the major hypothesis, few scholarly efforts have been directed at a critical evaluation. Yet, the undeniable evidence with respect to important differences in behavior and operating results between stock associations and mutual associations in the savings and loan industry indicates that there may be good reason for viewing this major work with some degree of caution. Indeed, there appear to be a contradiction in Mr. Berle's overall position with respect to the lack of potency of shareholders. In dismissing "shareholder democracy" as a "shibboleth," he observes that "when shareholders vote, they vote by dollars, not by men." He distinguishes between "democracy or mere maximization of profit." In the small institutions where there are only a few shareholders, they "want larger profits and especially if they hope to sell their stock they want them still larger. This may be called democratic. It may also be called a much more simple desire to make some money fast."[16] His point is that the influence of shareholders is only felt in a smaller corporation. Presumably, in the large corporation, no one shareholder can amass enough shares to have influence on the management.

But as indicated in the proxy fights of Montgomery Ward, New York Central and MGM, all large corporations, there are times when shareholders are sufficiently motivated to concentrate their strength and challenge management. Presumably, where management is not challenged, stockholders are satisfied with their performance. Surely, one would not infer that democracy is not present in the United States simply because one party remained in power for several decades. To the extent that elections have been free and honest, the electorate has preferred the incumbents to the alternative. There may be even more reason why the electorate should maintain in office the management of a large corporation. Even Mr. Berle has stated that the policyholders "want to be governed not bothered. They don't know who is a good manager." He dismisses "the right of deposit ownership to choose management" as "entirely meaningless. ... Further, the larger your institution grows, the less possible it is, perhaps even the less desirable it is, to have the equivalent of political parties to mobilize depositors' votes. Does anybody really think that makes sense?"[17]

The most disturbing aspect of this rejection of the democratic principle in corporations is that it applies *a fortiori* towards democratic political institutions.

---

[g]"The right to sell is a vote. And the stock market—Wall Street—is the polling booth. If the price of the stock goes up it registers stockholder—investor—satisfaction. If it goes down, it registers dissatisfaction in the marketplace."[14]

There are many who would accept the ancient Aristotelian principle that while democracy is not a "good" form of government, it also does not have the potential power for "evil" that some of the so-called "good" governments have. With all its faults, one may prefer the allegedly less efficient form of organization as more consistent with other goals. Furthermore, it is difficult to see how an organization, in the absence of the competitive discipline upon the exercise of authority, can be either socially desirable or economically efficient.

But there is another reason for not putting too much weight on the diffusion thesis of management control. The corporation may be in a competitive industry where management must cover expenses to survive: market share is maintained only by competitive struggle. There is no opportunity for diversion. If profits are not maximized, expenses will exceed revenues; and both the management and the firm will lose out. Only protected noncompetitive firms can ignore profit considerations. The qusi-firm requires two conditions: (1) the absence of property rights; and (2) the absence of competition.[h] Given these two conditions, management may divert—because there is a well to draw from, viz., the monopoly profit.

The hypothesis that diffusion of ownership in the modern corporation leads to management control can be tested in consideration of (1) the details of stockholder treatment; and (2) a comparison of the fortunes of stockholders to that of savers in a mutual (where management is in control). The tenfold, twentyfold and hundredfold increase in dividends that has been witnessed for some public corporations is hardly consistent with either neglect of shareholders or the Baumol thesis that only competitive dividends are paid. Increases of such magnitude are far beyond the requisite amounts for raising capital and treating stockholders as another class of bondholder. Obviously, stock prices would not reflect earnings through the price-earnings ratio if shareholders were not to ultimately share in the earnings' growth. The empirical manifestation of a management-dominated corporation is a low stock price. A management which is so foolish as to permit the value of the stock to erode away makes itself vulnerable to "raids" by groups of investors looking for just such opportunities.[19] Unlike the mutual, the stock company has shares that can be purchased in the open market. Management must purchase them itself and become an owner-manager or it does not remain in power.

The owners control management—not the other way around. The latter is characteristic of mutuals not stock. The empirical test for management control relates to managerial self-interest. Nepotism is practiced for that is one way to convert power into personal gain—by sharing its benefits with members of one's family. Management changes are less frequent because in the mutual, managements are self-perpetuating and omnipotent. Managements make payments in

---

[h]Cf. the statement by Williamson: "The assumption of profit maximization followed from the assumption of perfect competition as a necessary consequence . . . once one departs from the large numbers case, its great a priori plausibility is no longer secure. Instead, application of this assumption to situations that explicitly assume a degree of monopoly would seem to require separate justification."[18]

kind, in the form of amenities: beautiful secretaries, attractive furnishings, assistants, company dining rooms, etc. (All are frequent and involve greater costs relative to sales or assets than they do for stock companies). The diversion of income to suppliers, customers and management-owned affiliates is common. It is sufficient to note that the mechanism of diversion is grounded in monopolistic restriction so that savers receive smaller dividends while borrowers must pay higher interest rates.

Relevance of the Baumol Hypothesis for the Mutual. This hypothesis deals with oligopolistic firms dominated by management. The latter rather than maximizing profits are said to substitute sales or revenue which "have become an end in and of themselves."[20] They will avoid opportunities to increase profits which are extraordinary but unrepeatable: where one year the firm may earn 20 percent, the management will be asked to explain why profits fell to 12 percent the next year " . . . as a result, businessmen may be even tempted to avoid extraordinary profit. . . . Absentee ownership, then, means that management must curb, somewhat, its spirit of adventure because gambling comes close to being a heads-you-win, tails-I-lose affair. Even relatively riskless but extraordinary and temporary profits can be unattractive."[21]

These firms are said to operate under two constraints: they must cover their costs and pay a dividend sufficient to attract new capital. But the Baumol firm is not identical with the mutual since in the latter it is not necessary to provide information as to profits or to report to stockholders. A similarity to the mutual exists only in that the latter must also cover expenses and earn an income sufficient to pay dividends to savers. But this constraint is no more than that paid by any stock company to creditors, e.g., bondholders. The stockholder is in a different category.

The management in a mutual does not maximize profit because alternative choices yield him greater utility. These are forced on him as a result of the constraint which precludes his combining control with property in the association. This constraint does not exist in the Baumol corporation.

The manager of a mutual might continue to deal with a supplier even where it means a loss to the association because (a) it leads to larger size and thereby justifies a larger salary; or (b) it may be part of a diversion technique. The problem created by the separation of management from ownership is also illustrated in what may be the development of more amiable relationships between managers and labor unions. They may be far more willing to meet the demands of the union than are family-owned enterprises. This may be what Keynes referred to as "the tendency of big enterprise to socialize itself."[22] But "since management wishes to avoid stockholder criticism, the public conduct of the firm is best kept beyond approach."[23] A squeamishness by management towards the stockholders is hardly consistent with either domination or socialism. It would have no place in a mutual for management is under no pressure

from irate stockholders, large stockholders or stock market analysts. It is only in stock companies that one finds pressure to keep expenses down and make management "responsible." In return, management may receive stock options.

Management in the Mutual as a Self-Perpetuating Autocracy. Once the management has achieved control, it is practically impossible to be removed. This means that the ordinary internal correctives will not be operative. There will be no stockholders to object to the managerial policies nor public information as to those policies. Management controls the information to be made public. Nor is there reason why the best employees would be recognized and promoted. Top management has far more reason to prevent it. First, since it does not share directly in profits, it will take "payment in kind" which all too frequently means hiring only attractive individuals who cause no trouble and create no threat to the autocracy. Assistants will be picked because of their compatibility to the perpetuation of the autocracy; not because they can increase the profits of the association. It is no accident that the mutual associations are managed by "Wasps"; that they are all members of an exclusive club which goes under the name of the United States Savings and Loan League. The accidental few with different ethnic backgrounds that have risen to the highest position in a mutual have been distinguished not only by their rarity but also by their isolation. For all their rank, they have received about as much acceptance as a non-Aryan at a 1935 Nuremberg rally of the Nazi Party.

Capital Investment. The actual amounts of capital[24] invested in stock companies in both the savings and loan and insurance industries is relatively small compared to the amount generated by net earnings. Inasmuch as private savings generated the growth both in the savings and loan and insurance industries,[j] it has been questioned whether organizations of the profit-seeking capitalist type should be permitted. But one reason for encouragement of stock companies is that their incentive system is thought to bring about an allocation superior to one where property rights are absent. Incentives external to the firm emerge in management-dominated firms. The general impact is that activity is withheld so that both savers and borrowers are served less efficiently. Profit, on the other hand, is the price paid for rational allocation of resources: it is a signal to correct disequilibrium situations. In noncapitalist enterprise, those in power positions are constrained. Rather than correcting market disequilibria, they create them. Consequently, it is not particularly germane that little new capital should have

---

[i]"In the main, stockholder investment is retained earnings—some retained under regulatory requirements, some retained in lieu of federal income tax payment, some retained voluntarily." At the end of 1966, permanent stock, surplus and undivided profits for the California Stock Association, were $232.5 million which came to 1.3% of assets.[25] For all the United States, permanent stock savings and loan associations, the permanent stock at the end of 1966 was $209.8 million or 0.7% of total assets. It should be noted that this ratio does not include surplus and undivided profits.[26]

[j]Having regard only for the three largest life insurance companies, the original capital invested in Metropolitan was $500,000, Prudential $91,000, and Equitable $100,000. Though dividends were limited for the companies residing in New York, stock dividends were declared as a surplus. In the case of Prudential, a New Jersey company, $5.5 million had been paid out in dividends by 1909; and a surplus of $13.3 million had accumulated by 1904.[27]

entered the industry.[k] It is sufficient that capital should have been reinvested; that resources should have flowed to markets where capital was in scarce supply; and that property rights should have been granted management so that there was neither the ability nor the incentive to direct the organization towards external objectives.

Quasi-firm

The discussion has so far shown that the mutual savings and loan association is a mutual in name only. The saver-members neither participate in the decision making nor "own" the savings and loan association.[l] Nor is there the slightest evidence that their directors and management show greater interest in public service and "advancing the welfare of the community"[30] than do their profit-seeking brethren among the stock companies. The management of the mutuals run their association for themselves. Their problem is simply one of conversion of power—which is subject to no discussion or question within the association—to their personal ends, either pecuniary or nonpecuniary. The association is a vehicle to these ends; it has no vitality of its own; no independent goal. In this sense, it is not a conventional firm.

An enterprise run by a group without property interest or the right to share in profits has external objectives rather than internal. In this sense, it is a non-firm or what will be referred to as a "quasi-firm." Its existence is clearly necessary to the management in the same sense slaves were in ancient societies or animals are on a farm. They are inputs required for the particular activity but foreign or external so far as main objectives are concerned. In the mutual association, the association is not a firm but rather an input directed to the personal gains of a self-perpetuating autocracy.

The objective of management, given its power and thus freedom from having to account to stockholders, is conversion of that power into personal gain of both a pecuniary and nonpecuniary nature. There are roughly three ways in which it will react to its inability to share in profit directly:[m] wages; payments

---

[k]In referring to deferred tax reserves, Professor Shaw suggests that, "There is another result that Congress may not have had in mind, because it was concerned with mutual associations. This result is that tax deferred loss reserves displace investment by guaranteed stockholders in stock associations. Stockholder investment is diverted out of associations, potentially into other elements of the interest structure."[28]

[l]It is just as true of them as what has been said of depositors in savings banks, "they are creditors rather than part-owners of the institution."[29]

[m]Some observers have suggested that management or rather "the servants of the institution should share in what they have helped the association earn." And even thirty years ago, it is reported that many associations were "working out profit-sharing plans as well as retirement plans for their staff."[31]

in kind in the form of amenities taken in connection with employment; and diversion of what might have been association income to management-owned affiliates.

Salary Maximization. There is no regulatory control over salaries to top management in the federally-chartered associations—all of which are mutual. The only rather vague requirement is that the compensation be "reasonable." At one time, this meant that it be no larger than one-tenth of one percent of the dollar value of assets. In a $50-million association, this would have meant a salary to the chief executive officer of about $50,000. It is generally believed that salaries have been "rather modest." It would seem to be so where the chief officer received $150,000 in salary for running a billion-dollar association.

The chief officer of a joint stock company might take lower wages in return for both stock and stock options. The capital appreciation will be taxed at the lower capital gain rate though the initial offering is considered by the Internal Revenue Service as income and taxed accordingly.

In some quarters, it has been observed that the compensation of the chief executive officers in a mutual should be larger than that for officers in a stock association because the former lack the opportunity to acquire stock and share in the profits.[n] Indeed, it is urged that they be paid larger amounts just so the mutuals will attract the most efficient managers.[33] For reasons which have been discussed elsewhere, it is extremely doubtful that this is done. The management of a mutual is too good a thing to lightly surrender. Nor does the hothouse atmosphere of restricted competition require the intensive pursuit of superior management. In any case, to the extent that such considerations carry weight, the less is the difference and hence advantage of the mutual over the permanent stock company. The admission that higher wages must be offered to mutual management to compensate for capital stock gains made by stock management is simply a denial of the validity of the distinction between mutual and stock associations.

But there is another implication in the mutual's restricting management to salary. Mutuals solicit savings and buy mortgages in competition with stock companies. Restriction of managerial income to salaries may represent a form of exploitation: they pay savers approximately the same dividend as the stock, but they do not permit their managers the other pecuniary benefits. Either their managers are not as efficient, or they are not getting what they should. But as we shall see, management has other means for increasing both pecuniary as well as its nonpecuniary wealth. In addition, it is difficult to understand the argument that management should receive more income on competitive grounds when it is so abundantly clear that the mutual does not operate in a competitive environment.

---

[n] "... executives of state chartered stock associations may expect to derive gains from stock options while the officers of federally chartered mutuals participate in institutional growth through associations salary advances."[32]

Limits on executive compensation whether in the form of regulatory scrutiny or Internal Revenue penalties distinguish the mutual from the stock company in that the inducement to profit maximization is that much weaker. The mutual management will have that much less incentive to expand when prices rise relative to his marginal costs. The increase in profits will hardly add to his personal estate as it would in the stock company. He may therefore be expected to work less hard in order to live a little longer.

Even granting that at a relatively smaller asset size, management might seek to grow because it can increase compensation, there are differences in the form the growth would take as compared to a stock association. In a purely competitive market, growth may occur through reducing costs, thus making it marginally attractive to expand. But where salaries are tied to asset size, as in the mutual, the increase in assets is relatively slight compared to the increase in effort required to reduce expenses. Where size was not increased, it would be hardly worthwhile for management to reduce expenses, particularly if the reduction was in salary and amenities.

Sales Maximization in the Mutual. The theory has been advanced by Baumol and others that a managerial-dominated corporation will emphasize growth for its own sake. The mutual savings and loan association provides a limiting case of the Baumol model: power without ownership. Yet, mutual spokesmen claim the higher growth rates of stock associations are due to the pressure of stockholders. It is a fact not only that stock associations grow faster but that their highly diffused stockholder-owners desire it. The evidence reviewed elsewhere,[34] shows that there is truth in the position of the mutuals on their slower growth rates as compared to the stock.

Yet, there is something to be said for the theory that mutuals will place considerable emphasis on growth. Thus, Grebler and Brigham have commented on the tendency

to avoid deposit losses and potential deposit losses are probably stronger in the savings and loan industry which has a large admixture of mutual institutions, then it would be in an industry consisting only of stock corporations, as the rewards to managers of mutual organizations are far more dependent upon the size of their associations than upon their profits.[35]

But these considerations make sense only in the context that mutual managers are confined to but one choice in their efforts to convert power into personal gain. They can also gain through diversion of income to affiliates. But to do so requires that they withhold services and that they should restrict as monopolies.

Thus, to this extent, their rate of growth will be less than stock companies who do not operate under a handicap such as the necessity for diversion in order to convert managerial power into pecuniary gain. The stock companies can simply maximize profits and grow, if that is what the situation requires. Emphasis on growth in Baumol and Grebler and Brigham is misplaced because it ignores

the California Federal Savings and Loan Association alone, it was $7.8 million.
rather important alternative methods available to management. Of course,
management may seek to grow; but it will do so in a context of constraints that
make the problem one of reconciliation of a variety of methods. Growth is
sought, but only as a monopolist—and without sacrifice of other methods for
enhancing gain.

One final comment: when dealing with a quasi-firm, the profit index of rationality has no place. Growth may be a substitute as in the Baumol model. It may
even be rational, given the absence of property rights in the firm by the management. But there are ways to compel or induce profit maximization by management. Management may be given a stake in the firm so that a community of
interest is established. Profits also are an important prerequisite for growth since
they provide the principal source of funds needed to finance capital expansion.
"There may be little conflict between the goals of profit and growth if long-run
growth requires long-run profits . . . profits . . . are widely regarded as the firm's
scorecard of success or failure."[36] Thus, the Baumol concept of "profitless
growth" is neither necessary nor probable. It is not necessary because management can be furnished a property right in the corporation. It is not probable
because the major method or means to growth is through profit.

It has been observed that in the insurance business the "methods of compensating agents made the writing of new business and the consequent growth
'inherent in the business.' "[37] But this is no basis for censure. Growth is often
consistent with profit maximization and thus rationality. It is one test. There are
other tests. Insurance officials attributed their emphasis on growth to the belief
that it was socially desirable to extend the benefits of life insurance to the entire
population. Yet, growth is a rational goal once ownership is divorced from
control. The insurance officials who compared their role to religious and educa-
tional leaders were not much different from those politicians who think it necessary that the United States should be the first nation to put a man on the moon.
Once economic goals based on "consumer sovereignty" are rejected, one goal is
as good as another.

The Growth Objective is Based on Monopolistic Restriction. Substitution of a
growth goal for profit maximization suggests that the enterprise can ignore
profit considerations within a rather wide range.[o] Obviously, it must have a
sufficiently large margin if it is to undertake unprofitable decisions and investments. Presumably, this power is monopolistic if there is to be no detrimental
effect on management. This tells something about a management and organization which can absorb losses and survive. Obviously, it has no competitors to
fear; it need not worry that others will act differently or have lower costs and so

---

[o]"From the long-run point of view, profit no longer acts as a constraint in the calculations
of the sales maximizer or the growth maximizer. Rather it is an instrumental variable—a
means whereby management works toward its goal. Specifically, profits are a means for
obtaining capital needed to finance expansion plans."[38]

underprice. Pursuit of the growth or nonprofit objective is a choice reserved only to monopolies, i.e., to firms which have the power to practice withholding or restriction.

The sales-maximizer is an enterprise which has the "fat" to ignore profit considerations. It is characteristic of the quasi-firm for its suggests that the enterprise is oriented towards external objectives. Obviously, such a firm is not in pure competition; nor is it one fighting to survive in competition with rivals. There is a certain sense in which it is ridiculous to refer to the Baumol model and the mutual as sales-maximizers. The greater sales is simply a matter of higher cost operations and different objectives. Were these firms competitive, they would not operate plants or products at a loss. That they can do so testifies to their monopoly or semi-monopolistic situation. By not responding to profit considerations, they can sell more. Or they could sell at nonmarket-clearing prices—as with the chronic shortage of Rose Bowl tickets. The lower prices make for larger sales than a profit-oriented monopolist would permit, but not larger than the competitive level.

For the mutual or quasi-firm, the advantage of a non-equilibrium price is that the enterprise has an excess demand—a waiting line or queue. Advertising and promotional expenditures can accordingly be reduced so that more funds are available for wages, amenities and diversion. It is to be noted that California federally-chartered associations in the three years 1962-1964 had an average ratio of advertising expenses to average assets twenty percent smaller than that of the stock associations.P Presumably, they advertised in the first place because they were in a competitive market with aggressive stock associations.

The apparent difference between the Baumol firm and the quasi-firm is explained by the fact that the former are implicitly assumed to be monopolistic. It follows that the separation of control from ownership in this model leads to an increase in sales. The quasi-firm, on the other hand, is compared to a competitive firm. Thus, in order to divert, it must restrict as would a monopolist. The differences between the two models is more apparent than real. It depends on what is compared. The Baumol firm is monopolistic with its management logically preferring to offer a somewhat larger output. The quasi-firm is a shade more sophisticated: it offers the minimum price but not the equilibrium output.

The Internal Revenue Service is far more of a check than the regulatory authority since it would notice if salaries are out of line with that paid in other industries and thus question the expense as actually a part of net income. But observe the surplus reported by California federally-chartered associations for 1962: divided among the 69 associations, there was $620,000 for each.q Or for

PNet income after taxes but prior to payment of dividends was $290,000,000. Allowing for a 10% allocation to reserves and $218,000,000 for dividends this last residual of $42.8 million divided among sixty-nine associations comes to approximately $620,000 per association.
qNet income after taxes but prior to payment of dividends was $290,000,000. Allowing for a 10% allocation to reserves and $218,000,000 for dividends this last residual of $42.8 million divided among sixty-nine associations comes to approximately $620,000 per association.

Such sums could not be pocketed in salaries to the top officials. They represent a residue left after wages, amenities and diversions. It is clear that they do not represent additions to the personal estates of their managements.

Amenities in Lieu of Income Payments

Progressive taxes and regulatory supervision restrain mutual management from appropriating the entire net income in the form of direct income payments. Though the association's growth and success ultimately redounds to his benefit in that he may pay himself a higher wage and incur greater expenditures on amenities, he will not share in the growth of net worth as do his stock compeers.

But this is not to say that he lacks choices; that he does not have alternative methods for creating an estate, and for converting power in the mutual into opportunities for personal gain both pecuniary and nonpecuniary. Consequently, given the progressivity of the income structure and the pressures to maintain wages at "a modest level" (which in practice relates them to asset size), management is constrained to take rewards in forms other than direct wage payments,[r] e.g., valuable pension schemes and health benefits. The lack of vigorous competition in the industry ensures it that margins will be relatively high. Indeed, as size increases, potential profit is likely to be far in excess of what the manager may take home directly in the form of a salary.

The manager may be expected to "trade-off" increases in salary as compared to increases in the amenities with which he surrounds himself. In the case of a salary increase, he may have to share from fifty to seventy percent with the Internal Revenue Service. Though the expenditures paid for by the association may be "second best," he enjoys them to the extent of one hundred percent of the amount. They, at least, do not have to be shared with the IRS. The disadvantages are as follows: the expenditure is limited to the conditions in which he works and so is restrictive. First, he could have spent a direct monetary payment in accordance with his personal preference function. Second, as a company expenditure, it does not represent a buildup in a personal estate. It should be noted, however, that the Internal Revenue Service does scrutinize business expenses where they may be a substitute in lieu of salary. In the case of company-provided automobiles, it has held that that part of the mileage used for transportation to and from the place of business was taxable as ordinary income.

---

[r] Cf. Bodfish who says that "In studying compensation policies for management, it should be kept in mind that one of the major incentives any person has is his desire to provide security for his family upon his retirement from active business or upon his death . . . Hundreds or even thousands of business firms have had excellent results from bonus plans which give every employee an interest in carrying on his job as efficiently as possible and thus promoting the general interests of the institution. Savings and loan business might well study the application of this principle. One suggestion is that bonuses be related to reserve allocations."[40]

In any case, if the tax rate for marginal income is 50 percent, the utility from that fifty percent has to be compared to the "second best" at one hundred percent. Obviously, management adjusts its expenditures from salary so as to exclude those which the association could pick up. The problem is identical to that facing the consumer in comparing taxed articles to nontaxed articles. The change brought about in the relative prices affects the consumption of goods to the detriment of those taxed. In this case, the manager is encouraged to substitute articles acquired through his association for those which he must pay for himself: company automobiles, company dining rooms, long vacations with pay, conferences at resorts, etc. One obvious trade-off is leisure as against work and worry. The contractual basis of payments in both salaries and amenities divorces the executive return from his activity: the substitution of work for leisure is unrewarding. In a conventional firm, the marginal disutility of work is equated to the marginal utility of income. In the mutual, contract terms make the latter zero, or at least substantially less than that for stock management. Not only does stock management earn more *in toto* but it is under pressure by stockholders to work more. Both incentives and pressures differ.

The alternative to an amenity is reinvestment of earnings. The fact that the manager of a mutual takes it as an amenity indicates that there is an economic loss. In a free market, where there were no restraints on managers securing property interests, the funds would be invested until their marginal yields were equated to alternative investment possibilities. The transfer under mutuality from such investment to consumption is accordingly wasteful as it represents a less than optimal allocation of resources. This is a different form of "waste" than described above where the manager was constrained to choose the "second best" because of a wage maximum. In the latter, the manager-consumer is encouraged to consume more of the article or service because the cost to him is reduced relative to those things he could acquire from taxable income. The waste consists in reducing his private marginal costs as compared to the marginal social opportunity costs. His marginal private opportunity costs are less; therefore, he consumes more than he would had there been no constraints of the type discussed.

On the other side, both net earnings and the growth of the association will be that much smaller since the former is responsible for the latter. Mutuals expand at a slower rate than do stock associations—not only because they are more conservative but because they have less to gain from expansion and more to gain from expanding the expenses of the association. In this sense, they only *appear* to be more conservative because they have higher costs, and, they have higher costs because it is rational to take the rewards of management in that form. But expenses raise prices and thus restrict. In monopoly, restriction may come first: the price impact is secondary. But the sequence is immaterial so far as the consumer is concerned: in each case he is offered less.

Some conception of the magnitude of expenditures on amenities is given by a recent study of the savings and loan industry. It is reported that during the fifties, fifty-five percent of all associations built new main or branch office or both. Twenty-three percent of the new main office facilities were erected in the last half of that decade. "A 1960 association office was much more likely to devote some space to activities not strictly business than had ever been the custom before. Community rooms were no longer a news item; an employees lounge and dining room were an accepted part of the new office pattern."[41] Inasmuch as mutuals had over eighty percent of the total assets of the industry, this description can be taken as characteristic.

Differences in Attitudes towards Expenses in the Mutual. In the simplest instance, where salary is contractual, there are the obvious advantages to management in *maximizing* expenses *per se*. Since the management of the mutual is a law on to himself, he need not account for expenses; and because the profit does not directly go into his personal estate, a more cavalier attitude toward them is probable. But there is a worse danger. Should the management pass on the benefits of cost economies to savers in the form of higher dividends, competition is invited from other associations which may not have achieved the same superior level of efficiency. The higher dividend simultaneously increases the total costs of continuing in business. It may not be so easy to reduce the dividend rate should business fall off at some future time.[42] In this, he is in the same predicament that all competitive firms are once they have lowered the price level: they cannot easily restore the old higher price.

When faced with a choice, the mutual management will obviously find it to its advantage either to not concern itself with cost economies or to use the increased margin for increasing the amenities to be enjoyed as prerequisites of control. Furthermore, increases in the dividend may attract more savings, thereby requiring more lending. The pressure to increase loans leads to the assumption of more risk, and more headaches for management. Clearly, it is simpler when management contents itself with the enjoyment of its amenities rather than cost-reduction activities which may create problems.

Expenses and the Sources of Capital. The advantage of the mutual today, whether it is in the savings and loan or insurance industries, is that generally it is an older well-established organization which has grown with the great expansion of the two industries. The capital was basically derived from the savings of the public. For rather unique reasons, it has not been necessary to develop other sources of capital—particularly, investment capital.

But, inasmuch as they operate in sheltered industries, it is quite probable that the large, established mutuals have taken a rather leisurely attitude towards expansion. They might have grown at faster rates. The experience of the stock savings and loan associations, as well as stock insurance companies, suggest this to be so. The reason the mutuals have failed to duplicate the phenomenal growth of the stock companies may be traced to the mutuals' attitude towards expenses.

The primary source of capital for new growth is net earnings which have benefitted from favorable tax treatment.[43] If expenses are inflated by a specific organizational structure, the amount available for reinvestment will be that much less. The fundamental question concerns whether the mutual has the capacity to generate the necessary investment capital from earnings to the same extent as profit-oriented enterprise. Given the constraint on management's direct receipt of profits and the logic which diverts income through expansion of expenses, it is inevitable that the mutual shows net earnings lower than a stock firm. Nor for obvious reasons can a mutual—as presently structured—be expected to attract new capital from the investing public. In the savings and loan industry, the higher expenses of the mutual reduce the development of interest-free earning assets in the form of their net worth or additions to reserves and: reduce (1) the ability to pay higher dividends (and thus to attract new savings); and (2) the ability to promote, through advertising, information of that higher dividend. The tax-free aspect of amenities and the lack of control over them means that earnings which would have gone into growth have been diverted towards management. Investment in activities that might have generated more income and profit is avoided because management is not permitted to directly receive the profit.

Absence of Profit Incentive Reduces Resistance to Cost Pressures from Suppliers. There is little point in management losing sleep in bargaining with labor unions who threaten a strike when that management has no ownership in the enterprise nor shareholders who will hold it responsible. One would expect to find the most violent labor disturbances and strife in management-owned firms.[44] For similar reasons, management would hardly resist demands for higher wages. This is probably even more so in a nationalized firm than in the mutual. The constraints operating in the quasi-firm easily explain the differences in behavior.

Unlike the ordinary firm, there may be no penalties imposed on the inefficient employee in a nationalized enterprise. In a mutual, management can and might discharge the employee but the compulsion to do so is less than in a stock company. Nothing much is gained. It is more likely that he would be kept in the mutual if he had the right credentials with respect to background. But the greatest factor making for inefficiency in the mutual is that the manager himself cannot be replaced!

In general, there is less resistance on the part of management to supplier price pressures. The manager has little to gain. Indeed, he is the winner when he is the recipient of favors from the supplier, or when he owns the supplier either partially or wholly. Aside from this rather obvious form of diversion, there will be less resistance to collusive conspiracies among suppliers.[r] This is to be expected even more among government-owned organizations. There is less incentive among the purchasing agents to "beat down the price" and more incentive (of various persuasions) to remain on good terms with the supply houses.

The climate of the quasi-firm favors inefficiency. After all, to the extent that management is encouraged to take income in the form of amenities, it "wastes" employees. When beautiful secretaries or ethnically agreeable individuals are preferred, noneconomic considerations are forced to the forefront. There is a Parkinson's Law[46] here: redundancy of help is one of the more agreeable forms in which to take the privileges and dispensations of control in the enterprise. Redundancy makes the work easier for top management; it also makes it more pleasant. The objective is simple: reduction of the work load. The trouble is that the redundancy may eventually reach diminishing returns. There may be so many employees that nothing is done. It is pertinent to note here an incident related by Gibbon[47] of the Tartar khan who succeeded in wrangling a tithe from his tribesmen in order to institute corruption.[s] The money was to be used as bribes to secure action. Such may be the only method open to management in some quasifirms.

Nepotism. One obvious amenity available to management in a mutual is nepotism. Management has valuable assets in its autocratic control of the association. This control can be, and often is, passed on to one's heirs. It has the great advantage that as a lifetime source of income, both direct and indirect, it may be inherited without the necessity for paying inheritance tax.

Nepotism develops in a mutual and in other quasi-firms as a legitimate form of converting managerial power. But there are drawbacks: the best men are prohibited simply by accident of birth from rising to top positions. Given the noncompetitive environment of the mutual, the costs to the economy are high.

Nepotism is peculiarly a child of mutuality. With the constraints on the appropriation of profits and the sale of control, nepotism becomes one of the more obvious devices for the conversion of managerial power into personal gain. In a sense, it represents a form of capitalization since the control may be passed on to the members of one's family. On the other hand, since there are no shareholders or minority groups that may contest managerial decision, the em-

---

[r]Westfield said ". . . that it can be in the interests of the regulated private power generating companies to pay a higher rather than a lower price for the plant and equipment it purchases and that the regulated industry is not at all harmed by the inflated prices that result from conspiracy."[45]

[s]Corruption is the back door to the rational allocation of resources through really fluctuating prices in a market system. Under a system of privileges and obligations as illustrated by medieval feudalism and other forms of tribal relationships, arrangements are legal and social rather than economic. In the above example, corruption represented a form of economic incentive. The same phenomena exists in the United States at all political levels.

ployment of relatives and close friends may be added with impunity.[t] Indeed, the implications are broad and dangerous. In this connection, the words of a great economist may be cited:

I believe that the seeds of the intellectual decay of individualistic capitalism are to be found in an institution which is not in the least characteristic of itself, of which it took over from the social system of feudalism, viz., the hereditary principle. The hereditary principle and the transmission of wealth and the control of business is the reason why the leadership of the Capitalistic Cause is weak and stupid. It is too much dominated by third generation men. Nothing will cause a social institution to decay with more certainty than its attachment to the hereditary principle. It is the fear of this that by far the oldest of our institutions, the church, is the one which has always kept itself free from the hereditary chain.[49]

Diversion through Management-Owned Subsidiaries

The most effective device for circumventing legal controls on managerial appropriation of association income is not through compensation or amenities but rather through the ownership of subsidiaries which have dealings with the association. An effort to take what would be association profit in the form of compensation is not only obvious but undoubtedly would bring criticism, if not removal by the Federal Home Loan Bank Board, as a violation of the charter with respect to mutuality. Similar considerations limit diversion through the use of amenities. But more important is the obvious incentive by the management to secure the potential profit in direct monetary income. An infrastructure has been created for the special purpose of diverting potential association income.

The mechanism for diverting association income to management has had to overcome little or no problems. After all, management in a mutual savings and loan association is a power unto itself determining both the output and the prices charged both for the services rendered and the prices paid suppliers. Consider a disequilibrium situation, in which there are only mutual associations in each market and entry restricted by the regulatory authority. This is not to say that entry is not in fact also restricted for stock associations; nor that stock associations do not in fact operate under the same regulatory constraints. The point of the present discussion is simply to show the logic which is involved in

---

[t]Nepotism was one of the major complaints against the life insurance companies prior to the famous Armstrong investigation. It was common among the smaller companies as well as the larger ones. "None of the great company presidents, for instance, could match the errant nepotism of the head of the Security Mutual of New York: this worthy admitted that this wife, son, wife's nephew, son-in-law, "and my wife's sister's husband" were on the payroll."[48]

the creation of the diversion mechanism by the management of a mutual savings and loan association.

Associations in growth periods receive prices in excess of operating costs. Where a stock association, operating under normal profit-maximizing incentives, expands because marginal revenue is in excess of marginal costs, the mutual need not and would not. By not doing so, behavior is similar in nature to a restrictive monopolist. A reluctance to move toward profit equilibrium is expected of all mutuals regardless of the market situation. This relative insensitivity of mutual output to profit establishes a margin greater than that for the profit-maximizing equilibrium and is as permanent as is the disequilibrium from which it is derived.

But not only is there less reason for the mutual to offer the equilibrium output, there is also no reason why the market would be permitted to determine prices. Where under conventional profit maximization, reduced output would imply an excess demand, or "shortage," which would force prices up, the mutual sets prices on the basis of expenses. Its optimal price is considerably less than one which clears the market. Figure 8-1 illustrates the difference in behavior. The elasticity of supply is reduced by regulatory control over entry. With demand and supply in equilibrium, the price = OK and is competitive. When demand increases from D_1 to D_2, a profit-oriented industry would expand along the supply curve to a new equilibrium at the intersection of S and D_2 where the price = OL and the larger output is OB. The mutual simply does nothing with

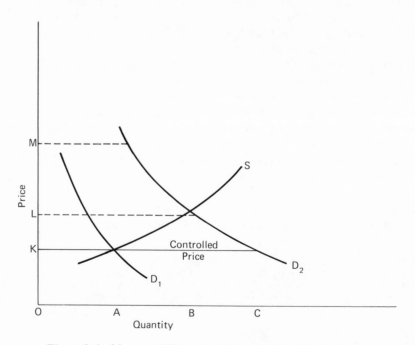

Figure 8-1. Managerial Diversion Through Price Manipulation.

respect to adaptation of output. Nor need it "accept" a higher price. Output remains at *OA*. But since the demand has increased, the quantity buyers seek is now *OC* larger than *OA*. In normal conditions, competition among the buyers would force the price up to *OM*. But the mutual management will not permit this competition.

The conversion mechanism rests on the manager's power over output and price. Diversion of income to affiliates owned by the management requires permanent disequilibrium or restriction coupled with prices below those which would clear the market. Given the shortage, management sets nominal prices and bargains with individuals over the premium they must pay. The price of a loan includes more than the interest rate and fees—the purchase of related services. The stock association with no necessity for diversion will produce a larger volume and the price will be lower[u] by the value to the borrower of the related services which are secured in free and therefore *more* competitive markets.

So far as management is concerned, the mutual savings and loan association is but one key element in an integrated operation involving the provision of services both to the suppliers of the association and the customers of the association. In this context, the ordinary objectives of mutuality, i.e., the highest possible dividends to savers, consistent with the provision of necessary reserves, and the financing of new construction and home buying has been superseded in favor of the management goal of maximizing both pecuniary and nonpecuniary income by means of ownership and control of a variety of related activities.

Disequilibrium or "Shortage" Crucial to the Diversion Process. The mutual management rations loans on the basis of private deals with borrowers. For example, management may be more willing to lend to borrowers who purchase insurance from its private insurance company. The borrower gains a loan he would not otherwise receive. The value to the mutual is illustrated: in 1964, 4.13 percent of the assets of federally-chartered associations in Los Angeles were held in the form of cash on hand or in commercial banks. For the five largest federals with an average of $642 million in assets, each averaged $27 million. With certificates of deposit selling at 4.0 percent, the return would have been $1,000,000. If the management of a large federal decided to forego an interest which cost him nothing in favor of a demand deposit, the bank would hardly hesitate to extend reciprocal courtesies.

The placement of savings and loan association cash flows is not inconsiderable. When "loans repaid" are added to net savings for 1964, the five largest federals would have had about a $148 million flow; and the next five $56 million. Commercial banks can create many opportunities for acknowledging appreciation. Lines of credit readily become available to the savings and loan association officials, and may be used to purchase options for speculative land appreciation—an arrangement not permitted officers of the savings and loan association with their own institution. Or relatives and business associates in

---

[u]Cf. the judgment "that the fee-interest ratio is highest where associations provide collateral services."[50]

other fields, on the reference of the savings and loan official, may secure loans for which they would otherwise not qualify. Whether it be commercial bank deposits or the sale of insurance, escrow, or trustee relationships is immaterial; management is in a position to exploit the margin between prices and cost in a bargaining arrangement similar to a tie-in sale.

Many techniques are available for management to divert income to affiliates. It is not necessary always to own affiliates. Income can be diverted to suppliers or borrowers who repay favors with similar concessions. Management may purchase mortgages from their privately-owned mortgage brokerages at inflated prices. By offering higher than the going market price, an excess demand is created for mortgage money. The price bid is disequilibrating because mortgages are available at lower prices. When they pay more, they attract an excess supply from brokers. This permits management to ration on a personal rather than market basis.

The seller of the mortgage owes something in return to the manager. He may cut the manager in on a part of a profitable construction loan. All this is possible only because the mutual operating in a noncompetitive market has a monopolistic margin with which to bargain. In this connection, it should be noted that if the mutual actually operated at greater efficiency than a stock company, it would have smaller expenses which would yield both higher income to the association and higher dividends to savers. But in that case, it would not be able to divert because there would be nothing to offer suppliers or borrowers.

In many respects, the development of the mutual has been similar to that of the Roman Catholic Church. Both had their antecedents in a self-governing mutually operated establishment. Both saw the emergence of a professional class of managers (priests and bishops) who seized absolute control. It would be no exaggeration to say that the manager of a mutual is today as "infallible" as the Pope in Rome. But this is not all. There is a parallel between the sale of benefices and sacraments in the church throughout the Middle Ages and the infrastructure of the savings and loan industry. The side activities are identical in nature to the "simony" which Luther preached against and which Protestantism sought to correct. Though they are part and parcel of the mutual, they have no necessary role in the conventional firm because their external orientation is inconsistent with profit maximization.

Nonprice Rationing. By holding to a price which covers costs while at the same time holding back output or loans, the quasi-firm management creates an excess demand. Borrowers are compelled into making better offers of a nonprice type if they are to secure a loan. Refusal of management to accept simple price bids forces the borrower into side deals. This is the mechanism of diversion and the origin of the infrastructure.

There are other gains from this rejection of the price mechanism. The impersonal nature of the latter is replaced by an allocative mechanism which permits management to decide who shall have the loans. Obviously, primary consideration is given to bids which offer to deal with the affiliates. The entire infrastructure gains also. The playdown of profits and equilibrium prices is not without reason. High and higher prices are objectionable per se. It is also ideologically appealing to hold on to "low" prices, i.e., disequilibrium prices. A mutual which takes a stand against high prices fits into the American way of life in the same way as do motherhood and the Fourth of July.

The public in the form of savers, borrowers and congressmen are informed that the mutual does not seek large profits at their expense. It is not a profit-seeking institution as are the stock companies. The result is that shortages must appear. When they do, management achieves a position for deciding who will receive the loans! It is able to substitute personal allocation for the impersonal price system. Both the low price and profit is to the manager's interest—not to the borrower's. The attack on profit conceals the diversion and inefficiency of the institutional arrangement. Once profit and price is rejected, there is no basis for allocation other than what suites those who allocate. The quasi-firm is non-market oriented.

The disequilibrium shortage offers another advantage to management: because it can sell all it wants, there is no pressure to "drum up" new business. Not only is the shortage the basis for the diversion mechanism, but life is made easier. Within limits established by restrictions on nonsavings and loan association competitors, the mutual may calmly sit back and let the business come to it. It need not worry about the quality of product or the servicing: buyers have no alternative but to accept the "deal" on the terms it sets. The quality of the product suffers because of the absence of competitive pressures. Service may deteriorate for the same reason, and the expenses of the business will be that much higher.

Chronic Shortages and the Quasifirm. The chronic shortages and inflation which characterize both the socialist and "mixed" economies of the last few decades are attributable to a refusal to permit consumers to competitively determine prices. Price control and shortages are characteristics of a regime of quasi-firms geared to external considerations. Either the prices are regulated as with public utilities, the industries are nationalized, or the firms mutuals. In each, property or ownership is divorced from management.

The literature provides abundant recognition of how management gains in regulated industries. Indeed, it has been recognized that regulation has become a device to permit management to appropriate the monopoly gain. Regulation rather than protecting the consumer against monopoly profits has merely transferred the profits from shareholders to the management. " . . . Separation of ownership and control may allow the managers, rather than the owners, to capture all or part of the monopoly gain."[51] Where compensation to management is not regulated,

... they are able to insinuate themselves into an ownership position not indicated by shareholdings. ... The corporation is admittedly a monopoly that would, apart from the regulation, make greater profits than it does. Any expense that can meet the approval of the regulatory authority will not adversely effect the return of the shareholders. ... The gain to the managers is not at the expense of the shareholders.[52]

Though the major reason advanced for price control is the protection of the consumer, this is hardly the real reason. Controlled prices imply control by someone. The power rests with those who allocate: when the market is not permitted to perform that function, an excess demand is created at the controlled price. Someone must ration. Prices are always too low, which is to say that demand is larger than supply. But paradoxically, (effective) prices will also be too high because in the absence of competition, there is no necessity for efficiency; and costs must be covered. So prices will be higher, but they will not be high enough! This is the paradox of price control under a regime of quasi-firms—not unlike socialism.

Prices approach the monopoly level because there is no cost discipline—no penalties for inefficiency. Indeed, there are rewards when the relationship between the economic and political are so intimate. Not only is management not constrained to keep costs down, it is too much trouble and there are no inducements. In any case, the manager of a socialist enterprise is sacrificing nothing. The only difference from the conventional profit-seeking monopoly is that the monopoly rent goes to the owners of inputs rather than to the firm. This is because it is a quasi-firm.

There is another problem in the quasi-firm. Though the manager may be expected to prefer the disequilibrium because he can sell all he produces, he is also a buyer of inputs. Not only can he dispose of all he produces, his suppliers have no compulsion for providing the quantity and quality he requires. An expert manager has to develop skills in finding suppliers rather than in finding new markets. And in war conditions, he comes to rely on ten percenters, experts in getting wanted supplies not to be found in the market. Nor surprisingly are they found in the market because the latter is not permitted to function openly. In the socialist or controlled economy, the ten percenter takes precedent over what is pejoratively described as the huckster from Madison Avenue. Though it is fashionable to condemn the latter, it is by no means clear that he is inferior to the former. In any case, neither have a function in pure or perfect competition. The queues, shortages, quality deterioration and fixers of the wartime conditions or socialist regimes are hardly an improvement over Madison Avenue. At least the latter appeals to consumers who in the final analysis decide what they want and how much they are willing to spend on securing information.

Incentives in the Absence of Property Rights

The absence of a property right in the association and therefore the opportunity to share in its profits is both the principal difference between the stock association and the mutual and the principal problem of the latter. In lieu of property rights and profit sharing, a different incentive system has emerged. That it is not a profit system is conceded by all mutual spokesmen.

The theory of incentive in the mutual is that salaried management will act at least as efficiently as management in a stock association. But there is no reason why this should be so. If the management is not efficient, there are no safeguards to ensure that he will either be brought up to the mark or discharged. Because the management of a mutual is a self-perpetuating autocracy, it can remain inefficient without penalty.[v] Should he feel no concern for advancing the welfare of the community or should he be lacking that requisite honor referred to by A.A. Berle, there are no means for correcting his deficiencies.[w]

But though some mutuals are run by benevolent managers, there are others lacking these virtues who are more concerned with more mundane objectives. These latter may be likened to the priestly sellers of holy relics during the Middle Ages. They have used their offices for personal gain and have exploited the trust bestowed upon them by an ingenuous laity by creation of a superstructure designed to appropriate for themselves the gains of restricted activity. They have taken possession of the allegedly nonprofit-oriented mutual and exploited it for their own profit.

Management on salary may be compared to salesmen on salary. The latter are notoriously poor producers. Unlike the commissioned salesman, they lack incentive to take to the bushes and drum up new business. They are paid without reference to what they produce; their rewards are divorced from their contributions. But this does not mean that salaried salesmen are insensitive to the opportunities for personal gain. On the contrary, they direct their attention along other lines. Indeed, in a sense, their activities are perversions as far as the firm is concerned. Frequently, salaried salesmen are found doing something on the side in order to pick up a little extra: service may be neither prompt nor courteous; important orders may even be forgotten. But he is always ready to provide some

---

[v]In some ways, mutuals are to be compared to defense industries. One observer has recently questioned whether the latter should be considered free enterprise claiming that they do not meet the ordinary requirements of private ownership; control of productive property; and determination of product and price by competition. Nor do their management and employees show a cost-cutting profit-making attitude. "Defense firms tend to make the most of costs to maximize them . . . This is so because the more they spend the more money they make. Defense firms and commercial firms have opposite attitudes towards technical progress: the former look hard for the latest wrinkle since their chief stock in trade is brand new products. Commercial firms prefer a more leisurely progress and move forward with demand."[53]

[w]"The objectives of the typical nonprofit organization are by their very nature designed to keep it constantly on the brink of financial catastrophe, for to such a group the quality of the services which it provides becomes an end in itself. Better research, more hospital facilities, more generous rehearsal time, better training for those engaged in these activities—all these are not merely incidental disiderata. They are fundamental goals in themselves and with objectives such as these, the likelihood of surplus funds is slim indeed. These goals constitute bottomless receptacles into which limitless funds can be poured. As soon as more money becomes available to a nonprofit organization, corresponding new uses can easily be found in still other uses for which no financing has been provided will inevitably arise to take their place."[54]

additional product to the buyer—one not carried by his firm (and which curiously offers him a commission). The phenomenon of tie-ins thrives in a sellers' market when, for various reasons, demand is larger than supply. But salaried personnel will contribute to the disequilibrium. Buyers rather than doing without the product are compelled to purchase the tied product by paying the little extra to the salaried salesman.

It is, therefore, to the interest of the salesman or salaried official to create a situation where the little extra can be picked up. Price control in the form of controlled salaries for salesmen or managers of mutuals will generally be associated with disequilibrium. Where it is possible by creating the conditions for disequilibrium, they insure that customers will want to deal on the side. It is to their rational interest to fail to respond to profit maximization and price bids. They drag their heels in the interest of pushing the sidelines.

The commissioned salesman is different. A community of interest has been established between him and his product or firm. He has a property interest in the fortunes of the firm since he shares in profits. He will not want to carry sidelines because they interfere with the sales of the firm's product. Nor will the firm permit him. In any case, it is neither to his interest nor the firm's. In contrast, in the mutual, there is no control over the manager's decision to build up a side business: the managing officer is a law unto himself. It is significant that for many years the Federal Home Loan Bank Board encouraged these relationships.[x]

It is relevant that the California savings and loan association with the lowest expenses does not have its loan solicitors on a salary but on a commission. In this way, they are partners in the enterprise and have an incentive to seek out the business while keeping down the expenses. Some of them earn as much as $30,000-$40,000 annually—far more than most salaried loan solicitors receive. Nor is it surprising that this should be a "stock association."

Inefficiency among stock associations is corrected by new entry and through purchase of inefficiently operated units. In the mutual, there is no incentive for the first and no possibility for the second. Contractual payments divorce management incentive from profit maximizing. Progressive income taxation further penalizes the salary recipient. Management therefore is induced to seek substitutes for monetary remuneration in the form of higher expenses—payments-in-kind. Removal from the pressure of the marketplace inevitably reduces operating efficiency and when coupled with less incentive implies that the mutual will be less concerned for the minimization of expenses than a stock association. Diversion to affiliates will also mean that less attention will be spent on the affairs of the association. In addition, the necessary condition for diversion or side dealing

---

[x]"In the savings and loan industry, the so-called corporate opportunity prevails, whereby, for example, the director of the savings and loan association can also be the principle officer and director of an insurance company which insures—provides the fire and hazard insurance on same, at least, of the mortgages that are written."[55]

is that shortages be created which lead to monopolistic margins between costs and prices. Finally, risk is reduced because as a threat to control, it might increase the chance for financial insolvency.

But for management to make side deals, it is essential that the buyers should not be able to find alternative sources of supply at higher prices. That is, there must not be competitive suppliers willing to accept price rationing. The most favorable situation is a homogeneous organizational structure: if all associations are mutual, each management has everything to gain by refusing to respond to price competition; and nothing to lose because it is not managerial profits which are lost. But where stock associations are present, there is a high probability that at least one association will respond because it is motivated by price incentives. If the mutual is unresponsive to price offers and insists on side deals which increase the effective price to customers, the stock association may simply expand volume to meet demand. It is no wonder that mutuals are so vexed with stock associations and charge that they do not belong in the savings and loan industry. It is to the interest of mutual managers, if not to their saver-borrowers, to eliminate the stock association.

The Infrastructure

Shaw in his brilliant seminal study describes the infrastructure as "an assortment of firms engaging in such activities as holding, developing, and selling real property; insuring property, title to property, and property owners; supplying junior finance, etc."[56] The subsidiaries or affiliates making up the infrastructure sell services that mortgage borrowers require in addition to finance—escrow, title insurance, property insurance, property management.[57] But they also sell services which associations will buy: the most common, of course, is mortgages from mortgage brokerage firms.

Clearly, the optimization problem in an integrated operation is vastly different from the simple management of a mutual savings and loan association. Expressed euphemistically, this would mean that decision making and integrated operation entails a reconciliation of the various goals of independently operated enterprises. The decision-making function is simply to relate each decision in the subsidiaries to the overall goal of the integrated operation. This will mean that the interests of one sector or enterprise at one level of operation will often be sacrificed in order to attain the goal of the integrated operation.

The original goals of mutuality cease to have a place. The integrated operation is a device or mechanism by which a management, operating under constraints with respect to profit-taking, has created a combination of a number of related activities all directed to the goal of maximizing its own welfare.

Viewed in another light, the mutual savings and loan association involves apparent self-dealing and conflicts of interests[y] once it becomes an integral part of this integrated operation. As the association grows, the opportunities for the development of the infrastructure with the ownership of subsidiary enterprises by the management becomes more lucrative. Obviously, as the side activities increase in importance, a question arises as to the distribution of time and effort the executive allocates between the association and his outside interests. It is suggested that the failure of the mutual savings and loan associations to have grown as rapidly as stock associations is at least due to their preoccupation with the development of their wholly-owned subsidiaries. These permit them to increase pecuniary income and other forms of wealth faster than mere compensation allows in the mutual savings and loan association.[z]

Shaw does not believe in mutualism for the California savings and loan industry. There might be a case for mutuality if that were the only alternative to the industry's present pattern of private enterprise. "Mutualism is not preferable to decentralized private enterprise in a competitive contest."[59] He notes that the California federal association "in common with state associations, . . . are interlocked through common management or management ownership with the infrastructure."[60] Mutualism is not the only way of meeting abuses or problems of the industry. "National experience in banking suggest competitive private enterprise can turn in a better performance under efficient regulations."[a]

Conflicts of Interest in the Quasi-firm? Regulatory authorities, interested in conflict-of-interest situations, believe that they explain the development of slow assets (i.e., delinquent and foreclosed loans), and thus endanger insolvency. Where slow assets are not indicated, scrutiny for possible conflict-of-interest is probably cursory. But the major form of such conflicts is ignored by the Federal Home Loan Bank Board. Yet they are inherent in a separation of a controlling management from an ownership interest. The entire paraphernalia of the infrastructure with its management-owned insurance companies, mortgage brokerage,

---

[y]"At present certain activities of directors fall into a shadowy area of conflict. Frequently, savings institutions employ corporations to conduct specialized activities for them. It is not unusual for an association to employ a corporate agent to originate loans and to pay this agent a percentage on each approved loan. The directorate of the corporate loan agent and the directorate of the savings association in some cases would reveal identical membership. It is difficult to distinguish the substance of this transaction from that conduct which if done directly would be felonious."[58]

[z]In a number of instances control has been transferred in California federals by means of a "sale" of the mortgage finance company. This was reported in instances involving the Beverly Hills and Wilshire associations.

[a]Shaw's judgment is that "the pattern of alliances effects federal as well as state associations. . . . State mutual as well as state stock associations are intertwined with related enterprise through management control. It appears to be the prospect of private profit in a subsidiary enterprise that motivates the same display of aggressive enterpreneurship in some mutuals as in stock associations." p. 16. "Within the narrow market that it may create, the association can establish a relatively high degree of monopoly power and use it, especially in discriminating schedules of fees and charges on its captive mortgage market."[61]

escrow, title and trustee companies is not only not questioned by the Board but has been at times actively encouraged. This infrastructure deals with the associations: there is no fiction of arm's length bargaining. All this phenomena would represent serious conflict-of-interest in a firm. Indeed, they would hardly be tolerated for a moment as witness the immediate sacking of the president of Chrysler Corporation when it was discovered that he had an interest in supplier companies dealing with Chrysler.[b]

It is clear that the Board implicitly recognizes that the mutual association is a quasi-firm. Preoccupation with conflict situations is restricted only to the more obvious self-dealing which threatens solvency such as loans to management, relatives or third-party fronts. By far the larger class of self-dealing, viz., that connected with the infrastructure is tolerated, not to say encouraged. It is suggested that in distinguishing between the two kinds of conflicts and calling one a conflict and ignoring the other, the Board has implicitly recognized that the mutual is a non-firm or quasi-firm; and that no other behavior is to be expected.

On the other hand, the Board is not consistent. The conflicts of interest neither recognized nor condemned are inevitable in the quasi-firm. The management has power. Given a lucrative opportunity, it will use that power for personal gain. Profits will be transferred from the association to managerial-owned creatures within the infrastructure. It is no accident that all the problem cases the Board has noted have originated in a conflict-of-interest. This is to be expected in a mutual or nationalized firm. It is standard and rational behavior for the quasi-firm. Where a firm by definition has a single goal—profit maximization—the quasi-firm is oriented towards outside or external goals. Or in the case of nationalized firms, the enterprise is a battleground of warring parties—management, labor, suppliers and, least effectively, consumers.[c] In contrast, the firm resolves or at least reduces conflict because control is invested in property rights. It is a more sophisticated and civilized unit for organizing resources.[d] In the

[b]In a suit brought by Chrysler, Newburg and his partner-neighbor, Ben Stone, "were charged with having taken unfair advantage of Newburg's position and influence. Stone and Newburg were said to have set up a new firm, Press Products, Inc., with Newburg taking half the stock and Stone and his wife, the other half. The firm produced automotive parts, including door hinges, deck lid (trunk) hinges and hood hinges. Press Products supposedly was able to secure orders from Chrysler, its only customer, through the influence and assistance of Newburg."[62] After investigation by the Board of Directors, the latter stated that "Chrysler will receive from Mr. Newburg profits in excess of $450,000 made by him from interests in vendor companies."

[c]Kaysen's comments on the large corporation are pertinent: "The ideology of corporate management which describes (stockholders) as one among a number of client groups whose interests are the concern of management—labor, consumers, and the 'public' forming the others—is in this particular realistic."[63]

[d]"When it is assumed that the firm operates in competitive markets and under certainty, then the given and known production functions and price parameters yield only one unique optimizing solution. In principle, it therefore makes no difference who directs the operations of the firm, since the constraints and alternative uses are known." In the dynamic world of uncertain prices and production functions someone has to take a position on the outcome of the future events. The owners of equity by assuming that risk acquire the right to make the decisions.[64]

quasi-firm, there is an absence of property rights; and, depending upon whether it is mutual or nationalized, either continual conflict or diversion of earnings results.

Externality of Objectives. Given the limitations of the salary contract, the manager need not be a profit maximizer. It may be in his interest to exploit his power position by offering higher than competitive prices to suppliers. The latter would compete for the privilege of dealing with him by offering perfectly legal deals. Thus, the manager might enter a mortgage brokerage firm as a partner or place a relative in the firm. Or the mortgage brokerage firm may show appreciation for the good prices received in the sale of mortgages by loans either directly to him or his candidate for speculative land appreciation. Such pay-offs are not revealed in the books of the association and may easily escape the scrutiny of the Board: they are private transactions of the mortgage brokerage firm.

Manipulation of the association according to exterior goals is the consequence of the dilution and suppression of clearly defined property rights. The conflict-of-interest problems which seem to arise with such regularity are nothing more than outside suppliers reimbursing management for permitting them to charge what the traffic will bear. The association is exploited in the same way a monopolist exploits the competition among his buyers. Management identifies with an external supplier or buyer. Because he is in absolute control, there is no discussion and no questioning his behavior. For example, it has frequently been charged that American Telephone and Telegraph Company circumvents rate regulation of its operating subsidiaries by having another subsidiary, Western Electric, supply parts at monopolistic prices.[e] This has two alleged effects: (1) the unregulated Western Electric is able to receive monopolistic profits; and (2) the operating firms can petition for higher rates on the basis of higher costs and thus secure a higher return on invested capital.[66]

Use of the quasi-firm in this sense suggests that exploitation signifies. It is the denial to economic units, e.g., the mutual savings and loan association, of a right to an economic life of its own; and it is caused by a conflict of objective between the supplying firm (or management) and the firm as an independent entity. There is also a side effect: other supply groups also experience a contraction in the demand for their services. Part of the market is foreclosed. In this sense, both the association and the economy loses: savers receive less for their funds because the higher operating costs limit the activities of the association; and borrowers must pay more.

The orthodox firm is not merely a production unit: it survives and prospers only because it is efficient—and it must be more efficient than the alternative uses for that expenditure of money and resources. Thus, it is not sufficient to

---

[e] ". . . the power of a public utility may be extended from a service field in which the monopolist is subject to regulation into a field of equipment manufacture in which there are no corresponding checks upon the use of business power."[65]

produce; it must produce at minimal costs and with an absence of hanky-panky along the way.

Management will develop outside interests and outside connections when it is not permitted inside interests, viz., property and profit-sharing. When this is the case, management will develop an external orientation, e.g., privately-owned companies, close relations with suppliers such as commercial banks and mortgage brokerage houses or intimate political affiliations. In a nationalized steel enterprise, shortages are chronic so that management can direct more steel to one customer rather than others. The latter in turn may make a good financial contribution to a specific political candidate or party. Someone or institution is paid off. Thus, the cycle is completed with power created and converted to personal gain.

The failure to resolve conflicts-of-interest is the distinguishing mark of the quasi-firm. In this sense, it may be said to be archaic. The firm, in the orthodox sense, is an advanced efficient instrument for securing maximum efficiency, i.e., the resolution of conflict. The mutual and nationalized enterprise represent regressions to a less efficient state. By externalizing the costs to management, the mutual inevitably becomes a vehicle for restriction. In contrast, economic progress has meant developments in an opposite direction. A firm represented the internalization of many of the expenses: management was made responsible through the institution of property and its accompanying reward—profit. Once management is provided with property, it is no longer to his interest to ignore the costs of restriction.

Impact of Managerial Policies. To the extent that management inflates salary or spends more on amenities, total expenses in the mutual are higher. This means that net earnings after all expenses, dividends and taxes will be less than otherwise. The effect is to reduce the amount available for allocation to reserves and thus to that extent slow the rate of growth relative to what it might have been under a different set of constraints. Similarly, the quasi-firm may be expected to take a different attitude towards the sale and purchase of loans and participations. To illustrate, sale by California federal associations to eastern savings and loan associations provides additional funds for lending in a capital deficit market. Additional loans or higher growth rates generate greater income as loan fees increase with the increase in the volume of loans made. This leads to more business for infrastructure affiliates such as mortgage brokerage houses and insurance companies. On the other hand, the eastern purchaser eliminates his origination expenses while increasing income. The margin available for salary and amenities (but not for his affiliates) is enlarged.

The diversion model must initially take account of two characteristics of the mutual. First, to all intents and purposes, there are no legally specified owners in the sense that there is in the orthodox permanent stock company. Management is not an owner; and, therefore, not permitted to assert a claim to the profits of the mutual. Second, management is in absolute control of the association and has to account for its actions to no one. Thus the problem it faces is how to convert power to personal gain? The most lucrative technique is the creation of an ingenious and elaborate mechanism for both the generation of monopoly income and diversion by means of privately-owned subsidiary companies. There is nothing sinister or underhanded in this mechanism. Public officials have encouraged it. An industry historian has not only noted it but sees no occasion for censure:

It seems desirable that the compensation of management and staff should come directly from the institution itself, although hundreds of examples could be cited where outstanding success has been achieved in the development of savings and loan associations with a substantial portion of the compensation coming from side line, but related activities.[67]

Diversion and Monopoly

In the economist's model, efficiency of performance is a function of the intensity of competition. In regulated or nationalized industry, competition is not permitted or is severely limited. Furthermore, once there has been an alteration or dispossessing of owners, there is little incentive to compete. Competition is regarded as gratuitous because of its intimate relation to ownership: the change in ownership, or the failure to specify it in terms of power and control, makes it meaningless in the mutual or nationalized enterprise. Whatever the form of ownership in a nationalized industry, it is different from that associated with the permanent stock company, or even the individual proprietorship and partnership. That ownership or property right which gives profit to the owner is abandoned in favor of mutual or social ownership. The distinguishing characteristic of the latter is its separation from control over the enterprise.

Quasifirms do not exist in competitive industries for another reason: they are externally oriented which reduces their chance of survival. Nor have they anything to offer management because returns are just sufficient to keep the number of firms in the industry stable. Management receives a competitive wage equivalent to that to be earned elsewhere; and the owners of capital would be expected to send more resources into the industry only when returns are larger than they are in alternative opportunities. The combined amount going to management and the owners of capital would be less than that which now goes to management. The present management of mutuals receives a higher return because entry is curtailed while competition is dampened, if not outright suppressed.

In a competitive market, there is no reason why a borrower or seller should give the management of the mutual anything extra in return for the loan or the mortgage. Price competition limits the payment to the price. Extra payments or side deals arise when there is disequilibrium. Though a mutual might price at the competitive level, management retains the decision to control output or the number of loans, i.e., control of the volume of activity. He need not be a profit-maximizer or strict marginalist. He can set an output less than that which would clear the market.

The infrastructure is one of the mechanisms for diverting the monopoly profits in the savings and loan industry. If there were no profits, there would be no infrastructure: borrowers only buy insurance from the affiliate because they get the loan. When an association operates with competitive margins and outputs, it has nothing to offer the borrower in return for the insurance. By creation of excess demand, he gains the profits of restriction in the price charged the borrower for insurance, i.e., he allocates in the latter's direction. It is a tie-in sale.

A stock association would compete for reasons not attractive to a mutual. This is so even where it is conceded that *on the average* sellers do not gain from competition when their margins are reduced. But an individual competitor can increase his market share and thus his total profits at the expense of his less aggressive rivals. But it is profit which is enlarged—something the management of the quasi-firm or mutual cannot directly enjoy. Though the total profit is larger, the management does not benefit because through reduction in the margin, he has lost his power to ration. For example, in a competitive market, he could not refuse to purchase certificates of deposit paying maximum interest rates as against carrying his cash as a demand deposit in a commercial bank at no interest. In the interests of survival, he would be forced to act identical to his competitors.

It is to be expected that borrowers at a mutual would receive better prices and terms than they do at stock associations. This would appear in the former reporting less income from interest and fees. But borrowers must pay for these concessions on the loan by the insurance and related items that they must purchase. Nor are state laws against forcing difficult to evade. The borrower is in the loan office, and has indicated whether he is receptive to giving his insurance to the affiliate. If not, it is relatively easy to vary the other terms or to delay or fail to get approval of the loan. In general, the applicants are likely to be carefully screened so that the loans with more favorable terms go to those who deal with the infrastructure.

Some idea of the value of the insurance affiliate can be gained by considering the twelve largest federally-chartered associations in the Los Angeles-Long Beach area at the end of 1965. With total assets of $2,970 million, the average association had $247.5 million. If the average mortgage is assumed $15,000, each had 16,500 mortgages. Suppose that each association sent its affiliate one-half of the insurance business on a three-year contract of $30 per policy written, this would have come to $10 per year on $82,500 for each association. With a screening which is one hundred percent effective, it would have meant $165,000 for each management affiliate. Insurance is but *one* of the many side deals which may be worked out with suppliers and borrowers.

Corruption and the Quasi-firm. Corruption and bribery are not accidental phenomena. They are the consequence of power without property rights. They are as inevitably associated with the quasi-firm as husbands are with the institution of marriage. Whenever price is not permitted to ration, as with rent control, shortages result: apartments are allocated on a black market. Tips, bribes, the purchase of unwanted furnishings and the corruption of apartment house superintendents represent efforts at improving on a disequilibrium situation.

Under government ownership, prices are often controlled so that shortages develop. Nonprice rationing, which consists in allocating the scarce resource in one direction rather than another, is pejoratively described as corruption. Yet, such efforts are nothing more than genuine efforts to improve upon a less than optimal allocation of resources. The perennial problem of bribery is the consequence of a refusal to permit price and competition to operate, coupled with a separation of management from ownership. It is a competitive bid where open price competition is inhibited. If there were no shortage, there would be no necessity for the bribe. In a mutual or quasi-firm, the manager feathers his nest by creating the circumstances that lead to side deals. By contrast, in the competitive market, with price free to allocate, there is no necessity for a buyer to engage in a tie-in transaction with the management. Kickbacks are neither tolerated by stockholders or the marketplace. A firm which makes use of them is similar to one which insists on racial discrimination. Its costs must be higher because it is not buying on price alone. It cannot survive in a competitive market because a buyer can always find an alternative source of supply at a lower price.

When all prices are public and identical, there are no possibilities of deals. Their appearance in the savings and loan industry is the result of government restrictions on entry and competition, and separation of management control from a property interest. The infrastructure would not survive removal of governmental controls and the link-up of management with ownership.

Effect of Prohibition of Management-Owned Affiliates. A suggested solution to the problem posed by managerial diversion is an outright prohibition of ownership of affiliates. But the problem does not have its origin in management-owned affiliates. On the contrary, the affiliates are organized because management has power without ownership. Were it not permitted to own insurance firms or mortgage brokerages, it continues to be advantageous to create shortage situations as well as to divert. Management does not have to own the affiliate to benefit. After all, it is hardly in a position to own a commercial bank yet it gains from dealings with one.

The large mutual insurance companies are carefully scrutinized by public officials. The slightest indications of self-dealing, as reported in the affairs of Shanks (Metropolitan) and Parkinson (Equitable) led to the forced resignation or dismissal of both chief executives. But such squeamishness is besides the point. The chief executive and directors continue to have tremendous power. They determine how to place their cash flows. The opportunities for self-aggrandizement are manifest. Decisions neither have to be made public nor clearly against their policyholders' interest. Their position opens doors not available to the ordinary citizen. They can graciously place their funds in a certain bank. The latter can and do call attention to opportunities for both quick and large profits. They may become corporate directors in other industries simply because of their position and the vast sums they control. No matter how scrupulous, they have within their hands the power to allocate. It is highly improbable that they can be precluded from personally benefiting.

It would seem preferable to move in an opposite direction. Rather than a denial of property rights in affiliates, management should be given the opportunity to secure property rights in the savings and loan association. By this step, the incentive for monopolistic restriction would be removed. The association would cease to be a quasi-firm with its externalization of managerial costs. Competition rather than monopoly would be encouraged with gain to both savers and borrowers. Management would have no incentive for diversion and greater incentive to provide what savers and borrowers want. Less attention would be devoted to side deals and payments-in-kind; more would be devoted to making the association an efficient competitive firm. Instead of making deals based on how the affiliates would profit, the manager would have an identity of interest with the association. The objective would be to satisfy the borrowers; not to select special kinds of borrowers simply because they are profitable to affiliates. The power of management would be used to enhance the profits of the company; not the income of the management.

Impact of Stock Associations on the Mutual

The stock savings and loan association poses one major problem for the mutual. Its management neither has the incentive nor the power to divert income to privately-owned affiliates. It therefore seeks profits and competes—both anathema to the quasi-firm. Where a mutual might offer a lower interest rate to a borrower in return for his insurance, the stock association would meet the competitive rate while under no necessity for insisting on the insurance business. Or the stock association seeking maximum profits would place cash in those banks paying the highest interest rate on certificates of deposit. This enhancement of earnings as compared to the mutual permits the stock to pay higher dividend rates. It is no wonder that mutual spokesmen refer to the stock associations with hatred and venom.

The emphasis on profit-making possibilities and growth leads the stock association to offer higher dividends. By reducing the spread between dividends and gross operating income, the margin for diversion is squeezed. The stock are indifferent to such concerns since their only interest is profit maximization. They can also increase their returns by increasing market share. Thus, a decline in the profit margin is quite consistent with an increase in total profits arising from larger volume.

The difficulty that the stock poses for the mutual is that at competitive prices, the mutual must restrict loans so that there is a shortage. But there is no shortage when a stock association stands by ready to make a loan refused by the mutual. The mutual might survive if it were able to charge different prices (i.e., higher prices than the stock). The experience of the federals in California is relevant. Their infrastructure may have escaped unscathed because (1) it was a rapidly expanding mortgage market; and (2) competition compelled them to adopt the techniques of the stock associations. Thus in an expanding market, they would not be expected to increase interest rates or fees as much as the stock. They could insist on tie-ins at better rates than those offered by the stock (who in any case were sold out, *ex hypothesi*). They would make more deals with commercial banks for their cash and with mortgage brokers. In fact, their greater conservatism is simply a more selective process in which they *deal* more with borrowers and suppliers. The result is that they have grown less rapidly. Not surprisingly, they have reported smaller earnings since in part their earnings have been diverted. Protected both by legal and geographical barriers to entry and a booming market, they not only survived, they even grew—but not as fast as the stock associations.

The stock associations and their holding companies pose a threat for the mutual. They have not only made the mutuals compete in their own geographical markets, but through national advertising, they have penetrated into areas where competition had been considered as rare as a privately-owned firm in the Soviet Union. Their competition both with respect to dividends and advertising promotion has been tough and original. They have forged new means to cope both with the problems of the money market and the negative effects of government regulation. They have been responsible for a new form of uncertainty in that competition makes the future more difficult to predict. Their concern for profit and expansion has hardly been consistent with the preference for the quiet life on the part of mutual management. Indeed, their successes have brought a form of warfare where there once was nothing but unchallenged restriction and diversion.

One indication of the federals' aversion to competition is found in the absence of the smaller federal establishments among those leading the dividend rate up. That large establishments with a significant share of the market should avoid dividend rate increases is hardly astonishing: they have to pay the higher dividend to *all* savers, and because they are large, they would take a significant number of savers away from rivals, thereby forcing retaliation. The result would be that the larger establishment is not likely to gain as much from competition as the smaller. Yet federal establishments are singularly absent among the price leaders—no matter how small and insignificant they are.

That the federally chartered dislike competition is revealed in the judgment by Hoeft, the founder and chief executive of Glendale Federal, the second largest in California. He refers to "a few bad boys in the savings and loan industry," California and Nevada associations, who have gone in for unbridled advertising in Eastern newspapers. When an Eastern bank goes to four and seven-eighths percent, "they are probably doing it under pressure to protect their institution from raiding of the advertising associations in the western part of the United States. . . . It is unfair to those eastern institutions."[68] A Federal Home Loan Board official said that every case of an increase in the dividend has been led by either a new or younger establishment. That this should be so is hardly surprising. How else is the young and smaller association to grow except by competition? But it does reflect an antagonism on the part of both mutual and government officials towards competition.

The mutuals seek at all times to identify the savings and loan industry with themselves. They belittle competition and profit seeking as having no place in an industry devoted to the encouragement of thrift and home financing. They suggest that mutuality is a substitute for competition and have used the regulatory agencies to suppress it as when they were able to have certificates of deposit beyond five percent of assets eliminated as part of the liquidity requirement for insured associations. Since certificates are saleable in the market, one can only infer that they have done this to protect their infrastructure along the lines suggested above.

9

Expense Manipulation in the Mutual

The hypothesis to be tested is that the mutual form of organization in the savings and loan inudstry exhibits significantly different forms of behavior and operating results than do stock associations. The phenomena is principally indicated in expenses and earnings. It should be noted that if the management of the mutual savings and loan association endeavored successfully to absorb what would otherwise be profits in the form of expense, the expenses would be higher than those for stock associations. This is because the mutual management is constrained in such a way that it can take or divert profits only through either reducing net income as when the association deals with management-owned subsidiaries; or boosting expenses as an attempt to take out the profits in the form of higher wages or amenities; or providing free services for management-owned subsidiaries. But, where management is 100% successful in using expenses as the mechanism for appropriating profits, it would in no way differ from the stock form of organization. It is suggested that the hypothesis of identical behavior is unacceptable. That the mutuals do act differently is attested to by strikingly dissimilar operating results. Both a model and the data with respect to the confirmation of the hypothesis will be developed in the ensuing chapters.

Rather than permitting expenses to get out of line, managements of mutuals have been compelled, for competitive reasons, to keep, at least their appearance, on a par with that of stock associations. When expenses are expressed as a ratio of assets, the mutual associations' expenses are not only not higher but they very often are lower than the stock associations' expenses. This has been achieved by doing less: fewer "loans made" are generated; and, as a result, their growth is slower.

Mutuality and Expenses

Expenses represent a principal form by which the management of the mutual is able to enjoy the benefits of his position of control over the association. The evidence indicates that the federally chartered associations which, of course are mutuals, generally keep expenses at a level such that solvency problems do not develop. This is accomplished both by an avoidance of undue risk as well as by maintaining a lid on the buildup of expenses.

As Table 9-1 indicates, there is a close relationship between the ratios of expenses to assets and new loans to assets. The simple correlations were +0.69

171

Table 9-1

New Loans and Expenses as a Percentage of Assets: Largest States, 1962

Leading States	New Loans/ Average Assets	Rank	Expenses/ Average Assets	Rank
California	37.5	1	1.30	1
Florida	20.6	7	1.25	4
Illinois	21.9	5	1.20	6
Indiana	21.6	6	1.28	3
Massachusetts	13.4	13	0.95	12
Michigan	18.7	11	1.23	5
Missouri	22.1	4	1.10	8
New Jersey	19.9	8	0.98	11
New York	15.9	12	1.06	10
Ohio	23.3	3	1.30	2
Pennsylvania	18.6	10	1.08	9
Texas	23.8	2	1.11	7
Wisconsin	19.0	9	0.81	13
U.S. Mean	24.6		1.17	

Source: Federal Home Loan Bank Board, Combined Financial Statements, Members of the Federal Home Loan Bank System, 1962, and Savings and Home Financing, *Source Book*, 1963, Washington, D.C.

and +0.54 for 1961 and 1962, respectively. The reason, confirmed by data to be presented later, is that a major contributor to expenses in a savings and loan association is the origination of new loans or loans made. A management which seeks to maintain control over the level of expenses will take a more conservative view toward the origination of new loans. The latter depends upon both the total amount of new net savings received and available for new lending and the loans repaid, or the turnover of mortgages. It is difficult to vary the loans repaid or turnover rate very much. Therefore, the main variable within the control of management is the growth rate which may be increased or diminished depending upon decisions with respect to dividend rate, advertising, promotion, and the sale of loans.

Management Attitudes towards Risk Exposure. Some indication of the problems involved in assuming higher risks and causing higher expenses and, therefore, a loss in income was noted in a statement by Elwood Knapp, a former president of the United States Savings and Loan League. "In Pennsylvania, for example, if we make an 80% loan and later have to foreclose, 16% of our 20% equity is swallowed up just in foreclosure cost. So while the mortgage process has improved in many ways, mortgage lending has taken on some additional risks."[1]

High rates of growth entail an increasing proportion of unseasoned loans. Such loans involve risks in the sense that the borrower has not yet attained sufficient equity or established a sufficiently large investment which would preclude his walking away from his mortgage. In the event that he makes a decision to abandon the obligation, the savings and loan association is left holding the property with no income and the certainty that it will incur extra expenses arising from the foreclosure and the ultimate resale of the property. Though high growth rates may be associated with higher income, they undoubtedly also involve a higher exposure rate to risks.

The mutual is to be contrasted with the stock association. Where a mutual would seek to avoid the threat to solvency, the owner-managers of the stock association might and often do take on the risks when they consider that the revenue will more than justify the additional costs involved. This is particularly so because stock associations are by nature profit-maximizing institutions. They will, therefore, decide on loans which while involving risk may be more than offset by the additional revenue that they bring. Even where the loans later turn sour, they are matched against other equally high-risk loans which have provided higher income and therefore higher profits to the association. The same reasoning is not expected from the management of the mutual. In the first place, he is not permitted to take the profits in the same way. In the second place, the only threat to his survival as the autocrat of the association is through undertaking such risks for a highly dubious profit which in any event he will not be permitted to seize—at least in a direct sense.

Management under a Wage Constraint

The managerial wage or salary bears a rough relationship to the total assets. It is said that in previous years, there was a rule-of-thumb which permitted management to pay itself a salary about equal to one-tenth of one percent of total assets. As savings and loan associations grew and prospered through the fifties and sixties, some grew to such size that had the old rule been in operation, those managing the largest mutual associations might have earned as much as a million dollars or more. There seems to be an unwritten rule which subjects top managerial salaries to some scrutiny by the Federal Home Loan Bank Board.

In addition, as salaries rise, the individual becomes subject to steeper tax rates under the system of progressive income taxation. But the influence of the Internal Revenue Service is both more pervasive and limiting than the actual constraints caused by the progressivity of the tax structure. The Internal Revenue Service is interested in the mutual savings and loan associations because of their earnings or potential earnings. Accordingly, it is a far more industrious inspector of the books than officials from the Federal Home Loan Bank Board. Extremely high salaries may represent attempts to divert what is otherwise corporate profit into the pockets of the mutual officials. They are likely to be identified by the Internal Revenue Service experts. A salary of which a large part was actually profit would not be allowed. Thus, there are two checks upon the power of the management of the mutual to divert profits directly to itself in the form of salaries or wages.

Figure 9-1 portrays managerial decision making in the mutual. This is a conventional model in which management chooses that combination which will yield the highest utility. The choice is between a salary and expenses that may be made on amenities that are the consequence of a particular position of control. Among the typical amenities are those expenses involved with the pleasantness of one's work. For example, a pleasing and attractive secretary or several secretaries; expensive office furnishings with rugs, furniture, curtains, refriger-

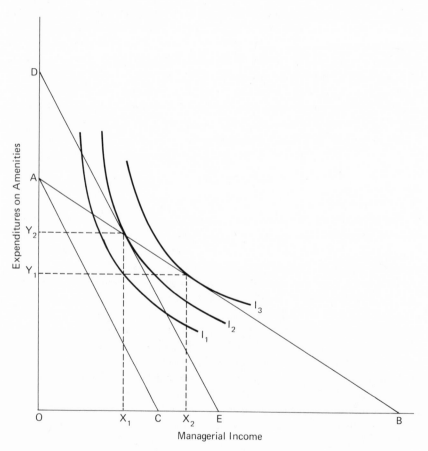

Figure 9-1. Managerial Decision-Making under an Income Constraint.

ator and other facilities; paid and lengthy vacations; an expense account and trips at the association's expense; use of an association automobile; and, in some cases, the use of an association-owned yacht, cabin in the mountains, helicopter and airplane. The figure reveals a series of indifferent curves which from the origin represent successively higher levels of utility or satisfaction. From A on the vertical axis, there are two straight lines with different slopes to the horizontal axis: AB and AC are constant outlay curves or price lines which indicate the different combinations of amenities and managerial input which may be purchased at different prices or salaries for management. A shift of the price line from AB to AC is equivalent to an increase in the relative price of management. DE is the price line when OX_1 of income and OY_2 of amenities is the optimal combination. AC is another with the same relative prices as DE.

Where there are no constraints on management, e.g., in a stock association, the manager-owner would be expected to make that selection between amenities and income which places him on the highest indifference or utility curve, I_3. In the chart, this is indicated at the point where the constant outlay curve is tangent to the highest indifference curve–I_3. Here, management spends Y_1 on amenities and receives X_2 in salary. We assume that the amount spent on amenities is larger than zero simply because of the requirements of any civilized society with respect to the conditions in which one works.

Now consider a mutual with a constraint on management. For the reasons cited, suppose that the management of the mutual is *limited* to an income less than X_2, e.g., X_1. Management would move up the constant outlay curve, AB, to the point where, while it meets the constraint that it receives no more in income than X_1, the same *total* expense is incurred because of an increase in the purchase of amenities from Y_1 to Y_2. The substitution of amenities for income is revealed by the line drawn parallel to the abscissa which crosses the Y axis at Y_1 as well as I_1 directly above X_1. The constraint initially resembles an increase in the price of management, e.g., due to growing scarcity.

However, the combination of X_1 and Y_1 on I_1 is not optimal in view of the options available to management. Since management controls the association, it has a choice among expenditures. Expenditures on amenities are expanded to the amount indicated at Y_2. At this point, the management is on the higher indifference curve I_2. But this new combination is, of course, associated with less utility than the original combination on I_3.

With this combination, the outlay curve, AB, crosses the higher isoquant I_2 so it is not an optimal situation. But the manager is not free. The slope is less than that for the isoquant. Had this been an optimal combination, the appropriate price line would have been tangent to I_2 and is shown as DE which reflects different relative prices. The lower price line AC shows the same relative prices as DE. Thus, the effect of the constraint is similar to an increase in the price of management as compared to amenities taken in lieu of income.

The consequences of placing a ceiling on the pay of the management is similar to a price increase in a free market arising from an increased scarcity. This is true with respect to all forms of price control: by creating excess demand, the effective prices are forced up and have the same impact as price increases induced by increases in scarcity or natural disasters. Unfortunately, the impact of wage control here has been to change management's optimal combination: management is not as well off as before. But so far as the association is concerned, there is no net gain because total expenses are identical to what they would have been had management been free to fix its salary. The limit on managerial income fails to save funds for the savings and loan association: it merely forces a substitution of other forms of satisfaction. Management is worse off and spends on amenities what it would have taken in salary. The economy is also the loser as the profits might have been reinvested, and forced mortgage rates down to the benefit of the borrower.

Externalization of Expense

But salary is not the only item controlled or scrutinized by the Internal Revenue Service. Total expenses are also checked since often they represent an attempt to avoid taxes. The expenses of the mutual association which may go into amenities are likely to come under fire by the Internal Revenue Service. It follows that the management of the mutual has reason to look about for other methods for taking advantage of its position.

Figure 9-2 shows a production possibility function. The decisions open to management are indicated by the two axes. The Y axis shows *external* resources; and the X axis *internal* resources. Isoquants convex to the origin reflect given levels of output; or, as is the case with the savings and loan association, new loans. The two parallel lines, AB and CD, represent constant outlays or isocost curves. The lower, AB is tangent to isoquant I_1 while the upper CD, cuts the isoquant in two points. The two curves CD and AB show maximum and minimum profit levels and can be viewed also as revenue lines: maximum expenses are those derived from revenue and the difference between maximum and minimum expenses is the difference between the upper, CD, and the lower, AB and equal to AC on the Y axis.

The isoquant is convex to the origin simply because there is increasing difficulty in the substitution of external resources for internal resources. This follows from the general properties with respect to the diminishing effectiveness in the substitution of one type of resource for another.

In the chart, with the abscissa representing internal resources, the optimal combination for that particular size (as shown by new loans) is manifested where the isoquant is touched by the lowest outlay curve. Perpendiculars dropped to the two axes from this point indicate the efficient proportion, Y_1 and X_2. In the diagram, AB is the constant outlay curve which touches that particular output

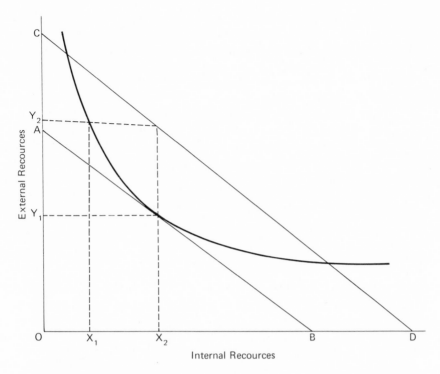

Figure 9–2. Managerial Substitution of External for Internal Expenditures when under an Income Constraint.

and indicates the optimal or least cost combination. *CD* represents the income. That this income is greater than the expenses is the result of the protection provided firms in this industry by the Regulatory Commissions in the form of controls on price competition and entry of new associations. When management is allowed to receive profits, *BD* represents the quantity of internal resources that could be bought with profit.

It is rational for a sophisticated management to reduce the jobs or functions which it must perform. The burden of adjustment of fluctuating profits is shifted to external suppliers. For any given level of output, management fixes expenses at the conventional ratio. For that level of output or assets, there is an optimal combination between the use of internal resources, for which management is responsible, and the external which it may buy. Where there is an absence of regulation, the optimal combination appears at X_2 and Y_1. Assume that due to restrictions on entry, the savings and loan association receives a profit equivalent to an outlay curve *CD* which lies to the right of *AB*. The acceptable internal expenses are X_2. When management is not permitted the profits, it preserves the same expenditure while cutting the use of internal resources. The same output is offered as in the unregulated case. Consequently, it moves up the isoquant to the left. The substitution of external resources for internal resources is indicated by the increase in expenses and consequent sacrificing of profits and is shown by the coordinates of the point on the maximum revenue CD, X_2, and Y_2. X_1Y_2 is a combination using fewer internal and more external resources under a profit constraint. It is these coordinates which tells us how much of the external resources can be purchased when X_2 continues to be spent on internal resources including management. But, to maintain the same output as before, the increase of external resources to Y_2 will consist of a substitution for actual internal resources which are reduced to X_1. Management now receives the same income in the way of expenses as before, but has fewer internal resources to manage and presumably less to do. The balance of the expense, X_1X_2, is left for managerial income and amenities.

The analysis shows that, beginning with profit and property right restrictions, the mutual, or quasi-firm, differs from the ordinary firm. Management has power, but it cannot take profits directly. It is induced into transferring activities to outside organizations in order to keep more of the permissible expenses for itself. The regulatory authority may fix the ratio at some reasonable amount. But management's response is to substitute external resources at the sacrifice of profits and income. The resulting expense level is expanded with amenities encouraged and managerial internal inputs reduced per dollar of investment. This is a euphemism for saying that inefficiency is the result of a control over profits; and the inevitable consequence of the elimination of private property rights.

The buildup of amenities, i.e., payments in kind, are inevitable under mutual organization, i.e., wherever management has power but nonownership. They result from allowing some permissible expense ratio; and are an incentive to the transfer of all possible activities to external institutions. In the ideal case, from the point of management, they are preferably transferred to wholly-owned managerial subsidiaries. Even where management is not permitted to "own" subsidiaries, a diversion would continue to external institutions in order to reduce its own inputs. This is rational in the quasi-firm because it is oriented towards entirely different directions from the profit-seeking firm. The basic difference is that in the latter there are not external objectives. Therefore, it is the objectives of the management that are critical.

By a shift of functions to outside resources, management surrenders profits; but, by the same move, internal expenses are reduced thereby permitting larger expenditures on amenities. While profits may be maximized under the conventional solution, management is truly better off with a nonprofit maximizing solution. In making this shift, management maintains the stability of the expense-to-asset ratio: it is able to hold the output or assets constant while shifting performance of the functions to outside suppliers. The result, of course, is that association income is sacrificed. Since assets do not alter, the expense ratio can be maintained while actually less is done internally per unit of assets. This means management can *divert* income which might have been used to cover expenses incurred in growth of both assets and income.

Expenses may be expected to be fixed for several reasons. First, the evidence shows that though mutuals have been able to keep their expenses in line with the stock associations, they have also exhibited less activity. But this was according to expectation. Another reason for expecting the expenses of the mutual to remain related to that of the stock is that in certain areas they are competitive with the stock and thus cannot allow their expenses to be too much out of line. Finally, unless expenses are comparable to the stock, there is no support for the null hypothesis that mutual organization is not significantly different from the stock. That is, the fixity or rough equality of expenses of the mutual as compared to the stock is a very essential part of that hypothesis. If expenses are significantly greater, there is reason to reject the hypothesis that the mutual form of organization makes no difference so far as the allocation of resources are concerned. There are good reasons for believing that this is not the case. That is, the mutual form of organization has a unique impact. The variations in the constraints operating on management are substantial: management does possess control but lacks ownership and so is motivated to follow rather unorthodox procedures.

There is one other point. Though the management of the mutual has power, it does not own. In seeking to capitalize this control, it is up against constraints which prevent direct milking of the association. The constraints force management into second best choices, e.g., amenities as compared to direct income payments; the use of external resources where internal resources would generate more income. This means that a mutual will show smaller actual dollar expenses relative to both wages and amenities received by management. Rationality consists in minimizing the input of management relative to the fixed wage. With expenses controlled at some fixed percentage, adjustment is made in the association income. Thus when mortgages are acquired with services provided by suppliers, the price paid to the supplier, e.g., the mortgage broker, is higher and the return to the savings and loan association is less. By the same token, the savings and loan association no longer has to incur the expenses involved in originating the new loans. Management can then appropriate the sums for itself. The limits on expenses are such that adjustment is made by management in the association income. The object of management is to reduce expenditures on items other than itself; but the minimization of expenses is only achieved by a corresponding loss of income. The savings and loan association's expenses are reduced only by hiring someone else to perform the function—at a price.

Management trades income for expenses. As the association gives up income, it is also able to reduce expenses. The ways to reduce expenses are: (1) through legitimate economy; (2) through reduction of activities such as the origination of new loans; (3) through arranging for outside suppliers to perform the functions.

The constraint means that for a certain asset size, expenses are limited. But there is no requirement that a certain income must be earned. Obviously, income must be sufficient to cover dividends to savers and the expenses to be absorbed by management. Different levels of income are equally consistent with both the size of the association and solvency.

The regulations on both the salaries and amenities of management induce an economy in the use of internal resources similar to rational changes in methods when the prices of inputs alter. Or, had the prices of external resources fallen, the relatively cheaper set of resources would have been substituted. Paradoxically, the salary constraint is identical to an increase in the relative price of management: its share is reduced to that extent. Thus, it is rational to substitute external resources. The effect on the economy is identical to a natural calamity.

The principal effect of the constraint on management is that through the transfer of activities to outside firms, association income is reduced. It is to management's advantage since by holding the expenses-to-asset ratio constant may reduce its own input. Disintegration is, therefore, a consequence of mutual or quasi-firms and arises from the absence of a managerial property interest. It is directly contrary to economic progress which takes the form of an internalization of costs.

The Cost to Savers. To the extent that the management of the mutual association successfully inflates expenses, there is obviously less return to the association. Reserves will not build up as rapidly as in a stock association. The result is that the total volume of assets for which no interest has to be paid is smaller. By the same token, the reduced growth in reserves also retards the overall growth of the association. Higher expenses imply smaller allocations to reserves, lower growth and ultimately less return to the association. The upshot is that the association will not have as much ability to pay higher dividends to saver members. Thus, there are two forces operating against the interests of the latter. First, the management of the savings and loan association is only threatened in his position of complete autocracy by threats to solvency. The consequence is that management avoids undue exposure to risk. Risk increases vulnerability and is a threat to maintenance of control. Second, the padding of expenses, endemic in management-dominated enterprise, means that less funds are available to allocate to reserves.

A major factor in the level of dividends is in the ability to generate new loans. Indeed, income, itself, depends upon ability to turn over mortgages; to grow and generate additional new loans as well as earning the fees which go with loan origination. The higher expenses of mutual organizations limit the opportunities for growth by precluding development of the necessary reserves that make growth possible. This ultimately impedes the ability to earn the higher income which alone makes for higher dividends.

The difficulties which associations have faced in parts of the country other than California have been the consequences of the mutual form of organization with its characteristic inflated expenses. Had those expenses been on a par comparable to that of stock associations, they would have had less trouble in meeting the California dividends. For the same reason, there would have been less necessity for exerting pressure upon the Federal Home Loan Bank Board to set maximum dividend rates in order to inhibit industry competition.

Part IV: Regression Results: Expenses and Return

10 The Measurement of Expenses

Until recently, it was widely believed that the conventional firm in the American economy was oriented toward profit. Though ownership in the large corporation may be widely distributed, and not withstanding an apparent separation of ownership from control, profits were the driving force behind managerial decision making. This is because they are also an index of rationality. In that sense, they are a signal for either positive or negative action in that they provide management with a feedback mechanism. Expenses, on the other hand, are not a primary element, either with respect to performance characteristics or as an item of significance in themselves. Indeed, an enterprise could rationally incur higher expenses simply because they generate additional profits.

The Peculiar Status of Expenses in a Mutual

It is because the management of a mutual savings and loan association has the power to make decisions, but lacks the power to take profits directly, that expenses play a peculiar role. One of the ways to circumvent this constraint is through control over expenditures. These may differ from a stock association in the following ways. First, for obvious reasons, the management would be expected to take a higher salary. Second, as indicated above, to the extent that salaries are limited, a manager would enjoy his position of management on the premises of the association. That is, he would take what, in effect, is income in the form of amenities on the job. Third, he might own one or several companies operating in a related area, possibly in the mortgage business, so that he could have the association incur expenses for the performance of services that under other conditions would be performed by the outside firm. All such instances bolster the expenses of the mutual as compared to the stock association. Expenses represent the principal media by which the management is able to enjoy its position of decision making within the mutual.

Interpretation of Statistical Data. The data as presented by the Federal Home Loan Bank Board and the various state savings and loan commissioners require some sophistication in interpretation. To a considerable extent, the reports represent the objectives and incentives of the particular organizations which make up the industry. Obviously, there will be differences between federally or

185

state-chartered mutual savings and loan associations and state-chartered stock associations. Again, biases are introduced when stock associations are owned by large public holding companies. It has been noted by Grebler and Brigham that associations

have a certain amount of leeway in their accounting practices, and within limits they can treat expenses in such a manner as to cause their reported profits to be relatively high or low. If it is true, for example, that the public affiliates are under pressure to report higher earnings in order to stimulate the prices of their holding company stock, they have some opportunity for doing so.[1]

It is quite clear that a corporation with an eye on the stock market has ample reason for reporting higher income since stocks are valued in terms of the earning ratio: the higher ratio, when a given multiplier is applied, obviously inflates the stock value. We would expect stock associations to pay considerable attention to their accounting procedures with respect to reported income. Furthermore, there is considerable logic in building net earnings simply because it is one of the tests of efficiency. To the extent that mutual associations exhibit a rather casual attitude, they represent less efficient economic institutions in the role of financial intermediaries.

Homogeneity and Aggregation. A problem arising when using citywide data is that the aggregation of the results for a number of associations may conceal different intracity market structures. To illustrate, Philadelphia might contain many relatively small associations, each typically less than $25 million in assets. On the other hand, Cleveland, with the same new loan volume, might have only a few large associations, each typically greater than $150 million in assets. It is possible that the differences in expenses would reflect differences in relative size rather than organization or product mix. To ignore this problem is to implicitly assume that the market structures in each city are homogeneous. It was therefore necessary to test for the influence of size differences.

Three different measures of size was devised. The hypothesis was that if allowance is made for variations in product mix, differences in the market structure would show some palpable impact on the expenses. The first and most obvious test was a simple one of the number of associations. The question was whether a variation in number would effect expenses. Unfortunately, the number criterion is unsatisfactory because it fails to reflect the differences in concentration when several large firms with 90% of the industry's assets are surrounded by a hundred very small firms. To meet this problem, two additional tests were devised.

The second test was a simple concentration index in which the largest three, five and ten associations were represented by their percentage share of total assets. The third test merely took their actual assets and hypothesized that in areas where the assets of the largest three, five or ten associations were large, there would be some effect on expenses: assets were a proxy to reflect the influence of concentration on market structure.

Determinants of Expenses

When expenses are broken down in terms of their component parts, it is seen that "the most important operating expense is compensation, which takes about half of each expense dollar."[2] The apparent reason is that the savings and loan industry is basically a service industry: services are provided with respect to financial intermediation. On the one hand, the association in exchange for savings creates shares. On the other hand, the funds derived from the savings' shares are used to finance both home purchase and the construction of new homes. Most of such activities involve payment for services rendered within the association in this financial intermediation.

Differences in expenses between associations may be due to a number of factors. Recent investigations have dismissed the importance of the size of the association. For example, Kendall concludes that "though there are significant variations in the operating ratios of associations, the variation cannot be attributed to the size of the institution."[3] "Apparently, economies of scale are not so readily available to mortgage lending institutions dealing in essentially local markets. . . . Competitive influences may well raise expenses in the larger cities as associations seeking to match one another in services rendered to customers, but the differences are not revealed as significant by the figures." Apparently, it is an imperfect market, insomuch as competition is generally expected to reduce expenses, i.e., the needling effect of maintaining low expense ratios in order to survive. However, at least one view, derived from "monopolistic competition" theory, has argued that "monopoly" influences, in an imperfect market, would raise expenses.[4] But this can hardly be laid at the door of competition; nor has the theory itself been substantiated operationally.

The differences in the expense ratios are attributed by Kendall to the following: (1) the number of services offered to customers; (2) differences in efficiency in handling transactions; (3) the number of separate offices maintained by the institution; (4) temporary overstaffing due to anticipated rapid growth or to other major changes in the near future; (5) percentage of relatively low-yielding loans among the earning assets, e.g., VA and FHA loans; (6) percentage of funds held in the form of lower earning liquid assets. There is also some recognition that there may be "some variation in expense ratios among different sized associations caused primarily by differences in services rendered."[5]

Significance of the Expense Test

It is necessary to inquire not only into the factors behind the use of an expense test but also to evaluate the kinds of expenses. In its 1963 report, the California

Savings and Loan Commissioner suggested a number of tests which allegedly would indicate superior performance. The first test referred to the ratio of expenses to assets: a firm would be considered superior if it had a ratio less than that of the average firm in its size class. For reasons to be discussed later, it is argued that this is a most infelicitous measure inasmuch as it fails to recognize variations in the product mix which respond to the ratio of new loans to assets, the increase in savings, the extent of participation sales and purchases, etc.

Another test noted by the Commissioner was the extent to which an association "has held advertising costs in check."[6] Such a judgment with respect to advertising is egregiously narrow. It fails to recognize the importance of advertising as a competitive weapon—one of a battery of competitive devices that may be chosen from time to time in order to improve an association's competitive market position. Associations that show a higher ratio of advertising expenses may also show a lower level of expenses, both with respect to total assets and absolutely when allowance is made for the product mix. The point to be noted is that advertising is but one of a number of marketing techniques. Each of the alternative techniques involves expenses and some may be preferable for certain purposes as compared to others.

Net Worth Not Significant in
the Mutual

Net worth does not have the same significance in the mutual as it does in the conventional stock corporation or savings and loan association. In the latter, net worth represents both the original paid-up capital plus the reinvestment of earnings. As such, it is the value at any one time of the shareholder's interest in the organization. Investment decisions by management in a profit-oriented enterprise presumably will take into account the rate of return on this net worth. But, in the mutual association, members are not shareholders in the orthodox sense. Though they maintain shares, which may be likened to time deposits in a commercial bank, their interest is in (a) the safety and liquidity of the funds deposited with the association; and (b) the rate of return on those funds. The insurance of those funds by the Federal Savings and Loan Insurance Corporation, as well as efforts by the associations, have converted the shares into liquid assets. This means that the members of a savings and loan association can have immediate access to those funds: the funds can be withdrawn without notice. Given these elements, the saving member of the association takes no further interest. Indeed, they are more properly understood as creditors rather than as owners of the association.

The upshot of this apparent creditor status for the saving-member is that the professional manager is actually responsible to no owner in the ordinary sense. Responsibility consists only in maintaining good relations with the regulatory authorities as represented by both the Insurance Corporation and the Federal Home Loan Bank Board (which since they are one and the same person apparently wear different hats for the different functions).

The consequence is that the management, subject to the constraint that it cannot directly and obviously convert profits into its own pocket, is free to make decisions in its own interest. It need not have the same objective in building up the net worth of the association. In this, it is to be contrasted to the conventional stock association where owner-managers have an interest in net worth because it represents the development of an equity interest in an estate which not only represents wealth for owners but is generally taxable at the lower capital gain rate. This is undoubtedly one of the advantages the stock form has over the mutual form. This being so, funds that might ordinarily go into net worth are likely to be siphoned off in the form of wages and amenities. It follows that, if one is to evaluate the relative performance of mutual associations as compared to stock associations, the ratio of net income to net worth may not be meaningful simply because the net worth is not maximized under the same set of objectives. Other things being equal, if two associations, one a stock association and the other a mutual, earn the same net income, the mutual association might show a higher ratio of return to net worth not because it is more efficient in generating profits, but because it has less incentive to expand the denominator, net worth.

Table 10-1 shows the changes in net worth (reserves) for federally chartered and state-chartered associations existing in California, 1953 to 1962. The California state-chartered associations are almost exclusively of the stock type of organization. The absolute change for the stock associations, during the ten-year period, at $608,000,000, was about twice that for the federally chartered asso-

Table 10-1
Changes in Net Worth and Assets for Surviving California Associations 1953-1962: Federal Compared to Stock

	1953	1962	Absolute Change	% Change
Net Worth				
Federal	97,676	417,243	319,567	327.
State	93,633	701,567	607,934	649.
Total Assets				
Federal	1,440,404	6,097,108	4,656,704	323.
State	1,234,591	9,141,204	7,906,613	640.

Note: The changes include growth through merger and acquisition.

Sources: Federal figures—*1963 Roster of Members*, Federal Home Loan Bank of San Francisco; State figures—*69th Annual Report*, Savings and Loan Commissioner; *Combined Financial Statements: 1962 and 1953* Federal Home Loan and Bank Board.

ciations. In percentage changes, the increase was 649% as compared to 327%. Undoubtedly, the difference is somewhat understated simply because the federally chartered associations operating in the same market as the stock associations had to take on some of the characteristics of the latter in order to remain competitive. It is quite likely that, in the absence of competition with stock associations, the increase in net worth would have been less. We conclude that the test of relative efficiency, net income as compared to net worth, is not meaningful when dealing with mutual associations.

Expenses and Efficiency

The difficulty here arises because the usual tests of net income on net worth or net income on assets are not relevant for the mutual type of organization. Other tests must be utilized. A test which might be appropriate for one type of organization may be inappropriate for the other kind of association. Thus, in the mutual, expenses take on a significance which they do not have in the stock association because the management in the latter has an opportunity to build an estate in the form of the net worth of the organization. Though expenses are one of a number of tests of relative efficiency for the ordinary profit-maximizing institution, they acquire a unique status in the mutual organization. Indeed, the investigator is faced to resort to other less orthodox tests in order to examine the significance of the mutual form. For example, he may look at the growth of assets or net worth; again, consideration may be given to the rate of return on savings. This latter test would seem at first glance to be of the utmost significance in a mutual organization which is allegedly owned by the saving members. But since those saving members have either little reason to take interest in the management of the mutual or little power to do so, the test is without significance. On the other hand, when it is relevant to compare the performance of the mutual with that of the stock association, it might be quite inappropriate to use expenses as a test because of the other management objectives.

Indexes of Efficiency Only in Terms of Objective. The indexes of efficiency are meaningful only in terms of the objectives of the organization. To illustrate, expenses might be taken as illustrative of relative efficiency or inefficiency. It has been observed that

a particular savings and loan firm may adopt a deliberate policy of seeking loans which are relatively expensive to make but which offer relatively high yields and the association may also be actively engaged in the selling of loans or participations. The cost variables of this association would be abnormally high, indicating that it was inefficient, but this might not be the case at all if its higher interest rate and the service charges and loan fees earned on the mortgages sold more than offset its higher expenses, it will have a high rate of return on its assets and one could argue that the association is actually more efficient than another with lower costs but lower returns on assets.[7]

On the other hand, a simple profit margin test with income expressed as a percentage of assets or savings is not satisfactory simply because the margin of profits is not the only test of efficiency. One has only to recall the extremely efficient and profitable retail operations of supermarkets operating on exceptionally low profit margins but earning high absolute profits because of the volume of operation.

It is necessary to be cautious therefore in interpreting expenses either absolutely or relative to assets since the objectives of the enterprises often differ along the lines described. Skepticism would seem to be appropriate before acceptance of the observation by the aforementioned authors that "when annual expenses are expressed as a percentage of average assets or average savings capital held during the year, California associations emerge as relatively high-cost institutions."[8] A group of associations are not relatively inefficient unless there is also reason to believe that the functions performed by the associations are also similar. Furthermore, the lumping together of mutual and stock associations is itself misleading as this discussion will show.

In the abstract, the level of expenses is meaningless. They achieve concreteness only when related to functions performed and objectives of the enterprise. Even if, for example, the stock associations showed higher expenses than the mutual associations, this would not in itself suggest an objectionable level of those same expenses. Expenses may generate income which is profitable. It is, therefore, all the more significant if, with a test meaningful for mutuals, it is possible to show similar conditions prevail for the stock association. Thus, under the case most favorable for mutual associations, i.e., when the test is expenses, an initial effort at making a meaningful comparison is attempted. Other tests are to be considered in a subsequent chapter.

A rational firm will take on additional production or sales when the incremental or marginal revenue exceeds marginal cost. Even though both total costs and average costs increase, the extra income will more than compensate for the extra costs incurred by the expansion. In the savings and loan industry, this is particularly the case when associations are in a market situation permitting the assessment of fees running to amounts of five percent or more of the loan (as is the case with some construction loans).

Table 10-2, which looks only at the 11 states, where data for stock associations are available, compares the ratio of expenses and net incomes to assets. It is noteworthy that in all the states where the expense-to-asset ratios were high, there was also a high ratio of net income to assets. Ability to generate higher income in terms of assets was associated with higher expenses. In seven of the states, the federally chartered associations showed smaller expenses in terms of assets. But, in nine of the states, stock associations showed a higher net income in terms of assets.

Table 10-2

Expenses and Net Income as % Average Assets: Federal Associations Compared to Stock Associations, Stock States, 1962 and 1963

	1962				1963			
	Expenses/ Average Assets		Net Income/ Average Assets		Expenses/ Average Assets		Net Income/ Average Assets	
	Federal	Stock	Federal	Stock	Federal	Stock	Federal	Stock
Arizona	1.53	2.05	4.59	4.85	1.57	1.97	4.09	4.79
California	1.28	1.31	5.11	5.77	1.36	1.42	4.62	4.93
Colorado	1.19	1.48	4.79	5.08	1.39	1.60	4.25	4.41
Idaho	0.98	0.65	4.61	4.85	0.96	0.92	4.23	4.51
Kansas	1.00	1.23^2	4.59	4.42^2	1.06	1.22^2	4.08	4.13^2
Nevada	1.18	1.41	5.08	8.76	1.17	1.80	5.24	6.68
Ohio	1.30	1.28	4.19	4.40	1.31	1.31	4.03	4.21
Oregon	1.19	1.96	4.47	4.45	1.25	1.54	4.56	4.16
Texas	0.99	1.19^2	4.59	4.78^2	1.07	1.22^2	4.36	4.29^2
Utah	1.58	1.52^2	4.75	4.52^2	1.76	1.65^2	3.95	4.07^2
Wyoming	0.99	1.87	4.44	4.72	1.05	1.18	4.16	4.49
All U.S. Associations[1]	1.17		4.54		1.21		4.23	

Notes:

1. Insured associations.

2. Includes state-chartered mutuals as separate data not available.

Source: Federal Home Loan Bank Board. *Combined Financial Statements.* Members of the Federal Home Loan Bank System, op. cit., 1962, 1963.

A profit-oriented enterprise might be expected to show higher expenses because they may be associated with even higher income. Accordingly, comparisons between stock associations and mutual associations should make allowance for income and profits generated. On the other hand, a mutual organization would report higher expenses simply because expenses represents one of the principal means by which the management finds it possible to convert control into some form of pecuniary wealth. As indicated elsewhere, management would use expenses as a device for diversion of income: the association could perform services at little or no cost for management's wholly-owned subsidiary firm; or the association in buying mortgages from a mortgage broker might pay higher prices, thereby enhancing the latter's profits. In this particular form of diversion, management diverts part of the net income of the association.

Regulation and Expenses. The regulatory authorities may have occasion to carefully scrutinize expenses when associations are beginning to exhibit problems. Initially, they would ask for a more detailed breakdown of the expenses. Problems arise when the association has difficulties in meeting its announced dividend rate. In these circumstances, one of the factors contributing to those difficulties is clearly the level of expenses tolerated by the mutual management.

The Measurement of "Output"

The evaluation of expenses requires that they be related to the functions performed. In the usual industrial company, expenses are incurred in the production or output of specific products. To illustrate, an automobile company will turn out so many units of automobiles during a given period for which it has expenses; or a steel company so many tons of steel; a steel container company so many units of steel containers; or a bottle manufacturing company so many units of glass containers. The problem is to specify the unit of output in the savings and loan association during the period for which the expenses have occurred. A savings and loan association is similar to other financial intermediaries in the sense it creates or produces services which are important for the monetary system.

Professors Gurley and Shaw have contended that in the commercial bank the input is the security against which the output is a demand deposit.[9] The analog for the savings and loan association is somewhat different in that what is created is the savings and loan share. This is against money or a draft on a commercial bank. But there is some question whether this is the proper emphasis for a savings and loan association. According to one authority, the main function of the savings and loan association is to promote the housing industry.[10] In this sense, the orientation is rather toward mortgages rather than toward savings. If this is so, the latter could be regarded as the input with the loans or mortgages as the output.

On the other hand, if one attempts to specify the product of the savings and loan association in terms of the mortgage market, there is a danger of downgrading the savings market. Surely the savings and loan associations create shares for which they receive funds. They are also actively engaged in vigorous competition with commercial banks, insurance companies and other financial intermediaries. And, it is here that the regulatory authorities play a most important role by (1) control of the flow of savings; (2) limitations on brokers' savings; (3) prohibition of new savings and loan associations from increasing the share rate and existing associations from going beyond the ceiling; (4) pressures on associations seeking to increase the rate; and (5) regulations aimed at restricting the growth of savings. It is therefore misleading to place the entire emphasis with respect to product on the mortgage market.

Commercial banks and savings and loan associations are similar in that where the former creates a demand deposit, the latter creates a share. In the two instances, the gain to the institution comes from the uses of what is created. In creating a demand deposit, a commercial bank makes a loan from which interest is earned. A savings and loan association borrows and pays interest. It is the output or production of shares which make possible the loans which ultimately pay interest. The saving input is converted into a security which is held against the share as with a commercial bank security as against the demand deposit. With the savings and loan association, three parties are involved instead of two (note that a time deposit is in this sense identical to a savings and loan share). The savings and loan association exchanges shares for savings: savings in turn are exchanged for a mortgage. But, just as with the commercial bank, the savings and loan shares are considered a liability while securities are assets.

The fundamental problem concerns a definition of the appropriate market for the savings and loan association. It is clear that the savings and loan association actually operates in two principal markets: (a) the market where it competes for savings; (b) and the market in which it competes for mortgages, i.e., where loans are originated as savings are invested.

Output as Assets. At this point, a digression is useful with respect to the conventional expression of expenses. The Federal Home Loan Bank Board following industry usage has treated expenses both as a percentage of assets and savings capital and gross operating income. The usual procedure is to take the ratio of the total operating expenses for a given year to the average assets or savings capital for that year. The latter denominator has been preferred in recent years because it was believed that some associations increased their borrowings at the end of the year either to inflate their size or to show smaller expense-to-asset ratios.

A word also should be noted with respect to the process of averaging the assets or the savings capital. Presumably, the reason is that the expenses incurred during the year should be related to the average amount of assets for that year. This procedure is considered in the present study to be unnecessary. Averaging reduces the base against which expenses are set when an association is growing. Unless there are good reasons why this base should be reduced, there would appear to be no basis for the procedure. A judgment to average must depend upon a prior specification of the output of the savings and loan association.

One of the problems involved in averaging is illustrated in the following. Suppose two associations have identical expenses with respect to the placing of new loans on their books: association A begins with mortgages of $100 and expands to $130 by making $50 worth of new loans, $20 for replacement and $30 growth; B with $300 worth of mortgages also makes new loans of $50 to maintain its portfolio at a zero growth rate. When the identical expenses of $1 for $50 of loans is expressed as a percentage of average mortgages for A, the ratio comes to 0.87, but B, which has a base three times A, has average expenses of 0.38. The latter associations' new loans are a necessary replacement to its portfolio as repayments come in (i.e., B is a mature association). A is lending new savings and thus the expenses on new loans represent a greater percentage of last year's assets (which entered through the averaging process). The significance of this illustration is that the expenses have to be related to the functions which they perform, rather than to some arbitrary base.

The Expense-to-Asset Ratio. The conventional measure of expenses is secured by taking a ratio of total operating expenses during the year to the average assets. Now what is the meaning of this ratio? Are we to infer that when one association or region has a higher ratio as compared to another it is less efficient?[11] Certainly, such an inference would be invalid unless evidence was provided that the two associations or regions were performing identical functions. Or, even were there reasonable similarity in their product mix, one could certainly not infer relative inefficiency if the high-cost associations were earning higher income. Therefore, the value in using this ratio ultimately must depend upon the purposes or objectives involved. If it is supposed to be a basis for a judgment as to relative efficiency, adjustments of the type already indicated would be necessary. For our purposes, we want to find out what the expenses are in order to evaluate the relative efficiency of mutual associations as compared to stock associations. Clearly, it is necessary to allow for the variations in services performed or product mix.

There are a number of problems involved in using the expense-to-asset ratio. For example, assets may be increased by the aforementioned borrowing from the Federal Home Loan Bank Boards—all of which increase the denominator relative to expenses and make for a lower ratio. The asset denominator also assumes that all the expenses for the association were for servicing: that each mortgage on the books makes an equal contribution to the expenses. But we know that there are other expenses: origination expense, promotion of new savings, servicing of mortgages which have been sold to associations in other areas. Not only are the expenses not limited exclusively to the servicing of mortgages, there is no reason for believing that each mortgage makes an *equal* contribution to expenses. Particularly, in the case of participations, the amount of servicing required on certain accounts may be greater than that on other accounts. The same factor may be generalized with respect to the *kinds* of borrowers or mortgages held. Obviously, when the slow asset ratio is higher, i.e., when there is more real estate owned by the association due to foreclosure, some of the assets will be more expensive than others.

There are difficulties in the use of a ratio for comparisons either over time or between different areas in that changes may occur in the denominator in one period or there may be a difference in the denominator as between geographical areas. To illustrate, between 1950 and 1963, nationally, the average life of a mortgage rose from 4.31 years to 6.99 years, i.e., 62.2%. If the expenses expressed as a ratio remained the same for the two periods at 1.30, the ratio could be misleading. This is because with the increase in the length of time the mortgages remain on the book, the association does less in replacing loans and, *cet. par.*, should show lower expenses. Ignore for the moment, servicing costs and note that a meaningful comparison requires some deflation of the denominator.

It makes no sense to compare ratios unless denominators represent the same kinds of activities in the different periods or for the different areas. A denominator which allowed for the same average life for the mortgages would have used a weight of 2.11 which is proportional to the longer life. Similar adjustments would also have to be made for increases in the average size of mortgages: comparisons which fail to make allowance for such changes are equally meaningless. Thus, when allowance is made for the 1950-63 increase in the average loan balance of 165%, the comparable expense-to-asset ratio is 3.56 which is 140% greater than the figure 1.44 for 1950. Even, if allowance is made for an average increase in wages of 69%, the appropriate change from 1950 would have been no greater than 1.91. Adjustment would also have to be made to a 29% reduction in the new loans to assets in order to reflect a reduced amount of activity. This would lower the ratio again.

In comparing the California stock associations to the federally chartered associations, there are some further differences deserving comment. The comparison has validity since both obviously operated in the same market area. Thus, it is noteworthy that while compensation for the stock associations was 43.3% higher than the federal associations, their new loan activity was 104% higher. When compensation is expressed as a ratio to assets, the federals reported 0.55 while the much more active stock associations showed 0.51. The stock associations *total* expenses showed the figure 49.5% higher, roughly one-half of their new loan activity. The stock associations were able to make twice as many new loans with but 43.3% more compensation or 49.5% higher total expenses. This in turn gave the stock associations 81% more net income. This higher net income was associated with only 62.6% more in assets. Inasmuch as the federal and stock associations serviced about the same proportion of old loans, the differences in expenses must be attributed to new loans.

The misleading character of the expense-to-asset ratio is suggested by scrutiny of Table 10-3. The ratios are for the United States without California and Federal and Stock association in California for the two years, 1962 and 1963. The expense ratio for the stock associations at 1.31 and 1.42 is slightly higher than that for the mutuals in California; but it is considerably higher than the United States average. But the next column reveals what those expenses produced. In each of the two years, the California stock associations made twice as many new loans relative to their assets as did associations elsewhere. While their expenses were three to six percent larger than that reported by the federals, they generated thirty percent more new loans. But even more significantly, the extra expenses were associated with additional income according to column (3). Evi-

Table 10-3
U.S. Compared to California, Mutual and Stock Associations: Selected Variables

	(1) Expenses ÷ Average Assets	(2) New Loans ÷ Average Assets	(3) Gross Op. Income ÷ Ave. Assets	(4) Fees ÷ Loans Made	(5) Dividends ÷ Average Saving Cap.	(6) Allocation to Reserve & Surplus ÷ Ave. Net Worth
1962						
U.S. less Calif. Insured Members FHLB	1.14	21.3	5.55	1.49	4.01	12.6
Calif. Federals	1.28	31.8	6.38	2.32	4.59	18.1
Calif. Stock	1.31	41.3	7.10	3.14	4.84	22.0
1963						
U.S. less Calif.	1.17	21.2	5.48	1.29	4.04	9.3
Calif. Federals	1.36	34.9	6.31	2.14	4.72	11.8
Calif. Stock	1.42	45.1	6.60	2.77	4.78	15.4

Source: Federal Home Loan Bank Board, *Combined Financial Statements, 1961-1963* and *Source Books 1962-1964*, Washington, D.C.

dence with respect to fees in column (4) shows that the stock associations were able to collect more income by higher charges (relative to assets).

Perhaps the most revealing part of the data is that which reports on dividends paid to savers and additions to net worth. Each year, both dividends and contributions to reserves were higher. This behavior is hardly consistent with the judgment that their higher expenses indicates inefficiency.

Assets. Inasmuch as the conventional procedure consists of expressing the particular statistic in terms of assets, there would seem to be ample reason for placing that element on the other side of an expense regression equation. Rather than using it as the denominator in a ratio of doubtful validity, it is preferably treated as one of the variables on the righthand side of the equation along with new loans, new savings, the number of savings accounts and the number of mortgages. The basis for the decision must depend upon the purpose of the investigation.

The orthodox statement of expenses on assets follows from the effort to express expenses in some form that permits comparisons between financial units or areas of different size. It is widely believed that differences in expense ratios indicate variations in relative efficiency. For example, Grebler and Brigham concluded that the California associations were high cost because their expense-to-assets ratios were higher than the national average. This conclusion was maintained in spite of a recognition that product mix variations could be most important. As noted earlier, the expense-to-asset ratio implicitly assumes that the *ceteris paribus* condition is met. Otherwise, the comparisons are entirely without meaning. There is no reason, however, to make the assumption that each association and area is homogeneous with respect to activities performed. If assets are to enter the model as an explanatory variable, they must appear on the righthand side of the equation. In that event, assets must be considered in terms of the contribution they make to expenses.

The assets of savings and loan associations are revealed by their balance sheets. The principal one is, of course, first mortgages held. Other assets of relatively modest significance are: buildings and furnishings, cash and bonds and stock in the Federal Home Loan Bank. It is obvious that assets contribute to expenses through the investment in mortgages. On the liabilities' side, the major item of expenses results from the acquisition and servicing of savings accounts.

Assets and liabilities involve expenses of two types: the acquisition and servicing of mortgages; and the acquisition and servicing of savings. Data are directly available with respect to each component. There is no necessity for considering an aggregate such as either assets or liabilities. Indeed, assets is not a good variable because it *includes* the two functions that are more properly treated separately—loan acquisitions and their servicing. Thus, the inclusion along with new loans and the number of mortgages is to double count since the actual activities, for which assets is at best a proxy variable, are new loans and their servicing. The same comments are appropriate for liabilities as a proxy for the acquisition and servicing of accounts.

Expenses and Assets

The expense-asset ratio is exclusively concerned only with the marginal expenses. To illustrate, compare a savings and loan association to a vineyard. A grower might be expected to *maintain* the number of vines intact during the year. In some instances, he would make additions. Though the vines planted in previous years produce income, they require servicing or harvesting. The principal expense, however, is in the cost of land, seed and planting in an earlier period. There is also a normal attrition rate in the vines: as they age, some portion must be replaced so that new plantings originate in both additions and necessary replacements. It is incorrect to treat the expenses from those new vines as the total expenses incurred in that year relative to all the vines. The two varities of expenses should not be lumped together. The current expenses relate only to (a) the servicing of existing vines; (b) the replacement of vines that have died; and (c) net additions.

The *total* costs of the vines are not just the costs incurred this year. This years' costs are the direct costs of cultivation, harvesting and replacing plus those from new vines, etc. These latter are but part of the *total* costs for all the vines. Isolation of the costs incurred this year in terms of the new vines would provide some idea of the cost only of the new vines. It is misleading to relate these costs to *all* the vines which includes those planted in previous years.

Changes in costs are not exclusively related to changes in vines since (a) some growers may be replacing old vines with new and different kinds of vines which may be more expensive and involve more land because of different grapes and methods; (b) due to differences in the grape, the life of the vines may vary. Thus, a higher replacement rate might be associated with higher prices and, consequently, a higher income-to-expense ratio, i.e., if the replacement rate increased; or if it is higher initially.

The total costs for all the vines might in some instances be computed as this year's costs multiplied by the number of years it takes to equal the present amount of the vines. When this year's planting represents 60% of the expenses and each vine lasts five years, each of the extra four years' 10% sums at unity. If the annual total expenses are 1% of assets, and one year's new plantings represents on the average 20% of the assets, it must be multiplied by five to yield 5%. Returning to savings and loan associations, it could be argued that the expense-to-assets ratio actually does indicate the average costs of the assets on the books. Sixty percent is the cost of the new loans and the 40% is divided equally among the older assets—their service cost. But another savings and loan association or area with a different turnover or ratio of new loans to assets would have higher expenses. But these are not the entire expenses involved: they are simply the variable costs. Their total cost are the costs of acquisition amortized over their entire life.

It follows that a distinction should be made between the variable and fixed cost. First, there are acquisition costs for the new loans. Second, are the servicing costs, prepayment costs, deposit costs, promotional costs, and the costs of running and maintaining the buildings and furnishings. The critical question is the relevant expenses for *all* the assets. Consider the case where there are no costs other than for acquisition. In the vineyard example, there would be no expenses to the grower (e.g., where the vines are contracted out, as with the harvest, to another individual or firm). All costs are attributable to the replacement of vines lost through normal attrition. Since there are no other expenses, expenses are related to new vines only. Or new loans. When expenses are compared to the relevant assets, it is to the new loans. But it will not make any difference if the denominator is total assets for in that case *all* the expenses are related to the acquisition of those assets. It follows that the ratio of total expenses to total assets will equal the ratio of current expenses to the new loans.

Total Expenses and Replacement Expenses

If expenses are compared to *all* assets, either of two procedures is necessary. First, it is essential to explicitly state that the expenses are only partial in the sense that they are incurred in order to maintain an investment intact (for example, a stable growth rate). Or, second, *all* the expenses incurred in acquiring *all* of the assets must be included. That means that current expenses must be multiplied by the number of years the average asset lasts. If one-third of the yearend assets were acquired during the preceding year, current expenses are multiplied by three; if one-fifth, by five. When total expenses are treated in this sense, the result is identical to using a ratio of expenses to new loans. If expenses are taken as a ratio to assets and multiplied by the reciprocal of new loans over assets, this merely cancels the asset figure in both the denominator and numerator: adjusted expenses over assets are made equal to expenses over new loans. With vines, it is the same as taking the preparation expenses and relating them to the new investment in land and vines (or seedlings).

The usual ratio of expenses over assets tells nothing more than the replacement expenses for maintaining the investment. It is permissible to say that such were the expenses for the period; but it is incorrect to relate those expenses to all the assets. In the illustration, the expenses are only incurred for replacing *part* of the total assets. They are not the total expenses for all assets. Introduction of service costs does not change the argument.

In the savings and loan association, the current operating expenses relate to

(a) replacement of loans paid off; (b) growth; and (c) the service costs from handling mortgage and savings' accounts; and (d) expenses arising in connection with delinquent and foreclosed loans. It follows that if New Jersey has a smaller expense ratio to assets than California, it could be due either to less turnover, slower growth, or relatively fewer scheduled items because of either a smaller percentage of unseasoned loans or different legal arrangements involved in the initiation of foreclosure proceedings. The smaller expense ratio need not reflect less efficiency, but rather less of the other variables. The proper measure of expenses includes the expenses from *all* loans and allowance for these other factors.

The conventional expense-asset ratio covers the four items enumerated above. While the third could appropriately be linked to *all* assets, it still only indicates what the cost is this year for such expenses. The first two also tell how much of the expenses in a given period went for replacement and growth. But why relate to all assets since the latter two were for only part of the assets? Thus, for certain purposes, the expense-to-new-loan ratio is more appropriate. If, however, *all* the assets must be used, *all* the expenses related to them should also be included. It follows that at today's rate of expenses and the rate at which we turn over the loans, we should be able to get the total expenses. The conventional expenses-to-asset ratio merely indicates the expense of replacement at an unknown growth rate plus possibly the influence of scheduled items. It is useless for comparing different regions or savings and loan associations since the information is incomplete. It does not reveal what the replacement or turnover rate was; nor the rate of growth. Nor does it provide the information actually seen, *viz.*, the average costs of placing and carrying all assets. The error consists in using the wrong denominator, *all* assets, when the expenses or at least the major part, are for the new loans. When all the assets are used, all relevant expenses have to be introduced since the principal item was the origination cost.

The Asset Base Overstates the Influence of Assets Acquired in a Previous Period

One major defect of the expense-to-asset ratios is that the bulk of the assets were acquired in previous periods. The same defect would also apply to the expense-to-gross operating income ratio because most of the mortgages contributing to gross operating income were acquired in previous periods. This means that typically expenses are related to an item which, in terms of dollar value, made little contribution during the current period. Relating expenses to total assets implicitly assumes that the numerator and denominator apply to the same year. This is clearly not the case since the bulk of the expenses must be set against only *part* of the assets. The other assets involve relatively minor expenses with respect to servicing of mortgages and savings accounts.

It is generally recognized that these expenses are considerably smaller than those from the origination or placing of new mortgages on the books. Actually, to be consistent, if assets acquired in previous periods are relevant, then we should also add the past expenses from placing those assets. Only then does the time period for expenses correspond to the time period for assets. With expenses, it is incorrect to consider only current expenses as against total assets. This is misleading and deceptive: the actual expenses of making loans are considerably higher and are properly related only to the new loans. In the absence of a showing that both the numerator and the denominator apply to the same time periods, and that there is reasonable homogeneity in the ratios, there is good reason for rejecting this particular test of relative efficiency.

It is as if industrial firms specifically recorded their expenses for one year not relative to that year's production, but to a multiple of the previous years' production. The expenses per unit of output in a savings and loan association will depend upon the relative importance of new loans generated during that year. Of course, yield has to be related to all the assets, but doing so does not justify application of the same denominator to expenses. The relevant question so far as expenses are concerned is the origin or purpose of those expenses. The bulk arose because of new loans—not from servicing.

To provide another analogy, suppose each of two firms make an investment on the premises. If the expenses, as related to the premises, are $1 for A and $2 for B, it does not follow that B is less efficient than A. We must first know whether A and B were in identical industries, providing identical products and services. Thus, B may generate four times as much business in the year as A, so that the expenses as compared to the gross operating income for A is 10% and B 5%. Expenses must be related to what they do, not just to an arbitrary base such as assets.

The general practice involving the quoting of expenses on assets is presumably in order to permit comparisons between associations and areas. But the underlying theory is that it is assets which explain the expenses. When expenses are expressed relative to these assets, they are supposed to mean something in the sense that if A has a higher ratio, it is less efficient. If there are other more important elements in expenses than simply the assets, the conventional procedure is not only meaningless, it is misleading. When assets are supposed to explain expenses, it is assumed that when the expense-to-asset ratio is different, there is a difference in efficiency. The expectation is that equal efficiencies produce equal ratios.

The problem is also indicated in the following illustration. Suppose, for example, the new loans-to-asset ratio is 5%. If, *mutatis mutandis*, the expense-to-asset ratio is 1%, the entire cost involved in this portfolio over its life of twenty years would approximately come to 20%. Alternatively, one could take the 1% on assets and divide by the new loan-asset ratio: 1% over 5% for the new loans each year; or one might multiply the twenty-year period by 1%. Now, suppose in another city, savings and loan associations have a new loan ratio of 20% and the expense-to-asset ratio is still 1%. Since there are four times as many new loans, the expense per dollar of new loans is one-fourth or 5%. Expenses should be related only to the associations *current* activities. When they are related to a previous activity for which they have been made, the only effect is to diminish the ratio. They are a subtle method for understating their true level.

It will be shown in subsequent pages that the product mix is the crucial element. Use of the expense-to-asset ratio is not only misleading, but it understates the expenses of mutual savings and loan associations as compared to the actual functions they perform. The fact that they show a lower expense-to-ratio, as compared to alternative measures, is an indication that this conventional ratio is not necessarily the appropriate measuring device. The major defect is that it understates actual expenses as compared to the services performed by the mutual associations. Actually, it is rational for the mutual associations to relate expenses to assets. By performing less services during the year, they are able to keep expenses down so that they seem reasonable. The ratio on assets is simply a means to bring in assets acquired in previous years: with little or no expenses, they deflate the expense ratio.

Table 10-4 reveals the rather extreme fluctuations for the expense-to-assets ratio, e.g., when Massachusetts is compared to California. These variations are associated with large differences in the new loans-to-assets ratios. The same is

Table 10-4
New Loans and Expenses as a % of Assets: Largest States, 1962

Leading States	New Loans/ Average Assets	Rank	Expenses/ Average Assets	Rank
California	37.5	1	1.30	1
Florida	20.6	7	1.25	4
Illinois	21.9	5	1.20	6
Indiana	21.6	6	1.28	3
Massachusetts	13.4	13	0.95	12
Michigan	18.7	11	1.23	5
Missouri	22.1	4	1.10	8
New Jersey	19.9	8	0.98	11
New York	15.9	12	1.06	10
Ohio	23.3	3	1.30	2
Pennsylvania	18.6	10	1.08	9
Texas	23.8	2	1.11	7
Wisconsin	19.0	9	0.81	13
U.S. Mean	24.6		1.17	

Source: Federal Home Loan Bank Board, Combined Financial Statements, Members of the Federal Home Loan Bank System, 1962, Washington, D.C.

true when growth of assets is substituted for new loans. On the basis of 1962 data for insured savings and loan associations, a smaller new loan-to-asset ratio for Massachusetts at 64% was associated with a 27% smaller expense-to-asset ratio, i.e., a 1% lower new loan-to-asset ratio was associated with only 0.4% lower expenses-to-asset ratio. As later data will show, expenses have their principal origin in loan acquisitions or originations. The servicing costs are incidental and fairly stable; and so far as variances between associations and cities are concerned, it is the composition of the total product—with new loans and new savings the critical determinants in expense differences.

Finally, use of expenses over assets actually involves a judgment that assets are the output of the savings and loan association. To a considerable degree, the assets of an association are mortgages. The latter is more meaningful. When mortgages are viewed as the output of the association, it becomes clear that error is involved. The mortgages on the books at the end of the year (or averaged) are definitely not the current output related to the current operating costs. These mortgages have been acquired in previous years. It is true that there are some expenses in connection with servicing, but they hardly represent as much as 25% of total cost. Nor do they provide much assistance in explaining variances between different areas. The annual output of the association is a composite made up principally of new loans with the servicing of mortgage and savings accounts of secondary importance.

Expenses Measured as a Percent of Gross Operating Income

All that has been said with respect to expenses over assets is equally true for the expenses-to-gross operating income ratio. The trouble with both is that they are ratios. This means that while there is no change in real expenses, variations in the denominator, assets or gross operating income change the ratio. There could be a decline in expenses/assets and expenses/gross operating income when an association purchases loans from mortgage brokers. Internal expenses may be less, but the net income is also reduced. This is particularly rational in a period when incomes are rising as interest rates and fees are both moving upward. Thus, where there has been no actual decline in expenses, the change on the income side reduces the ratio. This phenomenon is particularly relevant for eastern associations: when they buy participations in California mortgages, average yield and income is enlarged and expenses reduced since they have neither origination nor servicing costs.

The income figure is further inflated by income derived from previous years. Would it not be more appropriate to take, for example, only fee income which reflects supply and demand forces? Though expenses could be relatively high, the fee-income ratio would fall when income was inflated by demand forces.

Even new loans have the defect of double counting, as with shifts from construction to home purchase loans (where the savings and loan association may be a short-term financier or interim financier as well as long-term). All such differences make the comparisons based on expenses over assets confusing as well as erroneous. Rarely are the conditions so identical as to permit meaningful comparisons. Simply because Los Angeles has a higher expense-to-asset ratio than New York, it does not follow it is less efficient. Additional information is required with respect to the product mix. In California, the expense-to-asset ratio is 0.35 and 0.24 larger than that for Massachusetts and New York; but the new loan-to-asset ratio is three times that of Massachusetts and twice that of New York.

Number of Mortgages

The use of the *number* as a substitute for the dollar volume is no improvement. Number has all the defects associated with assets, plus additional ones as well. To illustrate, when they are related to a specific period. If expenses in the savings and loan operation were only for servicing mortgages, it would be quite proper to use either the dollar value of mortgages, assets or another proxy. But use of the number of mortgages errs simply because the loans are not homogeneous.

There are various types and kinds of loans. There are also a variety of borrowers and lenders for whom the savings and loan association may service the mortgage. To illustrate, refinancing is often cheaper than putting a new loan on the books because the credit worthiness of the borrower has already been established, the residence appraised, and the loan by this time is seasoned. Loans also vary as to the location and materials of the residence to be financed. Loans on multiple units such as apartment houses are different from the single family dwelling; and, of course, loans for other purposes, e.g., churches, YMCAs and bowling alleys, have their peculiar characteristics. But in any case, the number of mortgages is allowed for in a multiple regression analysis as one of the independent variables contributing to total expenses.

New Loans

The savings and loan association performs a number of services or functions. Obviously, an association initiates its activities through creating shares in return for the deposit of savings. The next step is to achieve a certain level of those savings so they can be put to work in such a way that they will return a yield sufficient to cover both the dividend paid to the savers and the expenses involved in running the operation. This means that it must act as a financial intermediary in the assembling and lending of savings for both new construction and the purchase of homes. A principal activity as well as contributor to the expense of a savings and loan association is the origination of loans. Not only must the applicant's credit worthiness be investigated, the prospective site and home must be appraised as well as the general area in the light of prevailing economic trends. Once the loan is approved, there is a further problem of servicing: mortgage payments must be collected when due; the property must be insured; and, ultimately, arrangements are necessary for the termination of the mortgage contract. But these latter expenses are relatively incidental as compared to the initial costs involved in placing that loan on the books.

The association's output is largely focused on the volume of new loans. They also are the major source of income to the association. Apart from the mortgage interest, income in an association is derived from fees[b] in loan origination, commissions, and prepayment penalties. If one function were to be chosen as the output, new loans would clearly be more appropriate than assets. But it is not necessary to choose one. The appropriate test of efficiency is in terms of the various functions performed by the association, each considered in terms of their relative contribution. New loans are not only an item entering into expenses: they are of major significance in explaining the variance in expenses between different associations and areas. Subsequent analysis will confirm this judgment.

There is, however, a problem involved in treating new loans as an independent determinant or variable in a model involving expenses. It is difficult to use them simultaneously with assets. It is therefore necessary to ascertain the relative importance of each. One difficulty in including both assets and new loans in the same model is that the assets whether taken as an average figure for the year, or year-end, include the new loans made during that year. This means that there is considerable overlap and multicollinearity between the two. In order to avoid this overlap, year-end assets can be adjusted by subtraction of new loans for that period. A net or adjusted asset or mortgage figure is derived. This is not completely satisfactory since the new loans, a flow during the year, also include construction loans which may not appear on the books at the year-end. However, a preferable method is to use the number of savings accounts or mortgages. Either is a reasonable proxy and reduces the problems arising from double counting.

Adjusted Expenses?

Some investigations subtract from operating expenses the amounts for advertising and promotion.[12] It is not altogether clear why this is necessary. Presumably, the reason is that expenses less advertising would appear to represent

---

[b]In the boom years, 1950-65, fee income averaged one-sixth of all annual income nationally and one-fifth in a rapidly growing state such as California.

the actual expenses involved in running the association. The advertising and promotion expenses are related to the growth of savings as well as new loans. But, inasmuch as concern is with *total* expenses, and since advertising is part of those expenses, there is no reason why the advertising should be excluded. It may be noted parenthetically that so far as comparisons between mutual and stock associations are concerned, exclusion of advertising does not make for significant difference with respect to the operating comparisons.

Absolute Data Preferred to Ratios

The problem is to derive an estimated expense figure for mutual savings and loan associations which takes account of variations in the product mix. Allowance must be made for the different kinds of output or services rendered by savings and loan associations. This calls for a multiple regression model which makes it possible to predict expenses from a set of variables, e.g., new loans, number of mortgages, number of savings accounts, real estate owned, etc. From the product mix, presumably, one can predict expenses.

Most students of financial organizations have treated expenses as a ratio in one form or another. Typically, they are related to assets. Not a few have concluded that higher expense-to-asset ratios meant not only higher costs but less efficiency.[13] Even a conscious awareness of the importance of variations in product mix has not precluded an adverse judgment on those operations reporting a relatively high ratio.[14] It is suggested that the proper method for treating the problem is to place assets on the righthand side of the equation. Instead of concluding that a higher ratio meant inefficiency, one would inquire into the differentiating elements which might have been responsible for the difference in the ratio.

The problem undoubtedly arises because of interest in *relative* performance. Information is sought with respect to how an association performs as compared to other associations; regulators are interested in the comparable performance of certain areas and types of organizations. All seek to make meaningful comparisons. But rarely is there allowance for the above-mentioned differences in activities or product mix.

If a ratio is to be used, it might appear that other ratios could be devised to take care of the problems with respect to variations in the types of activities. Thus, one might relate the expenses-to-asset ratio to average savings account, to average mortgage size, or the rate of growth and buildings and equipment as a percentage of average assets.[15] In the latter two instances, the denominator is identical with that used for expenses, while in the first two (the average size of the savings account and the average mortgage size) the numerator is close to the asset denominator. There is the usual danger that the expense denominator is related to its reciprocal on the other side of the equation. But, even more serious, the expression of all the variables in terms of assets contains an unacceptable implicit hypothesis that the variables, including expenses, are preferably expressed in terms of assets. Apart from the double counting, this hypothesis needs to be proved not assumed.

It may be that assets are important in determining the level of expenses in some unexplained way. It is relatively simple to test the hypothesis by using absolute data: assets are placed on the righthand side of the equation along with other factors which seem to have importance in determining the level of expenses. Clearly, such an approach necessitates the use of a multiple regression model.

11

The Sources of Data
For the Expense Model

This chapter discusses the problems faced in assembling the data necessary for the building of the regression models. The major issue concerned the limitations and shortcomings in the ways data are reported. Reliance was necessarily placed on two sources of information: city data which aggregated the results for associations and data of Los Angeles federal and stock associations for the year 1963. The difficulties faced are discussed in the following sections.

In each instance, the data are cross-sectional. However, it was possible to secure information for stock associations for the years 1961-1965. Fifteen areas reported the results for the stock. They were combined with the observations for thirty-eight Standard Metropolitan Statistical Areas for a total number of observations of fifty-three. In some instances, the stock observations were for geographical areas identical with that for mutual associations, e.g., Los Angeles, San Francisco, Oregon, Arizona and Colorado. Some of the mutual observations included a relatively small proportion of stock associations. But in no instance was the stock influence larger than fifteen percent of the total assets for the reporting area.

Selection of the Cities

One of the problems confronting an analysis of expenses in the mutual savings and loan industry is that data are not generally available in the form necessary to test the hypotheses. Generally, it is aggregated for federally chartered savings and loan associations within states. It is difficult, if not impossible, to secure data for individual mutual or federally chartered associations. The Savings and Loan Commissioner of the State of California does provide the operating results for the state-chartered (which are predominately stock associations); and, of course, the Federal Home Loan Bank Board, in its Combined Financial Statements, gives aggregate data for the *State of California* both with respect to the federally chartered associations and the state-chartered associations. However, there are discrepancies between the two sources of data. In recent years, the numbers reported by the California Commissioner have typically been higher than those of the Federal Home Loan Bank Board for their members. The California Savings and Loan Commissioner refers to all state-chartered associations. Inasmuch, as the latter exceeds the members in the Federal Home Loan Bank System, it is not surprising that the numbers should be higher.

Therefore, to analyze the performance with respect to expenses of mutual associations, it is necessary to have recourse to several series of data as provided by the Federal Home Loan Bank Board. The Combined Financial Statements of the Federal Home Loan Bank Board has separate reports for all member associations of the system within the state; the insured savings and loan associations; the federally chartered associations; the insured state-chartered associations; and the uninsured member state-chartered associations. In addition, the Board reports for member associations within the largest standard statistical metropolitan areas. The data combine the federally chartered and the state-chartered members.

The Combined Financial Statements also provide information with respect to real estate owned, contract of sale, total operating expenses, the dollar value of mortgages held, the dollar value of savings accounts and reserves. In addition, the Federal Home Loan Bank Board publishes a Source Book on the flow of savings under the headings of new savings, withdrawals and net savings. This information refers to those members insured with the Federal Savings and Loan Insurance Corporation, an arm of the Federal Home Loan Bank System. Not all members are insured with the Federal Savings and Loan Insurance Corporation. Additional data are furnished with respect to loans made which are further subdivided into construction loans, home purchase, and other loans.

One of the most important problems confronting the investigator results from the lack of purity in the cities. By this is meant that the data combine federally chartered associations with state-chartered stock associations in varying proportions. The only way to escape this impure mixture is to fall back on data with respect to federally insured associations within respective states. One set of results, therefore, refers only to areas in which mutual associations have been considered. Thus, there are 37 states in which all the associations are both insured and of the mutual type. Results are shown for these 37 states plus the results for the federally chartered or mutual associations in 11 other states.

There are drawbacks in relying exclusively upon state data. The principal is that the state data (an aggregate which combines the results for the entire state) lump together widely separated market areas. In order to deal with market areas in which the supply and demand conditions would be assumed to have some significance and homogeneity, it is preferable to refer to the standard metropolitan statistical areas. The Federal Home Loan Bank Board's Source Book provides the data with respect to both insured associations for the states as well as the 40 largest standard statistical metropolitan areas. The advantage of dealing with these largest cities is that they are meaningful economic units. The associations within them would be expected to respond to the same economic forces operating in both mortgage and savings markets. The individual differences between the market areas are not offset through that combination of different market areas which occurs when the state data are relied upon exclusively.

Within the states, there are difficult problems. A look at Table 11-1 shows the

Table 11-1

Distribution of Assets between Mutual and Stock Associations within Stock States, 1965

States	Stock % of State Chartered	Stock% of all Associations Federal and State Chartered
Arizona	100	47
California	97	60
Colorado	86	41
Idaho	100	10
Kansas	69	29
Nevada	100	84.1
Ohio	54	30
Oregon	95	28
Texas	77	46
Utah	73	38
Washington	10	2.5
Wyoming	100	7

Source: Federal Home Loan Bank Board, *Combined Financial Statements*, Washington, D.C. and respective states Savings and Loan Associations *Reports.*

distribution of assets between the federally chartered and stock associations within the states. It is significant that there are few states which could be called pure in the sense that the use of the Federal Home Loan Bank Board data with respect to the state-chartered institutions can be taken to indicate the performance of the stock associations. Not even in the largest state, California, do the stock associations embrace 100% of the assets of all the state-chartered associations. Colorado at 86% shows a larger difference; Kansas is 69% and Ohio at 54%. Thus, there are problems in interpreting data with respect to state-chartered stock associations within the states—since the performance of the stock associations is mixed with mutuals. Only the smaller Western states showed purity. It is also worthwhile to note that the percentages of assets held by the stock associations for all the associations within the states range from 2.5% to a high of 84.1% in Nevada.

Basis for Elimination of Certain Cities. The problem in dealing with the cities is that when the stock associations represent a substantial proportion of the assets or activity of associations within that city, they will obviously alter the operating performance. It is necessary to set up some mechanism which takes account of the specific contributions of the stock based on their significance in a particular market area.

It is not a simple matter of taking the stock share of assets, e.g., Ohio's at 30% and assuming that the stock influence is 30%. Obviously, a competitive influence may far exceed the actual market share at any one time. To illustrate, the California stock associations increased their market penetration from 41.9 in 1950 to 66.3% by 1964, (see Table 4-1). The problem is to concentrate on expenses in mutual associations. Therefore, a rule is necessary in order to discriminate with respect to both the inclusion and exclusion of certain cities on the basis of the importance of the stock associations in that area. Clearly, if stock associations are predominant in an area, the results from including such a city would reflect the competitive activity of stock associations. The question is what percentage of assets held by stock associations will exclude or not exclude certain cities.

Cities Embracing Mutual and Stock Associations., The accompanying Table 11-2 shows the share of assets held by stock associations in cities which permit that form. In four of the five California cities, included in the 40 largest standard metropolitan statistical areas, the proportion of assets held by stock associations exceeded 50%. It seemed clear that such cities should not be included in a

Table 11-2
Percent of Assets Held by Stock Associations in Cities Permitting that Form of Organization: 40 Largest, 1962

Chicago	8.2
Cincinnati	16.2
Cleveland	49.7
Columbus	37.8
Dallas	42.9
Dayton	7.2
Denver	28.8
Houston	91.0
Kansas City	11.4
Los Angeles	57.8
Phoenix	54.4
Portland, Oregon	35.8
San Antonio	12.2
San Bernardino-Riverside	57.8
San Diego	21.1
San Francisco	54.7
San Jose	99.0
Seattle	11.5

Source: State Savings and Loan Commissioners' Reports, FHLBB, *Combined Financial Statements.*

sample to be subjected to statistical tests. The reason is obvious—the stock associations in those four cities are not only in the majority but they clearly determine the set of competitive actions and responses. Inclusion in the model would create a problem of evaluating the particular significance of the high stock contribution. For similar reasons, Phoenix, Arizona, was rejected since the stock associations in that city at 54.4% would equally justify exclusion.

Other excluded cities, on similar grounds, were Houston where stock associations had 91% and Cleveland at 49.7%—which was on the margin but seemed to clearly show a large stock influence. The table shows a range in the remaining cities of 37.8% for Columbus, Ohio, down to 7.2% for Dayton, Ohio.

This left 25 cities in which all the associations were mutual plus six impure cities where the mutuals had more than 83% of the assets (see Table 11-3). The next question is whether stock associations in a city where their importance ranges from 17% to 43% will exert an independent influence on the outcome of the analysis. There is no question that since they are in the minority, and in some cases a very small minority, they do not represent a dominant influence in such cities. Therefore, though the observation is impure, the dominant influence would be the mutual associations. However, a few words are necessary with respect to the potential influence of the stock associations on the results.

Impact of Stock Associations when in Same Market

The impact of the stock associations in cities where they coexist with mutuals could take either of three forms. First, their influence could be negative in the sense that their activities would generally result in a lower level of expenses. If this were the case, it could hardly be said that inclusion of the stock associations had inflated expenses, thereby increasing the regression coefficients and causing an unfavorable comparison with the California stock associations. The problem of inclusion of stock associations arises only in another connection. But where the effect is to dampen the expenses, there is no basis for rejecting later conclusions with respect to unfavorable comparisons.

There is, however, another difficulty. Table 11-4 shows the ratio of loans made to total mortgages and provides a comparison of stock cities and pure mutual cities for 1963. If only the 25 pure cities are included, a substantial part of mutual associations in the nation are ignored. Furthermore, another bias is introduced: where one potential bias is the influence of stock associations, the table shows another, viz., a slower rate of activity among pure mutual cities. Where the latter is measured by the ratio of loans made to the dollar value of mortgages held, the 16 stock cities range from 21.4% to 70.8%, with an average of 41.6%. The mutual cities range from 16.9% to 37.3%, with the average of 24.6%. The stock average is 69% higher than the mutual. Consequently, exclu-

Table 11-3
Areas Represented in Sample by Type of Organization

Pure Mutual	Where Assets Held by Mutual Larger than 83%	Federal Associations Only	Stock Associations Only
Albany	Chicago	Phoenix-Tucson	Akron
Atlanta	Cincinnati	Colorado	Anaheim
Baltimore	Dayton	Los Angeles	Arizona
Birmingham	Kansas City	Oregon	Colorado
Boston	San Antonio	San Bernardino	Houston
Buffalo	Seattle	San Diego	Los Angeles
Detroit		San Francisco	Nevada
Indianapolis			Oregon
Louisville			Sacramento
Memphis			San Bernardino
Miami			San Diego
Milwaukee			San Francisco
Minneapolis			San Jose
Newark			Santa Barbara
New Orleans			Stockton
New York			
Norfolk			
Patterson			
Philadelphia			
Pittsburgh			
Providence			
Rochester			
St. Louis			
Tampa			
Washington, D.C.			

sion of the 16 impure cities excluded cities which have been more active in the loan market. When it is recalled that the principal activity of savings and loan associations is the financing of new construction, it is obvious that exclusion of these cities introduces a downward and equally objectionable bias.

It should be recalled that the purpose of the analysis is to consider the expenses of mutual savings and loan associations in *all* activities. Concentration simply on the pure mutual cities represent an exclusive preoccupation with cities operating on a less active basis. It is as if a study of the automobile industry excluded General Motors Corporation on grounds that it is not a pure automobile firm because it also manufactures refrigerators, diesel locomotives, and buses. The most important product turned out by General Motors is auto-

Table 11-4

"Loans Made" as a % of Total Mortgages, 1963: Cities Permitting Stocks Associations Compared to Exclusively Mutual Cities

Exclusively Mutual Cities[2]	"Loans Made" ÷ Total Mortgages[1]	Cities Permitting Stock Assns.[2]	"Loans Made" ÷ Total Mortgages[1]
Albany	19.0	Chicago	24.2
Atlanta	37.3	Cincinnati	25.6
Birmingham	24.3	Cleveland	32.2
Boston	19.5	Columbus	37.6
Baltimore	23.5	Dallas	39.7
Buffalo	16.9	Dayton	29.6
Detroit	26.6	Denver	32.0
Indianapolis	22.6	Houston	35.2
Louisville	24.4	Kansas City	21.4
Miami	21.7	Los Angeles	53.5
Milwaukee	26.1	Phoenix	70.8
Minneapolis	23.6	Portland	35.8
Newark	22.5	San Antonio	26.4
New Orleans	31.7	San Bernardino	59.9
New York	17.8	San Diego	37.6
Patterson	26.1	San Francisco	65.1
Philadelphia	22.3	San Jose	63.9
Pittsburgh	18.7	Seattle	31.8
Providence	26.0		
St. Louis	31.5		
Tampa	23.0		
Washington, D.C.	32.5		
Average	24.6	Average	41.6

Notes:

1. Total mortgages at beginning of year.

2. Insured associations only.

Source: Federal Home Loan Bank Board, Source Book, 1962, 1963, Washington, D.C.

mobiles; and, analogously, the mutual associations in these eighteen impure cities should also be considered in any study of mutual associations. It is unfortunate that these cities are not pure; but the stock associations are not the dominant influence. On the contrary, they represent a minority; and exclusion of the cities would simply mean a substitution of a restricted sample which failed to take into account the more active cities among mutual associations.

Furthermore, there are various reasons for including the six cities. The principal reason, of course, concerns the main hypothesis of this study. It is contended that the influence of stock associations is to damp down expenses in an area of both mutual and stock associations. The expenses for stock associations would not be expected to be higher since there are clearly other opportunities open to the owner managers of stock associations. On the contrary, the management of mutual associations, by the nature of the organization, are forced into taking both pecuniary and nonpecuniary income through the media of higher expenses. They either take higher wages or increase expenses which provide amenities for them, their associates and families. Unlike the stock association, there is no incentive for increasing profits; building net worth through allocations to reserves; and leaving an estate to their posterity. These constraints direct the activities of the management of the mutual associations into the pyramiding of expenses.

Accordingly, the only basis for exclusion is an alleged enlargement of the regression coefficients attributable to the stock influence. Three pieces of evidence refer to this particular hypothesis. In the first instance, a dummy variable was used. (See Chapter 13.) In impure cities where the stock proportion was greater than zero but less than 17%, there was competition. The value of one was assigned. The other cities, i.e., pure mutual, received a zero value. The results for the years 1961-1965 show that the competitive influence was positive. Expenses were in fact higher. This could mean that either the stock were less efficient; or that they were more efficient, and thus forced their mutual competitors into greater efficiency. In the latter event, the mutual management would benefit from the lower expenses by changing the composition of expenses such that it would receive higher wages, spend more on amenities or transfer the profits to wholly-owned subsidiaries which make up the infrastructure. Higher expenses here are not what they seem: they are the form which greater efficiency must take under the constraints of mutuality.

Of course, there is always the other alternative: the stock influence is to expand expenses. But other evidence suggests that this is not so. That the stock influence did not positively increase expenses was indicated by a multiple regression model using states which were exclusively mutual. The regression coefficients (see Table 11-5) were both of the same sign and magnitude as that for the cities when the impure observations were included. Even in the less satisfactory data for the states there did not seem to be a difference as compared to the cities where the data were impure. Finally, it is noteworthy that the stock associations have been increasing their market shares relative to mutuals in all of the states. Given identical market conditions, it is highly probable that stock expenses were equal or less than the federally chartered associations. There is one qualification for this judgment: the stock associations could have increased market share by assuming greater risks and carrying a greater proportion of bad loans.

Actually, there are two ways to grow. First, associations may grow relative to other associations simply because they are more efficient. By reducing expenses, one makes more funds available for additional loans. Or associations will promote new savings which may or may not lead to loans of inferior quality. Now if

Table 11-5
Expense Regression Models: SMSAs and States, 1963

	Constant Term	Loans Made	Number of Mortgages	New Savings	R^2
33 SMSAs	−1.299				.9830
Reg. Coef.		0.03059	0.05646	0.00735	
(s.e.)		(0.00562)	(0.01347)	(0.00236)	
Part Cor. Coef.		0.69930	0.60139	0.48794	
47 States	− .912				.9888
Reg. Coef.		0.02603	0.02200	0.01408	
(s.e.)		(0.00536)	(0.00367)	(0.00484)	
Part Cor. Coef.		0.83491	0.59621	0.66117	

the latter were the case, the consequences would be revealed over time in contracting income: an enlarged percentage of delinquent and foreclosed loans would yield less or no income. Table 3-5 showed the ratio of net income before dividends to average savings for both the federals and stock in the stock states for the years 1960-63. Stock associations not only did not experience a reduction in income, they also made higher allocations to reserves than the federally chartered associations. This evidence is inconsistent with a growth attributable to an undue proportion of poor quality loans. Both the growth data as well as the income data indicate that the stock associations do not add to expenses as compared to the federally chartered associations.

Furthermore, there is another set of evidence. When the Los Angeles federally chartered associations' product mix is related to the mutual multiple regression model, estimated expenses are either close to or below the actual expenses for those associations. For example, in 1964, while the SMSA mutual associations with a product mix identical to Los Angeles stock associations would have had expenses 17.5% higher than the stock associations, the Los Angeles federally chartered associations' estimated expenses would have been 13.3% less than they actually were. This difference of about 30% as compared to the stock reveals a large discrepancy between federally chartered and stock associations in the same market area when they are compared to mutual associations elsewhere.

Areas Selected

The sample, therefore, includes 25 pure cities, of which 24 are classified as Standard Metropolitan Statistical Areas (SMSAs). Only mutuals operate within their confines. Washington, D.C. was used instead of the Washington SMSA because the latter also took in adjacent parts of Virginia which permit the stock form. Six impure cities were selected because the mutuals clearly outweighted the relatively small stock sectors. Seven more areas were represented by their federal associations: Los Angeles, San Bernardino-Riverside, San Diego and San Francisco. In Arizona, it was necessary to resort to statewide information. But, inasmuch as there are but two federals in Arizona, the data refer only to the two cities, Phoenix and Tucson. Both the Denver and Portland (Oregon) SMSAs showed a proportion of stock assets which was considered too great. In order to escape possible stock bias, the federals for the entire state were used as a proxy. This was justified on the grounds that Denver and Portland dominated the statewide results for federal associations. In any case, they were thought a better statistic than the impure SMSA which included such a large proportion of stock assets.

Stock associations in the sample came from 15 areas, only seven of which were in areas not represented by either pure mutuals or federals. The Nevada stock associations were used since there was no SMSA and though the associations were in the two cities, Reno and Las Vegas, the latter had 92% of the state assets.

The total size of the sample came to 53 when the 38 mutual observations were combined with the 15 stock. In all, 45 cities or combinations of cities were selected. For certain purposes, the mutuals alone were used; and for others they were combined with the stock observations. Thirty-two of the areas were represented by pure mutual data. Six were substantially mutual. But it should be noted that in these six plus the seven federal areas (in all 13), some stock influence was felt so that only 25 were altogether isolated.

Competitive Influence of Stock Associations on Mutuals. In seven of the areas where federal data were available, separate stock data were also available. Such localities are not as pure as places which are exclusively mutuals. The federals obviously were influenced by competition: they could not act as mutuals in cities prohibiting the stock form. Indeed, there are numerous examples of mutual spokesmen complaining of the competition of the stock associations with their eye always adhered to the gyrations of the stock market. It is hypothesized that mutual associations in such a competitive environment will have to take on some, if not all, of the characteristics of the stock association. But that given the constraints of the organization, they will be compelled to resort to the conventional diversion tactics of the mutual. Ultimately, the impact of their behavior in the legal environment of mutuality is revealed in their expenses. The latter is, of course, the only visible part of that iceberg known as mutuality.

The decision was to include these competitive mutuals in the model both because as mutuals their behavior was an important part of the total picture and also because they would reflect the competitive influence of another form of organization. The results revealed an interesting paradox: because of their competition from the stock, it was expected that they would have to become more efficient to survive. On the other hand, this enhanced efficiency in the context of managerial diversion and mutual constraints allows an increase in expenses. It will later be shown that the stock influence is to reduce expenses. Thus mutuals surviving such competition are expected to benefit from reduced expenses by diverting income to amenities in the form of attractive furnishings, expensive trips and redundant personnel. Organizational structure or mutuality forces the more efficient associations into converting economies into higher and unnecessary expenses.

The California Stock Data

Due to different methods of reporting, the data for California stock associations are not altogether satisfactory. It was necessary to make adjustments in order to facilitate comparisons between them and mutual associations in the 38 areas. The number of mortgages, new savings and savings withdrawals, net savings and the number of savings accounts were secured in a straightforward fashion. Troubles, however, were encountered both with expenses and in real estate owned. One of the difficulties in the real estate owned data is that in California, it is possible for savings and loan associations to hold land for development. Therefore, the aggregate figure, as reported up through 1964 in the Combined Financial Statements of the Federal Home Loan Bank Board, included such a slow asset, even though it was not land or property acquired through foreclosure. The data provided by the Los Angeles Office of the Division of Savings and Loan for 1961-65 made it possible to break out the net foreclosed real estate owned for each of the California cities.

There are even greater difficulties in connection with estimating the expenses for the California stock associations. The Division of Savings and Loans reports a different expense figure than that in the Combined Financial Statements. Total operating expenses for 1963, as reported by the Federal Home Loan Bank Board, was $167,179,000 or 92.3% of the corresponding figure as reported by the Division of Savings and Loans at $181,221,000. One way to meet the difficulty is to assume that the ratio at the state level also applies in each of the cities, i.e., the federal data = 91.3% of the California. For example, Los Angeles stock expenses could be estimated on the basis of the same ratio as that which applied for the entire state. Another method was to take SMSA data and deduct the expenses of federal associations. Otherwise, it would have been impossible to make any meaningful comparison because of the different accounting procedures used between the two governmental agencies. The latter method was chosen.

The Expense Regression Model for Los Angeles Associations

The models discussed above assume that generalizations derived from aggregate citywide data appropriately describe the individual associations. But there is a danger that an aggregate model may conceal or distort important individual behavioral characteristics. It is, however, difficult to check on this possibility because the various state and federal agencies make only the aggregate data available. Indeed, they steadfastly refuse to provide data for *individual* mutual associations. The Federal Home Loan Bank Board in Washington, which supervises federally chartered associations, as well as insured associations, publishes only the aggregate information for Standard Metropolitan Statistical Areas and the various states. In the latter instance, it does separate federal and state chartered institutions. In a number of the states, the stock form is dominant, thereby making it possible to secure aggregate stock information.

Information for individual stock associations in California has been readily secured since 1961. As this study was nearing completion, data were secured for 23 federal associations in Los Angeles for the year 1963. The observations were included with those for 60 stock associations in a model devised to check on the results of the aggregative models. In addition, the data for stock associations in Los Angeles and San Francisco provided information with respect to product mix, so that expenses could be compared to mutual associations performing similar functions.

There are important differences between the aggregate data and that for individual associations. Twenty-five of the former observations are pure in the sense that they relate only to mutual associations: each market area is free from any form of competition with stock associations. Thus, 31 of the observations are wholly or substantially removed from competition with the stock form of organization. This means that the Los Angeles model will exhibit the effect of competition between the rival forms and, to that extent, is something less than a perfect check on models where the observations are only of the pure mutual type. Mutuals removed from the necessity of competing with stock associations would obviously behave in a different manner. It is, therefore, useful to gain information with respect to mutuals in models exclusively restricted to their form. The behavioral characteristics would be revealed in the models' parameters and could be applied to the product mix for Los Angeles and San Francisco stock associations. It is by such means that one gains light on their operating expenses, for it is only when they perform the same activities that their expenses can be compared.

The data for individual stock associations are, therefore, useful in that they provide the necessary information with respect to product mix, or distribution of activities, and permit a meaningful comparison of expenses with similar mutuals. In the absence of data relating to functions performed, comparisons are meaningless. But in addition, the information for individual associations—both stock and federal—does permit an analysis designed to ascertain the influence of organization. Unfortunately, the results are influenced by competitive interaction. It would have been preferable had the federal or mutual associations operated in a different market area isolated from competitive influences. Nonetheless, some conception of organization impact can be gained by the combination of the two methods outlined here.

12 Hypotheses with Respect to Expense Differences

When expenses are expressed in terms of assets, the most frequent and obvious hypothesis with respect to differences in expenses is a difference in relative efficiency. But even in the case of this particular ratio, there are other reasons why expenses should differ. This chapter discusses these alternative hypotheses and suggests a method for weighting each. It is to be noted, however, that when ratios are abandoned in favor of the absolute data, expenses vary in line with the total volume of operations as indicated by the dollar volume of new loans or the total volume of total assets, the number of mortgage accounts or the number of savings accounts.

The procedure was to select the most appropriate variables for explaining variations in expenses. Subsequently, the Los Angeles and San Francisco product mix was applied to the regression model in order to provide an appropriate expense figure for mutual associations with identical product mixes. In addition, the data for mutuals were combined with that for the stock with a dummy variable to ascertain the influence of organization.

Expenses as a Function of Annual Activity

Even with ratios, it is expected that there would be a variance between associations and regions simply because of variance in the composition of the portfolio: composition rather than absolute size of assets is important. Furthermore, total assets do not always pick up crucial expense determinants. For example, the variations in expenses associated with construction loans: typically, these occur during the warmer months and, as though they appear in loans made, they are not in the year-end mortgage portfolio. A measure of expenses which uses either year-end assets or mortgages will not give them, therefore, proper weight. The choice of the expense-to-asset ratio also implicitly assumes a homogeneity with respect to the composition of the portfolio. The validity of this assumption is questionable. Other investigations,[1] though recognizing the possibility that the product mix varies, have then proceeded to use a ratio which implicitly assumed that there was no variation.

Obviously, variances in the relative importances of the different functions performed by savings and loan associations and regions will account for differences in expenses. It has been observed, for example, "because of acquisition and setup costs, any association which is expanding at a high rate may be

223

expected to report higher costs than an association with a slower rate of growth":[2] the greatest variations occurred between state and federally chartered associations in California. While the former are smaller in size, they "appear to grow at a considerably faster rate. Their advertising and other operating expenses are high relative to the federal associations, but this is more than offset by their higher return on mortgages."[3]

Expense differences are not properly attributable to one variable such as assets or the number of mortgages.[4] Development of a model for estimating expenses must, therefore, take account of all the various contributory elements to those expenses. Unfortunately, multicollinearity precludes some important variables from attaining statistical significance in the regression model. But, since the objective is to allow for at least some of the various components that enter into expenses, omission of one or several variables on the grounds of intercorrelation does not seriously interfere with the objective of estimating organizational impact on expenses. It is sufficient that allowance is made for the variation in the composition of products or services. Predictions as to their relative importance is thereby made possible.

The expenses reported in a calendar year reflect not only the objectives of the particular association but also the varying kinds of decisions with respect to the services provided. For example, an association may achieve a relatively low expense ratio by having the appraisers and loan men on a commission basis. In such circumstances, the only expenses shown by the association would be that for the desks and use of the phone. *A fortiori*, employees operating on a commission would have that much more incentive to minimize expenses. And for the same reason, insofar as they receive a commission on the loan, the batting average for the association with respect to its own expenses would be that much higher.

The Influence of Higher New Loan Volume

Expenses reflect differences in the product mix or composition of the portfolio. To illustrate, take total United States insured savings and loan associations without California (Table 12-1). In 1962, the ratio of expenses to average assets was

Table 12-1

Expenses, Fees and Loans Made as a % of Average Assets: California Stock Compared to U.S., 1962

	Expenses ÷ Average Assets	Fees ÷ Average Assets	Loans Made ÷ Average Assets
California Stock	1.31	1.30	41.3
U.S. without California	1.14	0.32	21.2

Source: Federal Home Loan Bank Board, Combined Financial Statements, 1961, 1962.

1.14% as compared to 1.31% for California stock associations. The fees received by non-California associations was 0.317%, the California stock received 1.30%. Now suppose that fees equal the actual expenses incurred in placing new loans. For that year, the new loans-asset ratio for the United States less California came to 21.2%; California stock associations had 41.3%. If the 0.31% approximated the expenses of putting such loans on the books, the extra new loan volume for California would seem to justify additional expenses.

If the same ratio of fees to new loans for the United States less California is applied to the California stock associations, the amount earned in fees would have come to $55.9 million. Next, take the United States (less California) ratio of expenses to assets, i.e., 1.14% and apply it to the average assets for the California stock associations. This gives an estimated expenses for those associations, based on the performance of the mutuals throughout the United States (without California) of $103.7 million. The United States less California ratio of fee to assets, as applied to California, is $29,000,000. This is subtracted from the estimated fee for the California stock on the basis of the national rate which was $55.9 million and yields a remainder of $26.8 million. This is added to the estimated expenses for California at $103.7 million for an estimated value, allowing for the greater new loan volume, $130.5 million. When this is expressed on average assets, the ratio is 1.44% which is 10% greater than the actual rate of 1.31% for California stock associations.

The ratios of expenses and new loans on assets showed a simple correlation for the SMSAs of 0.60 and 0.55 for 1961 and 1962. In the model chosen, ratios were not used because it was believed preferable to take assets or a proxy of assets as an independent variable. The bulk of the assets in any one period were acquired in previous periods; and the expenses associated with the maintenance of those assets represents a relatively small part of the total expenses for the period. The expenses from originating new loans are a significant part of the total expense. The function of placing the new loan on the books consists in working with real estate agents, builders and mortgage brokers. Appraisals, the payment of commission, and orderly payments to builders are essential steps so that the mortgage transaction shall be consummated in order that income can thereby flow into the association in return for the lending of association funds.

Construction Loans

Construction loans may lead to double counting in the total volume of loans made. They are neither permanent mortgage loans on new houses or new loans for purchase of existing homes. They also include temporary loans to builders. Loans classified for the purchase of a home will include the loan both for construction and the purchase of the new homes. This leads to a duplication inasmuch as "loans reported once under the construction category are reported again under the purchase category."[5] There are, however, compensations in that the loan to finance construction is obviously not identical with the loan to finance purchase of a home. In each case, it is necessary to investigate the credit worthiness of the borrower or borrowers. Obviously, the property would not have to be investigated each time: the nature of the investigation and the expenses involved are different. In any case, construction loans frequently involve different types of loans as well as different types of borrowers. Very often, they are classified as speculative loans and cause greater expense which are caused by the necessity for continuous and close scrutiny of the builder. On the other hand, there are other construction loans not reported as "construction loans" which are limited to "one to four family units." Where there are more units they are classified as "other" loans. As they tend to be more expensive, they point up the lack of homogeneity.[6]

When new loans were divided into the three components, "construction loans," "home purchase loans" and "other loans" as reported by the Federal Home Loan Bank Board, little improvement resulted. The second component, home purchase loans, was not statistically significant. The aggregate, new loans, provided a superior measure of total performance.

Growth as a Cause of Higher Expenses

Another reason advanced for differences in efficiency is that a sustained period of high profits is thought to reduce the incentive towards operating at minimum costs.

During the postwar years of the tremendous growth of the state (California), the industry has been quite profitable and in such an atmosphere even inefficient firms have prospered. A firm which is successful does not have an especially strong motivation to reduce costs and operate at maximum efficiency, particularly if it has no solid basis of comparison against which to assess its own results.[7]

The same authors also note that "one group of institutions may report considerably higher operating expenses than another, but if the former are producing an expensive output mix (including such items as participations), are spending large sums to attract deposits to a capital deficit area, and are growing rapidly (which, as shall be seen, is quite expensive), a simple comparison of the two groups of associations is invalid."[8]

Turnover Rates

Changes in the turnover rate or the ratio of loans repaid during the year to the average mortgage portfolio will affect the level of expenses. Thus, for any given size loan portfolio, if the turnover rate should decline in that year, as compared to the previous year, expenses should also be expected to decline by the reduction in the necessary amount of "new loans" made. Table 12-2 shows the turnover rate for savings and loan associations both nationally and in California for the years 1951-66. A persistent decline in the average turnover rate from 22.8 to 11.5 is indicated.[9] There are a number of reasons why this turnover rate should fall, e.g., when the average life of the mortgage is increased as from 18 years to 20 or 25 years. Another reason would be an increase in the dollar size of mortgages written as occurs in inflation. Table 12-3 shows the trend in average loan balance 1950-68. In the early period, the average loan balance was $3,644. By 1968, it had increased by 240% to $13,396.[10] Larger loans are made; at the same time, smaller payments come in each year because of extension of the time period on the new mortgages.[a]

Table 12-2
Trend in Loans Repaid (Turnover) as % of Average Mortgages Held, 1951-1966

	U.S.[1]	California[2]
1951	22.8	36.3
1952	22.2	29.8
1953	20.8	25.6
1954	20.0	25.4
1955	20.7	28.1
1956	17.9	22.6
1957	15.5	19.7
1958	15.4	18.9
1959	15.5	20.4
1960	13.0	15.8
1961	13.3	17.8
1962	14.7	18.9
1963	14.8	20.6
1964	14.7	19.1
1965	14.2	16.2
1966	11.5	11.1

Source:
1. U.S. Savings and Loan League, Savings and Loan Fact Book, 1967, Table 60, p. 72.
2. California Savings and Loan League, Data Book, 1960, Table 24, p. 26; and Data Book, 1967, p. 22.

[a]"While the borrower in today's market is permitted to amortize his loan through monthly payments over an extended future period, very few mortgages actually last to maturity. Typically a U.S. family does not stay in one home that long, and the mortgage balance is prepaid on moving day. A new owner sometimes assumes the seller's obligation, but usually obtains a new loan. However, the significance of the term to maturity written in the contract is twofold: first, a longer time for repayment automatically lowers the total monthly payments, thus encouraging more people to buy homes. From the lender's view, it reduces the return flow of regular principal repayments which will require reinvestment in the future."[11]

228

Table 12-3
Trend in Average Loan Balance, U.S. 1950-1968

1950	$ 3.644
1951	3.851
1952	4.137
1953	4.555
1954	4.915
1955	5.351
1956	5.667
1957	5.966
1958	6.257
1959	6.966
1960	7.427
1961	7.800
1962	8.658
1963	9.473
1964	9.935
1965	10.092
1966	11.169
1967	11.803
1968	12.396

Source: United States Savings and Loan League, Fact Books, Chicago, 1962, Table 54, p. 60; Table 73, p. 79.

An increase in average size over the years automatically reduces the turnover rate, *ceteris paribus*. Extension of maturity further reduces that turnover rate as loans repaid represent a falling percentage of the new loans, particularly when the average size of the latter increases. The problem concerns the source of the funds. It is obvious that there are additional funds attracted into the savings and loan industry. In a stable industry, faced with inflation, repayments would not generate sufficient funds to maintain a fixed number of mortgages. Without the new funds, the industry would experience a contraction in activity, and would be compelled into making fewer loans. The general inflation of land values and building costs has meant that the loans repaid failed to generate sufficient funds. Thus, a declining turnover rate is a measure of the shortage of internally generated funds. The industry must literally run to stay in the same place. New funds have to be attracted. This means that the dividend rate must be increased; the promotional expenditures must be enlarged; and competition with other financial intermediaries must increase. It is, therefore, rather curious that the regulatory authority, the Federal Home Loan Bank Board, has put a damper on these possible courses of action. It has threatened associations that sought to advertise outside the local area; it has placed a maximum level on the dividend rate; and it has restricted the use of brokers performing the vital middleman function of collecting savings in capital surplus areas for diversion to capital deficit areas.

The effect of the turnover rate on relative expenses for different associations and different areas is indicated in comparisons between the national average and that for California for the six years, 1960-1965. After appropriate adjustments for participation purchases and sales, the national rate was 14.1% as compared to 20.6% for California.[12] The latter was 46% higher. This meant that whereas nationally associations were permitted to report income from fees and premiums equal to *their* turnover rate, California associations were allowed only two-thirds. The other third was placed in the account for "deferred credits." Recognition of regional differences would have permitted these associations to allocate 47% more fees to current income.

Furthermore, since twenty percent of the California stock associations' dollar value of mortgages had to be replaced each year, as compared to but 14% for the United States, stock associations are compelled into making more new loans merely to maintain their mortgage portfolio. If new loans are not placed on the books, cet. par., it is necessary to return this part of the repayments to their saving members. In order to avoid this latter alternative (which savings and loans characteristically refuse even to consider), replacements must be sought for the dollar inflow from "loans repaid." Thus, for this reason alone, simple comparisons on the basis of expenses to assets are meaningless in the absence of a showing of identical turnover rates.

It should be noted that savings and loan associations guard themselves against sudden increases in turnover rates through exacting prepayment penalties. But, though there is some compensation, it appears on the income side. Exclusive preoccupation with expenses conceals this legitimate though costly activity.

It might be suggested that a higher turnover rate could indicate bad lending as when the associations acquire "real estate owned" through foreclosure. This forces them to make new loans, i.e., to seek new borrowers. In California, however, the rate was higher both for mutual as well as stock associations.

Another factor contributing to a higher turnover rate is the construction loan. These short-term loans are repaid during the year. To this extent, they contribute to the relatively higher turnover rate of California associations.

The principal reasons for the higher turnover rate in California is not "real estate owned" but the mobility of the population which causes a high turnover of properties and the rapid growth of the state's economy. Growing prosperity has led to the development of new areas. High rates of family formations and immigration into the state have facilitated the turnover of single-family residences.

Variations in the turnover rate obviously change the denominator in any expense-to-asset ratio. The turnover rate is indicated by the ratio of loans repaid during any calendar period to the average mortgages for that period. Thus, when comparisons are made, it is necessary to consider whether the turnover rate has remained the same; or if an adjustment that allows for a change in this rate is necessary. If comparison is to be made between the United States mutuals and California stock associations over the period of 1950-65, allowance would have to be made for variations in the trend. While the national turnover rate fell over 40%, California's fell 20%. On these grounds alone, the higher percentage of new loans for California stock associations causes a higher average mortgage size. On the other hand, the decline in the turnover rate for Eastern associations means that for a given dollar volume of total loans, a decreasingly smaller amount are replaced annually.

The Servicing of Mortgages

Once the mortgage is placed on the books, some service charges appear with respect to their maintenance. These charges vary depending on the kind of mortgage, the type of borrower and co-lender as with participations. An indication of the relative importance of servicing of mortgages is revealed in the experience of mortgage bankers and mutual savings banks. Mortgage bankers in California indicate that their servicing expenses probably run about one-fifth of a point. Mutual savings banks reporting to the Federal Deposit Insurance Corporation pay an estimated 0.37 on the average value of their out-of-state mortgages.[13] It should be noted, however, that there is a margin between the additional interest income and the costs of servicing the mortgage. Mortgage correspondents or savings and loan associations are paid for the functions performed. Presumably, those who do the servicing earn some profit on the functions performed.

A chairman of the Federal Home Loan Bank Board, McMurray, stated that "one ought to be able to manage a mortgage portfolio for 1/2 percent or less of the mortgages involved."[14] If servicing expenses on mortgages is about a third of a point, McMurray's concern for some of the other activities in the savings and loan association can be appreciated. For example, he asks: "Why does it cost nine-tenths of one percent to service the share accounts? This seems to be a dubiously high figure, but it is the average for the United States. . . . The most efficient associations, in terms of size at least, are those in the $5 to $25 millions classes and even these suggest that the cost to service savings is about eight-tenths of one percent."[15]

For the reasons indicated above, it is remarkable that the Chairman sees expenses almost entirely in terms of the servicing of mortgages and share accounts. Not only are these not the major items in expenses, but there obviously are other items such as the generation of new savings and new loans as well as expenses of loan foreclosures. It is perfectly obvious that, by his test, the most efficient association is one with a low ratio of expenses to assets or share accounts. Such an association or area could achieve this low ratio simply by maintaining a relatively low growth rate; or by experiencing a downward trend in "loans repaid." It is curious that McMurray also noted that growth had been so rapid that insufficient attention has been paid to the expense side of the business. On the other hand, he properly noted that "the institution with an impeccable balance sheet, no losses but an inadequate income, is as ineffective and as much a drag on the economy as the institution which is reckless in order to obtain a high rate of return.[16] In his judgment, foreclosed homes "usually had too high appraisals; that poor credit checking was involved . . .; and mortgages with low down payments had a much higher foreclosure rate."[17]

There is no denying that the servicing of mortgages does involve expenses for the association. For this reason, the "number of mortgages" or "mortgage accounts" was introduced into the model as a variable. It was expected that it would offer some light on the share of expenses generated by the servicing function. But the attempt to allow for its influence failed because of the high intercorrelation with the "number of savings accounts." Since the latter had a higher T value as well as larger partial correlation with expenses, it was selected. On the other hand, when return is considered (as in a latter chapter), it was no surprise that "the number of mortgage accounts" was a better explanatory variable than the "number of savings accounts."

Advertising and Promotion of New Savings

Table 12-4 shows the relationship between advertising, new loans and expenses as a percentages of assets. The table is submitted simply because the ratio is the conventional test; and the simple correlation between new loans, advertising and expense is fairly obvious. Furthermore, there is ample evidence from the California experience, as well as from other growth states, that advertising expenditures can be quite significant. Indeed, expressed relative to assets, they were as high as 0.19 in California as compared to 0.12 in the rest of the nation; and for the California stock associations at 0.21, they represented 16% of total expenses.

The Servicing of Savings Accounts. Savings accounts also have to be serviced. Indeed, one of the major items of expense is the provision of facilities which will both attract savers to the association and, of course, permit the services involved in withdrawals, the payment of dividends and net additions to the savings accounts. These expenses may also be described in terms of their turnover. Preferably, the association would prefer them to grow without turnover. The latter is often expressed as a ratio of withdrawals to the amount of new savings which in 1965 was 78.5% for the United States. In New Orleans, it was as low as 62.0% while as high as 94.1% in San Diego. The turnover ratio, which measures the stability of funds, is the money withdrawn expressed as a percentage of total savings at the beginning of the year; and indicates the rate at which the total

Table 12-4

Expenses, Advertising and New Loan as a % of Average Assets, Largest States, 1962

Largest States	Expenses Assets	Advertising Assets	New Loans Assets
California	1.30	0.19	37.5
Florida	1.25	0.12	20.6
Illinois	1.20	0.15	21.9
Indiana	1.28	0.11	21.6
Massachusetts	0.75	0.08	13.4
Michigan	1.23	0.12	18.7
Missouri	1.10	0.13	22.1
New Jersey	0.98	0.07	19.9
New York	1.06	0.08	15.9
Ohio	1.30	0.12	23.3
Pennsylvania	1.08	0.11	18.6
Texas	1.11	0.12	23.8
Wisconsin	0.81	0.09	19.0
U.S. less California	1.14	0.12	20.6

Source: Federal Home Loan Bank Board, *Combined Financial Statements*, Members of the Federal Home Loan Bank System, 1962, Washington, D.C.

stock of savings is turned over in a single year. In 1965, this rate was about 30%, i.e., the average life of the savings was about three and one-third years.

Variations in the Size of Savings Accounts. Expenses in connection with savings accounts are of two types. Other things remaining the same, the expense in servicing a savings account is identical, whether that account is very small or very large. Or put another way, the expense per dollar of the savings account is obviously smaller, the larger the savings account. Again, expenses on savings accounts will vary depending upon the activity of those savings accounts. Thus, an account which is active in which both additions and withdrawals are made in any one period will be more expensive to service than one which is both stable and relatively inactive. Some indication of the variation in such items between regions is found in comparing the San Francisco Federal Home Loan Bank District to the national average in 1964. The former had 18.2% more accounts in the $10,000 or larger category (than the national average). 7.8% of the accounts were responsible for 33% of the total savings. The national figure showed that 6.6% of the accounts were larger than $10,000 and accounted for 31.4% of the savings. The Indianapolis District reported that the accounts with balances over $10,000 came to 40.8% of the total dollar savings. Such accounts represented 7.4% of the total number of accounts.[18] So far as the average account size in

California as compared to the United States, the former was 134.6% of the latter.[19]

One possible advantage that would accrue to California stock associations in a comparison with mutual associations in other parts of the country is the average size of their accounts. To the extent that California accounts are larger and less active, California has a cost advantage. A study by Stanford Research Institute found that "the average size of all California accounts from savers located outside of California was $4,338, an average which fell gradually to $2,307 per account for savers living within two miles of the office."[20] While 20.6% of the savings in federal associations in Southern California came from out of state, the ratio for the stock associations was 17.0%. Analysis of expenses in terms of ratios such as expenses on assets or savings capital must therefore consider both the average size of the accounts and the activity. This problem is met in multiple regression models through reliance upon absolute data. Size of accounts is handled through consideration of a variable indicating the "number" of savings accounts. It is hypothesized in a multiple regression analysis—which is a surrogate for the *ceteris paribus* restriction—that the independent influence of variations in the number of accounts is positive. Similarly, activity is indicated by another variable referred to either as "new savings" or "withdrawable savings." The greater the number of accounts or the more active they are as reflected in the New Savings, the larger is the impact on the level of expenses.

Consequently, it makes a considerable difference whether accounts are on the average relatively large and relatively inactive. In both cases, it is to be expected that expenses would be lower than where average accounts are smaller and more active with respect to New Savings and Withdrawals. It is to be noted that the aforementioned study reported that for the Southern California stock savings and loan associations 31.6% of the accounts above $5,000 had 66.1% of the savings for those associations. On the other hand, 42.6% of the total number of accounts, which were less than $1,000, came to but 4.6% of the total savings: more than two-fifths of the total number of savings accounts contributed an insignificant part of the savings.[21] On March 1960, 9.6% of the accounts had 15.4% of the savings. The average for such accounts was $4,359 or about 60% larger than the average account for the entire state.

One obvious implication of this statistic is suggested in a consideration of the sources of larger accounts. Obviously, the ability of an association to attract the larger account will, to a considerable extent, depend upon two factors: (1) the payment of a higher dividend; and (2) the advertising of that dividend in areas where the dividend rate is lower. The importance of these accounts for the association is that, on the one hand, they are stable and, on the other hand, due to their larger size, they are less expensive accounts. It is also significant that the ability to attract such accounts rests on two competitive weapons which today are not only in considerable disrepute with the regulatory authorities but at least one of them is actually banned. We refer here to competition by means of higher dividend rates and also through advertising. It is to be noted also that the advertising plays a considerable role in attracting accounts which come from more than five miles away. In the period studied by the Stanford Research Institute, 35.0% of total accounts were more than five miles away and generated 53.3% of total savings. In Los Angeles, 12.1% of the out-of-state savings accounts generated 20.2% of the total savings with the average account at a level of $4,731–75% larger than the state average.

Variations in the activity of savings accounts lead to differences in expenses. A proxy measure for this determinant of expenses is the ratio of withdrawals to savings at the preceding year-end. In 1965, the Los Angeles Standard Metropolitan Statistical Area rate was 39.0% while Milwaukee's was 21.8%. It is significant that Los Angeles was 79% higher.

Expenses of Foreclosures and Resales

When an association is forced to foreclose on a property, considerable expense is borne both with respect to the foreclosure proceedings and ultimate resale. Expenses from such activities are indicated by two balance sheet items in the Combined Financial Statements: "real estate sold on contract" and "real estate owned." While they do not represent all the so-called "slow assets," they are a good surrogate. Unquestionably, they do make a contribution to expenses; and have increasingly done so in recent years.

Loan foreclosures contribute to expenses not only in that the savings and loan associations must incur extra servicing activities; but higher salaried personnel possessing superior skills must be employed to supervise the foreclosed properties.[b] When a loan becomes delinquent and ultimately foreclosed, and is later transferred to another borrower under "a contract of sale," the work and expenses involved will be more than that for a loan on which payments have been maintained. Decisions involving considerable experience and judgment are required from specialized personnel.

The data relating to foreclosures and associated activities are derived from the Combined Financial Statements of the Federal Home Loan Bank Board. It is reported for the largest SMSAs as well as the states. There are some problems in connection with the use and interpretation of these data. In those areas where there is a larger proportion of FHA insured and VA guaranteed loans, associations will transfer the properties to the respective government agencies. The expenses in connection with the loans are also transferred. Areas where government insurance or guarantee plays a larger role in the total assets of associations will, cet. par., show a smaller ratio of loans foreclosed: and, therefore, the expenses involved in foreclosures will be that much less.

---

[b]The Federal Home Loan Bank Board considers these "real estate expenses" and therefore excludes them from its reports. But it is difficult to believe that it is completely effective as management must concern itself with such unwanted problems.

Table 12-5 shows the ratio of conventional loans to mortgage loans held, December 31, 1963, for the 40 largest Standard Metropolitan Statistical Areas. The range is from 50.0% in Detroit to 98.7% for the San Bernardino-Riverside-Ontario area. It is obvious, that in Detroit, San Antonio, Albany, Baltimore and Boston, the real estate acquired through loan foreclosures will be relatively less than in Los Angeles, San Bernardino or San Jose, California. The average percentage for the 40 cities is 82.1.

There are other factors which contribute to variations in the importance of loan foreclosures. Kendall has observed:

The legal framework through which savings and loan associations operate in a specific state and the legal conditions facing associations in a state, can have a bearing on the growth record of the business. Certain lenders consider investments in mortgages in specific states relatively unattractive because of legal restrictions such as lengthy redemption privileges granted to homeowners or strict usury laws at a relatively low ceiling. The result of such provisions can be to leave local markets to local lenders. Where such conditions exist in rapidly growing localities such as the Chicago metropolitan area, savings associations find their lending opportunities relatively greater than would be the case elsewhere because large Eastern companies consider foreclosure laws in Illinois quite restrictive.[22]

The document which relates the lending association to the home buyer is called a first trust deed in California and 21 other states, and a mortgage elsewhere. In each instance, the lender "secures" a note from the borrower at the time the property is purchased. This provides for repossession if there is a default on payments. But, to recover the property secured by the mortgage, the lender must go to court. The proceedings may take as much as and longer than a year. Because of the time involved, as well as the expense, mortgage holders are reluctant to start foreclosure proceedings. "With the fast moving first trust deeds, the process is quite different. Fall behind in your payments and you can be out of your house in four months."[23] When a house is purchased through a savings and loan association, the association pays the money to the seller of the house and the trust deed is given to a trustee, e.g., Guarantee Title and Trust Company. "The trustee has the power to sell your property if you default on your payments.[24]

Payments are made to the savings and loan association and can be declared delinquent if later than 15 days, although the usual practice is to extend the period to 60 to 90 days. The savings and loan association has the choice of determining when to order the trustee to start foreclosure proceedings. The trustee notifies the borrower and a 90-day period is given to make up the payments. At the end of that time, the trustee posts a public notice of sale, and 21 days later, the house goes on the block. "During the last 21 days, you can recover your house only by paying off the entire loan, plus the costs involved in the foreclosure proceedings."[25]

Table 12-5

Conventional Mortgages as a % of Total Mortgages Held December 31, 1963

40 Largest Standard Metropolitan Statistical Areas[1]	Percentage
Albany, Schenectady, Troy	66.0
Atlanta	88.9
Baltimore	71.5
Birmingham	87.2
Boston	64.1
Buffalo	76.9
Chicago	95.8
Cincinnati	94.6
Cleveland	93.5
Columbus	88.7
Dallas	88.7
Dayton	92.8
Denver	85.5
Detroit	50.6
Houston	90.0
Indianapolis	81.8
Kansas City	67.6
Los Angeles, Long Beach	93.5
Louisville	90.8
Miami	90.8
Milwaukee	82.7
Minneapolis	83.5
Newark	76.0
New Orleans	96.9
New York	76.1
Patterson	73.2
Philadelphia	81.7
Phoenix	89.2
Pittsburgh	90.2
Portland, Oregon	95.5
Providence	70.4
St. Louis	90.0
San Antonio	56.0
San Bernardino, Riverside, Ontario	98.7
San Diego	94.5
San Francisco	95.3
San Jose	94.0
Seattle	88.5
Tampa	82.6
Washington, D.C.	91.0
Average, 40 SMSA's	82.1

Source: Federal Home Loan Bank Board, *Source Book*, 1964, Table 15, p. 24.
Notes:

1. Total Mortgage loans held by these 40 largest SMSAs was $53.9 millions and represented 61.6% of all loans of insured associations in the United States.

The chief operating officer of a large California holding company has stated that "the experience of our Trustee Division has been that of each four default proceedings instituted, only one results in the need to actually acquire the property. The results of our experience have been that the properties we did have to acquire have been sold at a profit."[26] In states that use mortgages, Franklin Hardinge, Vice President of the California Savings and Loan League, comments that the number of mortgage holders who actually redeem their property during the much longer foreclosure period is a fraction of one percent. Though the California foreclosure rate is higher than elsewhere, "the reason stems from the faster foreclosure proceedings here ... this factor makes the comparisons drawn by the Federal Home Loan Bank Board unfair to California associations."[27] It should be noted, however, that there have been more foreclosures in California on houses that have never been occupied than in other states.

Two difficulties appear in connection with interpretation of the data with respect to loans foreclosed. Policy decisions with respect to the kind of "loans made" or the proportion between conventional loans and government insured and guaranteed will determine the relative importance of foreclosed loans as an item in the determination of expenses. Variations between the states with respect to the ease and speed with which properties may be foreclosed affect decisions with respect to the instituting of the legal proceedings to foreclose. In states where the length of time is lengthy and the legal proceedings costly a savings and loan association may forego the proceeding. The consequence is that both the proportion of loans foreclosed and the expenses that would be connected with them will be avoided because of the hazards of entering into a legal jungle.

Mutuality and "Slow Loans." While the above discussion has indicated the extent to which loan foreclosures may be concealed, another problem relates to the alleged ability of mutuals in keeping a low ratio of slow assets. When regression coefficients from the mutual multiple regression model are related to a stock product mix, the objection is that a mutual association would not incur "real estate owned" of such a magnitude. The evidence is derived from taking a ratio of "real estate owned" plus "contracts of sale" to average assets. Invariably, it can be shown that stock associations have a higher percentage both nationally and in California.

This test is unwarranted because the ratio derived from relating scheduled items to assets is meaningless. The level of assets is not the only, or even a crucial item, in the determination of "slow loans." The proportion of "unseasoned" or "new loans" is far more significant. Thus, an association which is growing rapidly would be expected not only to show more new loans, cet. par., but a higher percentage of unseasoned loans and, consequently, a higher proportion of "real estate owned" and "contracts of sale."

A product mix with a high new loan activity is also one with a high "real estate owned." Indeed, there is a high multicollinearity behind "new loans" and "real estate owned" suggesting that one or the other might be safely left out of the regression model. In 1965, the simple correlation for the 35 mutual cities was 0.8. Further support for the intimate relationship between new loans and "real estate owned" plus "contracts of sale" is provided by comparing the ratio in Los Angeles to Chicago. When the slow items are related to the new loans for the previous two years, Chicago reported a percentage of 10.77 in 1965 and Los Angeles 9.27. Yet, the former city is almost exclusively mutual.

But the relevant question concerns the extent to which "slow loans" contributes to expenses. In order to make meaningful comparisons, product mix must be comparable. In any one year, the activity of mutuals is not measured by their assets but rather by the loans they originate and service, the new savings they attract and the savings accounts they must service and finally, the "slow loans" which must be examined and ultimately eliminated. Attempts to predict the "slow loans" from a multiple regression model which embraced these other variables were defeated by the above-mentioned multicollinearity. Resort was necessarily to a simple correlation between "real estate owned" plus "contracts of sale" and the new loans of the previous years. The obvious advantage of the correlation method over the mean values for the mutuals is that the means underestimate the higher values and overestimate the lower values in the sample. Using the correlation method, the 1963 estimate for the mutual cities, given the Los Angeles stock associations new loans, was 21% higher than the actual "slow loans" for those same stock associations. In 1965, the simple correlation was 0.72 with the T value at 6.3. The estimated "slow loans" for the same new loan volume as the Los Angeles stock associations came to 51.6% of the actual amount. New loans was selected because it had the higher T value and coefficient of determination.

Profitability. But even if it should turn out, that by some meaningful test, mutuals would, for the same product mix, show a lower level of "slow loans," it does not follow that they are more efficient or more responsible. A high ratio of "slow loans" is not a per se indication of poor performance. On the contrary, undue concern for the alleged quality of loans may effectively frustrate the association in fulfilling the intermediation function. Indeed, the return may be so low as to make it vulnerable to competitive increases in the dividend rate. Associations must earn a return sufficient to permit them to add to their reserves for meeting bad times.

There is an additional factor connected with the unexpected acquisition of "bad loans." An association may compensate for their appearance through earning higher fees. When this is done, the potential loss of income and the higher expenses associated with the "slow loans" is offset. Indeed, income or return is the other side of the coin. Risk more than compensated for is not risk. In 1963, when the slow loans were set against the two previous years' fees, the estimate was almost three times the actual Los Angeles stock association's REO, or 172% larger. For the fees earned by the Los Angeles associations, mutuals would have had to contend with almost twice as much in the way of "slow loans." When this was done again in 1965, $R^2 = 0.64$ and R = 0.80. (Table 12-6). The slow loans were related to the fees of the two preceding years. Two years turned out to be a better variable than three years since when the latter was used R^2 fell to 0.46. With fees of $176 millions, the estimated "slow loans" was $254.7 millions as compared to actual "slow loans" for the Los Angeles stock associations of $321 millions. That is, the latter stock associations had about twenty-five percent more.

The amount of "real estate owned" and "contracts of sale" is only one of the factors in a judgment of economic performance. The two principal activities of the associations are the collection of savings and their conversion into mortgages. In the latter function, they can never be sure that some proportion will not turn sour. Indeed, they have been officially encouraged in line with civil rights policy to increase loans to members of minority races who fail to pass the usual tests for mortgage loans. It is, therefore, rather remarkable that their regulating agency, the Federal Home Loan Bank Board, should so roundly criticize associations who report a higher ratio of "slow loans" to assets—even going so far as to refuse "advances" to associations which fall into that category.

In the absence of evidence relating to earnings, it is immaterial that an association should report a higher percentage. Obviously, there are variations in the risk offered by loans of different categories. But the higher-risk loans may be more profitable. When an association makes such loans, while it is covering for a larger proportion of delinquencies and foreclosures, it is more than carrying out its function in financial intermediation. After all, though commercial banks have rather assiduously avoided the small and personal loan market, this has not prevented other companies from assuming this specialized lender's role. The higher rate of delinquencies and bad loans, as compared to commercial banks and other more conservative institutions, has been associated with earning a higher return on invested capital.

Table 12-6
Regression for "Real Estate Owned and Sold on Contract" to Fees, etc. Mutual Savings and Loan Associations, 1963 and 1965

Year	Constant Term	Premiums, Commissions, and Fees, Regression Coefficient	Standard Error	R^2	Standard Error of Estimate
1963	0.26135	1.76663	(0.30824)	.4703	12.73300
1965	0.87920	1.44834	(0.17854)	.6401	14.26223

Source: Federal Home Loan Bank Board, *Combined Financial Statements*, 1961-63.

The accompanying Table 12-7 provides estimates of "slow loans" on the basis of net return for the years, 1963-1965. Ratios were calculated for the means for 35 mutual cities. "Slow loans" were taken as a percentage of net return. This percentage was applied to the actual net return for the Los Angeles stock associations for the three years. Finally, the estimated "slow loans" were compared to the actual. Only in the last year, 1965, did the stock associations show a higher "slow loan" figure than the estimates derived from the mutual ratios.

"Slow Loans" as an Independent Variable. It is not altogether clear that "slow loans" properly belong in the multiple regression model. There are at least two reasons for their exclusion. First, the Federal Home Loan Bank Board, which is the principal source of the data for the cities and the states, definitely states that expenses in connection with them are "real estate" expenses; and do not belong in the "operating" expenses of savings and loan associations. Obviously, foreclosure of properties would mean that the lender would become responsible for maintenance, watering, and general caretaking. To the extent that they are recognizable and thus chargeable, they can be eliminated from the operating expenses of the savings and loan association. But, where they become a "headache" to the management of the association, they are not so identifiable and are properly seen as a contributor to total costs. On the other hand, inasmuch as management's salary is a "sunk cost," for which the association has contracted, there need not be additional or marginal expenses arising in connection with increased managerial exertions. Where the management is driven to hire extra help, they can be charged off as a nonoperating or "real estate" expense.

The second reason for excluding slow loans is that they are not strictly speaking an item in the product mix. That is, an association does not deliberately seek to produce or generate the "slow loan." Obviously, they are to be avoided or at least minimized after allowance is made for their income potential.

Table 12-7
Estimates of "Slow Loans" on the Basis of Net Return, 1963-1965

	1963	1964	1965
"Slow Loans"[1] as a % of Net Return for Mutuals[2]	104.5	110.0	135.1
Net Return, Los Angeles Stock Associations[3]	$ 87.7	$114.1	$117.5
Estimated "Slow Loans," Los Angeles Stock Associations on Basis of Mutuals' %s	91.6	106.3	158.8
"Slow Loans," Los Angeles Stock Associations[3]	$ 63.0	$ 96.6	$318.0
Estimated "Slow Loans" as % Actual	145.5	110.0	49.9

Notes:

1. "Slow loans" are "real estate owned" plus "contracts of sale" averaged for the year.

2. Ratios are derived from means for 35 mutual cities.

3. In millions of dollars.

In the multiple regression model, the willingness of an association to make such loans is indicated by the "new loans" relative to the other variables. It is not, therefore, surprising that "slow loans" should be so intercorrelated with these other variables since it is not, strictly speaking, independent of them. For these reasons, little is to be gained by treating "slow loans" as an independent variable. But, in order to meet all objections that would arise on the aforementioned grounds that mutuals have comparatively less of them, they were included in some of the models. As the subsequent discussion of the results will reveal, their impact on operating expenses was relatively slight.

Finally, it may be noted that "slow loans" were not significantly related to the return of associations. For the five years, 1961 through 1965, they did not provide additional explanatory information in the multiple regression models. This means that they were neither positively nor negatively related to the profitability of the associations. It may be inferred that when associations took such risks, they at least compensated for them. But it is more than likely that it was the *level* of new loans which was the more important variable in the "return" regression equations. This suggests that they had no identifiable impact on risk taken by associations.

Buildings and Furnishings

It is questionable whether "buildings and furnishings" should be introduced into regression models as an independent variable. Some students have done so[28] on the rather obvious grounds that they constitute an important part of the expenses of savings and loan associations. It is the thesis, however, of this study that they are a substitute for profits and thus properly belong in the analysis of profit or return rather than in operating expenses. Given the control exercised by management, and the constraints on the direct seizure of profit, mutual management is likely to exercise its power through expenditures on building and furnishings. It is hypothesized that stock associations, not so constrained, would show a lower expense when adjustments are made for activities performed.

The Federal Home Loan Bank Board reports the expenditures on buildings and furnishings in the "Income and Expenses" Section, Part II of its annual "Combined Financial Statements." Thus, there is no necessity for using "buildings and furnishings" as indicated in the balance sheet as a proxy for predicting the relative importance of the annual expenditures for such items. So far as the multiple regression model is concerned, it would be a simple matter to merely deduct these expenditures from the total operating expenses. Thus, the various independent variables, e.g., new savings, new loans, the number of savings accounts and the number of mortgage accounts could be related to this net figure for expenses.

The principal doubt with respect to treating "buildings and furnishings" as a variable lies in the fact that unlike the other variables, it does not represent a function or activity of the savings and loan association. They are not "product" in the sense new loans and savings and mortgage accounts are. New loans cause the association to incur expenses since they are a replacement of "loans repaid" plus the growth in savings which must be invested if the savers are to be returned a dividend. New savings are a necessary activity also since the savings and loan association must find them to replace withdrawals and to grow. Advertising and brokerage expenses result. The new savings and mortgage accounts, as well as the old ones, must be serviced. The expenses for "buildings and furnishings" are a "reported" expense for the above activities. They are not a functional operation of the association.

A further problem concerns the high multicollinearity of buildings with the other variables. With the exception of the stock organizational variable, the simple correlations were all in excess of 0.80. Not surprisingly, the correlation with the stock organization slope variable, new loans, was +0.27. This further confirms the hypothesis that the combination of managerial power and constraints on overt profit seizure diverts net income into these displays of wealth. They are one of the proxy forms by which management enjoys its amenities. In a sense, they are also an organizational variable in that they represent a peculiar characteristic of the mutual.

Some idea of the bias introduced into the analysis by treating "buildings and furnishings" as an independent variable is revealed by the 1964 regression coefficient. Of the mean expenses, 26.8% would have been "explained" by this item. Yet, the actual building and furnishings' expenses for that year for California federal associations came only to 12.2%; the California stock associations' ratio of expenditures on this item were 8.0%; and all United States federals showed a figure of 12.1%. In 1961, the multiple regression model yielded a regression coefficient for buildings of 29.2%. The corresponding ratios were: California federals, 9.3%; California stock associations, 7.1%; and U.S. federals, 10.6%. Clearly, the "buildings" variable in the model was picking up other factors, particularly the mutual organizational influence. It is significant that when this variable is dropped, very little is lost. The change in the coefficient of determination, R^2, is slight. Nor is the F value altered materially.

Buildings must, therefore, be rejected because first, they are not an independent activity in the product mix; second, they are highly correlated with variables that are more appropriately included in the model; and, third, they represent a form of diversion by management and, to that extent, are an organizational variable rather than one which describes any one of the various functions performed by an association and which would account for some part of the expenses. They are more properly seen as one of the ways management succeeds in diverting association net income; and are, therefore, more properly treated in the next chapter which discusses other tests of performance.

Dividends

Total operating expenses are derived from compensation, advertising and promotion, maintenance of building, e.g., light, heat, and furnishings, insurance premiums, etc. In addition, the savings and loan association must, of course, pay dividends to the saving members. However, the Internal Revenue Service permits savings and loan associations the right to deduct the dividends as an expense or cost. Thus, after gross operating income, total operating expenses are deducted to yield a net operating income before interest charges. The interest charges on advances and borrowings are next subtracted to yield the net operating income before income taxes. In the period 1952-62, savings and loan associations were permitted to transfer a substantial portion of their earnings to various reserves on a tax-deferred basis. By the Revenue Act of 1962, Congress provided a new schedule of income tax payments by associations. A regular corporate tax rate is paid on 40% of an association's income after deduction of expenses and interest paid to saving members.

The curious aspect of this tax law is that the interest or dividend paid is treated as an expense of the association. This, of course, puts the savings and loan association in a position comparable to commercial banks which pay interest on their time and savings deposits. Thus, the latter pays a corporate tax after the interest paid on such deposits. But when a mutual savings and loan association or a savings bank is permitted to treat these interest payments or dividends as an expense before taxes, problems arise in the interpretation. When the mutual is permitted to treat the payments on savings accounts in the same way as commercial banks and stock savings and loan association, a question is raised as to its difference from stock organizations.

If the mutual is actually owned by the members, the return paid them would be identical to that given shareholders; and is properly treated as net income after taxes. The savers or holders of investment certificates' operating expenses would be deducted as a cost prior to taxes. This practice of permitting the mutual associations to treat interest or dividend payments as an expense makes the concept of mutual ownership meaningless. Curiously elsewhere, the Internal Revenue Service requires savers (those who have share accounts in savings and loan associations) to treat their dividend return as an interest rather than as a dividend from an investment. They are not allowed to claim the dividend inclusion privilege.

The Sale and Purchase of
Mortgages

Expenses are also influenced by the extent to which an association or a region sells or buys part or all of a mortgage. In the savings and loan industry, such purchases and sales are characterized under the heading of "participations." California is the major net seller of participations while the remainder of the country, particularly the eastern part of the nation, is a net buyer. By 1963, after a FHLBB program initiated in 1957, California had made net mortgage *sales* of $1,348,000,000. This was 13.2% of its average mortgages for 1963. In contrast, the Boston Federal Home Loan Bank District, representing the six New England States, had net *purchases* of 9.4% of average mortgages held. There was a 23% differential between the sales made in California and the purchases in Boston (see Table 12-8). Obviously, the California associations, and particularly the stock associations, had larger expenses simply because of the much greater proportion of mortgages they serviced for associations in other parts of the country. On the other hand, expenses elsewhere were that much less: they reflected neither servicing nor origination expenses on purchased mortgages.[29]

There are various reasons why associations enter into participation purchases and sales. In 1963, on participations sold to eastern buyers, a prime loan yielded 5 1/4 to 5 1/2%. "The seller, who continues to collect payments on the loan, keeps the difference. Last year California savings and loan associations sold $673.1 million compared to $441.5 million in 1962."[30] One advantage of participation sales was noted by a San Francisco Federal Savings and Loan Association which decided "they didn't want to pay the relatively high dividend rate on savings and dropped it to 4.75%. 'As a result,' says President E. Ronald Long, 'saving deposits dropped about $500,000 in January alone.' And because the average cost of the money the association is using now is lower than the cost of new money, Long figures it is cheaper to generate new lending assets through participation sales than it is to pay the current high saving dividend rate."[31]

Table 12-8

Net Participation Sales as % of Mortgages Held at Beginning of the Year: 1963

Federal Home Loan Bank Districts	Net Sales	Mortgage Loans Held	Net Sales ÷ Mortgages
Boston	−216 262	2 303 594	−9.39
New York	−373 304	8 111 098	−4.60
Pittsburgh	−117 483	3 959 858	−2.97
Greensboro	45 452	10 982 014	0.41
Cincinnati	− 74 635	7 352 851	−1.02
Indianapolis	− 54 739	3 652 542	−1.50
Chicago	−279 693	9 123 061	−3.07
Des Moines	−114 435	4 627 885	−2.47
Little Rock	− 55 622	4 803 095	−1.16
Topeka	−190 486	3 158 373	−6.03
San Francisco	1 471 369	17 475 260	+8.42

Source: Federal Home Loan Bank Board, Source Book, 1963.

Thus, when an association wants to avoid a higher dividend rate or reduce the dividend rate, it may sell part of its mortgages to eastern buyers. This practice is advantageous both for the seller and the buyer. The seller's price is less than he would otherwise have to pay in the local saving market where he might be forced to raise his dividend rate or increase advertising expenses. The buyer increases average yield since he only purchases western mortgages at yields in excess of that offered at home. The seller gains not only from the cheaper money: he also receives the origination fees and by keeping part of the mortgage he has an override that may give him an effective yield close to 10%.[32]

Data revealing the purchase and sale of loans were secured from the Federal Home Loan Bank Board for the years 1961 through 1964. The totals were introduced into the 1964 model to ascertain the effect on expenses and return. When only mutuals were considered, the "T" value of the net participation regression coefficient was insignificant at -0.753. When the stock areas were also included the T fell even further to 0.176.

Differences in Accounting Procedures. Expenses may also differ entirely apart from the functions performed because of differences in accounting methods. Often, special arrangements may be worked out with suppliers. One association may use loan brokers paid directly by borrowers and receive only the balance of a fee paid at the loan origination. It does not have the expenses since they have been taken over by the loan broker. In contrast, other associations, which have their own employees perform the function, receive the entire amount of the fee. Both fees and expenses are obviously higher. Differences in accounting procedures also cause differences in expenses that have nothing to do with operating efficiency, e.g., some associations may own a building and charge all of the expenses, including that for tenants, to operating expenses. When such is the case a ratio such as expenses over assets[33] is clearly and erroneously inflated.

Size of Association

Chairman McMurray of the Federal Home Loan Bank Board has commented that it has long been held that financial institutions should experience declining rates of cost per dollar of assets as size increases. Noting that it seems to be so in banking, he observes that

it does among savings and loan associations, which some studies we are making reveal, until you get above the $25,000,000 class. Then, expense ratios which have been falling suddenly take off and start rising again . . . associations with $100,000,000 and over in share accounts do show a little better performance than the $50 to $100,000,000 group, but only about the same performance as that of many smaller associations with less than $25,000,000 in share accounts.

. . . There is some peculiarity in some of the operating performances. Advertising expenses, for example, tends to rise rather sharply for some of the larger associations so that the ratio of advertising expenses to income, and to share accounts or assets, increases quite substantially. Office building expenses seem to be higher, too, and in some cases compensation expenses, which you would expect to decline as the association grows, shows only a minor decrease.[34]

Now, for reasons indicated earlier, little significance can be attached to studies which relate expenses to assets, share accounts or income. There is nothing surprising in a finding that unadjusted ratios yield no indication of the contribution of size. A multiple regression analysis makes provision for variations in the product mix in loan originations, new savings, withdrawals, and real estate owned and acquired through loan foreclosure.

With respect to advertising expenditures, it is necessary to consider total income, as well as expenses, rather than advertising expenses alone. The large association may find it more profitable to make a direct appeal to savers through the use of the various media such as newspapers, magazines, TV and radio. Such a procedure may be uneconomical for the smaller association. This means that the latter would preferably and rationally use broker savings on which a commission must be paid and which do not figure in expenses. In the typical language of marketing specialists, the function of generating the new savings has to be performed one way or another with an expense involved in each instance. Thus, no significance can be attached to the higher ratio of advertising to total assets or share accounts as found possibly for the larger associations. This would simply mean that different policy decisions are optimal in large organizations as compared to the smaller ones. In either case, a marketing function is performed involving the attraction of savings into the association.

Variations in the efficiency of different size establishments is usually inferred from variations in average costs. But this would be correct only in the event that all other conditions remained the same, e.g., each had the same turnover rate for savings accounts and mortgages; the growth rates with respect to savings and mortgages were equal; and each had the same proportion of slow or bad loans. In the absence of data relating to the product mix, there is no warrant for judging that differences in average costs of different size establishments indicate a meaningful discrepancy in relative efficiency. Furthermore, the test of efficiency in terms of a ratio between annual expenses and assets is misleading for the above reasons as well as other reasons cited earlier.

If we wish to measure the influence of size, regard must be had for variables other than assets. Associations should only be judged in terms of what they actually do—not merely in terms of assets held. Thus, a savings and loan association has two principal functions plus a number of derived ancillary functions. First, as a financial intermediary it actively seeks and collects savings. Second, these savings are invested in mortgages. Both activities entail the association in servicing the savings and mortgage accounts. Thus, a difference in relative efficiency of different sized firms will be reflected in how they perform these functions. No importance can be attached to expenses in terms of assets: the necessary information relates to the expenses which result from the functions performed. Nor does it make sense to test for the influence of size while holding growth or new loans constant as was done in one study.[35] We are necessarily concerned with the efficiency of firms with respect to their growth or origination of new loans just as we want to know how efficient they are in attracting new savings. Growth is not something apart from efficiency. On the contrary, efficiency in "growing" is one aspect of efficiency. As the former chairman of the FHLBB noted,[36] a low expense ratio may merely mean that the association did nothing, i.e., it failed to serve its community in savings and lending markets.

Similarly, it has been suggested that size is an independent variable and, consequently, might explain differences in expenses. To illustrate: stock associations, on the average, may be larger and this fact would account for lower expenses. There are, however, two points which may be made of this hypothesis. First, if size is correlated with efficiency (and this is by no means established), and only the stock were found to have taken advantage, it would further support the hypothesis that they were more efficient. Obviously, the failure to exploit such economies is an indication of an indifference with respect to the level of costs. Second, one must not assume the problem away by taking it for granted that (a) large units are more efficient; and (b) that the stock are typically larger than mutuals. This is not the case in Los Angeles or elsewhere in the nation. Indeed, there may be reasons why mutuals would grow larger by merging where stock would not. The sale of control of a mutual through sale of the valuable infrastructure is a way for management to capitalize control of the association.

Expenses may also differ because of variations in the degree of vertical integration. In the savings and loan industry, this means that some associations might engage in forward integration by operating their own mortgage business. They originate loans in the place of real estate or mortgage brokers. Other savings and loan associations, using mortgage and real estate brokers, are able to shift the burden of such expenses onto the latter. Obviously, their costs will be that much lower. It has been suggested that in the Southern California area, the reason Home Savings and Loan Association, the nation's largest, has expenses equal to one-half the average for other stock associations is a less integrated arrangement. Home Savings pays solicitors on commission. With the borrower paying the solicitor, no expense is recorded by Home. To the extent that there are variations in the usage of brokers, reported expenses will vary between associations. In these circumstances, differences will not reflect relative efficiency.

Large Associations, Number of Associations
and Relative Concentration

Allowance must be made for variations in the typical size of associations in each of the areas. A city with a relatively large volume of dollar assets could differ from another city of equal size simply because it had a few relatively large associations in contrast to one with many small associations. The "average" size of the association would not pick up the factor that might account for differences in expenses attributable to large units simply because the several large associations are surrounded by many small associations. It is necessary to allow for a concentration test. For example, the amount of assets controlled by associations over $100,000,000, over $50,000,000 and over $25,000,000 was believed an indication of the relative importance of large associations. In addition, the number of associations in the particular area might itself be significant, after allowance is made for other scale items such as the dollar volume of new loans or the number of mortgage accounts and savings accounts.

First, the number of associations was treated as an independent variable. Table 12-9 reports its statistical significance in terms of the usual T values for 1962 and 1963. In both years, as the number of associations increased, expenses and profits declined. This would seem to suggest that while smaller associations, cet. par., had lower costs, they also received less in their return. When "average size" is substituted for numbers, this result is further confirmed with respect to profits for 1962 and expenses for 1963. The trouble is that neither numbers nor average size allow for an asymmetrical distribution of firms within the market area. One very large firm surrounded by a large number of small firms is consistent with such a result.

In order to allow for an asymmetrical distribution, the influence of relatively large size was tested for directly by the introduction of another variable: the percentage of assets controlled by associations in that area having more than $100 millions in assets, more than $50 millions; and more than $25 millions. As

Table 12-9

"T" Values for Number of Associations, Average Size and Concentration in Expense and Profit Models

Variable	1962		1963	
	Expenses	Profits	Expenses	Profits
Number of Associations	−2.289	−4.253	−1.871	−1.949
Average Size	0.722	2.273	2.275	−1.031
% of Assets held by Associations larger than $100 million	−0.451	0.742	−0.163	0.175
% of Assets held by Associations larger than $50 million	−0.698	1.972	0.295	1.220
% of Assets held by Associations larger than $25 million	−0.509	1.692	0.395	1.303

the table reveals, size as measured by these variables was not statistically significant.

Scale Economies in the Los Angeles
Data for Individual Associations

The regression model for eighty-one Los Angeles savings and loan associations is presented in Table 12-10. The number of mortgages was statistically significant as compared to the number of savings accounts. The T value for the latter was 1.08973. Inasmuch as information was sought with respect to the possible existence of decreasing costs and increasing returns, the data were transformed into logarithms. Constant returns occurs if the regression coefficients sum at some value close to unity.

The sum of the regression coefficients in the expense model came to 0.92106. The question is whether this is sufficiently different from unity to suggest the prevalence of decreasing costs as size expands. Using a method suggested by Tintner,[37] the hypothesis tested was that the production function was actually nonlinear. With the critical F value at 6.96, the test function F at 9.24 suggests that the hypothesis that there is a linear homogeneous production function must be rejected. But this was not the case with profits.

When the mutual associations were removed from the sample, the remaining 60 stock observations showed statistically significant sums of the regression coefficients different from unity. Expenses summed at 0.87335 and profits at 1.09312 (see Table 12-11). Both were significant at the 99 percent confidence level. That is, there was less than one chance in a hundred that the results could be ascribed to randomness.

The contrast between these results and that from the city data could be

Table 12-10
Expense Regression Model for 81 Los Angeles Savings and Loans Associations, 1963: Logarithmic Form

Constant Term		0.82568		
R^2	0.9715			
Variables		Regression Coefficient	Standard Error of Reg. Coef.	Partial Correlation Coefficient
Loans Made		0.25285	0.07672	0.35366
Number of Mortgages		0.46822	0.06133	0.65886
Real Estate Owned and Contracts of Sale		0.02687	0.01326	0.22648
Addition to Saving Capital		0.17312	0.04000	0.44470

Table 12-11

Regression Models for 60 Los Angeles Stock Associations, 1963: Logarithmic Form

	Expenses		Profits		
Constant Term	0.72411		−1.04592		
R^2	0.9611		0.9332		
Variables	Regression Coefficient	Standard Error		Regression Coefficient	Standard Error
Loans Made	0.41711	0.07459		0.81128	0.11005
Real Estate Owned	0.06763	0.01652		−0.03516	0.02568
Number of Mortgages	0.38861	0.06556	Number of Savings Accounts	0.31700	0.11018

attributed to aggregation. Another hypothesis is that mutuals use expenses as part of their diversion technique. Given the absence of clear-cut ownership arrangements in the mutual institution, exploitation of decreasing costs or increasing returns is highly unlikely. Whatever the potential gains. they are likely to be diverted to the infrastructure.

Variation in the Size of Loans

New loans or "loans made" indicate the extent of origination activity. The variable is the dollar value of the loans made during the specified period. As with all variables, there are difficulties in connection with its use. One rather obvious problem arises, when in comparing two associations or areas with identical dollar value for new loans, the average size of the loan differs. One area might lend a million dollars with the average loan at $15,000. The other area lends the same amount but the average size is $25,000. Though identical functions are performed in origination, the "number" of "loans made" in the latter case would be less. Accordingly, it would be incorrect to treat the area where the average size of loans made was higher as more efficient simply because, after making allowances for the other variables, expenses were lower.

Both the absolute price of the home purchased and the loan to price ratio is critical in determining differences with respect to loan size. The Federal Home Loan Bank Board has in recent years sought to provide data with respect to averages in the different principal cities. The two California cities, Los Angeles and San Francisco, show a purchase price 34% higher than the U.S. average.[38] Census data for 1960 also revealed that the purchase price for homes in Los Angeles had a median value 14.4% higher than that for all SMSAs. Making allowance for the higher purchase price yields an adjusted loan index for Los Angeles, as compared to the nation, of 86 to 75. Further adjustment of an additional 12%, to take account of the greater loan to price ratio, brings the figure to 96 which is 128% of the SMSA average on conventional loans for savings and loan associations.

The 1960 census indicated that the Los Angeles-San Francisco total showed an average mortgage size of loans made for 1959 and part of 1960 of 31.2% higher than that for the inside SMSAs. Or put another way, the latter average mortgage size was 76.2% of that for Los Angeles-San Francisco. If both years are adjusted for the higher average size of loans made, there is no impact upon *trend* in expenses as compared to the other variables for the specific period. Thus, for the SMSAs, expenses increased by 56% as compared to a 40% increase in loans made. In contrast, the expenses for the California stock associations increased only slightly more than 50% of that for the new loans. Thus in one case, the ratio is 140% while in the other, it is 55%. Had the SMSA expenses increased at the 55% for the California stock associations, their expenses would have increased 22%: the total expense increase would have been $343,360,000 instead of $439,842,000. The difference comes to $96.5 millions or, divided among the 1,059 associations, it would have been $91,107. It is highly likely that this represented a four-year transfer to the management in those associations. It is, therefore, irrelevant that the average size of loans made in California was higher.

There are some difficulties in using the Federal Home Loan Bank data because they represent a combined figure for commercial banks, mortgage finance companies, mutual savings banks, insurance companies and savings and loan associations. It is preferable to refer to the census data which deal exclusively with savings and loan associations. The obvious defect in the use of a combined index is that there is no information with respect to the relative importance of the different financial intermediaries in each of the standard metropolitan statistical areas.

One further caution is necessary in considering the significance of the different size loans. If one area has a preference for larger size loans, larger appraisals or higher loan-to-price ratios, there may be some association between this preference and a willingness to assume risk. Higher loan-to-price ratios may be associated with a higher proportion of scheduled items or slow assets. To the extent that this larger size involves the assumption of greater risk, this could mean higher expenses inasmuch as a greater proportion of more highly skilled and higher salaried personnel may be required. Again, the larger size loan and also the higher loan-to-price ratio is often associated with a higher proportion of unseasoned loans which may lead to higher risk and ultimately higher expenses.

There are other reasons why the size of loans made varies. Some regions, for example the West Coast, have experienced much higher rates of growth and also an inflation in both land values and construction costs. This means that the loans have to be larger or the down payments increased. If the same loan-to-price ratio is maintained, either the borrower or the lender must find more money. Since "loans repaid" have been falling historically, new funds are required by the association. Inflation increases the competition for savings. In California, this led not only to higher dividend rates but to the commandeering of money brokers so as to tap the relatively less competitive sectors of the nation. Larger associations also advertised in eastern newspapers and magazines.

Evidence presented (in Table 3-3) showed that the mutuals lagged their new loan activity as compared to both the increase in expenses and to stock associations in the period 1950-1964. Where California stock associations increased lending activity by 5% more than expenses, California federals permitted their lending to fall off by 22% and associations in the remainder of the United States by 35%. They increased lending by 65% of the expense increase. It is no wonder that the mutuals were quick to resent the growth of the California stock associations. The latter made it increasingly difficult for mutuals to divert funds.

Another factor at work, not only on the West Coast but elsewhere, involves a trading up with a pronounced increased preference for both larger homes and superior quality. To the extent certain areas have been characterized by these preferences, there would be a larger average size in "loans made."

Lack of Homogeneity. Mortgage loans are not homogeneous. Multiple regression analysis indicates that mix is far more significant in determining the level of expenses than the number of mortgages or the average mortgage size. It should be noted that average mortgage size is a ratio involving dollar volume or value of loans divided by the number of loans. However, with exception of the census data for 1959, annual data are not readily available to indicate the average size of "loans made." Instead, it is necessary to resort to a proxy variable, *viz.*, average size of mortgages "held." Or reliance can be placed on the 1959 data with reference to 1960 or 1961 when the differences are not too great. Either way, there is little difference with the results.

The hypothesis is that when the dollar value of new loans, the number of savings accounts, new savings, and real estate owned are held constant, average mortgage size is negatively correlated with expenses (Table 12-12). Though the sign was negative, it was not statistically significant. It is, however, not surprising that average size had little to do with expenses: larger loans may often increase expenses simply because of the greater detail required as with large apartment houses, bowling alleys, and churches. The relationship is not simple. Other variables seem to be not only more significant but far more important in explaining variations in expenses.

Factors in Different Size Mortgage Loans. A principal reason for larger average size is growth, as in areas where inflation and general prosperity have pushed up land values. New and higher priced homes are of larger importance than they would be in areas where there is a relatively larger proportion of loans for purchase of existing homes. Where there is more growth, both construction loans for one to four family residences, and multiple-unit construction loans of the more general community type are more important.

Table 12-12
Expense Regression Models with Average Mortgage Size: Mutuals

Year	Constant Term	Regression Coefficients and Standard Errors for Independent Variables					
		Number of Savings Accounts	New Savings	REO	New Loans	Average Mortg. Size	R^2
1962		.00760	.00933	.14482	.02198	−.09163	
	0.8600	(.00307)	(.00311)	(.04259)	(.00462)	(.17521)	.9895
1963		.00638	.01419	.12492	.01901	−.25398	
	2.4320	(.00340)	(.00356)	(.02802)	(.00471)	(.21511)	.9916
1964		.00831	.01288	.13580	.01476	−.25135	
	3.1990	(.00425)	(.00377)	(.02118)	(.00561)	(.26345)	.9890

Sources: FHLBB, Combined Financial Statements and Source Books, FHLB of San Francisco.

On the other hand, there are offsetting disadvantages to lending on higher priced homes. As prices mount, entirely different problems develop: the lender finds it increasingly difficult to resell the property in the event that there is foreclosure. Higher valued loans, therefore, involve both greater risk and greater expenses of reselling. Higher valued loans may also be due to more liberal appraisal. The temptation in this direction is obviously much greater in a growing area simply because mistakes are canceled out by the general inflation.[40]

Larger average size of "loans made" may also be due to a greater amount of refinancing. In California, where the population is relatively more mobile and where the turnover rates are higher, this is the case. The price is higher also because of general inflation. Another factor is that inflation in the value of the land and the home increases the equity of the owner which in turn permits refinancing for a variety of reasons, e.g., education, travel, or purchase of a new auto, etc. This represents a much less expensive source of cash. But it may distort the size of loan simply because reported as a "new loan," it may be counted to the full amount of $20,000 when, in fact, the actual increase in cash is only $5,000.

Average size is also influenced by loans for multiple-dwelling units. Where the new construction is turning towards apartment houses of increasing size, the average size is increased. It follows that the area cannot be compared to other areas without adjustment for variations in the proportion of financing for multiple units.

On the other hand, there are different kinds of expenses involved in apartment house financing, particularly where the loan is speculative in that close surveillance of builders is required at all times. This means that while the size of the loan may be considerably larger, there is an offset because it is a different kind of loan. Expenses are undoubtedly higher.

There is no simple relationship between number of loans and expenses. Some savings and loan officials have remarked that the larger loans carry higher risks. Not only can they not be sold as easily, but other lenders may not want them at all. There are inherent disadvantages: greater investigation may be required because more money is risked per borrower. As individual loans, the association has not acquired the same knowledge and experience it may have gained from tract loans or loans in older areas. To this extent, though the average mortgage size might be higher in California, the expenses involved would also be more: the loans are generally in new areas and are with new people from other states whose credit worthiness has not been established. Thus, there is good cause for distinguishing them from loans where the mortgage is at least five years old; where the borrower has had a loan from the savings and loan association; and where the loan is on a *known* property.

Average Size and Number of "Loans Made." The average size of "loans made" is a ratio in which the dollar value of "loans made" is divided by the number of "loans made." As indicated, these data are not available. Therefore, a proxy is substituted derived either from the 1960 census or the ratio of "loans held" to the number of mortgage accounts. But reliance need not be placed on a ratio. Since the regression model uses variables in their absolute form, the same precedent can be followed with respect to size of "loans made." It is sufficient to take "number of mortgages" as an independent variable. However, while the number of mortgages "held" is available, there is no information with respect to the number of "loans made." For this reason, as a last resort, the census data and the proxy variable were used.

Suppose there are two associations, each with $1,500,000 in mortgages and annual expenses of $15,000: the expense-to-mortgage ratio is 1.0%.[41] Now A has 100 and B 150 mortgages, so that the average size of the former is $15,000 and the latter $10,000. Though the ratio of expenses to mortgages are identical, is it necessary to make an adjustment for the number of mortgages? Or for the average size? To answer affirmatively is to assume that the critical item is the number of mortgages. In other words, that all mortgages are homogeneous. Thus, if we adjust the mortgage base by the difference in average size, we would increase it by 50% and thus cut the ratio by more than 50%. In effect, we are saying that the correct test of expenses is not related to the dollar volume of mortgages but rather to the *number*. The consequence is that an adjustment for variations in size of mortgages implicitly assumes that the determinants or functional relations between the determinants in the product mix are homogeneous. But, we know that there are differences in the activity of different savings and loan associations and between different regions, e.g., turnover and growth rates vary, construction loans may represent a larger percentage in the category of new loans as between regions; and there are variations in the activity of savings accounts and mortgage accounts attributable to difference in the extent of participation sales and purchases.

There is another rather substantial objection to an adjustment on the grounds of variations in size. The relevant question concerns expenses as related to dollars invested. Thus, it is immaterial for certain purposes that the East may make smaller mortgage loans on the average. Indeed, it may indicate nothing more than their competitive disadvantage with respect to their capacity to profitably invest savings. This obviously would confirm the original argument concerning the ability of not only mutual associations but eastern associations to compete for a scarce resource, *viz.*, money. In terms of dollars invested, expenses may well turn out to be higher in the east; and it would be irrelevant that mortgage prices were higher on the West Coast since the only question, so far as economic efficiency is concerned, is optimality in the use of a scarce resource.

If it were necessary to adjust for differences in the average size of "loans made," the critical variable would have to be number. In that case, number should have been used in the first place; or, at least, a proxy for number rather than a ratio. There are two reasons favoring a decision to make no adjustment: (1) when comparisons are made within the same state and, presumably the same market areas, rather significant differences are revealed between mutual and stock associations; (2) the conventional use of mortgages and assets is based upon dollars rather than number. Presumably, the acceptable reasons are that the number of mortgages is not as good a test as dollars of assets or mortgages. This is because mortgages are too heterogeneous to be treated as identical. Furthermore, dollars are generally thought a better common denominator and are widely preferred in investigations. Finally, the multiple regression models do not show that there is a significant relationship between the average size and expenses.

Deflation of "loans made" is legitimate only if the *ceteris paribus* assumption is met at the expense level as well. It is probable that there is some interdependence between higher average size of "loans made" and higher expenses. This might be the case where construction loans play a greater role since they are more expensive loans. Also, larger size may entail higher expenses because of (1) reduced liquidity; (2) greater risk of insolvency due to smaller liquidity; and (3) the greater care and expense necessary for the loan. Some verification for this relationship may be found in the correlation of schedule items and expenses in California. But higher expenses are also incurred because the additional revenue is more than compensating.

To attach importance to the average value is to implicitly assume that all mortgages are alike, that they are homogeneous and involve identical expenses. When the mortgages in one area turn over at a rate of 20% as compared to 14.3% elsewhere, the latter have a 40% longer life. The consequence is that there are two effects: (1) expenses for maintaining the portfolio intact are reduced; (2) but, since the mortgages remain on the books longer, they are reduced in value and thus the average mortgage size is less. There is an analogue to trees and vines which differ by their length of life: some might last four years, others eight years. If it is assumed that there is an equality in the cost of replacement, it follows that those which last half as long must have some compensating feature, e.g., their fruit may be twice as valuable. This suggests that when turnover rates differ, the mortgages may not be homogeneous. For such reasons, associations will often exact prepayment penalties, e.g., in California, an association may receive six months interest on the original value of the loan.

Junior Mortgages. Mortgage loans are often accompanied by second or "junior" mortgages which arise when the buyer or borrower does not have sufficient funds to make the down payment required by the lender of the first mortgage. Variations in the relative importance of junior mortgages affect the number of mortgages. But, junior mortgages are not usually made by savings and loan associations. The 1960 United States Census reported that in Los Angeles junior mortgages represented 21.4% of all mortgages as compared to 16.9% for mortgages within the Standard Metropolitan Statistical Areas. To the extent that the number of junior mortgages is greater in one area, the results are altered.

Adjustments. If adjustments are to be made, they should not be restricted only to those created by variations in the average size of loans made. If it is conceded that greater average size inflates the activity of one particular area or association, it must also be recognized that the use of other measures such as expenses to assets deflates expenses simply because the denominator includes assets acquired in the past and not contributing significantly to current expenses. It has also been observed that there are offsets to the larger loans in that while they may involve relatively lower handling costs, they represent "a larger percentage of total assets than does a smaller loan. The seriousness of a default and therefore the degree of risk, from the standpoint of that association are related to the size of the loan."[42] Because of such considerations, associations are limited in the maximum loan they may make. And, for similar reasons, single family homes are considered safer than tract homes.

For all of the aforegoing reasons, it was not believed that adjustment for average size of mortgages was necessary. None of three proxies turned out to be statistically significant. In any case, "number" of mortgages seemed to work out as the preferable method for handling this problem. It is admitted that each mortgage is unique and that any attempt to treat them as homogeneous is a dangerous assumption. It was felt, however, that there was insufficient evidence for hypothesizing that either California or stock associations differed from mutuals with respect to the extent of the heterogeniety.

Having made this choice, the next step is to consider each of the various independent variables in their absolute form without their adjustment in any form whatsoever to assets or any other denominator. The problem of comparing different size units is to some extent met either by assets or some proxy form. The impact of size can then be derived from the various regression coefficients.

Variables and Symbols

Table 12-13 lists the 24 variables and symbols introduced into the expense and profit regression models. They are also subdivided into components in some cases. Due to multicollinearity, the number of useful variables was typically not larger than five or six. The three principal equations were:

$$(1) Y = a + bL + cN_0 + dS + eT + f(Q \times L)$$
$$(2) R = a + bL + cM + dT + e(Q \times L)$$
$$(3) J = a + bL + cN_0 + dS + eT$$

Table 12-13
Variables and their Symbols

Y	=	Total operating expenses for area
A_0	=	% of assets held by associations larger than \$100 millions
A_1	=	% of assets held by associations larger than \$50 millions
A_2	=	% of assets held by associations larger than \$25 millions
D_0	=	Value of construction loans during the period
D_1	=	Value of home purchase loans during the period
D_2	=	Value of other loans during the period
L	=	Value of total loans made
N_0	=	Value of total new savings
N_1	=	Value of total savings, withdrawn
P	=	Value of participation purchases to date, 1959-1964
F	=	Fees, premiums and commissions
R	=	Additions to surplus and reserves
M	=	Average number of Mortgage Accounts
S	=	Average number of Savings Accounts
T	=	Average value of real estate owned plus contracts of sale
G	=	Number of associations
H	=	Average size of association in area
J	=	Average value of investment in buildings and furnishings
K	=	Net additions to total savings during the year
Q	=	organized as a permanent stock company
U	=	% of conventional mortgages
I	=	Spread
V	=	Gross operating income
Z	=	Dividends paid
E	=	Value of average mortgages
F	=	Value of average assets
W	=	Average size of mortgages
B	=	Value of average savings capital
Z/B	=	Average yield on savings

The T values for rejected variables are presented in Table 12-14. As indicated, the reason for their rejection was that they "added" little to the explanation. Higher multicollinearity reduced their contribution; or other variables were more powerful in the models.

The dollar volume of "loans made" or "new loans" is among the more important variables in accounting for the level of expenses. The series which reports the data also breaks down this figure into its various components, construction loans, home purchase, and other loans. Each was tested independently and was rejected as statistically less significant than the aggregate, "loans made." In addition, construction loans on one-to-four-family residences was combined with "other loans," which include construction of units of more than four families as well as commercial buildings. Even here, significant results were not attained.

Similar decisions occurred with respect to savings flow. Both the aggregate flow (referred to as "new savings") and its components ("withdrawals" and "net savings") were tested. In this case, both the aggregate figure and the components were statistically significant. However, it did not seem to make much difference whether the aggregate or the components were utilized so far as the coefficient of determination, R^2, was concerned.

The number of mortgages was treated as an independent variable because it is both an indicator of the size of operations and the required servicing of mortgages "held." With few exceptions, the sign was negative because of intercorrelation with the number of savings accounts. Expenses rise in connection with the servicing of the savings account. This variable was statistically significant generally within the 99% confidence level. In most years, it was preferable to the number of mortgages. Though consideration was also given to "other assets," as an independent determinant of expenses, it also was rejected as lacking statistical significance.

Table 12-14
"T" Values for Rejected Variables

Symbol	T	Year
A_0	−0.451	1962
A_1	−0.698	1962
A_2	−0.509	1962
D_0	7.851	1962
D_1	1.438	1962
D_2	2.381	1962
G	−2.289	1962
H	0.722	1962
N_1	−0.898	1962
P	−0.753	1964
U	1.587	1963
W	−0.523	1962

13 The Regression Analysis: Expenses

Hitherto, the discussion has been concerned with problems which originated in efforts to compare differently located associations of varying product mix. It was decided that the appropriate method was to use a multiple regression analysis in which each of the various contributors to expense were placed on the right-hand side of the equation. In addition to the choice of independent variables, there is another problem: that of allowing for the influence of organization on the level of expenses.

The Measurement of Organizational Influence

To a very large extent, the method chosen depends on the extent and character of the data. One problem is the refusal of the Federal Home Loan Bank Board to make data available with respect to individual savings and loan associations. Indeed, it is as jealous of its secrets as if it were the Soviet agency responsible for missile sites. Information is available only for cities and federally and state-chartered associations on a statewide basis. When there are both state-chartered mutuals and stock associations, there is a problem with respect to separating the contribution of each. In most cases, the separation cannot be made. This means that no data are available for stock associations in those states and cities. Of twelve states chartering stock associations, the data exclusively represented stock only in five. In the other seven, the mutual share of assets ran from 14% to 90% (see Table 11-1). Eighteen of the forty largest standard metropolitan statistical areas allowed stock associations to operate; but the mutuals' share of assets ran from 1% in San Jose to 92.8% in Dayton (see Table 11-2).

Because the California Savings and Loan Commissioner takes a different attitude with respect to the dissemination of information, data were secured with respect to stock associations in nine California cities. Akron and Houston showed a stock influence over 90% and provided two more additions to the sample. Finally, the state-chartered associations in Arizona, Colorado, Nevada, and Oregon completed the stock sample of fifteen.

The Los Angeles regression model included 60 stock associations and 21 federal or mutual associations. Both the SMSA and Los Angeles models suffered from a deficiency of one or the other types of organization. This meant that running separate regressions for each and comparing the parameters, while not

259

impossible, would be subject to rather wide sampling error. The conventional procedure for handling this difficulty is to combine the observations while identifying the organizational factor by means of a "dummy" variable. A third method consisted in applying to the stock data for Los Angeles and San Francisco, the most important of the stock areas, the regression coefficients derived from the mutuals. Both these procedures were adopted for this study. They afford a check on each other.

"Dummy" Variables. A "dummy" variable is utilized when the investigation seeks to ascertain the contribution of differences not expressed in quantitative form. In the present instance, concern is with the impact of either the stock or the mutual form of organization on expenses. When an observation possessed the stock characteristic, it was given a value of "one" and its absence was represented by "zero." In its simplest form, the influence of the characteristic would be revealed as an addition or subtraction from the intercept and is the result of the dichotomy between "one" and "zero." The impact is shown in the ability to shift the function up or down, depending upon whether it is positive or negative.

Intercept or Slope Variable? The above technique rests on the proposition that after allowing for the influence of other variables, there remains some unexplained residual which may be attributed to a qualitative variable expressed in the extreme values of "one" or "zero." The organizational effect is restricted to the intercept. But when there is reason to believe that the variable operates on the *slope* as well as the intercept, another procedure is necessary. In the present study, it was hypothesized that the organizational impact would be felt on the slope as well.[1] The critical area was "marginal costs" or expenses rather than some "fixed" item whose influence is confined to the intercept. Indeed, the problem at issue concerned the behavior of expenses for stock, as compared to mutual associations, where they varied in size and activity. There was no reason to believe that there was some irreducible fixed cost level below which no association or group of associations could operate. On the contrary, all previous studies of the behavior of costs suggested that a linear cost function would be appropriate for the savings and loan industry.[2] When allowance is not made for organizational influence on slope, there is an implicit assumption that marginal expenses are the same whatever the organizational form. This is nothing more than a naive attempt to assume the problem away.[3]

Selection of Slope Variables: Multicollinearity. Inasmuch as this is a multiple regression model, each of the variables on the right-hand side of the equation have some influence on the slope. The same procedure is followed as with the intercept dummy: each observation is multiplied by "one" if it is stock and "zero" otherwise. If there are four original variables, four additional ones would be created. When this operation was performed, high multicollinearity had the usual effect in reducing the "T" values. But in each instance, all had the same sign and were negative indicating that the stock influence was to force expenses down. It was felt that one of the slope variables would be sufficient to indicate the impact of organization on the slope. The variable with the highest value proved to be "loans made." The other important slope "dummy" was "new savings." When the simple or intercept "dummy" was used at the same time, it did not prove to be significant.

Statistical Significance of Organization. The above decisions with respect to the selection of the appropriate "dummy" variables have assumed that some statistical meaning can be attached to the standard errors of their regression coefficients. Pearson[4] has criticized this notion. Since nothing is known about the tetrachoric "r" and its distribution, he believed that the calculation of the standard error was meaningless. Though this may be so, it leaves the investigator of qualitative variables desperate. He must still face the problem of assigning some value to variations in nonquantitative characteristics. For want of an altogether satisfactory alternative, he is compelled to fall back on "dummy" variables though well aware of their shortcomings. At best, comparison of the results to other less satisfactory methods is a check. When they are consistent with each other, there are some grounds for believing that there is a probability that they indicate the correct sign. If the model shows, e.g., that the stock influence on expenses is negative, useful information is gained.

The consistency of the results from both methods, as well as with other tests, supported the general proposition that stock associations achieved lower costs with similar product mixes. Earlier chapters indicated that by a number of tests, some sophisticated and some crude, that performance differed between the two types of ownership arrangements. Reliance was not exclusively placed on either the multiple regression model or the dummy variable.

The Regression Models

The regression coefficients and their standard errors for the 37 mutual areas are presented in Table 13-1 for the years 1961-1965. Thirteen important cities had to be excluded because of preponderant stock influence. The regression coefficients are stable with respect to sign; and their variation from year to year is not pronounced. It should be noted that the equations included "buildings and furnishings" inasmuch as the model was exclusively mutual. Expenses on this item are an important part of the total income, pecuniary and otherwise, accruing to the management of mutuals. The intercepts were all positive but relatively insignificant as compared to the mean level of expenses. Coefficients of determination, all over 0.99, suggest that the variables included explain most of the variation in expenses.

Table 13-1
Regression Equations for Operating Expenses: Insured Mutual Savings and Loan Associations, 1961-65, 37 Areas[1]

	1961	1962	1963	1964	1965
Constant Term	0.13924	0.08410	0.09385	-0.11250	0.59095
R^2	0.9977	0.9973	0.9981	0.9975	0.9976
Standard Error of Estimate	0.74302	0.86843	0.85853	0.98930	1.00785
		Regression Coefficients and Standard Errors			
No. of Savings Accounts	0.00493 (0.00104)	0.00682 (0.00108)	0.00782 (0.00116)	0.01406 (0.00077)	0.00809 (0.00149)
New Savings	0.00961 (0.00154)	0.00706 (0.00174)	0.00988 (0.00181)	0.00117 (0.00050)	0.01017 (0.00161)
Loans Made	0.00845 (0.00204)	0.01021 (0.00203)	0.00812 (0.00177)	0.00891 (0.00205)	0.00838 (0.00283)
Real Estate Owned and Sold on Contract	0.22772 (0.03280)	0.10327 (0.02693)	0.08372 (0.01770)	0.01231 (0.01423)	0.05871 (0.01260)[2]
Buildings and Furnishings	0.23544 (0.03805)	0.33762 (0.03930)	0.20757 (0.03380)	0.28390 (0.03058)	0.18339 (0.02233)

Notes:

1. Excluded because of stock influence were Cleveland, Columbus, Dallas, Denver, Houston, Los Angeles, Phoenix, Portland (Oregon), San Bernardino-Riverside, San Diego, San Francisco, and San Jose and Washington, D.C. SMSA's. Data for federal associations was substituted in Arizona, Colorado, Oregon, Los Angeles, San Bernardino, San Diego, San Francisco and Washington, D.C.

2. In 1965, the FHLBB changed these items from "real estate owned" and "contracts of sale" to foreclosed "real estate owned," "contracts of sale, and loans to facilitate sale of foreclosed real estate."

The regression coefficients of Table 13-1 were applied to the product mix for stock associations in Los Angeles and San Francisco in order to estimate the expenses mutuals incur for the same product mix. An adjustment was necessary for the amount allowed for "buildings and furnishings" because mutuals have a different attitude towards these items than the stock. A multiple regression model was used to predict the amount spent on the basis of the various activities of savings and loan associations.

The estimated expenses were consistently larger than the actual expenses for the stock associations in the two cities (Table 13-2). The average excess for the ten observations was almost 28 percent. In every instance, the difference of more than three times the standard error of estimate suggests that the chances of securing such differences because of sampling fluctuation are less than one in a hundred.

The regression model for the mutual areas for 1963 revealed that a typical set of mutual savings and loan associations, operating with a product mix identical to that of the Los Angeles stock associations, would have had estimated expenses of $111,335,000 as compared to the actual expenses of the stock associations of $94,461,000. Is this discrepancy statistically significant? That is, are

Table 13-2

Estimated Expenses as Compared to Actual Expenses for Los Angeles and San Francisco Stock Savings and Loan Associations on the Basis of Identical Product Mix as Derived from Regression Equations, 1961-65.

	Estimated Expenses	Actual Expenses	Estimated ÷ Actual	Estimated less Actual ÷ Standard Error of Estimate
(in 000s)				
1961				
Los Angeles	65,299	53,794	121.41%	15.51
San Francisco	12,707	10,961	115.93%	2.35
1962				
Los Angeles	85,481	68,274	125.20%	19.80
San Francisco	15,676	12,834	122.14%	3.27
1963				
Los Angeles	111,335	94,461	117.86%	20.30
San Francisco	22,499	19,702	114.20%	3.26
1964				
Los Angeles	118,340	95,983	123.80%	22.61
San Francisco	41,164	30,478	135.06%	10.08
1965				
Los Angeles	144,706	102,490	141.20%	41.80
San Francisco	48,003	31,686	151.50%	16.20

such differences compatible with observations from the same universe and having the same sample mean? The null hypothesis is that the actual value for the Los Angeles stock associations is part of the same universe as that for the mutual associations and, therefore, the difference is not statistically significant. "T" is the estimated expenses less the actual expenses for the Los Angeles stock association divided by the standard error of estimate: the ratio of the difference is 16.9 divided by .86. The quotient is 20. The null hypothesis obviously would only be accepted at values of "T" smaller than 2.5. This means that the chances that the actual value is part of the same universe is clearly less than 1%.

Relative Importance of Determinants of Expenses. Some conception of the contribution to each of the explanatory variables to the "mean" expenses is provided in Table 13-3. The impact on expenses is also shown as a percentage of the mean. The most stable element was "loans made." The "number of savings accounts" was also as important but not as stable. The former generally contributed between 40 and 50 percent of the expenses, while the latter varied from 14 percent to 45 percent.

Table 13-3

Contribution of Independent Variables to Mean Expenses

	Year[1]	Mean[2] Expenses	Number of Savings Accounts	New Savings	Loans Made	Real Estate Owned	Organizational Slope Variable
	1961	9.83					
Contribution to expenses			1.68	4.36	2.83	1.09	−0.40
% of mean expenses			17.0%	44.5%	28.8%	11.1%	−4.1%
	1962	11.09					
Contribution to expenses			4.26	1.10	5.39	0.92	−0.90
% of Mean			38.4%	9.9%	48.6%	8.3%	−8.1%
	1963	14.70					
Contribution to expenses			6.66	—	7.07	—	1.31[3]
% of Mean			45.3%		48.1%		−8.9%
	1964	14.23					
Contribution to expenses			6.35	1.17	6.47	1.15	−0.86
% of Mean			44.6%	8.3%	45.5%	8.1%	−6.0%
	1965	15.05					
Contribution to expenses			2.23	6.55	6.38	1.08	−1.42
% of Mean			14.8%	43.5%	42.4%	7.2%	−9.4%

Notes:

1. Data derived from Table 13-5.

2. In millions of dollars.

3. "T" value at −0.52994 not statistically significant.

The organizational influence ranging from 4 to 9 percent of the mean expense is somewhat misleading. The stock observations came to only 29 percent of the total. Thus, their influence on the mean expenses was limited. In order to evaluate their actual impact, another measure is needed. Table 13-4 shows what the mean expenses would have been in the absence of either mutuals or stock. Mutual expenses were secured by taking the mean without the negative stock influence. Stock expenses were found by assuming that the mean organizational slope variable was for stock areas only. The ratios of the mutual means to the stock means are given in the fourth column of the table. In general, mutuals showed expenses 20-60 percent larger than the stock.

Table 13-4
Estimated Mean Expenses: Mutual Compared to Stock

Year[3]	Mutual	Stock	Mutual ÷ Stock
1961	10.23[1]	8.41[1]	121.6%
1962	11.99	7.90	151.8%
1963	—[2]	—[2]	—
1964	15.09	11.23	134.4%
1965	16.47	10.14	162.4%

Notes:

1. In millions of dollars.

2. Stock organizational variable not significant.

3. Data derived from regression models in Table 5.

Organizational Impact

The second technique featured an organizational variable in the regression models for the same years, 1961-1965. The results are summarized in Tables 13-5 and 13-6. The statistically significant variables were either the average number of savings accounts or mortgage accounts, the dollar volume of new savings attracted that year, the dollar volume of "loans made," the dollar volume of real estate owned and contracts of sale and the organizational slope variable on "loans made."

"Loans made" was not only the most stable with respect to its regression coefficient, it was the only one. The others varied considerably from year to year. But their signs were stable. The organizational variable was negative and significant for four of the five years. The one year it failed to be significant was 1963; but that year was troublesome for other variables as well. The major difficulty seemed to be the unusually high multicollinearity. Neither "new savings" nor "real estate owned" proved to be significant this year either.

Table 13-5
Expense Regression Models with Organizational Variable, 1961-1965

Regression Coefficients, Standard Errors and Partial Correlation Coefficients for Independent Variables

Year[1]	Constant Term	R^2		No. of Savgs. Accts.	New Savgs.	Loans Made	Average Real Estate Loan & Contracts of Sale[2]	Loans Made X Organization[3]
1961	0.27842		Reg. Coef.	.00557	.01369	.01464	.30798	-0.00749
		0.9954	S.E.	(.00131)	(.00170)	(.00226)	(.03799)	(.00122)
			P.C.C.	.52805	.76361	.68825	.76547	-.66703
1962	0.33480		Reg. Coef.	.01268	.00242	.02240	.17404	-0.01135
		0.9928	S.E.	(.00115)	(.00981)	(.00212)	(.03268)	(.00225)
			P.C.C.	.84893	.34103	.83928	.61415	-.59274
1963	1.30987		Reg. Coef.	.01832	4	.02395	4	-0.00303
		0.8357	S.E.	(.00510)		(.00791)		(.00618)

Year			Reg. Coef.					
1964	-0.05699		.01635	.00236	.02232	.10458	-0.00794	
		S.E.	(.00163)	(.00109)	(.00275)	(.02272)	(.00183)	0.9882
		P.C.C.	.82845	.30489	.76776	.56196	-.53837	
1965	0.24666	Reg. Coef.	.00547	.01422	.02391	.05051	-0.01590	
		S.E.	(.00257)	(.00272)	(.00418)	(.01479)	(.00266)	0.9916
		P.C.C.	.30026	.61080	.64559	.45038	-.66151	

Sources: Federal Home Loan Bank Board, *Combined Financial Statements* and *Source Books*, 1960-65, Federal Home Loan Bank of San Francisco, California Division of Savings and Loan Associations.

Notes:

1. Data are for Insured Savings and Loan associations: 53 observations in 45 areas. Twenty-four are exclusively mutual and in 6 the mutuals had greater than 83% of the assets. This makes for a total of 30 standard metropolitan statistical areas plus Washington, D.C. Other mutual observations are for federal associations in Tucson-Phoenix, Los Angeles, San Bernardino-Riverside, San Diego, San Francisco, Colorado and Oregon. Stock observations in Akron, Anaheim, Houston, Los Angeles, Sacramento, San Bernardino, Santa Barbara, San Diego, San Francisco, San Jose, Stockton, Arizona, Colorado, Nevada and Oregon.

2. Averaged for 1961-64. Year-end data in 1965 included "foreclosed real estate owned," "contracts of sale" and "loans to facilitate sale of foreclosed real estate owned."

3. The "stock dummy" = one; and the "mutual dummy" = 0.

4. Not statistically significant this year.

Table 13-6
Expense Regression Models with Organization Variable, 1961-1965

Year[1]		Constant Term	R²	No. of Mtge. Accts.	New Savgs.	Loans Made	Real Estate Owned Plus Contracts of Sale	Loans Made X Organization
1961	Reg. Coef.	.16202	0.9974	.02123	.01608	.01212	.32377	-.00863
	S.E.			(.00688)	(.00155)	(.00250)	(.04112)	(.00123)
	P.C.C.			.41212	.83614	.57975	.75587	-.71623
1962	Reg. Coef.	.02970	.9946	.06453	.00284	.01825	.25002	-.01182
	S.E.			(.00808)	(.00121)	(.00287)	(.03947)	(.00291)
	P.C.C.			.75890	.32340	.68006	.67860	-.50939
1963	Reg. Coef.	1.26996	.8318	.07251		.02162	.19723	-.00389
	S.E.			(.03289)		(.00959)	(.11886)	(.00682)
	P.C.C.			.31223		.31856	.24013	-.08671
1964	Reg. Coef.	-.66136	.9950	.08886	.00206	.01676	.14607	-.00462
	S.E.			(.00790)	(.00101)	(.00281)	(.01983)	(.00182)
	P.C.C.			.85668	.28896	.66130	.73590	-.34234
1965	Reg. Coef.	-.01219	.9921	.03114	.01394	.02218	.05869	-.01572
	S.E.			(.01178)	(.00252)	(.00422)	(.01483)	(.00242)
	P.C.C.			.36230	.63187	.61162	.50300	-.69135
	P.C.C.			.46036		.40037		-.07047

1. Sources and Notes are identical to those in Table 13-5.

This model combined the observations for mutual and stock cities and treated the stock data in cities where mutual data also were available as separate observations. Thus, where there are 45 localities, there are 53 observations, eight of the cities reporting data separately for both mutuals and stock. The intercept or constant term was not as stable as it was in the purely mutual models; and, in 1964, it became negative. Nonetheless, it was generally quite low as compared to the mean values for expenses. The coefficients of determination were close to the 0.99 level for all years but 1963. The latter year reported a value of 0.8357 which was not unexpected considering the fact that "new savings," "real estate owned," and the organizational variable were statistically insignificant. The two remaining variables "explained" 83 percent of the expense variations.

Expense Variations and Mutuality. A multiple regression model by taking account of a number of variables permits comparisons. When a model does not permit adjustments on the basis of variations in the product mix, or the differential functions assumed by different associations or regions, it is impossible to make meaningful comparisons. Conventional comparisons on the basis of expense-to-asset ratios are misleading for this reason. They implicitly assume that all associations are identical in terms of services performed and products created. The falsity of this assumption was indicated in Table 10-4 which showed how the new loan-to-asset ratio varied between different regions. In addition, there is the rather significant simple correlation between new loans to assets and expenses to assets. A measure which fails to take account of such variations is not worthwhile.

A major difficulty in the multiple regression analysis of mutuals concerns the concept of mutuality: its primary principles involves a denial of profit maximization. It is hypothesized here that mutual expenses will be higher because (1) there is no private property interest; and (2) a self-perpetuating management is expected, apart from the variations in product mix, to take out in expenses all it possibly can. This is a variant of Parkinson's law: expenses are what income permits. It would follow if mutuals always maximized expenses in line with income, one would not expect to find the variations in expenses associated with variations in the product mix as would be the case for institutions operating under normal profit considerations.

"Spreads" and Expenses

There is, however, a way in which allowance can be made for this aspect of the mutual while testing at the same time the general hypothesis with respect to mutuality. Since it is anticipated that the management of the mutual will take in expenses as much as income permits, the procedure is to incorporate another variable, potential income, which shows how much can be diverted into expenses. This mutual determinant of expenses is derived from the income statement. It is referred to by industry as "spread" and is the difference between the gross operating income and the sum of dividends plus interest paid to the Federal Home Loan Bank[a] or commercial banks. After allowance is made for all other factors, the higher the "spread," the higher are expenses.

The results from regression models with "spread" as an independent variable are summarized in Table 13-7. In all but one of the years, the regression coefficients were significant. In the later years, "spread" would have accounted for rather substantial proportions of the mean expenses for the areas. While it would be incorrect to treat it as an "explanatory" variable, the signs do support the hypothesis that large "spreads" are positively associated with larger expenses, after allowance is made for other factors. It should be noted that this conclusion is consistent with a negative sign for the organizational or stock variable.

The positive correlation revealed by this table suggests that after allowance is made for the various activities of the associations, e.g., new lending and new savings, the number of savings accounts, scheduled items and the influence of organization, there remains another factor operating on expenses. This is that brought about by the institutional arrangement of mutuality. High spreads will produce their counterpart in high expenses simply because management operates under a set of constraints with respect to the direct appropriation of income.

Comparisons between Mutual and Stock Associations. The regression analysis indicated that if loans made had been doubled in 1962, as compared to the mean for the series, expenses would have been increased by 65% for the states and, depending upon how many variables were used, from 25 to 59% for the

Table 13-7
Impact of "Spread" on Mean Expenses of Mutuals[1]

Year	R^2	Regression Coefficient	"T" Value	Contribution to Expenses[2]	Mean Expenses[2]	Spread Contribution as a % Mean Expenses
1961	.9911	0.06624	2.12	1.305	10.456	9.9%
1962	.9868	0.04392	1.06	1.040	11.934	8.7%
1963	.9972	0.36314	7.86	8.164	14.097	57.9%
1964	.9918	0.32697	3.53	8.093	14.892	54.3%
1965	.9965	0.44807	10.01	11.612	15.623	74.3%

Notes:
1. Data derived from mutual regression models with "spread" as one of the variables.
2. In millions of dollars.

[a]Shaw's California study failed to include this. Yet such payments are a most important substitute for dividend payments. For California stock associations, these payments came to 13.8 percent of expenses and 5.1 percent of dividends paid savers in 1963.[5]

SMSAs.[b] When the California and Los Angeles stock data, with respect to these variables, are related to the regression coefficients, a mutual area with the same product mix would have had expenses of 62.6% and 72.6% higher than what was actually achieved by the stock associations.[c] The results are shown in Table 13-8 "Operating Cost Regression Models, 1962-1964." It is to be noted that when the

Table 13-8
Operating Cost Regression Models, 1962-1964

	Constant Term	Loans Made	Number of Mortgages	New Savings	R^2
35 SMSAs 1962	−0.33062				.9850
Reg. Coef.		0.03433	−0.00514	0.01479	
(s.e.)		(.00423)	(.01158)	(.00262)	
Part. Cor. Coef.		0.82429	− .07947	0.71134	
35 SMSAs 1963	−1.47961				.9893
Reg. Coef.		0.03059	0.05646	0.00735	
(s.e.)		(.00562)	(.01347)	(.00236)	
Part. Cor. Coef.		0.69930	0.60139	0.48794	
35 SMSAs 1964	−1.46038				.9893
Reg. Coef.		0.02461	0.06718	0.00812	
(s.e.)		(.00648)	(.01725)	(.00384)	
Part. Cor. Coef.		0.56337	0.57320	0.35510	
48 States 1962					
(Mutual only)	−659				.9888
Reg. Coef.		0.03551	0.00868	0.01041	
(s.e.)		(.00353)	(.00554)	(.00178)	
Part. Cor. Coef.		0.83491	0.22985	0.66117	

Source: Federal Home Loan Bank Board, *Combined Financial States*, 1962-1964, and *Savings and Home Financing: Source Book*, 1963-1964.

[b]The differences in the results discussed here and earlier is attributable to the use of "number of mortgages" for "number of savings accounts" in the above models.

[c]When allowance is made for estimated greater average size of loans made by California institutions, the excess of the mutuals is reduced to 30 percent. But this adjustment is not thought necessary for all the reasons listed above and summarized as follows: (1) when size of loan is tested as an independent variable, it turned out to be statistically insignificant; (2) it is not necessary to make an adjustment when comparisons are made within the same market area, e.g., California where "average size of loans made" is roughly identical for both mutuals and stock; (3) an adjustment on the basis of average size does not solve problems: it only changes them because average size is a ratio of dollar volume of mortgages to number of mortgages. Mortgages are heterogeneous, differing as to expense involved in placing them on the books; risky loans often entail more work. Therefore, it seems preferable to eschew tampering with the lid of this Pandora's box. Even in a competitive market, the stock generated twice as much new loan volume with but 43 percent higher expenses. On the basis of the 1960 census information indicating differences in size of "loans made," California stock data were deflated by 23.8 percent. The difference was only reduced to 41.6 percent.

number of variables was enlarged, there was but a minor increase in R^2. So far as estimations are concerned, the addition of variables fail to change the results substantially. However, the enlargement of the number of independent variables did reduce the regression coefficients, particularly "loans made." This is not surprising since this variable would, because of intercorrelation, pick up the factors associated with "real estate owned" due to foreclosure.

A major difficulty arises because of the variation in the services or product mix of different associations and different areas. In certain years, the estimated expenses for a mutual would have been from 15 to 42% higher than the actual expenses for the Los Angeles stock associations. In contrast, the estimated expenses for the Los Angeles federal associations would have been from 4 to 29% higher. When the estimated ratio of expenses to assets for the California stock associations are compared to the estimated ratio of expenses to assets for the California federal associations, the ratio is 131%. That is, mutuals with the same product mix as the California stock associations would have had expenses 31% higher than that for the California federal associations. The actual difference between the stock associations and the federal associations in this state was but 2%. Had the California stock associations behaved as their federal rivals, the expense to asset ratio would have been 1.60. At such a level, they would have been 28% higher than they actually were.

The differences between California stock associations and mutuals elsewhere in the nation deserve further comment in view of the judgment of one study that California associations were "typically high cost."[6] It is clear that not all California associations should be lumped together in this fashion since there are very strong expense differences arising from variation in the ownership arrangement. But an even more fundamental criticism is that it rested on a comparison of expense-to-asset ratios. In the absence of evidence demonstrating that associations elsewhere in the nation perform the same functions or have identical product mix, such comparisons are misleading if not erroneous. Assets are not the product turned out by the association during the year. They are rather capital acquired over a number of years, including the present. Expenses must be related not to previously acquired capital but to current acquisitions and the servicing of capital acquired in the past.

*The Influence of Stock Associations
on Mutual Associations*

On the basis of the above tests, it is contended that the evidence supports the hypothesis that the stock savings and loan associations achieve lower expenses. It follows on the basis of the survival test[7] that mutuals in areas where they must compete with stock associations will be forced to acquire some of the same characteristics. Clearly, the competition would be expected to increase their efficiency. What then are we to make of the evidence cited above that Los Angeles federal associations have expenses closer to the estimates derived from the mutuals' regression model coefficients?

This apparent paradox between the greater efficiency of the competitive mutuals and their higher expenses is easily resolved. The constraints imposed on the management of mutuals diverts what would have been larger revenue and net income into expenses. With controls on their "take-home-pay," management diverts income into nonpecuniary amenities such as attractive buildings and furnishings, additional and redundant manpower, etc. Short of diversion into management-owned subsidiaries, there is no alternative.

The ability of management to spend more on "buildings and furnishings" has its source in the greater efficiency forced on management by the necessity of competing with stock associations. Unlike the profit-seeking enterprise, a mutual's efficiency may be indicated by the capacity to elevate the level of expenses. It should be noted that these higher expenses do not mean that competitive mutuals are as efficient as their stock rivals. Because the fruits of their efficiency is diverted into "second-best" options such as "buildings and furnishings," high salaries and expensive vacations, less is available for additions to "net worth." This means that they are not able to grow as rapidly—nor are they able to pay their savers as much as the stock associations.

Tangible evidence of the impact of the stock associations on the competitive mutual is also provided by their larger activity as compared to both assets and expenses. The California federals must also generate more new savings and new loans each year. Only in this way can they generate the income which they must earn if they are to remain competitive with the stock associations in the savings market.

One final point needs to be made with respect to an alternative hypothesis which has been put forth, *viz.*, that they are able to spend more money because they inhabit areas of high growth.[d] A higher return is attributed to the more favorable mortgage market in which they operate. But this is not relevant here since growth is included in the "loans made" variable, i.e., given the growth and turnover rates reflected in the level of "loans made," expenses are higher (and also return). Whatever the growth rate, there is, in addition, another factor operating on expenses: the competitive influence of the stock associations forcing expenses down. But success in the mutual allows managements to divert into expenses what would have been additions to "net worth" in the stock association.

In order to test for the influence of the stock associations on their mutual competitors, similar regression models were developed as described earlier. The fifteen stock observations were dropped; and "dummy" variables were assigned to the ten areas which experienced stock competition. It was hypothesized that

[d]Since "growth" is but one part of "loans made," it cannot constitute an alternative hypothesis. The expenses or "return" is higher after making allowance for the growth rate.

for the mutuals to survive, they would have had to develop an efficiency comparable to that of their competitors. But, given the constraints imposed on management, expenses would be paradoxically higher than those reported for the noncompetitive mutuals. That is, had they been stock, they would have reported lower expenses and higher return; but because of the constraints, they are forced into taking that "return" in the form of higher expenses.

The hypothesis would be confirmed in the event that there was a positive correlation between expenses and competitive influence. On the other hand, the greater efficiency which makes possible the higher expenses would not be carried over into profit or return. Statistically speaking, the "T" values would be significantly positive as between competitive influence and expenses while they would not be expected to be so for competitive influence and "return."

Table 13-9 reports the relevant "T" values for the years 1961-65 for both relationships. They were significant at the 95 percent confidence level for expenses and competitive influence. Indeed, there is a pronounced increase in the significance during the period. The hypothesis with respect to "return" is only partially verified as the results are mixed. In the first years, the "T" values are significant and positive. Only in the last three years is the hypothesis confirmed. It may be that there is some relationship between the increase in "T" for expenses and the decline in "T" for return. It is remarkable that there should be such a pronounced negative correlation in the trend for the two sets of values.

In any event, it is clear that the mutuals made their expenses what their income or "spread" permitted. The difference in expense behavior as compared to that for "return" reveals the operation of the conventional constraints on the mutual managements.

The Los Angeles Model. The Los Angeles model was not only the source of additional information but inasmuch as it was based on 81 individual associations, it provided a check on the city data which aggregated data for the individ-

Table 13-9
Competitive Influence of Stock on Mutual: 40[1] Areas, 1961-1965

| | "T" Values | |
	Expense Regression Models	Return Regression Models
1961	1.84929	4.74574
1962	1.90584	3.92388
1963	2.10181	−1.15556
1964	3.19337	−0.76695
1965	3.49847	0.70606

Notes:
1. 41 areas in 1961 and 1962 as Memphis included.

ual associations. The regression coefficients and their standard errors for both "number" of savings accounts as well as "number" of mortgages are shown in Table 13-10. Because it was not possible to secure "new savings" from the federal associations, the growth in savings was substituted. The organizational slope variable, "loans made" had a negative sign similar to the aggregated city data. All the regression coefficients were significant at the 99 percent confidence levels. The organization impact on the intercept was not significant in the absolute model, thus giving further support to the absence of indivisibilities.

The significant variables for the individual associations were loans made, the number of savings accounts, the number of mortgage accounts, the growth in savings and the organizational slope variable which was obtained by multiplying loans made by the dummy variable. When the influence of the stock associations is removed from the mean, expenses are increased to $1,981,000 on the average for each federal. Had all the associations been stock, the mean expenses would have been $1,723,000. The federals add 15 percent to expenses. When mortgages

Table 13-10
Regression Equations[1] for 81 Los Angeles Associations, 1963

		A.			
R^2	0.9523				
Intercept	216.2				
			Independent Variables		
		Loans Made	No. of Savings Accts.	Growth in Savings	Organization Impact on Slope (L X Q)
Regression Coefficients		0.01654	23.39827	0.00223	−0.00507
(Stand. Error)		(0.00352)	(4.52670)	(0.00065)	(0.00145)
Part. Cor. Coef.		.47457	.51019	.36482	−.37297
		B.			
R^2	0.9498				
Intercept	173.2				
		Loans Made	No. of Mtge. Accts.	Growth in Savings	Organization Impact on Slope (L X Q)
Regression Coefficients		0.02301	69.17520	0.00224	−0.00647
(Stand. Error)		(0.00261)	(14.93560)	(0.00067)	(0.00142)
Part. Cor. Coef.		.71090	.46922	.35854	−.46437

Notes:
1. Absolute data.

are substituted for savings, the federal impact is to increase expenses 19.5 percent.

The model for the individual associations is not only consistent with the aggregate data, but it supports the general conclusions derived from them. Aggregation did not appear to distort the general hypothesis concerning the influence of mutuality on expenses.

The Gain to Management from
Higher Expenses

On the basis of the SMSA regression model for 1965, it was estimated that for the 37 mutual observations, expenses for an identical product mix to that of the California or Los Angeles stock associations would have been about 52 percent higher. If a more conservative estimate of 30 percent is used,[e] the value of the higher expenses to management can be estimated. The comparison is between the actual expenses of all United States federally chartered associations and estimated expenses on the basis of a product mix identical to that reported for the Los Angeles stock associations. The problem is to ascertain the value of control of a mutual to the top management. The results are confined to federally chartered associations with assets over $10,000,000 on the basis that the smaller associations do not significantly contribute to either total assets or to the principal functions carried out by savings and loan associations. Thus, it is an estimate of the value of control in a successful and well-established association.

Table 13-11 shows the calculations for 1965. The total assets for all federally

Table 13-11
Diversion Potential for Management in a Mutual Association

	Federal Associations in the U.S. with Assets Larger than $10,000,000	% of all Federal Associations
1965 Assets	$61,754,000,000	92.6
Number of Associations	1,181	58.7
Actual Expenses	$ 593,007,000	
Estimated Expenses on Basis of Los Angeles Stock Associations	$ 456,022,000	
Excess	$ 137,000,000	
Excess per Association	$ 116,004	

Source: Federal Home Loan Bank Board, *Combined Financial Statement*, 1965, op. cit.

---

[e]The average excess for the five years was 26 percent.

chartered associations was $66.7 billion. Federally chartered associations with assets greater than $10,000,000 had a total asset value of $61.7 billion which came to 92.6 percent of the assets for all federal associations. By number, associations in this size classification came to 1,181 or 58.7 percent of all the federals. The expenses in 1965 were $593.0 million.

On the basis of the regression model, federally chartered associations with a product mix identical to the stock associations would have $137.0 million more in expenses, i.e., 30% more. An excess of this nature was diverted to management in the form of higher salaries, nonpecuniary fringe benefits, and provision of services for privately-owned subsidiaries. Some indication of the value in dollars of the diversion to the management is indicated by taking the ratio of this total amount of $137.0 million to the number of associations, 1,181. The diversion potential per association comes to $116,000. Over a ten-year period, this amounts to $1.1 million for each federally chartered association.

14 Profits

Profits play a major role in growth since they provide the basis for future growth in that they represent the necessary reserves required for additional savings and lending. Thus, a major source of growth lies in the ability to keep expenses in check. Mutuals are not constituted so as to operate by reducing expenses and increasing profits, thereby building a platform for the further growth. On the contrary, expense manipulation is one of the principal methods by which management diverts association income to itself.

Some conception of the value of the buildup in net worth that can result from holding expenses down, or from more aggressive growth, was revealed by Table 10-1 which showed the changes in net worth for California associations which continued to exist from 1953 to 1962. Inasmuch as federal associations operated in the same market as stock associations, it is not unreasonable to assume that they had the same opportunities for growth. Had the federals grown at the same rate as the stock association, they would have accumulated $314.5 million more in net worth. The yield at 4.59 percent (as paid by California federal associations in 1962) would have come to $14.5 million which would have added 0.30 to dividends paid savers. Or, if the relative performance is compared to other stock states, the increase in dividend would have come to 0.21 for the federal associations. In any case, there is agreement with Professor Shaw's conclusion that cost economy "strengthens capital adequacy. At any given spread between marginal rate of interest and share rate, it increases the volume of intermediation that the industry would find appropriate for any given rate of return on assets and net worth."[1]

Problems in the Measurement of Return

In reporting on income and expenses, the Federal Home Loan Bank Board's *Combined Financial Statement* refers to the "allocation of net income" as between reserves, surplus, and dividends. In the subsequent analysis, the sum allocated to reserves and surplus is described as the return. One of the first considerations is to make the return comparable for different areas and types of organizations. The usual procedure is to take a rate of return or net earnings on assets, savings capital, or net worth. The California Savings and Loan Commissioner's 1963 report, which suggested as one test of superiority the ratio of profits to dollar assets, is relevant here.[2] But the usual problems arising in connection with using a ratio are further compounded by including assets in the denominator. Assets vary rather widely and are consequently an unstable denominator: they are high on financial statement days; they may be inflated with short-term loans which are never converted into actual construction. For a short-term loan to a builder, the funds may come entirely from Federal Home Loan Bank loans.[3] There are also problems with the numerator part of the ratio which originate in variation in the product mix. Given the opportunity to originate new loans, sell loans and service them for distant associations, income will be higher than where this is not possible.

California associations possess more favorable opportunities for increasing income because of the relatively faster economic expansion in their area. As a consequence, they can secure both higher interest income as well as higher fees. Another factor is "the relatively larger portion of recent loans in the portfolio of California associations, which is a concomitant of growth."[4] Mortgage rates have been rising the last two decades, so that

one would expect a group of lenders with a continuously large share of new loans in their holdings to show a higher average earnings ratio than a group with smaller additions to their mortgage investment. The same is true for fee income, which is a function of the volume of new loans as well as the amount charged. . . . Related there, though, is the share of construction loans in total lending activity, which has been unusually large in California. Because of greater risks or larger costs involved in construction loans, or both, fees charged on such loans are generally higher than on other mortgage transactions.[5]

But, it should be added, that "growth" requires explanation. It is symptomatic not causal—the result of conscious managerial decisions having their origins in organizational structure and incentives.

Expressing the return on net worth is also misleading since the mutuals do not have the same incentive in its expansion as management and owners in a stock association. A more interesting question concerns whether or not management in the mutual will seek to maximize profit as opposed to the rate of profit. Thus, in eschewing the latter, management is free from dependence on a denominator, itself the effect of the activities of the association. The assets grow because of the decisions made by the association. When a mutual maximizes net worth, it is at the expense of managerial compensation, amenities and the diversion mechanism.

Growth in Net Worth

A different attitude towards net worth in mutuals is indicated by Table 14-1, where the growth in reserves for the period 1959 to 1964 for the federal is compared to the stock associations in states permitting the latter. The per-

Table 14-1

Growth in Net Earnings, 1959-64: Federal Compared to Stock, 12 Stock States

	Reserves Plus Surplus, 12-31-59(000s)	Reserves Plus Surplus, 12-31-64(000s)	Increase	% of Increase
Arizona				
Federal	9,379	17,622	7,883	88.3
Stock	531	16,205	15,674	2,951.8
California				
Federal	271,369	528,463	257,097	94.7
Stock	355,966	1,059,297	703,331	201.8
Colorado				
Federal	30,565	54,465	23,900	78.2
Stock	15,431	38,079	22,648	146.8
Idaho				
Federal	8,841	16,055	7,214	81.6
Stock	510	1,636	1,126	220.8
Kansas[1]				
Federal	26,173	50,025	23,852	91.1
Stock	10,323	18,687	8,364	81.0
Nevada				
Federal	2,393	4,774	2,381	99.5
Stock	523	24,504	23,981	4,585.3
Ohio[1]				
Federal	169,793	268,010	98,217	57.8
Stock	96,621	158,886	62,265	64.4
Oregon				
Federal	19,851	37,277	17,426	87.8
Stock	5,077	16,527	11,450	225.5
Texas[1]				
Federal	52,816	104,310	51,494	97.5
Stock	34,096	91,054	56,958	167.1
Utah[1]				
Federal	7,286	15,004	7,718	105.9
Stock	7,898	19,015	11,117	140.8
Washington				
Federal	57,597	102,937	45,340	78.7
Stock	809[2]	4,158	3,349	414.0
Wyoming				
Federal	5,536	8,443	2,907	52.5
Stock	60	389	329	548.3
Total				
Federal	661,599	1,197,385	545,429	82.4
Stock	527,845	1,548,737	920,592	174.4
U.S. Insured	4,016,339	7,513,269	3,496,930	87.1
U.S. All Federal	2,327,053	4,096,015	1,768,962	76.0

Notes:

1. Data refer to 1958 and 1963 as separate information on stock associations not readily available for five-year period 1959 through 1964.

2. Includes mutual associations which subsequently converted into state-chartered stock associations.

Sources: Federal Home Loan Bank Board, *Combined Financial Statements*, 1958, 1959, 1963, 1964; United States Savings and Loan League.

centage increase in the amount held in reserves plus surplus is shown in the last column. In 11 of the 12 states, stock associations reported relatively larger additions. When the 12 states are lumped together the stock added to their reserves at a rate more than twice that of the federals: and also twice that of all federals in the United States. Only in Kansas did the federals report greater additions.

But this table includes some state mutuals. Information for stock associations alone is provided in Table 14-2, which reports the growth in net earnings for

Table 14-2

Growth in Net Earnings, Mutual Compared to Stock: 1955 to 1967 (Pure Stock Data)

	Reserves + Surplus 1955	1967	(millions) Increment	% Change
Arizona				
Federal	4.6	20.4	15.8	343.5
Stock	1.6	18.6[1]	17.0	1162.5
California				
Federal	134.5	627.7	493.2	366.7
Stock	141.9	1320.9[1]	1179.0	830.9
Colorado				
Federal	17.6	65.2	47.6	270.5
Stock	5.5	48.0[1]	42.5	772.7
Ohio				
Federal	122.3	354.0	231.7	189.5
Stock	66.7	258.8[2]	192.1	288.0
Oregon				
Federal	11.0	48.6	37.6	341.8
Stock	2.9	21.8[1]	18.9	651.7
Texas				
Federal	31.1	139.5	108.4	348.6
Stock	17.3	223.4[1]	206.1	1191.3
Washington				
Federal	57.6	126.9	69.3	120.3
Stock	0.8	6.4[1]	5.6	800.0
U.S.				
Federal	1302.0	5142.1	3840.1	294.9
Stock	249.9[3]	1835.8[1]	1585.9	634.6

Sources: Federal Home Loan Bank Board, *Combined Financial Statements*, 1955, 1967; United States Savings and Loan League, Fact Book, 1962, 1968; Federal Home Loan Bank of San Francisco, Directory of Members, 1968.

Notes:

1. Includes cash dividends paid to holders of permanent stock, 1965-67.

2. Includes cash dividends paid to holders of permanent stock, 1956-67.

3. Includes mutual associations which subsequently converted into stock associations.

seven of the stock states for the period 1955 to 1967. The percentage growth for the stock associations was significantly higher in each instance. Of the five not included, only Kansas and Utah showed a federal increase larger than the stock.

Though mutuals do not have the same incentive for building net worth as stock associations, it is possible to make comparisons under certain circumstances. It is true that the management does not *own* the net worth in the mutual association. However, the difficulties attributable to diversity in objectives can be circumvented. In California, net worth, as a ratio to savings, is approximately equal for the federal and stock associations. This may be so because the Federal Home Loan Bank Board and the Federal Savings and Loan Insurance Corporation require that 10 percent of net income be allocated to reserves prior to dividend payments for most associations and particularly for growing associations. Since dividends have to be paid, there is an incentive in securing adequate net income.

Another way to avoid the problems in taking a return after dividends as a ratio to average net worth is to refrain from use of a rate. The difficulty with the rate is that the denominator is a result of decision-making activities in the mutual. Thus, the assets would be expected to grow because of both what the mutual does and how active it is. Reasons have been indicated that there is not the same incentive for maximizing net worth. One solution is to take reserves plus surplus at a specific moment of time for mutuals as compared to stock associations. In California, the assets held by California federal associations in 1959 were 80 percent of those held by the stock associations. But with respect to the allocation of net income to reserves and surplus, the federals' earnings were only 49.1 percent of the stock associations. Had they received an amount equivalent to their asset ratios, they would have added $25.4 million more.

Table 14-3 shows the additions to reserves plus surplus as a percentage of average assets and net worth for the five years, 1960-1964. The ratios are for the United States less California, the California federals and stock associations. In all years, the stock associations reported higher additions than both the federal associations and the United States. This is true whether the denominator is average assets or average net worth. Generally, the difference between the California federals and the stock associations favors the latter by 40 to 60 percent. Because the federal authorities require that ten percent of net income be allocated to reserve prior to dividends, evidence is also presented with respect to the contribution to reserves and surplus after making allowance for the necessary ten percent addition. The same differences exist: the stock associations' contribution is from 50 to 100 percent larger than the federal association: when the denominator is average assets; and identical differences exist when the denominator is average net worth. For comparisons, a set of rows indicates the relationship of net income to average assets. Here again, the stock associations outperform the federal associations.

To a considerable extent, the superior performance of the California stock associations over the California federal associations, as measured by additions to reserves and surplus, is a result of the greater new loan activity which caused

Table 14-3

Additions to Reserves and Surplus as a Percentage of Average Assets and Average Net Worth, 1960-1964

Ratio	Area or Type of Organization	1960	1961	1962	1963	1964
Reserves + Surplus	U.S.*	.80	.84	.87	.63	.64
÷ Average Assets	California Federal	.94	1.10	1.24	.78	.79
	California Stock	1.47	2.09	1.66	1.11	1.19
Reserves + Surplus	U.S.*	11.59	12.30	12.60	9.28	9.60
÷ Average Net Worth	California Federal	13.74	15.86	18.13	11.80	12.16
	California Stock	19.45	27.43	21.49	15.39	17.06
Reserves + Surplus less	U.S.*	5.65	6.20	6.30	3.20	3.38
10% Net Income÷Average	California Federal	7.10	9.02	10.81	4.83	5.02
Net Worth	California Stock	12.56	20.46	14.00	8.53	9.99
Net Income ÷	U.S.*	4.08	4.18	4.34	4.12	4.14
Average Assets	California Federal	4.55	4.73	5.01	4.62	4.65
	California Stock	5.19	5.32	5.77	4.93	4.94

*United States less California

Source: Federal Home Loan Bank Board, *Combined Financial Statements*, 1959-1964, op. cit.

higher operating income. It is likely that the federal associations were too busy diverting part of their gross income to report equivalent amounts. The five years, 1959 to 1964, were chosen because the California federal associations presumably had the same opportunities as the stock associations. With 44.5 percent of the assets at the beginning of 1959, the California federal associations allocated 23 percent of the increase in reserves plus surplus. Or put another way, the stock associations with 125 percent of federal assets earned 435 percent of the amounts taken in by the federals. The federal associations increased only 37.4 percent of what they could have, had they acted in a way similar to the stock associations. This is additional evidence that the federal associations are either diverting income or not taking full advantage of their opportunities.

Previous tables have shown that over the ten-year period, the stock associations were twice as efficient in allocating funds to reserves plus surplus. Inasmuch as the data apply to the same number of associations, i.e., associations in existence in 1953 as compared to 1962, it is to be presumed that the difference went to managers.

Estimated Potentials

Here, a comparison is made of the five-year period, 1959-1964. The return is related to assets and net worth at a time when the stock association assets were

25 percent larger than the federal associations. If the federals had been as efficient as the stock associations, their share of the 1964 return would have been the same as in 1959. Had the federal associations been able to secure 80 percent of what the stock earned, they would have received $139.0 million instead of $60.8 million, i.e., $78 million more. This meant that the savers could have been given 1.62 percent more in dividends—an increase of 21.9 percent. On the average, each of the 69 federal associations' chief officers had the possibility of diverting $1.1 million.

Table 14-4 shows estimates of federal associations' additions to reserve surplus on the assumption that they maintained a share equal to the assets share held in 1959. For the five-year totals, the savers would have received $251.3 million more or 84.9 percent of their 1964 dividends. This would have meant an increase of 4.03 percent on their average savings capital in 1964. Or, in terms of what it could have meant to the chief officers of the federal associations, each might have diverted as much as $3.6 million over the five-year period.

If the mutuals had been able to perform on a comparable basis to the stock associations, the returns would have increased *pari passu* with the ratio of their assets to the stock associations. The conventional relating of returns to average

Table 14-4

Estimates of Federal Additions to Reserves and Surplus on the Assumption They Maintain Their Asset Share of 1959: 1960-1964

	Additions to Reserves + Surplus (000s)	
	Federal	Stock
1960	$40,400.	$82,198.
	80% stock $63,758.	
	difference $25,358 equivalent to 0.72% higher dividend, i.e., 16.4% increase; or as diversion to chief officer gives each federal, on the average, $367,500.	
1961	$54,284.	$127,595.
	80% stock $102,076.	
	difference $47,792 or 1.18% more dividend; or 26.7% increase to chief officer $692,630.	
1962	$71,794.	$150,434.
	difference $48,553 or 1.02% more in dividend; or 22.3% more to each federal chief officer $703,660.	
1963	$52,949.	$130,387.
	difference $51,361 or 0.93% more dividend—an increase of 19.7%, $723,390 to each chief federal officer.	
1964	$60,752.	$173,747.
	$78,246 difference or 1.26% more dividend—an increase of 21.9%, $1,134,000 to each chief officer.	
Totals	$251,310,000 to savers or 84.9% of 1964 dividends or 4.03% extra dividend; to chief officers, $3,642,170 in 5 years.	

net worth or average assets is misleading and self-defeating inasmuch as it conceals the mutuals' failure to aggressively promote new assets and reserves. An increase in reserves promotes an increase in assets, since a certain percentage of reserves is required. Though the return relative to average assets and to average net worth may appear to be rather close for the federal and stock associations, it is the *absolute* return to institutions which is critical. The question is why did not the 69 federal associations make the same additions to reserves and surplus as the stock associations? The larger additions of the stock associations cannot be attributed to the increase in numbers from 155 to 203 in a period when the number of federal associations was relatively fixed, because the bulk of the additions made by the stock associations were generated by associations existing at the end of 1959. The increased number was in new and smaller associations which did not make significant contributions to total stock reserves and surplus.

Similar calculations can be made for the remainder of the United States. The basic assumption is that the California federal association had the same opportunities as the California stock associations. The federal associations could have had an asset growth of $8.6 million instead of $4.0 million (Table 14-5)—an increase of 213% of what actually was achieved. That is, the California federal association increased their assets but 46.9 percent of their full potential. Or, put another way, the actual increase could have been 113 percent higher.

Now, if we assume that the same percentage difference would also apply throughout the United States, this would have meant that the asset growth for associations outside of California would have been 113 percent higher than what they actually achieved; or $85.9 billion instead of the actual $40.3 billion. That is $45.6 billion more. If the same relatively low rate of return to average assets for the United States without California is assumed, as was actually achieved in 1964, additions to reserves plus surplus at the 0.64 rate would have come to $292 million which would have increased reserves in that year 4.9 percent.

Table 14-5

Estimates of Additions to Net Worth by U.S. Associations on the Assumption that they Acted Similar to California Federal Associations as Compared to California Stock Associations, 1959-64

	Asset Growth, 1959-1964 (000s)	% Increase
U.S. less California	40,326,715	79.9
California Federal	4,026,048	100.0
California Stock	10,766,588	213.4

U.S. asset increase estimate on % difference between California federal and stock	$85.9 billion
Potential not realized	$45.6 billion
Return on U.S. average assets, 1964 = 0.64%	

Increase in estimated reserves $292 million or 4.9% increment in net worth.

Table 14-6 makes similar estimates with respect to additions to net worth by United States associations under the assumption that they perform in the same ratio as the California stock associations relative to the California federal associations for the period 1950 to 1964. If the California federal associations net worth had increased at the same rate as the California stock associations it would have been 2,143 percent or an actual increase of $1.3 billion. This would have been 279 percent of what was actually achieved. Now it is not assumed that the associations in the remainder of the country would have the same opportunities as the California stock associations. But it is reasonable to expect that a similar ratio might have existed between the actual and the potential. Had the United States mutuals acted as California stock associations, the increase in net worth would have been 179 percent higher. This would have increased net worth by 1964 by $9.2 billion which was equal to 12.6 percent or 1/8 of the total dollar value of mortgages held by United States associations other than California. At the 4.14 percent paid by non-California associations that year, this extra amount would have yielded their savers an additional $383 million for an increase in the rate paid of 13 percent.

Two hypotheses might explain the smaller additions to the reserve plus surplus for mutuals. First, they are said to be more conservative: they do not grow as rapidly. But, if this is so, it would be expected that over time, the mutuals would earn more by virtue of their claim that they take a less risk, i.e., their conservatism would be justified operationally in a higher rate of return. Second, it is hypothesized that the mutuals divert potential return by various devices such as compensation, amenities and the use of the ancillary establishments. Again, mutual decision making might involve a selection of less expensive assets. But this is an opportunity cost in that they receive a smaller return. If this is so, mutual expenses should be less after allowing for product mix adjustments. The

Table 14-6

Estimates of Additions to Net Worth by U.S. Associations under the Assumption that They Performed in the Same Ratio as California Stock Relative to California Federal, 1950-64

	(000s)			
	Net Worth			
	1950	1964	Increase	%
U.S. less California	875,883	6,036,154	5,160,271	589
California Federal	58,434	528,463	470,029	804
California Stock	50,170	1,125,425	1,075,255	2,143

Estimate of U.S. on % difference between California federal and stock
  $ 5,160 million x 179% = $9,236 million

$14,396 million total estimated increase in net worth or 153% larger net worth

At the 4.14 yield on savings that year, savers could have received
  $383 million or an increase of almost 13%.

multiple regression models presented previously show higher mutual expenses. It appears that it is not management's conservatism so much as it is a rational policy for diverting part of the potential income of the association.

Regression Models for Profits

Profit or additions to reserves and surplus after taxes is another test of performance. If expenses are one side of the coin, return is the other. It follows that if mutuals have higher expenses, they would also be likely to show a smaller return. In order to allow for variations with respect to the product mix, a similar multiple regression model was developed as with expenses. The problem was to predict the profit or additions to reserve on the basis of the various inputs.

The most important variable with respect to return is "loans made." Whenever a loan is originated, fees are earned so that the higher the proportion of new loans to total loans the higher is the income earned. "Loans made" are also important in raising the income in another way: when interest rates rise, the more important are "loans made," in that there is a larger proportion of mortgages bearing the latest and higher yields.

Assets are not a satisfactory variable because, as was the case with the expense models, they involve double counting: "loans made" constitutes a large proportion of total assets. It was decided to use "loans made" and to substitute for assets the "number of mortgages." The latter would reflect the annual income from "mortgages held." Obviously, some double counting would be unavoidable, but the multicollinearity with "loans made" is much less.

A negative influence on return might be expected from "real estate owned" and "contracts of sale." Buildings and furnishings similarly might exert a negative influence on return. But for reasons explained before, they are a surrogate or proxy for organization. They add nothing to a regression model which treats the influence of organization directly.

The model hypothesized that net income, after dividends paid to savers, interest on advances, taxes and expenses, would depend positively on the volume of "loans made," the number of mortgage accounts, and an organizational variable for the stock associations. A negative impact is to be expected from the "slow assets." As with the expense models, the organizational effect would operate on the slope as well as the intercept. Because of multicollinearity, one organizational slope variable was judged sufficient to indicate the stock influence.

The regression coefficients and their standard errors for 38 mutual areas are shown in Table 14-7 for the years 1961 through 1965. The constant term is relatively slight. Coefficients of determination larger than 0.9 mean that more than eight-tenths of the differences in return may be considered explained. The standard errors of estimate range from 1.08 to 2.83. As only mutual data were used, there was no organizational variable.

Table 14-7

Regression Equations-Profits: Insured Mutual Savings and Loan Associations, 1960-65, 38 Areas[1]

	1960	1961	1962	1963	1964	1965
Constant Term	0.01875	−0.38244	−0.63890	−0.54747	−0.61149	−0.42808
R^2	0.9489	0.9585	0.9809	0.9928	0.9947	0.9729
Standard Error of Estimate	1.64488	2.82780	2.26397	1.07756	1.06023	2.43839
			Regression Coefficients and Standard Errors			
Loans Made	0.01582	0.02387	0.03082	0.01682	0.02435	0.02322
	(0.00443)	(0.00524)	(0.00364)	(0.00118)	(0.00141)	(0.00473)
Average Number of Mortgages	0.04923	0.04175	0.03943	0.04040	0.03593	0.03377
	(0.01021)	(0.01431)	(0.00953)	(0.00424)	(0.00398)	(0.01171)
Average Real Estate Owned and Contracts of Sales[2]	[3]		[3] −0.15756	−0.04747	−0.06793	[3]
			(0.05342)	(0.01506)	(0.01088)	

1. See Table 13-1, Chapter 13.
2. Ibid.
3. Not Significant

"Loans made" and the "number of mortgages" were the main explanatory variables. The regression coefficients were stable, fluctuating over a relatively narrow range for the five-year period. The relative importance of the variables is shown in Table 14-8. "Slow assets" was statistically significant in three of the five years.

Table 14-9, derived from Table 14-7 presents a comparison of estimated profits to actual profits for the Los Angeles and San Francisco stock associations. The estimates are secured by taking the same product mix as the stock associations and applying the regression coefficients derived from the regression models. The differences between actual returns and estimated are compared to the standard errors of estimate in order to ascertain their statistical significance. Only the Los Angeles associations were clearly so. With such mixed results, it is impossible to derive any meaningful conclusion.

The next step was to take the 45 areas utilized in the expense models plus an organizational variable. Table 14-10 presents the relevant results. The constant terms were relatively small and the coefficients of determination in excess of 0.97. "Loans made" and "number of mortgages" proved the decisive variables; and were fairly stable. The "slow assets" coefficient, though not significant for two years and rather unstable, was negative for all five years. The organizational influence was shown by a slope variable indicating how the stock acted on income generated by "loans made." With the exception of 1961, it fluctuated in

Table 14-8
Relative Importance of Explanatory Variables in Profit Models: 38 Mutual Areas

Year	Variable	"T" Value	Contribution to Mean Return	Contribution Mean
1960				
	Number of Mortgages	4.82051	3.801	60.6%
	New Loans	3.56849	2.457	39.1
1961				
	Number of Mortgages	2.91761	3.658	45.3
	New Loans	4.55578	4.807	54.7
1962				
	Number of Mortgages	4.13565	3.548	39.3
	New Loans	8.46442	6.918	76.6
	Real Estate Owned	−2.94945	−0.802	−8.9
1963				
	Number of Mortgages	9.52894	3.849	52.4^2
	New Loans	14.21878	4.382	59.7^2
	Real Estate Owned	−3.15175	−0.342	$−4.7^2$
1964				
	Number of Mortgages	9.03872	3.640	42.5^2
	New Loans	17.30266	6.205	72.4^2
	Real Estate Owned	−6.24322	−0.661	$−7.7^2$
1965				
	Number of Mortgages	2.88310	3.558	39.9
	New Loans	4.91143	5.779	64.9

Notes:

1. Real Estate Owned not significant, 1960, 1961 and 1965.

2. Totals add to more than 100 as they are ratios on the mean not percentages.

a narrow range. In each of the years, the influence was positive. The regression coefficient was significant at the 99 percent confidence level.

Table 14-11 estimates the contribution made by organization to the average or mean profits. First, the amount that stock organizations contributed to the mean profits is calculated. Since the organizational regression coefficient is multiplied by a mean, which includes the influence of the mutual areas, it was necessary to calculate a mean appropriate for stock areas. Accordingly, the average "loans made" for the latter are multiplied by the regression coefficient to gain the estimate had all areas been stock. Since the regression coefficient is positive, the stock influence is to increase average or mean profits.

Table 14-9

Estimated Profit after Taxes as Compared to Actual Profits for Los Angeles and San Francisco Stock Savings and Loan Associations on the Basis of Identical Product Mix, as Derived from Regression Equations, 1961-65

	Estimated Profits	Actual Profits	Actual Estimated	Actual less Estimate[2] ÷ Stand Error of Estimate	Standard Error of Estimate
1961					
Los Angeles	48,347	81,801	169.2%	11.83	
San Francisco	10,754	15,183	191.2	1.96	
1962					
Los Angeles	74,650	96,071	128.7	9.46	
San Francisco	15,902	15,883	99.4	–	
1963					
Los Angeles	64,119	90,264	140.8	24.25	
San Francisco	13,719	12,572	91.6	–	
1964					
Los Angeles	80,034	114,163	142.6	32.20	
San Francisco	23,960	13,457	56.2	–	
1965					
Los Angeles	71,447	84,710	118.6	5.44	
San Francisco	23,083	30,609	132.6	3.09	

(in 000s)

Mean profits for mutuals and stock and the ratio of the latter to the former are shown in the table. The difference attributed to stock organization ranged from 117 percent to 159 percent. The total for the five years came to $13.5 millions. This is the extra amount each area would have earned on the average, had all been stock. Divided by the average number of associations, it is worth $409,575 and is an estimate over a five-year period of what savers lost *in each association* as a consequence of the mutual organizational structure.

Los Angeles Associations. As a further check on the results, the same procedure was followed as with expenses. A model was derived from data drawn from the 81 Los Angeles associations. Both the absolute data and the logarithmic transformations are presented in Table 14-12. As with expenses, the absolute form is preferred. But unlike the models for the cities, number of savings accounts proved a better fit than number of mortgage accounts. The principal variable was again "loans made." In both forms, the stock organizational variable was positive and statistically significant at the 99 percent confidence level. Had the mutual associations also been stock, profits would have been 29 percent larger.

Table 14-10

Regression Equations for Profits: Insured Savings and Loan Associations, 1961-1965, 45 Areas—Inclusion of an Organizational Slope Variable

Year	Constant Term	R^2	Independent Variables	Regression Coefficients, Standard Errors and Partial Correlation Coefficients			
				Loans Made	Average Number of Mortgages Held	Average Real Estate Owned and Contracts of Sale[1]	Loans Made X Organizational Variable (Stock = 1 Mutual = 0)
1961	−0.75088	.9666	reg. coef.	.02360	.04534	—[2]	+.02236
			(s.e.)	(.00451)	(.01196)		(.00290)
			p.c.c.	.59904	.47643		.74077
1962	−0.45851	.9810	r.c.	.03112	.03710	−.15066	+.00609
			(s.e.)	(.00339)	(.00870)	(.04928)	(.00209)
			p.c.c.	.79791	.52439	−.40375	.38726
1963	−0.77631	.9928	r.c.	.01693	.04085	−.04432	+.00568
			(s.e.)	(.00173)	(.00614)	(.00218)	(.00127)
			p.c.c.	.80960	.69667	−.27983	.54530
1964	−1.00056	.9696	r.c.	.02156	.03625	[2]	+.01022
			(s.e.)	(.00395)	(.01102)		(.00281)
			p.c.c.	.61912	.42892		.46446
1965	−0.44745	.9896	r.c.	.02558	.03129	−.02353	+.00484
			(s.e.)	(.00422)	(.00998)	(.01594)	(.00263)
			p.c.c.	.66241	.41620	−.21055	.25993

Sources: Federal Home Loan Bank Board. *Combined Financial Statements*, 1960-1965; Federal Home Loan Bank of San Francisco, California Division of Savings and Loan Associations.

Notes:

1. Averaged for the year, 1960-64. In 1965, year-end data used and included foreclosed real estate owned, contract sales and loans to facilitate sale of foreclosed real estate.

2. Not statistically significant this year.

Table 14-11
Impact of Stock Associations on Profits, 1961-1965[1]

	Mean Mutual Profits	Mean Stock Profits	Stock Mutual
1961	$7,063	11,293	159.9%
1962	9,108	10,818	118.8%
1963	7,270	9,478	130.4%
1964	8,475	12,323	145.4%
1965	8,760	10,282	117.4%

Notes:

1. In thousands.

Table 14-12
Regression Equations-Profits for 81[1] **Los Angeles Associations: 1963**

Independent Variables	Absolute Data		Logarithmic Transformations		
Constant Term	−68.375		−1.41086		
	Regression Coefficients, Standard Errors and Partial Correlation Coefficients				
Loans Made	0.01515	(0.00361) 0.43203	0.87487	(0.11337)	0.66043
Number of Savings Accounts	13.06616	(4.62658) 0.30633	0.20397	(0.11615)	0.19626
Dummy Variable: Loans Made	0.00673	(0.00148) 0.45949	0.12516	(0.04464)	0.30438
R^2	0.9452		0.9086		

Note:

1. Sixty stock associations and 21 mutual associations.

Sources of Superior Stock
Performance

The superior performance of the stock associations is due to a number of factors. They are more aggressive in originating new loans, thereby earning not only more each year from fees but also raising average mortgage yield in periods of rising rates. They also show higher ratios of "slow" assets to assets. Though the evidence shows that this item had a negative effect on profits, this is *only relative to the level of "loans made."* The latter is positively correlated with the slow assets; and it appears as if there may be a causal positive relationship running from "loans made" to "slow assets" to profits. Thus, the better showing of the stock would have to be due either to lower expenses or to a willingness to make loans that the mutuals refuse. This does not mean that they need assume greater risk since it is compensated by higher profit. Variations in risk cannot serve as an explanation of differences in income.

A possible bias might have been introduced by the relatively high concentration of stock observations in the fast-growing and profitable West. As eleven of the fifteen stock observations, as compared to but five of the thirty-eight mutual observations, come from this area. The differences in return could be attributed to geography rather than to organization. But such a conclusion is unwarranted. The models do allow for the independent influence of "growth"; it is a component in "loans made." The hypothesis is that *given* the level of "loans made," the number of mortgage accounts, and "slow" assets, organization has a positive influence on profits. The greater activity and more rapid growth of the West Coast associations as well as other areas is allowed for in the model.

A similar problem is raised with respect to the influence of variations in local money markets. It is a well-known and established fact that western markets are characterized by a capital-scarcity: mortgage yields and loan origination fees are generally higher than elsewhere (Table 14-13). To what extent are the differences in return attributable to variations in money market conditions rather than to organization?

The problem is to find a satisfactory index of local money market conditions. The ratio of mortgage interest to average mortgages, as reported in the *Combined Financial Statements* of the Federal Home Loan Bank Board, is misleading. First, it is influenced by the "loans made"-to-mortgage ratio so that it may be larger when interest rates are rising, even though the cost of money is identical between two areas. Second, the composition of "loans made" may vary with the West Coast associations making relatively more construction loans. As the latter yield higher interest rates, the yields would be higher even when the interest rates both on construction and existing homes are equal. Finally, allowance for money market variations may be gratuitous in that while yields on mortgages are undoubtedly higher in California so are the rates paid by associations to savers. Indeed, the latter is but the other side of the coin: higher yields on mortgages make it possible to pay higher rates to savers. They are not independent phenomena. This is revealed by calculations derived from Federal Home Loan Bank Board data with respect to interest plus fees on both new and existing mortgage loans weighted by the relative importance of each. In 1963, the aggregate yield to California associations came to 7.05; the rest of the U.S. received 6.52 for a difference of 0.53 in California's favor. But 5.02 was paid out in dividends and interest on advances as compared to 4.37 for the United States federals or 4.24 without the California federals. Thus, though the California associations received 0.53 more on their loans, they paid out 0.65 or 0.78 more for their borrowed money! Whatever advantage California associations may have

Table 14-13

Average Interest Rate and Other Loan Terms on Conventional First Mortgage Loans on Previously Occupied Single Family Homes—Originated by Major Lenders in the United States by Selected Metropolitan Areas. June, 1964

Areas	Contract % Interest	Fees %	Terms of Contract in Years	Loan to Price as %	Average Purchase Price (in thousands)
Atlanta	6.01	1.35	19.2	73.3	$22.0
Boston	5.34	0.02	21.5	70.4	23.9
Baltimore	5.64	0.36	19.0	71.0	16.9
Chicago	5.53	1.07	21.5	70.1	24.9
Cleveland	5.84	0.45	21.0	71.4	21.5
Dallas	5.90	0.47	21.5	76.4	24.2
Denver	6.01	1.06	21.1	72.3	19.4
Houston	5.90	0.40	22.2	76.1	25.0
Detroit	5.68	0.40	22.5	69.8	21.0
Los Angeles	6.22	0.89	25.6	76.4	25.6
Miami	5.85	1.07	21.0	75.3	21.0
Minneapolis	5.68	0.26	20.8	71.2	22.5
New Orleans	5.98	0.01	21.6	70.0	22.2
New York	5.57	0.43	23.6	68.3	28.0
Philadelphia	5.68	0.24	20.0	68.9	17.2
San Francisco	6.09	1.06	24.8	74.3	25.0
Seattle	5.87	0.65	19.8	70.9	21.9
U.S.	5.89	0.52	20.2	70.9	19.3

Source: Federal Home Loan Bank Board, *Digest*, Aug. 1, 1964, Vol. VII, No. 1.

had in mortgage markets was more than offset by disadvantages experienced in markets from which they drew their savings capital.

The higher return of the stock associations is revealed by a number of independent tests. Not only have they increased net worth at faster rates, but they generally earned more when allowance is made for variations in the product mix. This was revealed by the multiple regression models for the 45 areas for 1961-1965 and for the eighty-one Los Angeles associations in 1963. This higher return rather than signifying a better mortgage market indicates a greater drive and ferocity on the part of the stock associations in exploiting the market opportunities. In many instances, the federals or mutuals had the same market opportunities. But they failed to show the same vigor in cutting expenses to generate the higher profit which permits additional loan originations, thereby yielding more fees and income. The stocks were willing to take chances with respect to the acquisition of "real estate owned" that the mutuals refused. A higher ratio of "slow assets" to total assets does not mean poorer quality loans if there is compensation in the former of higher rates and fees. Personal finance companies make loans that banks would not touch. It is true that the delinquencies are larger, but so are the profits. The latter have acquired an expertise from specialization while keeping expenses in check. In the same manner, the stock associations, having successfully exploited the high-risk mortgage market, have earned higher profit and have grown faster than their mutual competitors.

15 Conclusion

The seminal ideas which motivated the founders of the mutual savings and loan association were those of service, asceticism, personal frugality and savings and lending directed to home ownership. In the course of more than a century, the original goals have been superceded by novel concepts; and the zealous founders have given way to professional managers. The ultimate power which originally resided in the member-saver has (by his surrendering a proxy when opening his account) been transferred to management. The rule, originally designed to preserve democratic control, limiting the number of votes one member could control to fifty, has effectively diffused ownership. Subject to little, if any, pressure from savers, management is a self-perpetuating autocracy. Not surprisingly, one legal scholar concluded that "a shareholder has a vote until he cares to exercise it, and then he ceases to have a vote, if the board so decides."[1]

It is apparent that enthusiasm and dedication to the mutual ideal was not sufficient. Lacking the expertise and widely diffused in the ownership of savings, the members were in no position to guide the destiny of a modern association. The enthusiasm failed to survive; the "member" preferred to see himself as a saver interested only in safety. The corporate existence of "his" association ceased to interest him. The professional managers stepped into the breach. Indeed, by a series of developments, they helped along the separation of the member-saver into the present dichotomy between savers and borrowers. The organization no longer contains member-savers waiting for their turn to become borrowers and thus secure financing for home purchase or building.

The mutual savings and loan association, controlled by a professional management while subject to some constraints with respect to disposal of the association's income, is entirely free from interference from the saver-member. This power has permitted the substitution of a different set of goals and objectives from those originally conceived by the founders of mutual institutions. The original enthusiasm has been replaced by an elaborate infrastructure controlled by a self-perpetuating bureaucracy which successfully preserves its perquisites in a manner similar to that of the medieval monasteries. The early mutuals were as far a cry from today's institutions as were the same medieval monasteries from primitive Christianity.

To a considerable extent, the take-over by management was inevitable. As associations grew, not only did the original enthusiasm gradually die out, but it became increasingly difficult for members to continue to take an active part in the management of the organization. Absenteeism from meetings became not only general but rational. The member's stake was simply not sufficient to keep him vitally concerned. Given this absenteeism, it did not take long for management to substitute a different set of goals for the original ones. The comments of ancient Cato on absentee ownership are relevant: the owners of farms should always be on the watch to make sure that their bailiffs do not swindle them. A manager would always take advantage of a careless master.[2]

The member is not only separated from control: he is no longer an "owner." Indeed, the management has achieved a "property in office" which has historical parallels with the monasteries and with sixteenth and seventeenth century monarchic governments. They are likewise able to enjoy high salaries, amenities and other perquisites of office. The most important has been a regulatory environment which has permitted the establishment of ancillary establishments for the purpose of siphoning off association income. In short, management has replaced the original goals of mutuality with a vastly different set, pertinent to its own objectives. In doing so it has created a quasifirm. The latter has objectives external to itself and may be expected to act in a very different manner.

The quasifirm is essentially a management-dominated enterprise operating under a certain set of constraints. Since management is not allowed to appropriate the profits of the enterprise directly, it has created a diversion mechanism for the conversion of power into the various forms of wealth. The essential prerequisite to diversion is the *restriction* of output. It is pertinent to note here that *managerial restriction* is not the only form of restriction. The most commonly observed is that said to arise from the control of supply, or monopoly. But the latter is surely less common than that associated with externally oriented or quasifirms. In the latter, diversion can only take place via restriction. Hence, the management's primary decision concerns the form in which the restriction can occur. In the illustrations discussed in the preceding pages, the management of mutual savings and loan associations lend only in the context of a tie-in transaction, e.g., insurance. By insisting that the borrower purchase insurance from the manager's privately-owned subsidiary, the price of the service (or loan) is effectively raised. The increment to the price "restricts" the quantity loaned and is akin to monopolistic restriction. This form of restriction develops even where the ordinary monopoly elements are lacking, viz., control over supply. If competitive prices prevailed such that supply were equal to demand, it would be impossible for management to insist on the tie-in sale. Thus, the management firm both *requires* the restriction in order to maximize wealth and *causes* it by the tied sale.

Inasmuch as management operates under a set of constraints, it is not permitted to enjoy the same kind of direct income payments characteristic of conventional stock enterprise. Consistent with the theory of a positive supply function, it is expected that the offerings by management in nonprofit enterprise would be somewhat less—but wholly predictable on the basis of the supply function. The evidence provided by successive chapters in the study indicates that this is in fact so. Management-controlled firms grow at slower rates. It may be because expenses are higher: both salaries and that spent on amenities; or incomes are lower because of the diversion mechanism; or all the factors may operate simultaneously in the quasifirm. But it is clear that they restrict as *compared* to stock enterprise operating in the same market.

The principal hypothesis was that mutuals would show different operating results as compared to stock associations. A number of tests were offered so that it could not be said that undue reliance was placed on one test or one form of investigation. The results of the different tests and procedures were similar. In every instance, mutuals not only behaved differently: they lagged behind the stock in reducing expenses, increasing profits and in growth. While the regression models might have been subject to sampling error, the other tests clearly and strongly supported the conclusions with respect to the observed differences. It was also shown that similar differences existed between mutuals and stock in the insurance industry.

One of the consequences of management domination and the diversion mechanism is that essential markets and sources of supply are foreclosed. The top management posts are not open to competition or to use the words of mutual spokesmen, they are not "up for grabs by the wrong people." By insulating themselves from market competition, the managers have suppressed the possibility that inefficiency will be penalized and eliminated. Further, through insistence on tie-in deals, they deny loans to borrowers unable to pay the higher prices. Restriction of output, by necessarily raising prices, prevents some part of the borrowing market from receiving loans. Resource allocation is less than optimal.

The principal test concerned expenses. The conventional ratio of expenses to assets was rejected on the grounds that it was both misleading and irrelevant: misleading in the sense that "assets" were not the annual "output" of the association; and irrelevant in that expenses were a function not of assets but of the particular product mix. It was noted that an association generated new savings and new accounts; that it had to advertise for the savings; that it often used brokers; and that those new savings were invested in "loans made" each year for which fees were received; and, finally, the association had to service both the savings and mortgage accounts for not only itself but often for other associations located in other parts of the nation. To allow for variations in the product mix, multiple regression models were developed for five years for forty-five cities or areas; and also for individual mutuals and stock associations in the Los Angeles area. In all the models, the stock influence on expenses was statistically significant as well as negative. Mutuals had higher expenses as revealed by the hypothesis.

Similar regression models were generated with respect to profits or return. Again, the results were consistent with those for expenses. The stock associations reported more profits in each of the five years where the cities were used; and also in Los Angeles where individual associations provided the data.

The results of other tests were consistent with the above two. Mutuals made greater use of nepotism; and showed fewer management changes. Somewhat surprisingly, the mortality rate for mutuals in the Los Angeles area was slightly higher. Perhaps a habit of caution in this high-growth region may have had negative survival results. It is more than likely, however, that contrary to popular belief, mutuals are no more cautious. After all, it is *other* peoples' money they use.

But the most decisive difference in behavior was revealed in "additions to reserves." Taking only associations in existence at the beginning of the period, a survey revealed that the stock associations in California added twice as much as the federals. The remarkable aspect of this diversity in behavior is that the mutual had the same market opportunities. It is not surprising that the stock asset growth should have been twice as large, since growth is dependent on reserves which in turn depend upon the ability to earn profits. Nor was it any less astonishing that the market share of the California federals should have fallen from 60.6% to 33.7%.

Savers or customers also benefitted from the greater efficiency of the stock. It is consistent with the higher growth rates that the stock should have paid higher dividends and made more aggressive use of advertising, premiums and brokers. They also placed greater reliance on the relatively less expensive source of liquidity, Federal Home Loan Bank "advances."[3]

The relationship between the mutuals and the government in the form of the regulatory authority, particularly the Federal Home Loan Bank Board, was somewhat paradoxical. Whenever competition threatened to break out or become too virulent, the mutuals turned to the government. Punishment was meted out against the competitive aggressors. It might be said that the mutual "depended" on the government for its survival. But the relationship was more reciprocal than that. Evidence was offered showing that in a number of instances, officials who had been responsible for administering and regulating the industry had found high-paying executive positions or had become legal counsel. It would appear that it is not so much that the mutual is dependent on the government as it is that government is responsive to the mutuals. The chief manifestation of this phenomenon is found in the suppression of competition both within the industry and with respect to the stock sector.

If mutuality is characterized by public benevolence and stock ownership by private cupidity, it might be preferable for the nation to opt for the latter. Mutuality is a euphemism to shield powerful restrictive forces from the public scrutiny. Furthermore, if California experience is any guide, the mutual is an institution which can survive only at the cost of continued governmental restriction of competition; i.e., through creating for it a sacred-cow status similar to that of agriculture.

The remedy for the excessive margins of mutuality is obvious. If mutuals were converted into stock associations, not only would profit provide a basis for rational decision making, but the necessity for maintenance of nonequilibrium margins would vanish. Removal of the profit constraint on management eliminates the pressure to second-best choices such as nepotism, infrequent management changes, and tie-in deals—all of which increase the price to borrowers while reducing the interest paid to savers. The diversion mechanism is not only restrictive, it is inefficient.

Notes

Notes

Chapter 1
Introduction

1. Jerry Voorhis, Hearings before the House of Representatives, Committee on Banking and Currency (Subcommittee on Bank Supervision and Insurance), 85th Congress, *Federal Charter Legislation for Mutual Savings Banks*, page 296.

2. The Recent Commission on Money and Credit, *Mutual Savings Banking: Basic Characteristics and Role in the National Economy*, (National Association of Mutual Savings Banks), (Englewood Cliffs, New Jersey: Prentice-Hall, 1963), page 6, made the following observation: "Earnings of mutual savings banks serve two essential purposes—the payment of interest to depositors and the accumulation of reserves necessary for the protection of deposit."

3. *Report* of the Federal Home Loan Bank Board for the year ending December 31, 1961 (Letter of Transmittal, June 15, 1962), Washington, D.C., p. 55.

4. Cf. Stanford Research Institute, *The Savings and Loan Industry in California*, South Pasadena, California (prepared for: Savings and Loan Commissioner, Division of Savings and Loans, State of California), November 1960, II-2; Leon T. Kendall, *The Savings and Loan Business* (a monograph prepared for *The Commission on Money and Credit*), Prentice-Hall, Englewood Cliffs, New Jersey, 1962, pp. 4 and 5.

5. Cf. Saul B. Klaman, *The Post War Residential Mortgage Market* (National Bureau of Economic Research), Princeton, 1961, p. 165.

6. The Federal Home Loan Bank Board classifies a company which holds 10 percent or more of the guaranty stock of a savings and loan association a holding company.

7. In 1959, holding companies were prohibited from acquiring control (10 percent or more of the stock) of more than one insured association, or acquiring control of any insured associations in additions to those already controlled.

Chapter 2
The Relative Performance of Mutual as
Compared to Stock Savings and
Loan Associations

1. A.A. Berle and G. Means. The Modern Corporation and Private Property, N.Y. 1932, Book I, Chapter 4 and 6.

2. See J.A. Livingston, The American Stockholder, Philadelphia, 1958 (Lippincott, p. 144).

3. See Baumol, Business Behavior, Value and Growth, rev. ed., (New York: Harcourt, Brace & World, 1967), Chapter 6.

4. United States Savings and Loan League, Savings and Loan Annals, 1958, Report of the Subcommittee to study the acquisition of a federal association by state-chartered association, "The Two-Way Street," by Alex Mintz, Chairman, p. 371.

5. Ibid.

6. Ibid.

7. Ibid. Cited page 373.

8. Ibid.

9. Ibid., pp. 374-75.

10. Ibid., p. 377.

11. Ibid., p. 388; comment by William Prather (Legal Bulletin, May 1957).

12. Kendall, Saving and Loan Industry, p. 98.

13. William J. Baumol, *Business Behavior Value and Growth*, pp. 45-52.

14. Ibid., p. 52, note 15.

15. Ibid.

16. Compare O.E. Williamson, *The Economics of Discretionary Behavior*, (Englewood Cliffs: Prentice-Hall, 1964), and Anthony Downs, "A Theory of Large Managerial Firms," *The Journal of Political Economy*, vol. LXXIII, no. 3, June 1965; D.K. Osborne, "On the Goals of the Firm," *Quarterly Journal of Economics*, vol. 78, November, 1964; Robin Marris, *The Economic Theory of Managerial Capitalism* (Glencoe: The Free Press, 1964), especially Chapters 2 and 3; R.F. Lanzillotti, "Pricing Objectives in Large Companies," *American Economic Review*, vol. 98, December 1958.

17. See also Leo Grebler and Eugene F. Brigham, *Savings and Mortgage Markets in California*, California Savings and Loan League, Pasadena, 1963, Table VI-3, p. 149, where it is reported that where the federally-chartered associations had a ratio of buildings to assets of 1.56, the state-chartered had a ratio of 1.37 and the L.A. state unit was 1.19.

18. Cf. the judgment "that the pre-interest ratio is highest where associations provide collateral services." Edward S. Shaw, Savings and Loan Market Structure and Market Performance, A Study of California State Licensed Savings and Loan Association, A Research Study Prepared for the California Savings and Loan Commissioner, 1962, p. 38, also p. 121.

19. "At present certain activities of directors fall into a shadowy area of conflict. Frequently, savings institutions employ corporations to conduct specialized activities for them. It is not unusual for an association to employ a corporate agent to originate loans and to pay this agent a percentage on each approved loan. The directorate of the corporate loan agent and the directorate of the savings association in some cases would reveal identical membership. It is difficult to distinguish the substance of this transaction from that conduct which if done directly would be felonious," Marshall S. Mayer, Deputy Attorney Gen-

eral, State of California, "Civil and Criminal Liabilities of Directors of California Banks and Savings and Loan Associations," Journal State Bar of California, November-December, 1966, no. 6, p. 901.

20. In a number of instances, control has been transferred in California federals by means of a "sale" of the mortgage finance company. This was reported in instances involving Beverly Hills Federal and Wilshire Federal associations.

21. "Associations also often employ corporations to perform escrow, insurance, trustee, and real estate sales functions. It is not unusual for directors and officers of the association to be financially interested in these firms," Mayer, *Liabilities*.

22. In Eddy vs. Home Federal, a borrower sought a declaratory judgment to determine whether he had to purchase insurance from the *director of the association as required in the loan agreement.* The court held the agreement valid since the contract had been agreed to by both parties and did not contravene federal law. The court did not discuss the conflict of interest. "However, if the association had sought to recover the 30% commission earned by the director, the California cases leave little doubt as to the result." Ibid. It is quite clear that this was a rather typical instance of profits being siphoned off by the management of a mutual.

23. Joint committee of the Senate and Assembly, New York, Investigation of Life Insurance Companies, Report, Vol. X, pp. 30-31, 83-84, 132.)

24. Mayer, *Liabilities*, p. 901.

25. Shaw, *Structure*, p. 109.

Chapter 3
Differences in Expenses and
Operating Characteristics

1. Shaw, *Structure*, p. 37.

2. *Mortgage Markets*, p. 158.

3. Norman Strunk, United States Savings and Loan League, Conference on Savings, 1960, Chicago, p. 172.

4. Kendall, Commission on Money and Credit, p. 98.

5. Shaw, *Structure*, p. 141.

6. National Association of Mutual Savings Banks, 1963 Report, New York, New York, p. 3.

7. United States Savings and Loan League Conference on Savings, 1960, Chicago, Statement by Ted T. Greene, p. 156.

8. Shaw, *Structure*, p. 141.

9. *Wall Street Journal*, Pacific Coast Edition, March 31, 1965.

10. Ibid.

11. Stanford Research Institute, The Savings and Loan Industry in California, South Pasadena, California, Table 52, p. A-22, and Table V-III, p. A-23.

12. California Savings and Loan Commissioner, Report, 1963, p. 8.

13. Cf. Kessel, R., "Price Discrimination in Medicine," Journal of Law and Economics, v. 1 (1958), pp. 43-44.

Chapter 4
Relative Growth

1. Kendall, *Commission*, p. 97.
2. Ibid.
3. Stanford Research Institute, Table VIII-5, A-37.
4. Kendall, *Commission*, p. 97.
5. Ibid., p. 98.
6. Grebler and Brigham, *Mortgage Markets*, p. 141.
7. Ibid.
8. Shaw, *Structure*, p. 9.
9. Ibid., p. 109.
10. Ibid.
11. Ibid.
12. Grebler and Brigham, *Mortgage Markets*, p. 158.
13. Ibid., p. 84.
14. Shaw, *Structure*, p. 141.
15. Grebler and Brigham, *Mortgage Markets*, p. 158.
16. House of Representatives, Subcommittee on Bank Supervision and Insurance, Federal Charter Legislation of Mutual Savings Bank, p. 224.
17. Stanford Research Institute, V-5.

Chapter 5
The Mutual Savings and Loan
Association: Nature and
Development

1. Kendall, p. 4.
2. Stanford Research Institute, The Savings and Loan Industry in California (prepared for: Savings and Loan Commissioner, Division of Savings and Loan, State of California), South Pasadena, California, 1960, II-2.
3. Stanford Research Institute, III-3.
4. See Edward F. Shaw, *Savings and Loan Market Structure and Market Performance*, California Savings and Loan Commissioner, Los Angeles, 1962, pp. 31, 32; Leo Grebler and Eugene F. Brigham, *Savings and Mortgage Markets in California*, California Savings and Loan League, Pasadena, 1963, pp. 163-64.
5. See John Stafford, Conference on Saving, 1960 (United States Savings and Loan League), p. 170.

6. E. Sherman Adams, Vice President, First National City Bank, New York, "Implications of the Big Trend in Banking," address before the annual convention of the New Hampshire Bankers Association, Newcastle, New Hampshire, June 21, 1963. Cited in *Federal Charter Legislation for Mutual Savings Bank*, p. 91. Also, "Commercial banks are demonstrated to be the short term, low percentage, conventional home mortgage lender among the five major types," Federal Home Loan Bank Board, Release, August 1963.

7. See Josephine Heges Ewalt, *The Savings and Loan Story, 1930-1960: A Business Reborn*, American Savings and Loan Institute Press, Chicago, Illinois, 1962, p. 45.

8. Alan Teck, *Mutual Savings Banks and Savings and Loan Associations*, N.Y. (Columbia), 1968, p. 38.

9. Stanford Research Institute, III-I.

10. United States Savings and Loan League, Savings and Loan Fact Book, 1967, Chicago, Illinois, 1967. Tables 45 and 59, pp. 58 and 70. There were four times as many "saver-members" as "borrowers-members."

11. Testimony of P. James Riordan, Federal Charter Legislation for Mutual Savings Banks, p. 214.

12. Ibid.

13. The American Bankers Association, The Commercial Banking Industry, a monograph prepared for the Commission on Money and Credit (Englewood Cliffs: Prentice-Hall, 1962), page 82.

14. *The Theory of Social and Economic Organization* (translated by Talcott Parsons and A.M. Henderson), New York, Oxford, 1947, page 318.

15. Testimony of Charles K. Fletcher, *Federal Charter Legislation of Mutual Savings Bank*, p. 289.

16. Morton Bodfish and A.D. Theobald, Savings and Loan Principles, (New York: Prentice-Hall, 1938), p. 74.

17. California Savings and Loan League, Data Book, Pasadena, 1966, p. 14.

18. Durelle V. Trader's Federal Savings Association of Parkersburg, et al., 104 SC 2nd 230 (1958), (The Supreme Court of West Virginia). But a recent study on mutual savings banking concludes "An unqualified power of redemption does much to negate effectively voting rights," Mutual Savings Banking, p. 24.

19. Rules and Regulations of the Federal Savings and Loan System, Federal Home Loan Bank Board, Washington, D.C., page 9. (October 31, 1963)

20. *Federal Charter Legislation for Mutual Savings Banks*, p. 251.

21. Investigation and study of the Federal Home Loan Bank laws, Part 1A-Alice, House Subcommittee of the Committee on Government Operations, House of Representatives, 87th Congress, First Session, August 4, 1961, Washington, D.C., page 254.

22. P. James Riordan, *Legislation*, page 206.

23. Jerry Voorhis, *Hearings*, p. 296.

24. Federal Charter Legislation for Mutual Savings Banks, p. 214.

25. *Wall Street Journal*, 13 February 1967.

26. Federal Charter Legislation for Mutual Savings Banks, p. 290.

27. Journal of the State Bar of California, V. 4, Nov.-Dec., No. 6, 1966, p. 901.

28. Kendall, The Savings and Loan Business, p. 37.

29. Kendall, p. 28.

30. Comparative Regulations of Financial Institutions, p. 101.

31. E.g., see Federal Home Loan Bank Board, Annual Report, 1963, Washington, D.C., p. 37.

32. Shaw, *Structure*, p. 2, 38.

33. Stanford Research Institute, Table IX-I.

34. Harvey Pinney, "Corporations in the home loan group," 15 New York University Law Quarterly Review (May 1938), p. 505.

35. Shaw, *Structure*, p. 2.

36. Kendall, The Savings and Loan Business, p. 97.

37. Ibid., pp. 28-29.

38. American Bankers Association, p. 12.

39. Bodfish, pp. 73 and 74.

40. Charles F. Phillips and Delbert J. Duncan, *Marketing, Principles and Methods*, 4th ed., 1960 (Homewood, Ill.: Richard Irwin, 1960), p. 245. See also *Statistical Abstract of United States*, 1959, p. 485.

Chapter 6
Regulation and Competition

1. Elwood Knapp, *Conference on Savings*, 1960, p. 151.

2. Norman Strunk, op. cit., p. 155.

3. Cf. George J. Stigler and Claire Friedland, "What Can Regulators Regulate? The case of electricity?" *Journal of Law and Economics*, vol. 5 (October 1962), pp. 1-16.

4. United States Savings and Loan League, Conference on Savings, 1960, p. 155.

5. *Savings and Loan Journal*, May 1962, p. 13.

6. United States Savings and Loan League, Conference on Savings, 1960, p. 156.

7. E.S. Shaw, *Money, Income and Monetary Policy* (Homewood, Ill.: Irwin, 1950), p. 115.

8. Leo Grebler and Eugene F. Brigham, *Mortgage Markets*, p. 121.

9. Ibid., pp. 29-30.

10. Shaw, Saving and Loan Market Structure and Market Performance, p. 27.

11. Grebler and Brigham, *Mortgage Markets*, pp. 93-94.

12. *Commercial Banking*, p. 52.

13. American Bankers Association, Commercial Banking Industry, p. 52;

Grebler and Brigham, *Mortgage Markets*, pp. 41, 160. A. Phillips, Journal of Finance, March, 1964, p. 41.

14. Shaw, *Structures*, p. 136.

15. Cf. Federal Home Loan Banks Board, *Report 1963*, p. 37.

16. Leon Kendall, The Savings and Loan Industry, Commission on Money and Credit (Englewood Cliffs: Prentice-Hall, 1962), p. 30.

17. Shaw, *Structures*, p. 147.

18. Grebler and Brigham, *Mortgage Markets*, p. 130.

19. Los Angeles Times, 29 May 1964.

20. Cf. Shaw, pp. 101-2.

21. Federal Home Loan Bank Board Digest, vol. VIII, no. 2 (September, 1965).

22. Ewalt, pp. 117-18.

23. Federal Home Loan Bank Board Report 47.

24. p. 170.

25. *Federal Home Loan Bank Board Digest*, vol. VIII, no. 2 (September 1965).

26. *Wall Street Journal*, 27 June 1966.

27. Ibid.

28. Los Angeles *Times*, 1 July 1966. Italics supplied.

29. Los Angeles *Times*, 21 July 1966.

30. Fred Balderson, "Summary Report: Revision of the Standards of Applications for New Charters and New Branches in the Savings and Loan Industry of California," February 8, 1963.

31. Ibid., p. 3.

32. H.P. Gray, "Some Evidence on Two Implications of Higher Interest Rates on Time Deposits," *The Journal of Finance*, vol. XXXIX, no. 1 (March 1964), pp. 65-66.

33. Cf. A. Phillips, *Journal of Finance*, (March, 1964), v. 19, no. 1, p. 39.

34. Investigation and Study of the Federal Home Loan Bank Board, Part 1a—Alice, Texas, p. 101.

35. Ibid., p. 256.

36. Ibid., p. 285.

37. Ibid., pp. 290-91.

38. Ibid., Part 1b, p. 541.

39. Investigation and Study of the Federal Home Loan Bank Board, Part 1a, Alice, page 250.

40. Federal Charter Legislation for Mutual Savings Banks, p. 283. Italics supplied.

41. Horace Gray and Walter Adams, *Monopoly in America* (New York: Macmillan, 1955), p. 39.

42. Eugene Staley, The World Economy in Transition, London, 1939, page 287.

43. Federal Home Loan Bank Board. The Public Holding Companies in the Savings and Loan Industry, Washington, D.C., September 1959, p. 49.

44. *Savings and Loan Journal*, April 1961, p. 64.

45. Ibid., November 1962, p. 9.

46. Jack McDonald, Vice President of San Diego Imperial Holding Company, Address to New York Society of Security Analysts, September 1963.

47. Federal Deposit Insurance Corporation, Annual Report, 1944, pp. 10-11.

48. Federal Home Loan Bank Board *Digest*, October 1964, vol. 7, no. 3.

49. George J. Stigler, "The Theory of economic regulation," 2 The Bell Journal of Economics and Management Science 4.

50. Chairman Horne quoted Los Angeles *Times*, 1 July 1966.

51. Federal Home Loan Bank Board *Digest*, vol. VIII, no. 2 (September, 1965).

52. Elwood Knapp, Conference on Savings, 1960, p. 157.

53. Ibid.

54. Stanford Research Corp., XI-12.

55. Riordan, Federal Charter Legislation for Mutual Savings Banks, op. cit., p. 214.

56. Ibid.

57. Ibid.

58. Robert R. Mullen, Investigation of the Federal Home Loan Bank Board, Alice, Part 1a, p. 10.

59. The Federal Home Loan Bank Board, Savings and Loan Holding Companies (Washington, D.C.), May 1960.

60. Stanford Research Institute, The Savings and Loan Industry in California, V-21.

61. Hearings Before a Subcommittee of the Committee on Government Operations, House of Representatives, 86th Congress, 2nd Session (August 25, 26, and 27, 1960, Federal Home Loan Bank Board's Seizure of Long Beach Federal Savings and Loan Association, part 1, Washington, D.C., 1960, p. 740.

62. United States Savings and Loan League, Conference on Savings, 1962, Chicago, Illinois, p. 171.

Chapter 7
Management Control and the
Fiction of Mutuality

1. Bodfish, Morton A. and A.D. Theobald, Savings and Loan Principles (Prentice-Hall), New York, 1938, p. 30.

2. John Stafford, U.S. Savings and Loan League, (Chicago, Ill.), Conference on Savings, 1960.

3. E.g., the Mormon Church in Utah and the Christian Brother Monastery in California.

4. See chapters 2, 3, 4, 13 and 14.

5. Wall Street Journal, June 18, 1968.

6. Federal Charter Legislation for Mutual Savings, Banks, (hearings before the House of Representatives, Committee on Banking and Currency: Sub Committee on Bank Supervision and Insurance) 85th Congress, pp. 306-307 Congressman Abraham J. Moulter.

7. Ibid., p. 37.

8. Ibid., p. 51 — (Summary Statement)

9. Investigation and Study of the Federal Home Loan Bank laws, House of Representatives Subcommittee of the Committee on Government Operations, 87th Cong., 1st Sess. August 4, 1961, Washington, D.C., Part 1-A, p. 254

10. Federal Charter Legislation, pp. 309-311

11. Bodfish, *Principles*, p. 392

12. Conference on Savings, 1962, p. 169.

13. Federal Charter Legislation, p. 290 (Hoeft)

14. Crawford Testimony, Federal Charter Legislation for Mutual Savings Banks, p. 211.

15. Edward F. Shaw, *Savings and Loan Market Structure and Market Performance*, California Savings and Loan Commissioner, Los Angeles, 1962, p. 16.

16. Leon S. Kendall, Conference on Savings, 1960 (United States Savings and Loan League, Clt.III), p. 147

17. Ibid.

18. Investigation of the Federal Home Loan Bank Board, Part Ia, Alice, p. 557

19. Norman Strunk, Conference on Savings, 1963, p. 162. But it also suggests a non-competitive margin which managers tap through control of the infrastructure.

20. Shaw, *Structure*, p. 81.

21. Ibid., p. 2.

22. Ibid., p. 2.

23. United States Savings and Loan League Fact Book 1967, (Chicago, Ill.) Table 45, p. 58.

24. Charles F. Phillips and Delbert K. Duncan, *Marketing*, 4th ed., (Homewood, Illinois: Richard D. Irwin, 1960), p. 252.

25. R.J. Mischler, "Co-ops have Federal Income Tax Responsibilities," News for Cooperatives, March 1955, p. 14.

26. Cf. Mehr and Osler, Modern Life Insurance, (New York: McGraw-Hill, 1966), p. 616, n. 5.

27. Ibid., p. 616.

28. Ibid., p. 715.

29. Investigation of concentration of Economic Power, Temporary National Economic Committee, 76th Congress, 3rd Session, Study of Legal Reserve Life Insurance Companies, Monograph No. 28, Washington, 1941, p. 141.

30. United States Savings and Loan League, *Savings and Loan Fact Book 1967* Table 38, p. 51.

31. Federal Charter Legislation for Mutual Savings Banks, p. 179.

32. Ibid., p. 37.

33. Investigation of the Federal Home Loan Bank Board Alice. op. cit., p. 101.

34. Federal Charter Legislation for Mutual Savings Banks, (Courshon), p. 225.

35. U.S. Savings and Loan League, Annals 1963, statement by John de Laittre, p. 91.

36. Ibid.

37. Investigation of Concentration of Economic Power, Study of Legal Reserve Life Insurance Companies, op. cit. p. 14.

38. George J. Stigler, "The Economies of Scale," *The Journal of Law and Economics*, Vol. 1. October 1958, p. 56.

39. In Edward S. Mason, Editor, *The Corporation in Modern Society*, (Harvard, Cambridge, Massachusetts, 1959), p. 91.

40. John Lintner, "Distribution of Income of Corporation Among Dividends, Retained Earnings, and Taxes," *American Economic Review* Vol. 46 (May 1956) p. 100.

41. See Adolf A. Berle, Jr., and Gardner C. Means, the Modern Corporation and Private Property (New York: Mcmillan, 1934), Chap 6; also Carl Kaysen, "The Corporation: How Much Power? What Scope?" Mason, *The Corporation in Modern Society*, Harvard, Cambridge, 1959, pp. 85-105.

42. For a most penetrating critical and empirical evaluation of the Berle and Means thesis, see John Lintner, "The Financing of Corporations" in Mason, *The Corporation*, p. 171.

43. Paul A. Samuelson, *Economics: An Introductory Analysis*, 4th ed. (N.Y.: McGraw-Hill, 1958) p. 93.

44. Data derived from Stanford Research Institute, The Savings and Loan Industry in California, So. Pasadena, Calif., Commissioner of Savings and Loan, 1960, Table VIII-5, p. A-37 and Table XI-I, p. A-55.

45. Henry G. Manne, "Some Theoretical Aspects of Share Voting," *Columbia Law Review*, Vol. 64, December 1964, no. 8, p. 1445.

46. Ibid., p. 1441.

47. See Henry G. Manne, "Mergers in the market for Corporate Control," *Journal of Political Economy*, LKIII, April 1965.

48. Courshon Testimony, Federal Charter Legislation for Mutual Savings Banks, p. 254.

49. Testimony, Federal Charter Legislation for Mutual Savings Banks, pp. 309, 312.

50. Morton Keller, *The Life Insurance Enterprise, 1885-1910, A Study in the Limits of Corporate Power*, (Harvard, Cambridge, Mass. 1963), p. 273.

51. Stalson, *Marketing Life Insurance*, (Harvard, Cambridge, Mass. 1940) p. 559.

52. Stalson, p. 558. See also Keller, pp. 247-249.

53. Hoeft, Federal Charter Legislation, p. 290.

54. Hoeft, Progress Report to "our account holders," June 1964, Glendale Federal Savings and Loan Association, Glendale, California.

55. United States Savings and Loan League Conference on Savings, 1962, p. 169.

56. Federal Charter Legislation for Mutual Savings Banks, p. 309.

57. Evidence presented elsewhere refutes this allegation.

58. Provided in 12 U.S.C. 1728C., cited California Savings and Loan Data Book, 1968, p. 27.

59. Almarin Phillips, *Journal of Finance*, Vol. XIX, (March 1964), p. 41.

60. Wesley Lindow, (Irving Trust) United States Savings and Loan League, Annals 1964, p. 68.

61. See the discussion of the remarkable relationship between William Newburg, former president of Chrysler Corporation, and his outside supplier interests in James W. Kuhn and Ivas Berg, editors, *Values in a Business Society*, (New York: Harcourt, Brace and World, 1968), pp. 246-249.

62. Fred C. Stalder, past California Savings and Loan League President, reported in the Los Angeles *Times*, 15 September 1964, Part 3, p. 9.

63. Kaysen, p. 90.

64. Ibid.

65. In "The Corporation: How much Power? What Scope?" in Mason, *The Corporation*, p. 92. Cited in n. 41.

66. *Wall Street Journal*, 2 August 1968, p. 4.

67. "The Trade Union," in Mason, *The Corporation*, p. 127.

68. Federal Charter Legislation for Mutual Savings Banks, p. 104.

Chapter 8
The Quasifirm: Management-
Dominated Enterprise

1. William J. Baumol, *Business Behavior, Value and Growth* (Macmillan, New York), 1959, p. 90.

2. Preston Silbaugh, United States Savings and Loan League, Annals 1962, p. 292.

3. Baumol, *Business Behavior*, pp. 90, 95.

4. "Towards a Theory of Property Rights," *American Economic Review*, V. 57 (May 1967), No. 2, pp. 358-359.

5. Richard Caves, *American Industry: Structure Conduct Performance* (Englewood Cliffs, New Jersey: Prentice-Hall, 1964), p. 4.

6. Shorey, Peterson, "Corporate Control and Capitalism," *Quarterly Journal of Economics*, Vol. 49 (February 1965), p. 18.

7. For an interesting discussion, see the monograph by Mancur Olson, *The Logic of Collective Action: Public Goods and the Theory of Groups* (Harvard, Cambridge, Mass., 1965), pp. 55-56.

8. Cf. Baumol (1959), *Business Behavior*, pp. 48-50, also pp. 95-96.

9. Wilbur G. Katz, "Responsibility in the Modern Corporation," *Journal of Law and Economics*, Vol. 3 (October 1960), p. 84.

10. Baumol, *Business Behavior*, p. 96.

11. "The 'Higher Criticism' of the Modern Corporation," *Columbia Law Review*, Vol. 62, No. 3 (March 1962), pp. 404-405, note 15.

12. Adolf A. Berle and Gardiner C. Means, *The Modern Corporation and Private Property* (New York: Columbia University).

13. *Wall Street Journal*, 10 February 1967.

14. J.A. Livingston, *The American Stockholder* (Philadelphia, 1958), p. 60.

15. John Lintner, "The Financing of Corporations" in E.S. Mason, Ed., *The Corporation in Modern Society* (Cambridge: Harvard, 1959).

16. Federal Charter Legislation for Mutual Savings Banks, Hearings Subcommittee on Bank Supervision and Insurance, Committee on Banking and Currency, House of Representatives, 88th Cong., 1st Sess., Oct. 29, 30, 31, 1963, p. 318.

17. Ibid., p. 307.

18. Oliver E. Williamson, The Economics of Discretionary Behavior: Managerial Objectives in a Theory of the Firm, (A Ford Foundation Prize Dissertation, Markham Publishing Company), Chicago, Ill., 1967, pp. 17-18.

19. Cf. Henry G. Manne, "Mergers in the Market for Corporate Control," *The Journal of Political Economy*, Vol. LXIII, 2 (April 1965), pp. 110-120.

20. Baumol, (1959), *Business Behavior*, p. 47.

21. Ibid., p. 96.

22. John Maynard Keynes, *Essays in Persuasion* (New York: Harcourt Brace, 1932), p. 314.

23. Ibid.

24. For California Stock Associations, "Stockholder cash investment in the industry is negligible." Edward S. Shaw, Savings and Loan Market Structure and Market Performance (California Savings and Loan Commissioner, Los Angeles, 1962), p. 58.

25. Federal Home Loan Bank Board Combined Financial Statements.

26. United States Savings and Loan League, *Fact Book*, (Chicago, Ill.) 1967, Table 40, p. 52.

27. See Myles M. Dawson, Mutualization of Life Insurance Companies, American Academy of Political and Social Science Annals, Vol. LXX, (March 1917), pp. 67-71.

28. Shaw, *Structure*, p. 67.

29. Federal Charter Legislation for Mutual Savings Banks, p. 162.

30. Ibid., p. 4.

31. Morton Bodfish and A.D. Theobald, *Savings and Loan Principles* (New York: Prentice-Hall, 1938), pp. 393, 394.

32. Leo Grebler and Eugene Brigham, Savings and Mortgage Markets in California (California Savings and Loan, League, Pasadena) 1963, p. 109.

33. Bodfish, *Principles*, p. 391.

34. In Chapters 2 and 4.

35. Grebler and Brigham, *Mortgage Markets*, p. 91.

36. Caves, *American Industry*, p. 5.

37. Investigation of concentration of economic power, TNEC 76th Congress 3rd Session, Monograph No. 28, Study of Legal Reserve Life Insurance Companies, Washington, 1941, p. 10.

38. Baumol, *Business Behavior*, pp. 96-97.

39. The ratio for the federal association was 0.16 and for the stock associations 0.20, Federal Home Loan Bank Board, *Combined Financial Statements*, Washington, D.C., 1961-1964.

40. Bodfish, *Principles*, pp. 392-393.

41. Josephine Hedges Ewalt, *The Savings and Loan Story, 1930-1960: A Business Reborn*, American Savings and Loan Institute Press, Chicago, Ill., p. 330.

42. Cf. Baumol, *Business Behavior*, p. 96.

43. Cf. Shaw, *Structure*, p. 58.

44. See Armen A. Alchian, "Private property and the Relative Cost of Tenure," *The Public Stake in Union Power*, edit. P. Bradley, University of Virginia Press, Charlottesville, Va., 1959, pp. 350-371.

45. Fred M. Westfield, "Regulation and Conspiracy," *American Economic Review*, Vol. LV, 3, (June 1965), p. 424.

46. C.N. Parkinson, *Parkinson's Law and Other Studies* (Boston: Houghton-Mifflin, 1957).

47. Edward Gibbons, *The Decline and Fall of the Roman Empire* (New York: Modern Library edition, 1932), Vol. 2, p. 240.

48. Morton Keller, The Life Insurance Enterprise, 1885-1910: A Study in the Limits of Corporate Powers (Cambridge, Mass.: Harvard, 1963) p. 42.

49. John Maynard Keynes, *Essays in Persuasion*, p. 327.

50. Shaw, *Structure*, p. 38, also p. 121.

51. Manne, "The 'Highest Criticism' of the Modern Corporation," p. 404.

52. Ibid.

53. M.D. Robbins, Los Angeles *Times*, 24 September 1966.

54. W.J. Baumol and W.G. Bowen, "On the Performing Arts: The Anatomy of Their Economic Problems," *American Economic Review*, Vol. LV, 2 (May 1965), p. 497.

55. Testimony of Morris D. Crawford, Jr. Federal Charter Legislation for Mutual Savings Banks, p. 211.

56. Shaw, *Structure*, p. 2.

57. Ibid., p. 81.

58. Marshall S. Mayer, Deputy Attorney General, State of California, "Civil and Criminal Liabilities of Directors of California Banks and Savings and Loan Associations," *Journal State Bar of California*, November-December, 1966, No. 6, p. 901.

59. Shaw, *Structures*, p. 141.

60. Ibid.

61. Ibid., p. 121.

62. "Values in a Business Society: issues and Analysis," ed. by James W. Kuhn and Ivar Berg (New York: Harcourt, Brace & World, 1968), pp. 246-249.

63. "The Corporation: How Much Power? What Scope?" in *The Corporation in Modern Society*, p. 91.

64. Herbert G. Grubel, *American Economic Review*, Vol. LV, 2, May 1965, p. 77.

65. Corwin D. Edwards, *Maintaining Competition: Requisites of a Governmental Policy* (New York: McGraw-Hill, 1949), pp. 98-99. The Federal Communications Commission Report of the Investigation of the Telephone Industry in the United States, pursuant to Pub. Res. No. 8, 74th Congress, 1939, noted that sales are made at noncompetitive prices (see pp. 316-323) and Western Electric profits have been extraordinarily high (p. 544-566).

66. Cf. Harvey Averch and Leland L. Johnson, "Behavior of the Firm under Regulatory Constraint," *American Economic Review*, Vol. LII, No. 5 (December 1962), pp. 1052-1069.

67. Bodfish, *Principles*, p. 391.

68. Federal Charter Legislation, pp. 282-283.

Chapter 9
Expense Manipulation in
the Mutual

1. Elwood Knapp, U.S. Savings and Loan League, *Conference on Savings*, 1960, Chicago, p. 172.

Chapter 10
The Measurement of Expenses

1. Grebler and Brigham, *Mortgage Markets*, p. 150.

2. Kendall, *Conference on Savings*, p. 136.

3. Ibid.

4. Shaw, *Structures*, pp. 110-122; see also Grebler and Brigham, pp. 23-28.

5. Kendall, *Conference on Savings*, p. 140.

6. Savings and Loan Commissioner, 70th Annual Report for Year 1963, April 27, 1964, p. 8.

7. Grebler and Brigham, *Mortgage Markets*, p. 137.

8. Ibid., p. 105.

9. John G. Gurley and Edward S. Shaw, "Financial Intermediaries and the Savings Investment Process," *The Journal of Finance*, Vol. 11, No. 2, May 1956, pp. 257-266; also John G. Gurley, "Financial Institutions in the Savings Investment Process" in United States Savings and Loan League Conference on Savings, 1959, p. 11.

10. A.D. Theobald, and Morton Bodfish, *Saving and Loan Principles* N.Y. 1938, p. 182.

11. Cf. Grebler and Brigham, *Mortgage Markets*, p. 164.

12. Grebler and Brigham, *Mortgage Markets*, Table V-3, p. 106.

13. Shaw, *Structures*, p. 122.

14. Grebler and Brigham, *Mortgage Markets*, p. 130.

15. Ibid., pp. 136-144.

Chapter 12
Hypotheses with Respect to
Expense Differences

1. Cf. Grebler and Brigham, *Mortgage Markets*, pp. 105-109.

2. Ibid., p. 141.

3. Ibid., p. 146.

4. Ibid., p. 164.

5. Klaman, Saul. *Postwar Mortgage Financing*, National Bureau of Economic Research, New York, p. 159.

6. Cf. California Savings and Loan League, 1964 Data Book, Pasadena, 1964, p. 19.

7. Grebler and Brigham, *Mortgage Markets*, p. 131.

8. Ibid., p. 132.

9. United States Savings and Loan League, *Savings and Loan Fact Book*, 1967, Table 60, p. 72 (Chicago, Illinois).

10. United States Savings and Loan League, *Savings and Loan Fact Book*, 1969, Table 73, p. 79.

11. Federal Home Loan Bank Board, Office of Public Affairs, May 1963.

12. Source for the United States: United States Savings and Loan League, *Savings and Loan Fact Book*, 1966, p. 78. Source for California stock associations: Federal Home Loan Bank of San Francisco, information provided in letter to author.

13. Federal Deposit Insurance Corporation, *Reports*, 1960-1964, Washington, D.C.

14. *Savings and Loan Journal*, April 1963.

15. Ibid., p. 25.

16. Ibid.

17. Ibid.

18. United States Savings and Loan League, *1965 Savings and Loan Fact Book*, Chicago, Illinois, 1965, Table 7, p. 20.

19. Ibid., Table 11, p. 24.

20. Stanford Research Institute, op. cit., VIII-15.

21. Ibid., Table VIII-4.

22. Kendall, *Conference on Savings*, pp. 28-29.

23. Los Angeles *Times*, 20 March 1964.

24. Ibid.

25. Ibid.

26. Edward Johnson of Financial Federal, Los Angeles *Times*.

27. Ibid.

28. Grebler and Brigham, *Mortgage Markets*, p. 142.

29. Cf. the following: "Further, the higher income ratios of California associations reflect to some extent differences in the composition of assets." The larger percentage of assets are invested in mortgage loans and a smaller share in the government-insured loans with their smaller yield. "Finally, a group of institutions especially active in selling mortgage loans or participations, as the California associations do, is apt to show earnings from the origination and servicing of mortgages which do not appear in their own assets but magnify both income to asset and expense to asset ratios." Grebler and Brigham, *Mortgage Markets*, p. 143.

30. Los Angeles *Times*, 17 March 1964.

31. Ibid.

32. Ibid.

33. McMurray, *Savings and Loan Journal*, April 1963.

34. Ibid.

35. Cf. Brigham, E., "Economics of Scale in the Savings and Loan Industry," Western Economic Journal, vol. III No. 1 (Fall 1964).

36. McMurray, *Journal*.

37. Gerhard Tintner, Econometrics (N.Y.: John Wiley & Sons, 1952), pp. 89-91.

38. Federal Home Loan Bank Board, Washington, D.C., Release, October 24, 1965.

40. Cf. Grebler and Brigham, *Mortgage Markets*, p. 131.

41. The denominator here is mortgages. It could, with no violence to the logic, have just as easily been assets. Though total assets exceeds total mortgages, the difference is not critical for the above discussion.

42. Stanford Research Institute, The Savings and Loan Industry in California, Pasadena, 1960, XIII-7.

Chapter 13
The Regression Analysis: Expenses

1. Cf. J. Johnson, *Econometric Methods*, N.Y. 1963 (McGraw-Hill), pp. 221-228.

2. Brigham, "Economies of Scale . . . ," pp. 8-10; Kendall, *Conference on Savings*, p. 136.

3. Cf. Grebler and Brigham, *Mortgage Markets*, Ch. VI.

4. Pearson, Karl, "On the Probable Error of a Coefficient of Correlation as found from a Fourfold Table," Biometrika, 1913, V. 9, p. 22.

5. Cf. E. Shaw, *Structure*, pp. 111-114.

6. Cf. Grebler and Brigham, *Mortgage Markets*, p. 164.

7. See George Stigler, "The Economies of Scale," *Journal of Law and Economics*, V. 1 (Oct. 1958), pp. 54-71.

Chapter 14
Profits

1. Shaw, *Structure*, p. 105.

2. California Savings and Loan Commissioner *1963 Report*, Los Angeles, p. 8.

3. Grebler and Brigham, *Mortgage Markets*, p. 101, note 6.

4. Ibid., pp. 103, 103.

5. Ibid.

Chapter 15
Conclusion

1. P. James Riordan, Hearings before the House of Representatives, Committee on Banking and Currency, p. 206.

2. See F.R. Cowell, "Cicero and the Roman Republic," (Harmsworth, Middlesex, England: Penguin, 1968), p. 64.

3. Cf. Shaw, *Structure*, p. 68.

Index

Accounting procedure: as disguise for expenses, 245

Advertisements: and marketing functions, 246; as competitive weapon, 131, 233; as component of expense, 207; magnitude of, 47–49, 53

Affiliates, 6, 29

Alice Savings and Loan Association: conflict of interest, 95–97, 119

Assets: by ownership type, 61, 62; distribution of 211, 212; loan acquisition component, 198; volume of, 39, 40

Bank deposits, 28

Baumol model: and quasifirm profitability, 132; and separation of ownership and management, 135, 139

Baumol, William J.: hypothesis of, 22, 23

Berle, A. A., Jr., and Means, G. C.: hypothesis of, 11; on mutuality, 125; ownership and control, 137

Bodfish, Morton, and Theobald, A. D., 76n

Boston Federal Home Loan Bank District, 244

British Building Society, 71n

Buildings and furnishings, 241, 242

California: market changes, 60; net mortgage sales, 244

California Savings and Loan Commission: evaluation, 188; standards of, 51, 259, 279; on insurance, 126n

Capital investment: and stock companies, 140; restrictions on in mutual, 149

Capper-Volstead Act of 1922, 83n

Cities, by type of organization, 214, 215

Clayton Act of 1914, 83n

Coast Federal, rate increase of, 47

Commercial banks: rates of, 45

Committee on Banking and Currency, 80

Compensation, 53

Competition: and property rights, 4, 113; and power blocks, 81–83; control of entry, 88–91; lack of, 87; regulatory authorities, 97

Conflict of interest, 27; Chrysler Corp., 160, 161

Corruption: lack of property rights, 166

Data: availability of, 220

Disequilibrium: price control, 158

Disintegration: and lack of property rights, 180

Diversions: and externalized expense, 178; and monopoly, 164; and salary benefits, 158; and subsidiaries, 151–155; of fee income in Calif., 29, 30

Dividends: of federals and stock, 40–46, 74

Efficiency: and negative effect of profit, 226; as function of size, 247; an evaluation of, 171; as masque for diversion, 187–192; as source of capital, 148; disguised as external resource, 174–178, 180; in Calif. stock associations, 37, 38; regression analysis of, 259–278

Equitable Life Insurance Co., 125n

Failure rate: and organization form, 126

Federal associations, origins of, 63

Federal Home Loan Bank Act, 72n

Federal Home Loan Bank Board (FHLBB), 18, 60–67, 73, 77; and collusion with mutuals, 102; and harassment, 96; and interpretation of expenses, 194; and management power, 119; annual reports of, 294, 279; data of, 185, 234, 250, 259; rate control of, 92–95, 100; salaries, 106

Federal Home Loan Bank of Little Rock, 77, 113

Federal Home Loan Bank System, 61, 72

Federal Savings and Loan Insurance Corp., 16, 76, 77, 98, 99

Fee origination, 42

Fidelity Federal, 27

Financial Federation, 47

First Charter Savings and Loan Association, 99

First Savings and Loan Association, 47

Foreclosure, 67, 78; in cities, 234–236; loan size, 253

Furnishings: investment in, 23–26

Grebler, Leo and Brigham, Eugene F.: growth and mutuality, 36, 37, 65, 66, 143

Greef vs. Equitable, 15

Greenbaum, Michael, 92n

Growth: and concept changes, 73, 74; and efficiency, 64; and management, 66; differences in, 58; in number, 60–63; instrument of management control, 118–122; stockholder pressure, 143

Gurley, John G. and Shaw, Edward S., 193

323

About the Author

Alfred Nicols is Associate Professor of Business Economics at the University of California at Los Angeles. He received his bachelor's degree in philosophy from UCLA, and his M.A. and Ph.D. in economics from Harvard.

Dr. Nicols has contributed to numerous professional journals, including *The American Economic Review, Schweizerische Zeitschrift Für Volkswirtschaft and Statistik, The Journal of Business of the University of Chicago, The Review of Economics and Statistics*, and *The Quarterly Journal of Economics*.